Themes,
Dreams, and
Schemes

Themes, Dreams, and Schemes

BANQUET MENU IDEAS, CONCEPTS, AND THEMATIC EXPERIENCES

G. Eugene Wigger, CPCE

JOHN WILEY & SONS, INC.

New York • Chichester • Weinheim • Brisbane • Singapore • Toronto

Library of Congress Cataloging in Publication Data:
Wigger, G. Eugene.
    Themes, dreams, and schemes : banquet menu ideas, concepts, and
thematic experiences / G. Eugene Wigger.
        p.   cm.
    Includes bibliographical references.
    ISBN 0–471–15391–5 (cloth : alk. paper)
    1. Caterers and catering—Management.   2. Menus.   3. Meetings—
Planning.   I. Title.
TX921.W6   1997
642'.4—dc21   96–38128

Printed in the United States of America

10 9 8 7 6 5 4 3

Contents

1   The Theme and Scheme of Things   1

2   Raise Food and Beverage Management to a Higher Level   9

3   Don't Kneel to Propose   21

4   Creative Thematic Meeting Breaks   41

5	Breakfast Appetizers	71

6	Lunch/Dinner Appetizers	73

7	Soups	75

8	Salads	79

9	A Guide to Vegetable Dishes	81

10   Desserts   91

11   Breakfast Entrées   95

12   Seated Breakfast Menus   97

13   Buffet Breakfast Menus   103

14   Buffet Bruncheon Menus   113

15   Luncheon Entrées   117

16   Seated Luncheon Menus   125

17   Luncheon Buffet Menus   139

18   Dinner Entrées   147

19   Seated Dinner Menus   155

20   Buffet Dinner Menus   183

21   Signature Line Gourmet Dinner Menus   199

22   Reception Menus   213

23   Low-Cholesterol, Low-Fat, Low-Sodium Menus   243

24   The Fantasy Factory® Theme Menus   251

25   Kosher Menus   293

Foreword

Throughout human history feasting has played an integral role in human celebration. From life cycle events such as weddings, christenings, bar and bat mitzvah celebrations to major corporate incentive programs, the blending of food, beverage, decor, entertainment, and other elements results in the final experience that ensures happy memories.

The author of *Themes, Dreams, and Schemes* has literally and figuratively provided you with a detailed menu for special event success. G. Eugene Wigger, CPCE, one of the most respected and creative professionals in the event catering profession, has identified the strategies that will assist you in managing a high profit, high quality, event catering operation.

Throughout this valuable text you will discover numerous ways to actually save money while rapidly increasing your bottom line. Even more important, your staff will enjoy this process as it allows them to use their creativity to help you accomplish important financial and quality assurance goals for your organization.

While the back of the house operations are carefully considered, the major emphasis is on presentation, operations, and marketing. These are critical areas for modern event managers and often overlooked in previous texts. In this volume you will learn how to design a unique theme party, develop a winning proposal, and negotiate to ensure a win-win outcome with your client.

Included are over 375 possible theme experiences, the complete methodology for creating a themed event catering department, as well as literally hundreds of other valuable ideas. On each page there is at least one thousand dollars worth of consulting information and much more when you consider the potential return on your investment when you combine your creativity to implement these proven successful ideas.

A separate chapter on kosher theme dining experiences reflects the growing popularity and demand for this type of cuisine. Event caterers who serve this clientele will appreciate and use the valuable tips ranging from designing the kosher meal to preparing the Viennese table or selecting the appropriate kosher wine.

To my knowledge, this is the first book to thoroughly combine the creative thematic design of food with a variety of other event resources to provide a comprehensive reference for caterers, event managers, and any professional who desires one stop shopping. In one volume, the author has ingeniously woven each of these threads together to present you with a magic carpet to soar to new heights in satisfying the increasing demand for value-added special events. Thanks to Gene Wigger, you are on your way to creating your own themes, dreams, and schemes, and I know that your magic carpet ride will be one you and your clients will long remember.

Dr. Joe Goldblatt, CSEP

Founding Director
The Event Management Program
The George Washington University

Preface

Banquet menu ideas are limited only by the constraints of your imagination. Meeting planners and social clients alike have repeatedly expressed their displeasure with establishments not showing much imagination in their banquet menu repertoire. Most hotels and catering businesses have a banquet menu selection that appears to be a carbon copy of their competition, almost to the point of a cookie cutter approach.

The trend is for clients to look for something different, away from meat and potatoes and toward a more innovative approach to meeting and social menu planning.

Try different ways of preparing and presenting food, ways that will spice up the function and take the "blahs" out of menu planning. That doesn't mean inventing new foods, but it does mean trying new combinations and new serving ideas.

Food Is Food—The Difference Is the Show

This book is conceptual in nature and is a complete presentation of menu ideas and concepts. Therefore, actual recipes are not included, in order to allow for individual creativity.

Creative Menus and Innovative Thematic Ideas?

This book includes only a selection of the author's personal favorites. Your contributions to the next edition are welcomed.

Please send your own creative menus, thematic experiences, innovative support ideas, demiurgic meeting breaks, social event input, interactive music and entertainment options, and ingenious, sophisticated decorations and embellishments for possible inclusion in the second edition, with appropriate credit given to yourself.

Be you an on- or off-premise caterer, hotelier, chef, educator, convention planner, club manager, special event producer, incentive or corporate meeting planner, entertainer, decorator, designer, or supplier, send your creative input to G. Eugene Wigger, CPCE, Adam's Mark Hotel Dallas, 400 North Olive Street, Dallas, Texas 75201, (214) 922-0343, FAX (214) 922-0308.

Acknowledgments

Our best thoughts come from others.
—Ralph Waldo Emerson

This book, like any other, has a long ancestry. Many people and experiences have shaped my creative thinking over the years. In this respect, it is honest and accurate to say that work on this manuscript began a long time ago.

Despite this qualification, what follows is primarily the product of over thirty years of direct involvement in thousands of creative special events. During this period, I have profited immensely from working with many distinguished creative thinkers and doers. I'll always be grateful for their contributions to my professional development.

A very special acknowledgment of the photographic genius that is prominently displayed in the book goes to Sheila and Rob Hurth, Tiffany Photographic, Fort Lauderdale, and Joe Saget, Joe Saget Studios, Philadelphia.

All photographs displayed in this book were taken during the six years I served as executive director of catering of Marriott's Harbor Beach Resort in Fort Lauderdale. I was very fortunate to work with management whose support, encouragement, and belief in my abilities made me love my job and my craft. It was a rare and special privilege to work with such exceptional professionals as General Manager Ezzat Coutry and Director of Food and Beverage Franz Ferschke.

The three-dimensional props prominently displayed in the photographs featured in this book were co-designed and built by Fantastic Props, in collaboration with this author, for Marriott's Harbor Beach Resort.

This book is for all of us—the students of our craft, past, present, and future—who never cease in our efforts to become more professional, more creative, and more knowledgeable by the synergistic sharing of our life's work and passion.

Above all, I want to dedicate this book to my son, Corey Ryan, who has brought my life a new meaning with his love, creativity, enthusiasm, appreciation, and pure joy. He has indeed made my life a special event . . . one worth celebrating!

Chapter I

The Theme and Scheme of Things

The thematic event is certainly not a new concept, but it has indeed come of age. Most of today's clients expect a thematic experience, not only from a theme party, but also at breakfasts, luncheons, dinners, and even meeting breaks. They demand sophisticated props, creative foods that support the theme, appropriate staff costumes, and attendee and staff involvement—all at an affordable price!

Provide a Creative "One-Stop Shop"

Consequently, some of the world's most outstanding hotels and resorts have taken the innovative approach and developed complete on-property theme event programs. They provide a complete "one-stop shop" for the special event. Commitment to achieving such a program will bring about several results:

A. The hotel or resort can offer something that will give them a showbiz uniqueness.
B. Even if their banquet prices are higher, they can offer greater value by providing the thematic decor, props, and staff costumes at about half of what an outside supplier would charge.
C. The end results will be a much better performance by the hotel or resort, due to the repetitiveness.
D. The thematic experience becomes more fun with each performance, thereby creating more staff involvement.
E. A total staff effort generates improvement each time a special event is presented.
F. This one-stop approach allows the hotel or resort to control all aspects of the event, and thereby control the results.
G. Because the props are designed for easy installation by banquet housemen, the setup time is greatly reduced, thus allowing the hotel or resort to sell an additional function or two, instead of holding the ballroom all day for decorations setup.
H. If the hotel or resort must negotiate a lower price with some client group, there is still a built-in area over which the hotel has complete control, and hence a hard bargain will not affect the bottom line so drastically.
I. The client only has so many dollars in his or her budget to spend on the event. The more the client spends with an outside supplier, the less he or she has to spend with the hotel or resort.
J. And the hotel or resort will create a new profit center, which has the potential to generate many hundreds of thousands of extra dollars, more profit, and greater guest satisfaction.

Creating an Extra Million Dollars

Could your catering operation use the infusion of an extra million dollars? Of course. Who wouldn't answer "yes" to that question? Your operation cannot afford to overlook any possibility for greater profit, because you can't simply increase your banquet prices to reflect your increased costs of operation. I for one believe that you must invest in your operation if you want it to reach its full potential. In the six years, 1984–1990, that I was Executive Director of Catering at Marriott's Harbor Beach Resort, Fort Lauderdale, Florida, I developed a complete custom thematic program inventory for the resort, worth over a half million dollars, which included fully dimensional props, specialty linens, neon sculptures, show plates, tabletop props, scenery backdrops, coffee break canvas backdrops and props, and costumes. This extra profit center helped to make the resort one of the most profitable catering operations in the country by generating over an extra million dollars in revenue during one year, and most of that went directly to the bottom profit line!

Design a Theme Party That Is Unique

The best selling thematic experience at the South Florida resort was "The Florida Wacky Tacky Tourist Beachless Beach Party." The proposal for this, or any other theme party, should be presented in such a way that the client will get excited just by reading about the party. See this sample proposal in Chapter Three and see photos on pages 63–68 and on color insert.

The original purchase cost of the Wacky Tacky decor was about $65,000. The decor generated about one half the income of what an outside supplier would normally charge the client. Since we averaged about forty of these parties per year and we charged at least $8,000 for the decor, that one theme party alone generated an extra $320,000 or more per year. Of course, there were some expenses for extra labor and prop maintenance, but those expenses were minimal.

The cost of the food-only menu was $45.75 and because of the way the menu was "sold" to the client with the proposal, no one complained about the price, once they were able to experience the thematic event. In addition, such a party will generate beverage revenue with a four- or five-hour full open bar, and possibly specialty drinks.

Create a Signature Thematic Dining Experience

Every hotel and resort in America should create a memorable dining experience (not simply a dinner) that is unique to their operation. The staff must be committed to designing a superb dining experience that can serve as a reminder of their personal achievement and distinction. Pablo Picasso said, "Some painters transform the sun into a yellow spot; others transform a yellow spot into the sun." Transform a different kind of banquet into a magic memory.

Consider your clientele, their budget and desires, and create a dining experience that will live long in the memories of those in attendance. Almost every business group that visits a resort hotel will hold a final dinner or an ending luncheon, which gives you a great potential.

Also, don't overlook the social event potential. While at the South Florida resort, I designed a collection that I titled "The Achievement Series," which included three innovative thematic dining extravaganzas: the "Florida Fantasy Feasts," "Spot-

light on Excellence," and "Celebration" (see color insert photos). Ten different menu selections were available for each, a total of thirty innovative culinary memories. In my wedding package, I offered the ultimate wedding experience, which included the "Celebration" theme, and I called this offering my "Designer Wedding Celebrations."

When designing a memorable dining experience, first think of the visual impact. When the doors to the ballroom open, the attendees will decide at once if this will be a special event or not. I believe that a special event is not a different kind of banquet, but that every banquet should be a different kind of special event. Each of the three dinners I designed in "The Achievement Series" included floor-length table cloths, overlays for impact, napkins that matched the floor-length cloths, a unique centerpiece, a custom designed show plate, and a bandstand backdrop for that total finished decor look. Now that we have the visual impact, we need to brainstorm some challenging and innovative menu suggestions.

The Greek philosopher and gourmet Philoxenux once said, "I wish I had a neck like a crane so that I might extend the good taste of my food and make longer the moment of swallowing." You don't have to invent new foods to wow your clients; you do need to concentrate on the presentation. For example, offer double entreés (not a choice) such as:

> Fillet Tenderloin Steak with Wine-Laced Mushrooms, Over an Almond Eggplant Crouton, Served with Sauce Bérnaise, passed, and
> Four Large Shrimp stuffed with Crabmeat, Cooked in scampi butter
> • • •
> Petite Fillets of Beef Tenderloin, Veal Tenderloin, and Pork Tenderloin, Presented with Sauce Chanterelle, passed

Be sure to design menus that are upscale and challenging not only for the kitchen, but for the service staff as well. Remember the little touches: Serve all the women at the banquet round table first; when the guests enter the room, make sure that all servers are at their stations, facing the entrance, with a crisp napkin over the right forearm; provide freshly folded napkins with each course; have all servers introduce themselves before starting service, shake out the napkins and place one in each guest's lap; provide chilled forks with the salad course; and so on. And, of course, make it white glove service, providing the most special attention to every detail.

In a one-year time span at this South Florida resort, we sold 88 of "The Achievement Series" Dining Experiences, serving over 22,000 covers. Since we charged an extra $16.00 per person (all prices from 1990) for the decor, that's over $350,000 in extra revenue. At that rate, it doesn't take long to recover your investment. Also, this is in addition to the increase in average check. The dinners ranged from $37.50 per person for Chicken St. Jacques, a breast of chicken accompanied by large tender scallops laced with a creamed wine sauce, to $97.75 per person for Quail Ponce de Leon, braised quail with wild rice pilaf and quail eggs, sauce demi-glace au cognac and medallion of veal loin, sautéed, with twin lobster decorations.

Can We Go on Meeting Like This?

Give your meeting attendees a break—they deserve one! At the same time, you can help stamp out those ho-hum, humdrum, run-of-the-mill, hackneyed, stale, interminable, trite, world-weary, blasé, lethargic, everyday, meeting coffee breaks (see color insert)! You should provide a fresh interpretation of today's trend toward a more innovative treatment of the meeting interlude, imaginatively prepared and presented. These visionary breaks will undoubtedly reinvigorate any group's meeting message.

When I developed my meeting break program at that South Florida resort, I worked with a local prop company to develop a series of 8' × 24' canvas backdrops that could be displayed on specifically designed, quickly assembled, velcro-covered frameworks. These backdrops were augmented with large props that could be positioned around the meeting break stations. And there were tabletop props as well. My most popular break was entitled, "It's A Jungle Out There." See Chapter Four for this sample meeting break proposal.

Remember to keep the cost of these breaks affordable, so your groups will be able to provide one or more of these special breaks during their stay. Your goal should be to present ten to twelve of these breaks per week. My dozen thematic breaks were priced from $8.50 to $9.95 per person, of which $1.00 per person went toward the prop purchase. This pricing structure was not out of line, since an American Continental Buffet Breakfast at that time cost $7.50 per person.

Attendee and Staff Involvement

One of the keys to a great thematic party is involvement of both the attendees and the staff (see photos on pages 63, 66, 67, and 69 and color insert). The Wacky Tacky Tourist Party I spoke of earlier will only reach its full fun potential if all the attendees are encouraged to develop their own costumes, which will even allow them to change their personalities somewhat. Once they have made such a commitment, they will approach the party in a way that will assure its success. The same goes for the hotel or resort staff. Encourage them to create their own costumes and to develop their own characters.

In order to set an example of involvement and commitment, I appear at my theme events as an array of unique characters. I actually appear, perform, and entertain at my thematic functions. In fact, I have gotten so good that some of my clients have me entertain at their events that I do not plan. I have enhanced themed events for clients from Hawaii to Bermuda, and I even went to Washington, DC to entertain for a party hosted by the Marriott family.

That's Okay for You, But . . .

Oh, I've heard all the excuses. One of the most common is, "My clientele would *never* spend that much money!" Well, I for one believe that you should never underestimate your clients' willingness or ability to pay, but excite them into spending more money than they intended!

Or, "We have kitchen limitations!" At the South Florida resort where I served as Executive Director of Catering for six years, we were doing almost $11 million annually in catering revenue when I left in 1990, and they had forgotten to build a separate banquet kitchen. You must find ways to compensate for the shortcomings of facilities, staff, and equipment.

Or, "My clients always order the same thing and are afraid to experiment with different menus!" I believe that banquet menu ideas are limited only by the constraints of your imagination.

Or, "We don't have enough storage space now, even without the props!" This is always the case, but better utilization of space, such as putting a second level in the storage area for smaller items, is almost always possible. Be a creative thinker. At first I had a rough time getting management to build a prop storage area in the unusable areas of the parking garage, but once they saw how much money could be made, I was able to add four additional storage rooms.

The General Manager even helped me find the storage areas.

Special events should be designed with creative flair, to honor creative genius.

An Alternative to Prop Purchase—Creating a Partnership

If, after much thought and discussion with management, an alternative to prop purchase must be found, then pursue the development and creation of a complete theme program in partnership with a leading special event firm for design decor and a local talent agency for music and entertainment, leaving your hotel or resort responsible for the creative concepts and food and beverage service, thus providing the perfect backdrop for your clients' dreams to come true.

In addition, develop several thematic events whose decor is based on balloon art. Such decorations are affordable and memorable. Balloon sculpturing has become a sophisticated art, on the cutting edge of creativity. Here again, form a partnership with a local creative balloon art and sculpturing firm.

The theme program that emerges from forming these partnerships must be exclusive, as created, among the partners, and should qualify for special pricing. What you are doing is transforming the special event into an art form.

You can then use these ingenious partnerships as a market tool to sell your selected thematic events, showing clients how the total impact is enhanced by the innovative theme menus, costumes, entertainment, and elaborate, sophisticated three-dimensional props—all available at an affordable total per-person price. The package is presented as a program offered by the partner hotel or resort, rather than by the "approved vendor." Clients love it because it's an accepted program of their selected hotel or resort, it's easy for them, and it's offered at the right price, giving them value for the dollars spent.

The Theme Dream® Team is such a formed partnership, which allows one contact to provide the client with all the innovative special event elements he or she might want, at the best possible price. In forming such a team you become a partner in exceeding your customers' expectations, rather than just a partner in profit. A formed partnership can indeed control your client's costs, as well as the end results, while offering something truly unique.

A famed entrepreneur once advised that to be successful in business: Be daring, be first, be different!

375 Possible Theme Experiences

African Adventure	Fashion Show	50's Bash
Floridafest	Beach Party	Bahamarama
Wizard of Oz	New Wave	Miami Deco/South Beach
Everglades/Swamp Party	Murder Mystery Theatre	Archie/Comics
South of the Border	Goombay Fest	Street Party
Enchanted Forest	US Regional	2001—A Bar Mitzvah Odyssey
Famous Couples	Jungle Safari	Broadway/Opening Night
Construction, Blueprints for Success	Phantom of the Opera	Seasonal Decor—Christmas, Halloween, July 4th, and so on
Monster Mash	Hooray for Hollywood	
All That Glitters	Surfin' in the USA	You Light up my Life
Gypsy Holiday	You Are the Magic	40's Follies
Tex-Mex Western	Coney Island	Indy 500/Grand Prix/Cars
Balloon Sculptures	Electric Eve/High Voltage	Academy Awards
Casino/Monte Carlo Night	Wedding Decor—An Elegant Touch	Muscle Beach
Winter Wonderland	Rain Forest/Amazon	I've Got the Music in Me
Hawaiian Sands Luau	Born in the USA	All American Boy/Girl
Back to the Future	Island Clam Bake	Classical Movies
Animal House	The Magic in You	Game Shows
Carnival	Jungle Chic/Safari Nightclub	Olympics—Go for the Gold
Texas Rodeo	Hearts/Rainbows	Shape of Things to Come
Ports of Call	Planet Hollywood	Under the Big Top
Journey to Israel/Judaism	Medieval Castle Fantasy	1001 Arabian Nights
You Ought to Be in Pictures	Black/White/Black Tie	Out of this World
Hillbilly Hijinks	Captain Quinn's	Teddy Bears/Lollipops

//////

Treasure Hunt
All That Jazz
Excellent Adventure
Mardi Gras
Rhapsody in Blue
50's Sock Hop
60's Psychedelic/Sign of the Times
Gay 90's
Orient Express
Pirate Shipwreck
Great Gatsby
Hard Rock Café
Red Hot Night
Cruises/Travel/Bon Voyage
Roaring 20's
M*A*S*H®/China Beach®
"Calle Ocho"
One Singular Sensation
Fairy Tales
French Pâtisserie
Anniversary/Birthday
Sports Bar
Denim and Diamonds
Camelot
Alaskan Goldrush
Diamonds Are a Girl's Best Friend
Wacky Olympics/Sportsfest
Alice in Wonderland/Queen of
    Hearts
Far East/China-Japan
Casablanca
Welcome to _____
Baseball, Basketball, Snow Skiing,
    Soccer, Tennis, Golf, Fishing,
    Windsurfing, Football, Waterski-
    ing, Surfing, Skateboarding, and
    Boating
Midas Touch/All Gold
Bar and Bat Mitzvah
Campaign Theme
Gone With the Wind/Tara
Jeans and Jewels
Radio Active
Paint the Town Red
Circus/Bring in the Clowns
Garden Party (Long Island)
In Vogue
Rich Man/Poor Man
Polka Dots
Wrestlemania 13 (Bar Mitzvah)
Fire and Ice
Toon Town
Quest for the Best

Beverly Hills 90210
Party Animals
Beaux Arts
In the Pink
Copacabana
Shangri-La
The Secret Garden
Tropical Caribbean
Hats off to You
Australian Outback
Carousel
40's Big Band
New York, New York
Private Night Club
Teahouse of the August Moon
Italian
Movie Magic
Tropical Serenade
Candyland/Chocolate Factory
Margaritaville/Key West
Country and Western
Your Hit Parade
Space—The Final Frontier
Jukebox Saturday Night
Octoberfest
Enchantment under the Sea Dance
Babes in Toyland
Larger than Life (Oversize)
Life's a Beach
Peter Pan's Night Flight
Girl Talk
Masquerade Ball
Over the Rainbow
Southern Garden
Pub of the Isles (Scottish, British,
    Irish, etc.)
Patriotic
Stopping by Woods on a Snowy
    Evening
Stadium Club
Sentimental Journey
Casino (C&W, Riverboat, Gatsby,
    Roaring 20's, etc.)
It's a Small World
Participation (Carnival, Casino, Mo-
    nopoly, Olympics, Sumo, Sports,
    etc.)
Broadway Lights
Ice Cream Parlor
Great White Way (All White)
Cheerleading
Twilight Zone/Party Zone
International Fantasy

Bayou Barn
Voyage to the Bottom of the Sea
Continental Elegance
Comedy Warehouse
Puttin' on the Ritz
In Living Color
Dance the Night Away
Starlit Evening
Dixieland
Caribbean Holiday
Summer Camp/School Daze
Wacky Tacky Tourist
Cotton Club
Nostalgic Nights
Palms and Palladiums
Caesar's Bacchanal
Shop Till You Drop
Speakeasy
The Great Train Robbery
The Last Bar Mitzvah
Rio Carnivale (Brazil)
Country Fair
Hot Tropic
Caesar's Feast
Batman®
Addam's Family®
Flintstones®
Hollywood Backlot
Ali Baba's Island
Gatsby's Mansion
Night on the Nile
Gilligan's Island®
Comic Cabaret
Only the Brave, Rave!
Future World
Flip Side of the 60's
The Big Chill/Woodstock
Big
Tom Jones Theme Party
Tropicana
Red Baron Ball
Top Gun
A Night of Stars
Café la Crêpe
The Faces of America
Yo MTV Raps/MTV®
Out of the Blue
Mississippi Riverboat
White Knights
Indiana Jones/Temple of Doom®
Broadway Christmas
Jurassic Park®
Western Badlands

375 Possible Theme Experiences (continued)

Beach Olympics	Neon Nights	The Great Race
Power Picnic	Dynasty	Dancing Through the Decades
Night in Havana	Abracadabra	Star Search
Western Hoedown	Midnight in Moscow	California Dreamin'
Pirate Adventure	Dick Tracy Adventure®	A Christmas Carol
Aladdin's Palace	Frankenstein	Hullabaloo
Smoke and Mirrors	Whaler's Village	Rhinestone Cowboy
Les Miserables®	Bow Tie and Blue Jeans	Walk on the Wild Side
57th Street Delicatessen	Lullabye of Broadway	Mystery Cruise
Miniature Golf	Field of Dreams®	Club Mocambo
Guys and Dolls	Night in the Tropics	Journey into Your Imagination
Golden Games of Hollywood	English Hunt Club	City Slickers
Hot, Hot, Hot to the Top	Goldfinger®	Harbors of the World
Pow Wow	Polynesian Luau	Fan-ta-Seas (Underwater Fantasy)
Flamingo Bar and Grill	From Russia with Love®	Making Memories
A Very Sheik Celebration	Aztec Adventure	Neptune's Kingdom
Ja'Maican Me Crazy	A Night at the Apollo®	Fiesta
China Club	Make Your Own Rock Video	Dracula's Castle
The Pink Flamingo	Up, Up, and Away	Dancing in the Streets
Club Voodoo	Toyland	Your Favorite Musical Star
Electric Reef Party	Hollywood Squares®	FutureShock
Born to be Wild/Harley Bar	A Fair to Remember	Possum County Swamp
The Gold Nugget Review	Starlight Express on Broadway	Wild West Fest
In the Mood	Rhythm of the Night	An Enchanted Evening
Museum of Natural Mystery	Vienna in Three-Quarter Time	Blues Brothers® Jazz Club
Blue Moon	Concourse d'Elegance	The Boston Freedom Trail
Positive/Negative	USO Comedy Cabaret	Trash Disco
Roman Toga	Camp Corporate	Enchanted Forest
A Night at Versailles	A Night at the Diner (50's)	Christmas Around the World
Theater of Illusion	Renaissance Faire	Leader of the Pack
Headed for the Future	Luck Be a Lady Tonight	Southern Nights
Name That Tune	A Star Is Born	Black Horse Saloon
Urban Cowboy	Fantasy Island®	South Pacific
Super Heroes	Land Before Time®	Route 66
Caddy Shack	Disco . . . Inferno	Country Jamboree
Lifestyles of the Rich and Famous®	The Man of LaMancha®	Future Frontiers
A Night of Andrew Lloyd Webber	Motown Madness	Six Flags over Texas®
Star Wars®	My Fair Lady®	Mama Mia's Ristorante
A Dickens of a Christmas	What's Black and White and Red All Over?	Atlantic City Nights
Café Tangiers		Impressions of France
A Tropical Blizzard	Ghouls, Goblins, and Ghosts	Mexican Border Bash
Tropical Madness	Moonlight Romance	Premiere Party
Samba South Beach Club	Desert Magic	Great Frontiers
Masters of the Universe®	Mad Hatter's Tea Party	Club Beverly Hills
Picasso Party	Rock and Roll Hall of Fame®	Cajun Party
Purple Passion	Lights, Camera, Action!	Streets of San Francisco
America the Bountiful	Bonanza® Revisited	Ranch Party
Calypso	Chinese New Year	High-Tech Futuristic
Taste of the Globe	Caribbean Island Festival	State Fair
Conch Republic	King Kong	Spring Break Fever
At the Races	Romance of the 40's	
Gold and White	Festivale de Florida	

Some Entertainment Possibilities for Consideration

The entertainment should reflect and contribute to the theme concept. In order to consider the many forms of entertainment that may be available, we list many of them for your consideration. This by no means should be considered a complete list.

Celebrities	Fire eaters	Talking trash cans
National show bands	Limbo artists	Country cloggers
Local bands	Jugglers	Cheerleaders
Performing disc jockey	One-man bands	Marching bands
High energy entertainment	Gunfighters	Celebrity look-alikes
Fireworks productions	Bird man	Jugglers
Casino parties	Palmist	Strolling shows
Tributes	Rain makers	Marionettes
Video stage	Glass walkers	Skits and stunts
Full orchestras	Helicopter rides	Pony rides
Magicians/illusionists	Indoor fireworks	Hay rides
Comedians	Square dance callers	Sand art
Caricaturists/cartoonists	Choirs	Snake charming
Murder mysteries	Belly dancers	BMX trick bike show
Hermit crab races	Barbershop quartets	Monkey and organ grinder
Carnival rides	Hula dancers	Road rally
Company picnic specialties	Street musicians	Puppet show
Costumed characters	Face painters	Roof top balloons
Name acts	Ringmaster	Ventriloquist
Regional bands	Petting zoo	Caribbean revue
Character acts	Spin art machines	Guest speakers
Karaoke	Circus dog show	Fortune teller
Dance revues	Carnival high striker	Impersonators
Laser productions	Armadillo racing	Bull riding
Recording artists	Hypnotist	Boxing match
Impressionists	Treasure hunt	Simulators
Single entertainers	Searchlights	Strolling bands
Robots and aliens	Fire dancers	Jukeboxes
Psychics/ESP/witches	Mimes	Models
Specialty acts	Stilt walkers	Polynesian show
Artists	Trick ropers	Virtual reality
Circus acts	Exotic animals	Robotic boxing
Sport bar equipment/games	Monkey man	Remote control race cars
Carnival games	Clowns	Remote control boats
Balloon sculptor	Sword swallowers	
Unicyclists	Contortionists	

Chapter 2

Raise Food and Beverage Management to a Higher Level

In today's highly sophisticated, fast-paced, and ever-changing business world, meetings, conventions, and incentive travel programs provide a dynamic opportunity for creative expression. And planners of special events have a captivating combination of circumstances favorable to gathering people together to network, share problems, brainstorm solutions, sign contracts, or close deals. You can say everyone in attendance has innovative expectations. Breakfasts, luncheons, coffee breaks, cocktail parties, theme parties, banquets, white glove dining experiences—any occasion for eating and drinking is an opportunity to meet business goals. Design your special events to indeed be special, spend your dollars wisely and stay one step ahead of your increasingly sophisticated audience.

According to Henry R. Luce, "Business, more than any other occupation, is a continual calculation, an instinctive exercise in foresight." It is often said that it takes genius and courage to originate, not imitate. We all have dreams and fantasies about the future. But the best way to predict the future is to invent it. Successes are spawned from creativity, from generating and implementing ideas. What this is telling us is that our business food and beverage events must include creative genius, as our clients' business sophistication demands it.

Setting and Understanding Objectives

I have always enjoyed Yogi Berra's quotations on various subjects, as he has a very simple way to say and understand things. Yogi Berra might simply say that, "You can only achieve an objective if you know what it is." Understand the objective of every food and beverage event clearly. Maybe the objective is just to have fun. Understand clearly the meeting goals and dovetail in the attendees' needs.

Recruit the Hotel or Resort Staff

Make the hotel or resort staff a valuable member of your team. Recruit their ideas, creativity, enthusiasm, and commitment. Challenge them to provide some unique suggestions rather than to rely on preprinted menus or computer-generated menu suggestions. The catering executive should present menu proposals based on a client's budget and the function's objectives. The catering executive must have complete knowledge of what will work in his or her facility, as well as of the staff capabilities. He or she should be an expert in developing and executing contemporary menus that meet and exceed client expectations.

If you were hiring a catering executive, you would look for someone with great "people sense," creativity, knowledge of food and beverage trends, and the ability to listen. It is the catering executive's job to shape the client's needs and desires into a total food and beverage experience.

Hence it is the client's—the meeting planner's—job to communicate. The client should supply accurate estimates of what he or she can afford, should discuss the functional goals and the mood to be created, should provide records of past events indicating attendance patterns and menu selection history. The more information that the planner conveys, the more likely the client will get what he or she wants.

Initial Site Inspection Must Include Presentation by Director of Catering

Meeting or incentive planners must understand that food and beverage play a very important role in a meeting or incentive program; thus they should insist on a complete presentation by the Director of Catering on their initial site inspection visit. If you are that Director of Catering, it is very important to present what it is that makes your operation unique among your competitors. Even if your food and beverage prices are higher, you can generally secure the business if you can excite the client with your commitment, creativity, and enthusiasm. Most times you can excite the client into spending more money than he or she had intended—before the budget is set and firmed up. Don't just hand your menus to the planner but listen to his or her needs and goals, and then create a special event with those in mind.

Execution Excellence

A revolution is on: The corporate pursuit of long-term excellence. This excellence results from superior service to customers or clients and from constant innovation, both based on the consistent creativity of every person in the company. It also requires day-to-day acts of leadership at every management level, adding up to superior performance. Executive success has come from empowering every single manager and line employee to practice common sense in their decision-making. This benefits the customer first, then benefits the company with customer loyalty. More managers are staying close to their customers using an MBWA approach, "managing by walking around." New Age executives must possess six essential leadership skills: sensitivity, insight, versatility, focus, vision, and patience. Crisis-ridden catering executives must:

- Know their hotel's or resort's capabilities—and make the most of them.
- Motivate their people to peak performance.
- Respond positively to change from within and without.
- Develop long-term goals and see them through.
- Turn crisis into opportunity.

Hotels, resorts, and convention centers are anxious for more business. And there is more competition for the meeting and travel dollar. As a result, the meeting and/or special event planner should expect prompt attention to food and beverage requests. Every planner should push the catering and banquet staffs to deliver the best. Our reputations are only as good as today's performance. Be proud of your career and make sure your career is proud of you.

The Art of Negotiating Anything

In Herb Cohen's book *You Can Negotiate Anything*, he quotes a saying: "Power is based upon perception—if you think you've got it then you've got it. If you think you don't have it, even if you've got it, then you don't have it."

Your real world is a giant negotiating table, and like it or not, you're a negotiator. How you handle your daily encounters with other people in your personal and business life determines whether you prosper happily or suffer frustration and loss.

In a culture as business-minded as ours, the ability to negotiate well is a powerful asset. For meeting planners, it's a must. Fortunately, all successful negotiations turn on three simple things: the right attitude, good timing, and proper information.

Remember John F. Kennedy's words, "Let us never negotiate out of fear, but let us never fear to negotiate." When you're the meeting planner, you must never be afraid to ask for concessions. You might ask yourself, what's the right attitude when negotiating food and beverage? I am reminded of Herb Cohen's words, ". . . Successful collaborative negotiation lies in finding out what the other side really wants and showing them a way to get it, while you get what you want." "Win-win" may sound like a cliché, but all parties involved should gain something during the negotiation.

Obviously, the more a hotel or resort needs your business, the better the deal they'll cut.

A hotel that is just opening presents you, as a special event planner, with an excellent opportunity to negotiate. You cannot expect, however, that everything will go as smoothly as with an operation that already has a history of professionalism and excellence. If you are willing to take that risk, then this presents an excellent savings opportunity.

However, you can expect successful negotiations at other times such as off-season, when you're arranging short-term, repeat bookings, when you're planning large food and beverage programs, or when you're making multiyear bookings. And don't forget to ask for some concessions in order to close the deal.

You may be told "no" but better yet, you may receive a "yes"!

If You Want It, You Have to Ask for It

Leopold Fechtner once said, "No customer can be worse than no customer." This is the reason short-term negotiations are so often successful. The axiom's mirror image is also true, however, but there is always room for some sort of concession, such as:

- Hotel may guarantee the next year's group food and beverage menu prices with a maximum 4% or 5% increase, even though the rate of inflation may be higher than that.
- Hotel may credit master account for the opening cocktail reception with hot and cold hors d'oeuvres or with a maximum dollar amount credit.
- The hotel may increase the maximum number of room nights for future site and planning inspection visits.
- The hotel may provide additional travel staff rooms in addition to those provided by the usual comp policy of one for 50 paid.
- The hotel may provide extra suites.
- Complimentary coffee and soft drinks may be provided daily at the hospitality desk.
- Additional VIP room amenities may be provided.
- Complimentary newspaper might be provided each morning for all rooms.
- Complimentary round-trip limo service for ten (or more) VIPs might be arranged.
- All rooms with the best view or location may be provided.
- And so on.

Negotiate Only with Those Who Possess the Power and Authority to Negotiate

Don't pick only one hotel or resort at your preferred site location, and let each hotel know that the site will not be finalized until you can negotiate your best deal. Each property has its own hierarchy, and you should always politely insist on working with managers who can make decisions for the hotel or resort. When a manager tells you, "Let me talk it over with the boss and I'll let you know," assertively ask for a decision now: Either make the decision or let *me* negotiate with the boss.

Care—But Don't Care Too Much

Be willing to walk away from the negotiating table. Be willing to take chances. Care about the outcome but don't care too much. When making a site inspection, insist on a presentation by the Director of Catering, so you know what to expect from your food and beverage activities as well as costs, and then take these into final consideration on your site inspection and your site choice to follow. If there are some concessions that you need in order to close the overall deal, then ask now, before you have selected the site. Know your group's demographics, including information as specific as the percentage of males to females and your attendees' average age, economic bracket, education level, and employment status. Men usually eat more than women, especially red meat. With some groups the quantity of food is most important; with others, it's quality. These elements will help you control costs.

No-show records are especially useful, since they can prevent you from overbuying. You should generally figure a 10% no-show factor into your guarantees. Hotels and resorts will set up and be ready to serve 3% to 5% over and above the guarantee. This is where knowing your group will pay off. Remember, you pay for whichever is higher—your guarantee, or the number of people who show up.

Of course, you must establish a reliable budget in order to know how much you can spend per person, per meal. You should also understand the objectives of each food and beverage event. For example, if you are planning a "soft-sell" reception for exhibitors at a nurse's convention, don't create a cabaret-style evening with little cocktail tables, low lights, and a fun, low-cost menu of finger foods because in the dim lights, the exhibitors won't be able to read the names on the name badges.

Total Meeting Food and Beverage Budget Concept

As a Director of Catering, I much prefer the meeting planner to approach me with a total F&B budget. Tell the catering staff how much your budget is for all of your food functions and ask them to make suggestions and shift the monies around to give you the most for your dollars. They know where they can make adjustments, and when they know that you are not holding out on them, they will be more willing to work with you. I am certain your catering executive can make some cost-saving suggestions.

I suggest you plan your menus, whenever possible, directly with the Catering Director, and sometimes with the Executive Banquet Chef. Look at the hotel's or resort's printed menu or computer management menus and if there is not a large selection of creative choices, then set them aside. Then tell the hotel or resort management that you are there to plan each of the functions and negotiate some of the costs.

Ask them to be creative while helping you to reduce costs. Of course, ask what specialties they offer or would suggest. Also, don't overlook the possibility of reducing entrée portions by a few ounces or of offering a double entrée with a smaller portion of beef or veal and a small portion of fish, instead of a 12-ounce steak. Plate presentation can make up for smaller portions.

30 Smart Ways to Save on Food and Beverage Costs

There are smart—and not-so-smart—ways to save on food and beverage costs. Ordering the cheapest thing on the menu because you have a tight budget falls into the latter category. The last thing you want is attendees saying, "Gee, what a chintzy looking piece of chicken." Food and beverage can be one of the most costly components of a meeting. Here are some simple ways to take the sting out of the master account, while you do it right:

- Reduce the guarantee at breakfast by a few percentage points per day. The longer a meeting runs, the fewer people show up for breakfast.
- Keep things simple. Beware of sauces, flambés, and glazes—they involve more labor, the most expensive variable in food and beverage costs. And don't offer more than one choice of entrée. You can offer a double entrée of smaller portions but not a **choice** of selections.
- Know the cuts of meat and proper portion sizes. For instance, an 8-ounce, or even 6-ounce, filet mignon may be sufficient because filet has no fat or bone.
- Save on dessert. Serve petits fours or cookies and/or sherbet with a topping instead of something elaborate. Or have a dessert table so people can help themselves, and arrange to pay only for what is consumed by being brought to the dessert table.
- For receptions, serve hors d'oeuvres in bite-size pieces with cocktail forks and napkins. Making it awkward to pile up hors d'oeuvres can reduce consumption by as much as 30 percent.
- Don't provide plates for hors d'oeuvres.
- Cut the reception length to no more than 45 minutes, particularly if a meal follows.
- During the reception, have aperitifs passed, butler-style, by white-gloved waitpersons. Aperitifs, by design, awaken jaded tastebuds. They put an edge on the appetite, providing the perfect prelude to a meal. The selection should include a dry to semidry white wine, champagne, and chilled mineral water. When you change attendees' habits, they will respond differently. The consumption will be much less than if you were serving hard liquor, and your guests will be able to taste their food.
- Serve light hors d'oeuvres before a heavy meal or heavy hors d'oeuvres before a light meal.
- For buffets, have servers dole out expensive foods, like shrimp or sushi, rather than laying them out on a table. Attendees will eat less, especially if the server is of the opposite sex!
- Instead of a reception followed by a sit-down dinner, throw a cocktail party with substantial hors d'oeuvres and "action stations," like a pasta bar, crêpes station, and so on. It will cost more than a regular reception, but less than a reception and dinner.
- Set up a good follow-up system for a party or event RSVPs. Issue tickets for food functions to make guarantees more accurate. But never assume a group will remember printed instructions for ticket exchange. Make announcements, put up signs, have an information desk—spread the word in every way possible.
- Compute difference in cost: per bottle/per drink/per person; per gallon/per person. Generally avoid per person prices, as they are more costly.
- Have servers pass drinks to reduce bar bill.
- Use house brand alcoholic beverages.
- Count the empties of marked bottles after beverage service periods.
- Instead of cutting large sweet rolls in half, serve only the petite size.
- Select the same menu for simultaneous functions. Ask for a discount because your advance planning will save the hotel or resort money and increase their profits.
- Instruct the caterer not to uncork the wine ahead of time; uncork only as needed.
- Work with the Chef or Director of Catering to develop the best meal within your budget. Don't just plan all your menus from preprinted menus, if they are not most creative.
- Avoid labor-intensive foods, such as shrimp. If you put ten shrimp out per person during a reception, the attendees will eat them and want more.
- Avoid buffets, which cost more than sit-down meals.

- Serve smaller portions. Most meeting attendees will confess that they usually can't eat everything served at most meal functions.
- Be conservative. Instead of spreading out funds over many different events during a gathering, try to come up with just a couple of functions that really sizzle. Meeting-goers will have happier memories from one dinner that hits a home run than from plodding through several mediocre affairs.
- Rein in your ideas and go for the tried and true. Down-to-earth, Texas-style barbecues are clichéd by now, but still provide lots of laid-back fun. Sometimes, wicker baskets and mason jars work just as well as silver and china. After a long hotel meeting, hamburgers and hot dogs on an outdoor grill never tasted better.
- As the planner, you should know your group better than anyone, so you should also make the needed decisions. Whether planning a retirement dinner for 50 or a convention reception for 3,250, don't ignore your own food and beverage erudition and don't let the facility's catering executive decide how much food and drink your group needs, without any input from you. But to avoid problems you must do your homework; otherwise you have no choice but to rely on the recommendations of the catering executive. However, when you make your own decisions, there are some risks involved. Consider the locations of the kitchen and coffee break preparation areas, and ask if the banquet captains and coffee break captains carry two-way radios. The advantage of a per-person price is that it stabilizes budget considerations, but it does carry a price.
- Typically, food and beverage are priced on a per-person basis for only one reason—it's more profitable for the facility. Avoid Continental breakfasts on a per-person basis. Use your own consumer know-how to figure out how much your group would consume, and then order coffee and orange juice by the gallon and baked goods by the dozen.
- Insist the facility give you the option of ordering beverages, hors d'oeuvres, reception embellishments, and breakfast items by bulk instead of on a per-person basis. Make this insistence at the time of negotiating the overall facility contract, not after.
- What records will be used to determine payment? Ticket count? Head count? Plate count? Or quantities? Know this important factor up front.
- Roughly 60% of the cost of a plate of food served by a facility is for labor. Therefore, the number of servers becomes important in pricing food and beverage activities for meeting planner clients.

And, remember that even though it's important to have a solid history of your groups' eating and drinking habits, don't fall into the trap of ordering the same amounts of food from year to year. For example, if your meeting is in a different city, there may be other variables involved. The last city may have had great restaurants and other attractions, like Washington, DC or Las Vegas, and attendees may have skipped meal functions.

Food and Beverage Allowances

2–2 $\frac{1}{2}$ drinks per person per hour

2–2 $\frac{1}{2}$ 4-ounce glasses of wine with formal dinner

1 bar for each 100 guests—open bar

1 bar for each 150 guests—cash bar

1 coffee station per 60 guests

1 buffet line per 50–75 guests

1 $\frac{1}{2}$ baked goods, muffins, Danish, bagels, per person

1 $\frac{1}{2}$–2 cups of coffee per person, early morning

1–1 $\frac{1}{2}$ cups of coffee per person, midmorning

$\frac{1}{2}$–1 cup of coffee per person, afternoon, if soft drinks are also available

---

Alcoholic Beverages

One keg of beer equals 160 glasses

One fifth (25.6 ounces) equals 23 1-ounce drinks

One liter (35.6 ounces) equals 33 1-ounce drinks

One quart (32 ounces) equals 5 6-ounce glasses

One gallon of wine (64 ounces) equals 16 4-ounce glasses

One bottle of wine (24 ounces) equals 6 4-ounce glasses

Reception fare is more difficult to order in bulk fashion. Wine and liquor—particularly for large groups—are most cost-effective when purchased by the bottle, rather than by the drink or by flat rate per person.

Reception
Alcoholic Drink Estimator

Length of Reception	$\frac{1}{2}$ hr.	$\frac{3}{4}$ hr.	1 hr.	$1\frac{1}{4}$ hr.	$1\frac{1}{2}$ hr.	$1\frac{3}{4}$ hr.	2 hr.
			Drinks Per Person				
Guests							
25–59	2	3	$3\frac{3}{4}$	4	$4\frac{1}{4}$	$4\frac{1}{2}$	$4\frac{3}{4}$
60–99	2	3	$3\frac{3}{4}$	4	4	$4\frac{1}{2}$	$4\frac{3}{4}$
100–229	$1\frac{3}{4}$	$2\frac{1}{2}$	3	$3\frac{1}{2}$	4	4	$4\frac{1}{2}$
230–299	$1\frac{1}{2}$	2	$2\frac{1}{2}$	$2\frac{3}{4}$	3	$3\frac{1}{4}$	$3\frac{1}{2}$
300 & up	$1\frac{1}{2}$	2	$2\frac{1}{2}$	$2\frac{3}{4}$	3	$3\frac{1}{4}$	$3\frac{1}{2}$

Based on all male attendance and easy access to bars. With 50% female attendance, average is $2\frac{1}{2}$–3 drinks per hour; with 100% female attendance, average $2\frac{1}{2}$ drinks per hour.
SOURCE: American Hotel & Motel Association

Liquor Bottle Estimator

Bottle Size (Quarts)	Amount of Alcohol per Drink (Ounces)	Number of Drinks
4/5	1	25
4/5	$1\frac{1}{4}$	20
4/5	$1\frac{1}{2}$	17
1	1	31
1	$1\frac{1}{4}$	25
1	$1\frac{1}{2}$	21

SOURCE: American Hotel & Motel Association

Coffee Allowances

One gallon of coffee equals 22 6-ounce cups. For most coffee lovers, especially at early-morning functions, one cup just isn't enough. Another factor: many people today stay away from caffeine.

Suggested Quantities for a Group of 100

5 gallons of regular coffee
4 gallons of decaffeinated coffee
1 gallon of hot water with tea selection

As for bottled soft drinks, mineral water, and all-natural fruit juices—by all means have them available, but only agree to pay for them on an "as-consumed" basis. For more elaborate spreads, order individual containers of yogurt or serving-size boxes of cereal. Order enough for almost everyone, but the key is to order "by consumption." That way you will pay only for what your group actually consumes.

Hors d'Oeuvres

The industry standard for a two-hour reception is eight pieces per person for the first hour, and six pieces per person during the second hour. This is based on an average hors d'oeuvre buffet that includes cold food, such as fruit and cheeses, along with hot finger food.

Carving stations also lend themselves to bulk orders.

Whole roast steamship round of beef serves approximately 200 portions
Whole sliced marinated roasted beef tenderloin serves approximately 25 portions
Suckling pig serves approximately 125 portions
Whole smoked Nova Scotia salmon on display serves approximately 35 portions per side

Whole roast turkey serves approximately 75 portions

Whole sugar-cured baked ham serves approximately 75 portions

Whole roast baron of veal serves approximately 100 portions

Glazed corned brisket of beef serves approximately 75 portions

Another possibility is to order cheese and other cold tray items, such as fruit and cold cuts, by the pound rather than per person, if you as a planner are confident in estimating quantities. Or, you may want to order by bulk for items that are menu enhancers, and not the sole reception offering. Good examples of this are jumbo shrimp and crab claws. Stagger the quantities being brought to the buffet table or—even better—pass them.

The facility may not allow you to dictate how many pounds of tortellini you want on the pasta bar, but you can negotiate the amount somewhat.

If you order less than the catering executive recommends, try to find out which food items can quickly and easily be replaced. Also, stay in close contact with the banquet captain in charge during the function so you know when you are running low— not when you are out and the chafing dishes are empty.

Creating Memorable Dining Experiences

French Chef Fenard Point once wrote, "A successful meal is a combination of small things done well." That's certainly true when it comes to planning menus. Attention to the finer details— such as eating and dining trends, food availability, and kitchen staff talent—can transform the mundane into the memorable.

When creating menus, meeting and incentive planners should ask three key questions: What's hot? What's not? and What's possible?

Contemporary menus convey a sense of fun without eschewing the traditional. Here's a look at what's hot in food and beverage, with some sample menus reflecting today's trends.

Breakfast Trends

High Fiber Foods:	Muffins; Granola; Muesli; Cereal.
Personal Service:	Made-to-order Omelets or Frittatas.
Bread Baskets:	Fresh Croissants; Brioche; Hard Rolls.
Fresh Foods:	Seasonal Fruits and Berries; Freshly Squeezed Juices.
Beverages:	Freshly Brewed Decaffeinated Coffee; Herbal Teas; Cola.

Meeting Break Trends

Finger Foods:	Salsa and Tortilla Chips; Chicken Wings; Vegetables and Dip; Popcorn.
Fun Foods:	Dove Bars; Cracker Jacks; Ice Cream Sandwiches; Candy Bars; Chocolate Brownies; Peanut Butter Brownies; Giant Cookies.
Healthful Choices:	Fresh Fruit Kabobs; Low-fat Yogurts with Fruit Topping; Fruit-and-Nut Breads; Fruit Smoothies.

Lunch Trends

Light Lifts:	Cold Poached Salmon with Yogurt-Dill Sauce; Grilled Chicken; Pasta Primavera Salad.
Seasonal Foods:	Fresh Fruits; Vegetables.
Box Lunches:	Bagel Sandwiches with Deli Meats; Tomatoes Stuffed with Tuna or Chicken Salad; Gourmet Peanut-Butter-and-Jelly Sandwiches with an Apple and Chips.
Deli Buffets:	Kettle of Soup; Salads; Turkey, Ham, and Roast Beef Platters; Sliced Cheeses; Assorted Breads.

Cocktail Reception Trends

"Light" Liquor:	Light or no-alcohol beers; Fruit Smoothies; Wine Spritzers.
Mineral Waters:	Sparkling and nonsparkling specialty drinks: Flavored Margaritas, Piña Coladas, Fruit Smoothies.
Food Stations:	Stir-Fry; Pasta; Tempura.

Dinner Trends

Ethnic and Regional Foods:	Italian; Asian; Mexican; Caribbean; Cajun; and Others.
Wine Pairings:	Courses Paired with Specific Wines.
Traditional Favorites:	Prime Rib; New York Strip Steak; Smoked or Marinated Salmon; Chicken Breast; Rack of Lamb.

Dessert Trends

Platters:	Petits Fours; Cookies; Mini Pastries.
Local Favorites:	Key Lime Pie in Florida; Pecan Pie in Georgia; Sopaipillas Sprinkled with Cinnamon and Sugar in the Southwest; New York Cheesecake; Mississippi Mud Cake.
Fresh Fruits:	Raspberries; Whole Strawberries for Dipping in Chocolate; Mangoes; Papayas; Fresh Fruit Crêpes.
Make-Your-Own Sundaes:	Homemade Chocolate, Vanilla, and Strawberry Ice Cream; Butterscotch, Strawberry, and Hot Fudge Toppings; Walnuts; Sliced Bananas; Whipped Cream.

General Trends

Menu Trends of the Year:	The East/West Influence; the French Bistro; Wine and Food Matings.
Most Artfully Promoted Cuisine:	Mexican.
The Drums Are Beating but We're Still Waiting:	South American Cuisine.
Maybe in a Future Year:	Spanish Cuisine.
Hot from the Headlines:	Eastern European, Russian, and German Cuisines.

What's Possible

Special event planners and menu-makers are often influenced—and rightly so—by the latest crop of cookbooks, the hottest food magazines, and the most up-to-date food and beverage trends. However, it is critical that the inspiration of these wonderful sources does not result in menus that are beyond the kitchen's capacity.

Insist that the Executive Banquet Chef be included in the menu development process, since his or her talents, staff, and equipment will largely deter- mine what can be served. Developing a concept that can't be realized is asking for trouble.

Quality service is also paramount. Attendees want to feel pampered, and they know the difference between a service staff that is only going through the motions and one that pays attention to every detail. According to Peter Glen, in his book, *It's Not My Department,* "Service is the hottest subject in business right now, but most of the service is lip service, not customer service. It is time to stop whining and act!"

Observe and talk to the waiters to determine their strengths and weaknesses. Make sure the staff isn't asked to serve a flaming dessert unless they've had tableside service experience. Most important, make sure they understand that, whether your event is a luncheon for 30 people or a dinner for a few thousand, you expect good service to start before the first guest arrives and end only after the last has departed.

Achieving service success at its optimum level depends on management's being able to get the service staff involved and committed to its overall goals. As a meeting planner, you must also strive to recruit those you work with to become members of your team, with your clear-cut objectives foremost in their minds.

I Guarantee It

One of the hardest things you have to decide as a special event or meeting planner is what guarantees to give. This is where knowing your group and their history comes into play and proves to be so vital. Obviously, you must be prepared to serve as many guests as needed, but you'll want to avoid over-ordering. Hence it is essential that you pay attention to the group departure list in order to stay abreast of how many of your group remains for each meal. Guarantee formulas will vary with each group, but here are some general guidelines:

Breakfast

- On day one, reduce the guarantee by 10 to 15% of the guests in-house. The hotel or resort will set up and be ready to serve 3 to 5% over and above the guarantee.
- On day two, reduce the guarantee by 15 to 20% of the in-house guests.
- After several days, you may reduce the breakfast guarantees by 20 to 25% of the in-house guests.
- This is an area where keeping a close watch on your meal counts and adjusting as you go can save you more money than you might expect.

Lunch/Dinner

- Since most in-house guests will attend the luncheons and dinners, you can generally

reduce those guarantees by 5% or less, depending on what the hotel or resort sets as an average.

Meeting Breaks

- For early morning breaks, figure one cup of coffee for 80% of the in-house meeting attendees.
- For midmorning breaks, provide assorted soft drinks for 25% of the attendees, of which two-thirds should be diet.
- For afternoon breaks, provide coffee for 25% of the in-house meeting attendees. Since you should only be charged as consumed for assorted soft drinks, plan on one per person.

These guidelines will vary from group to group so they should be used as just that—guidelines—which you can adjust each day when giving your next guarantees.

To Tip or Not to Tip? This Is the Question

The meeting is coming to a close and it's almost time for your attendees to head home. They are packing your conference materials for that trip. It's time for you to handle one of the more delicate matters: who, what, and when to leave something extra for extra services rendered. After several long days of working with the hotel staff, badgering them for this, reminding them to do that, you feel you have become

almost a part of their team. But somehow, shaking hands and saying "thanks" doesn't quite make it.

Of course, you know it is their responsibility to provide you a high level of service; this is the reason they are on the payroll. However, I suggest you give a little extra whenever it is obvious that various personnel have gone *above and beyond what normally would be considered acceptable*. What I have found over the years is that people in the hotel/resort industry are almost always individuals who approach their careers with a great deal of passion. They do not need to be motivated with money, but instead really care about providing the highest level of service and really care about avoiding any disappointments for you while they meet and exceed your expectations. *But*, providing a little extra as a token of appreciation will be remembered. This is especially a good idea if you plan to return to the same facility. Now you ask yourself: Whom should you tip, how much, and when?

Who Receives the Gratuity/Service Charge Added to Each Food Function?

One question that no one seems to know the answer to is who receives the gratuity or service charge that is automatically added to each and every food function. The answer to this question will vary from hotel/resort to hotel/resort.

In some hotels/resorts none of the gratuity/service charge goes directly to the staff or management but goes in its entirety to the hotel or resort. However, the staff and management in these facilities usually receive larger salaries to compensate. This is done to benefit the employee: Since gratuity/service charge percentages cannot qualify as salary, depending on them as income makes it more difficult to qualify for home and auto loans or other major purchases. Also, the higher hourly rate of pay in these hotels and resorts provides a more steady income with less fluctuation. Other hotels and resorts, whose employees belong to a labor union, have the gratuity/service charge split determined in their union contract. For example, some hotels/resorts distribute 65% of the gratuity/service charge to waiters, waitresses, bartenders, and captains. The remaining 35% is distributed to supervisory, sales, and other banquet personnel.

Whatever the distribution arrangement, it really doesn't matter because it all is considered salary. Regardless of the salary paid to hospitality employees—it's never too much. When you consider the hours, stress, pressure, and the holiday and weekend work that is required, hotel and resort staff are paid too little almost across the board. Tipping should be considered something extra and unexpected. I know people who think that tips are written into the food costs in hotels and resorts and divided among key personnel. However, I feel that certain key people generally deserve more. These people need to be at your beck and call and can make or break a meeting. I feel they should be rewarded—and I'm sure you ask, how? In the hospitality industry, the words "tip" and "gratuity" are often used interchangeably, but there is a distinction. A gratuity is a charge added to a food and beverage item. The typical range is 16 percent to 20 percent and, like a tax, it is automatic and nonnegotiable. A tip is a cash gift or award, over and above a gratuity added automatically to the bill, given to staff members in appreciation for services rendered.

Budget for Tipping

The hotel staff all know who tips and who doesn't. Of course, good employees would never do less for any client, but a tip may make the difference between those who knock themselves out and those who don't. The professional planner knows it is customary to tip if service is exceptional, but many planners are not full-time professionals. Planners who believe in tipping regularly have learned that they have to budget for it. Many planners recommend that their clients provide an amount equivalent to 1 percent of their total meeting budget, excluding sleeping rooms, for tips.

This is only a general guideline. Another guideline is a range of $3.00 to $5.00 per person, based on the number of meeting attendees. For the smaller meeting $5.00 per attendee may be more appropriate, whereas for the larger meeting, $3.00 per attendee may generate enough monies. Even though it is budgeted for, you should never feel the tips need to be given out if service is below par.

Whom Do You Tip?

Needless to say, it is impractical and impossible to tip every person involved in each function. As the planner, you must determine what key players went the extra distance for you. Generally, ask the Convention Service Manager and the Catering Executive for a list of names of individuals who directly served each function and what function each employee served. Yes, there are some obvious choices. But there are also some not-so-obvious "back of the house" employees; some of these might well be the PBX Operators, the Executive Banquet Chef, Banquet Housemen, and the Shipping and Receiving Manager.

It is recommended that a handwritten or typed note be placed in an envelope with the tip and the individual's name written on the outside of the envelope. It is best to give these envelopes out yourself before departure. If this is not possible, then the envelopes can be given to the Convention Services Manager or the Catering Executive to be given out in your absence, following the meeting. Once you return to your office, the appropriate thank-you letters should be written to top management or to the corporate office, recognizing by name those individuals who went out of their way to make your conference or incentive program such a success.

An Example of Disbursing Tips

You project your company will spend $140,000 on meals, meeting room rental, A/V equipment, and other miscellaneous charges. Based on the 1% rule, you have $1,400 to disburse in tips. Or your conference is for 350 attendees. Allowing $4.00 per attendee will also give you $1,400 to disburse in tips.

Assuming all staffers went the extra distance, here's an appropriate disbursement schedule:

Convention Service Manager	$ 250
Catering Executive	$ 250
Banquet Manager	$ 150
Assistant Banquet Manager	$ 50
Meeting Break Captain	$ 35
Banquet Captains (4)	$ 140
Executive Banquet Chef	$ 50
Convention Floor Managers (3)	$ 150
Banquet Housemen (10)	$ 150
Shipping and Receiving	$ 50
Audiovisual Technicians (2)	$ 50
Front Desk Remote Clerks (3)	$ 75
Total Disbursement	$1,400

The following charges can be billed to a group master or handled by the individual attendees:

Housekeeping: $1.00 to $2.00 per room, per day (if the attendees are leaving the tip, they should leave the tip for the maid in an envelope or under an ashtray).

Bellman: $1.00 to $1.50 per bag or box.

The above suggestions are merely guidelines. Tipping is always subjective, and the planner must determine who has provided exceptional service and disburse tips accordingly.

One last thought to remember and to pass along: "Don't achieve to be happy but happily achieve!"

Chapter 3

Don't Kneel to Propose

Without a doubt, one of the hardest parts of being a catering or special event executive is planning and preparing the proposal or prospectus. Of course, this is when all your efforts are put on the line; your proposal will probably make the difference between a sale and no sale. I will not call preparing the proposal the most important development stage because I, for one, believe the execution step is the most important stage. We must always deliver more than we promise. But it's making the promise and how it's made that gives us our greatest challenge. It is amazing to me to see how little effort sometimes goes into the prospectus preparation. The menu may not be a reflection of the theme and no effort has been made to excite, inspire, and entice the client. Don't kneel and beg with your proposal but motivate, stimulate, and stir the theatrical blood; bring about a feeling that they can't wait to experience.

How to Write a Proposal

A proposal should be well thought out and researched to present a completely unique and memorable experience. When reading the prospectus, the reviewer should feel the event and look forward to sharing it with his or her attendees. If our proposals do not excite, we are missing an opportunity to be uniquely different.

First, set the mood of the special event and follow through as if you are telling a narrative, imaginary happening, or chronicle. Use vivid and picturesque descriptions, a word portrait that creates expectations. For example, if you are presenting a 50's theme menu and you are describing chicken and tuna salad plates, maybe you can make them seem special in this way:

The Light Touch

As rock'n'roll fills the era, allow these delectable items to fulfill your enjoyment:

The Marilyn Monroe
Two heaping mounds of Chicken Salad
Nestled on an English Muffin and dripping with Cheddar
Cheese Sauce

The Brigitte Bardot
A sumptuous Tuna Salad barely Covered in Cheese
and Sprawled on Toasty Muffin Beaches

The Esther Williams
One of Each—for those who can't decide

Or, if you are describing specialty drinks:

We All Scream for Ice Cream
Specialty Drinks

Special concoctions created for the "soda set." They'll jar your memory with the fun of a malt shop.

Sputnik
Vodka, Kahlua, and Ice Cream—
A delicious way to go into Orbit!

Chocolate Monkey
Crème de Banana, Crème de Cocoa, and Ice Cream—Go Bananas!

Snow Bear
Amaretto and Ice Cream—
Dare our bear!

Casa Blanca
Rum, Tequila, Kahlua, and Ice Cream—
A delicious way to "Play it again, Sam!"

Golden Chevy
Galliano, Crème de Cocoa, and Ice Cream—
The Rich Man's High!

Start with the name of the thematic experience to set the stage for excitement to follow. Since we were just talking about a 50's theme event, let's present a full prospectus describing the themed experience.

We could call this event, "Sock Hop Saturday Night," "Back to the Future," "Nifty 50's Sock Hop," "Bop Till You Drop," or "The Fabulous 50's/60's Junk Food and the Hop!"

The Fabulous 50's/60's Junk Food and the Hop

Brylcream and bobby socks. Remember those days? Sock Hops in the high school gym. Meeting after school at The Sweet Shoppe Soda Parlor for a soda, or at Paisano's Pizzeria for a slice or two of pepperoni pizza and a "warm" Coke, or at Hamburger Haven for an A&W Root Beer and a burger with everything, except onions.

Memories of the senior class sock hop come alive tonight . . . penny loafers, bobby socks, faded blue jeans, letter sweaters, poodle skirts, ducktails, and ponytails (see color insert). The Pep Squad and the Key Club have decorated the gym with the school colors, balloons, banners, posters, and lifesize photos of the rock'n'roll idols. Go "Back to the Future," where you'll recapture the essence of the past and project it into the promise and excitement of the future. There are plenty of games to play from the past, future, and today. Stick around after the games for the Enchantment Under the Sea Dance, where you'll be dancing the great Papa Doo Run Run. Get ready to do the Jitter Bug, the Hokey Pokey, and the Hand Jive.

Remember when it was ducktails for the cats, ponytails for the chicks, bobby socks and poodle skirts at the malt shop and White Sport Coats with

Pink Carnations for the Prom? Ahhh, those were the days! All the boys dreamed of Chantilly Lace and a pretty face. And breaking up with your steady meant Heartbreak Hotel. Ike may have been the President, but Elvis was the King. It was a time like no other in your life, and here's your chance, for one magic evening, to live it again.

Before you ask your guests to enter our 50's/60's Time Machine, we suggest that you give them plenty of advance notice so that they can get totally involved, providing themselves with outfits that will be the envy of everyone who isn't square!

So dust off your blue suede shoes, slick back your hair with a lot of that "greasy kid stuff" and get ready for the music of the 50's and 60's, with a swinging rock revival provided by the "in" disc jockey.

When you enter the party, you will find yourself back at your High School Sock Hop. We will re-create a high school gym with a hardwood gym floor, bandstand and an out-of-sight Disc Jockey providing the nonstop "sounds." This is where the fun starts. Of course, liquor can be served from the "Boys" and "Girls" locker rooms, graffiti and all.

After the "Bunny Hop," "Stroll" on over to the Sweet Shoppe Soda Parlor, "Pony" on over to Hamburger Haven, or do the "Mashed Potato" on your way to Paisano's Pizzeria. At each hangout, the appropriate 50's/60's junk food will be served.

Your guests will love stretching their imaginations and dressing up with the fashions of the 50's/60's, while your D.J. features the soulful music of greats like Elvis Presley, Little Richard, and Chubby Checker.

If you like, we can even arrange for dancers to teach and lead guests into the fun of the "Twist," the "Pony," the "Monkey," and the "Mashed Potato" . . . you name the dance of the 50's/60's, and chances are we already have it on the agenda! Also, upon request, we'll heighten the mood by flashing pictures of the era's stars such as Elvis Presley, James Dean, Connie Francis, and Marilyn Monroe around the room with the help of audiovisual aids.

It's a visit back to the days when the biggest problem was getting a shine on the old Ford and a date for the Senior Prom, and there are few people who wouldn't love to make the trip!

Take a trip back to the days of dancing in the gym and sharing sodas after school. The days of the Bop, the Stroll and the Peppermint Twist, when cool meant hot, hot meant stolen, and pimples were the end of the world.

So "Hang on Sloopy," start practicing those DA hairdo's, and start looking now for those letter sweaters, saddle shoes, and bobby socks; practice rolling Lucky Strike cigarettes in your T-shirt sleeves, and get ready for . . . the Hop.

Be there or be square!

HAMBURGER HAVEN

From the "Burger Joint" we will serve:

The Great Pretender

Miniature White Castle Cocktail Size Cheeseburgers with or without Grilled Onions

How Much Is That Doggy in the Window?

Miniature Hot Dogs with Mustard, Mayonnaise, Ketchup, Chopped Raw Onions, and Shredded American Cheese

Hang on Sloopy Gold Diggers

If chicken is your thing, try these young, Breaded Breast Chunks served with our Sweet-N-Sour Sauce, for dipping

Presley Boats

Cheddar-Bacon Potato Skins, Fried Golden Brown and Laced with Chives and Sour Cream

Tijuana Taxi

Golden Nacho Chips Patterned with Spicy Cheese, Seasoned Beef, and Jalapeño Slices Guaranteed to take you for a ride!

Chubby Checker

Mozzarella Cheese Stix, Tenderly Breaded then Fried to a Crispy Wonderfulness

Marlon Mushrooms

Deep Fried and served with our Spicy Horseradish Sauce. A Definite Contender

Alley Oop Rings

Generous Selection of Onion Rings Lightly Battered and Fried Golden Brown

• • •

HOT BEEFY COLLECTION

Great Prime Rib of Beef, Thinly Sliced, and Served with Numerous Personalities to please the most discriminating of tastes Each Selection prepared to order, piled high on our Buns and served with Chips and Pickle Spear, Au Jus on the side.

Create your own taste-studded morsels of star fame with the following selection of toppings:

BBQ Sauce
Horseradish Sauce
Mayonnaise
Monterey Jack Cheese
Cheddar Cheese
American Cheese
Sliced Tomato
Grilled Onions
Sautéed Sliced Mushrooms
Sliced Green Peppers
Bacon Pieces

Hot Beefy Gallery of Distinction Includes the Following Personalities:

(Written out on a large blackboard)

Joe DiMaggio

With BBQ Sauce

Gary Cooper

With Horseradish Sauce

Spencer Tracy

Mayonnaise, Lettuce, and Shredded Tomato

Buddy Holly

American Cheese and Grilled Onions

Clark Gable

Cheddar Cheese and Bacon Pieces

James Dean

Monterey Jack Cheese and Sautéed Sliced Mushrooms

John Wayne

American Cheese, Shredded Lettuce, and Sliced Tomato

• • •

Side Orders

Shoestring Potatoes
Boxes of Cracker Jacks

• • •

Coffee, with or without Caffeine
Tea, Up or on the Rocks
Soda Pop, With or Without Calories
to include:
Coca-Cola, Sprite, Cherry Coke, Big Orange,
and A&W Root Beer

PAISANO'S PIZZERIA

You haven't experienced a true slice of life until you have indulged yourself with a slice or two of Paisano's Pizza. The following Selection of Pizza with a Combination of Pepperoni, Italian Sausage, Anchovies, Mushrooms, Onions, Green Peppers, Romano, Parmesan, and Mozzarella Cheeses, and our own Homemade Sauce.
or
A Plain Cheese Pizza
for those of you with no Imagination

SWEET SHOPPE SODA PARLOR

Relive the old-fashioned Soda Parlor where you could take your best gal From behind the counter, we will serve: Vanilla, Butter Pecan, Strawberry, and Chocolate Ice Cream.

Guests will add the following toppings: Whipped Cream, Cherries, Chopped Nuts, Chocolate Jimmies, Strawberry Sauce, Hot Fudge Sauce, Butterscotch Sauce, Sliced Bananas, and Crushed Pineapple Sauce We will also offer Ice Cream on Sugar Cones.

THE FABULOUS 50's/60's JUNK FOOD
AND THE HOP PRICES
(Include Food, Decor, and
Staff Costumes)

From 150 to 250 Guests	$ _____	From 751 to 850 Guests	$ _____
From 251 to 350 Guests	$ _____	From 851 to 950 Guests	$ _____
From 351 to 450 Guests	$ _____	From 951 to 1,050 Guests	$ _____
From 451 to 550 Guests	$ _____	From 1,051 to 1,150 Guests	$ _____
From 551 to 650 Guests	$ _____	From 1,151 to 1,250 Guests	$ _____
From 651 to 750 Guests	$ _____	Over 1,251 Guests	$ _____

EXTRA ITEMS AND ARRANGEMENTS

Beverages:

Times/Location

We will provide _____ Beer stations dispensing Quart bottles of Beer, inserted into a brown paper bag, given to the guests and charged at $ _____ each, to the Master Account.

Additionally, from _____ p.m.– _____ p.m.

We will provide 1 Motorcycle Gang Member in leather jacket and motorcycle hat, located outside of the gym entrance, with a "Black Market" Station to "sell" ⅒ pints of various liquors. Each guest will sign an I.O.U. $ _____ will be added to Master Account for each ⅒ pint "sold."

The mixers, as well as water in plastic glasses, will be available at the Soft Drink dispensing Bars.

Also, we will provide _____ Nonalcoholic Specialty Dry Bar(s) serving:

T-Bird Sunrises, Hot Rod Smashes, and '57 Chevys at $ _____ each, charged as consumed and added to the Master Account.

If Alcoholic Beverages are to be served on the hotel premises (or elsewhere under the Hotel's Alcoholic Beverage License), the hotel will require that beverages be dispensed only by Hotel Servers and Bartenders. The Hotel's Alcoholic Beverage License requires the Hotel to (1) request proper identification (photo ID) of any person of questionable age and to refuse alcoholic beverage service if the person is either underage or if proper identification cannot be produced, and (2) refuse alcoholic beverage service to any person who, in the Hotel's judgment, appears intoxicated.

Service Charge:

_____% service charge on all food and beverages, added to the Account.

State Sales Tax:

_____% _____ State Sales Tax on all charges, added to the Account. By State Law, the _____ % Service Charge is taxed.

Linen:

We will provide 50's/60's tablecloths, with the compliments of the Resort.

Table Centerpiece:

We will provide Cracker Jacks, Potato Chips, and Soft Drinks Centerpieces, Complimentary.

Decorations:

We will provide elaborate three-dimensional props which measure 20 to 24 feet in length and 10 to 12 feet in height with stools and fast food style seating incorporated into the design.

The three-dimensional props include a walk-through facade of the high school gymnasium building. Dimensional brick walls with two doorways will give guests access to the "High School Hop." Alongside of these school doorways will be lighted marquees, hedges, and old bicycles tied by chains to the bike racks, enhancing the reality of the mood.

Outside the gymnasium are a variety of "Slow—School Zone" signs and a working traffic light.

Other elaborate three-dimensional props include Hamburger Haven, resembling the front of an Edsel with lighted headlights and eight 16 × 20 inch backlit transparencies of stars of the 50's; the Sweet Shoppe Soda Parlor, which resembles the side view of a '57 Chevy; Paisano's Pizzeria with the sides of the building being the backlit plexiglass panels in Italian colors and the entire building topped with the world's largest revolving Pizza.

The bandstand backdrop will span 24 feet and will be covered with shiny gold lamé fabric. High gloss musical notes are superimposed amongst revolving plexiglass records, all artistically lighted. A dimensional 6-foot lighted juke box prop is placed in the center of the design. Along the front of the bandstand platform 30-inch sculptured records will stand vertically, as if they were lined up in a record rack. Two-dimensional 8-foot Coca-Cola bottle look-a-likes will be placed to the right and left of the bandstand. The above decor is included in the per-person price.

• • •

OPTIONS: HERE ARE SOME ADDITIONAL DECOR CONCEPTS AND OTHER SUGGESTIONS:

Additional Decor:
- The Yellow Submarine Sub Shop:
  This free-standing sub shop will provide the setting for the sub sandwich service, which will be provided through the windows of the submarine.
- Arnold's Drive-In:
  A fully dimensional diner with a walk-through entrance. The pink and turquoise diner is complete with open windows. Once inside, guests can order their burgers from Arnold while sitting on stools at a counter. Black and white checkered screens will be placed behind the food stations.
- Two 10-foot realistic basketball backboards and hoops will be placed on each side of the gymnasium floor, which doubles as a dance floor for the Sock Hop tonight.
- Twelve 24-inch diameter decorative mirror balls will be suspended from the ceiling over the dance floor area. These balls will not revolve and will be pinspotted with theatrical colored lights from the perimeter of the room.
- Operative pinball machines.
- Non-coin-operated juke box.
- 1950's authentic cars.
- Gymnasium bleachers and/or lockers.
- Ceiling canopied in crepe paper ribbon (resembling High School Prom).

Centerpieces:
To further create your room atmosphere, we suggest upgraded table centerpieces that may consist of the following:
- 24-inch tall glass trademarked Coca-Cola bottles with oversized straws will adorn each table. Alternating tables will host (4) 45 records with balloons in red, blue, pink, and turquoise extending from the center.
- Roller skates decorated with balloon bouquets.
- Popcorn, hula hoop, confetti, and helium balloon clusters.
- Coke bottles with fresh flowers.

Participatory Events:
The most important and effective aspect of this 50's/60's theme event is participation. Each one of these booths and games is uniquely decorated, coordinating with the service that they offer.
- 60's T-Shirts:
  In this section a hippy-type costumed person will be doing air brushing on T-Shirts. This can be either a give away or a viewing booth. With a paint compressor, the hippy will create customized designs, tie-dye slogans, names, and so on. Across the top of the booth will be a sign saying "Six-T's Shop."
- The Hippy Hut:
  The Hippy Hut/Head Shop/Beads and Weeds/Candles and Incense. Within this section will be signs printed with all of the above titles. A costumed performer will be stringing beads and placing them around the guests' necks. He will also offer them a colorful assortment of Love Flowers. In addition, the aroma of burning incense will surround an area of colorful lighted candles.

- Beach Ball Bash:
  A thatched-roof chickee hut-look will serve as the booth for your 50's/60's lifeguard, complete with sunglasses, beach shorts, and zinc oxide. He will offer to all of the guests inflatable beach balls, which can be personalized.
- Sing Like a Star:
  This booth hosts the feeling of a 50's/60's recording studio, complete with a lighted "On the Air" sign. The function of this area is such that guests may select from an array of tapes with a selection of thousands of songs. Each person sings into the microphone along with the song of their choice and as a souvenir receives a taped cassette of their voice singing with the original soundtrack music as background.
- The "Flick" Coffee House:
  In this section, we suggest the catering facility in a quiet area, like the foyer outside the "gym," where a variety of coffees, as well as dessert, will be served. We will create a display passthrough booth for this purpose. On the side of the coffee house a folk guitar player in 60's attire will perch on a wooden stool.

Participatory Games:

- Starcade:
  Stop by the starcade for some cosmic activity. Step into the future and try your skill at the Starcade video games.
- Hit the Road Jack:
  Sit on the curb of the street, outside the house with the picket fence, and play jacks with three of your friends. Mr. Policeman is the judge to determine each round's winner.
- Let's Go to the Hop:
  Hop around the schoolyard on pogo sticks. He who hops and flops loses. The gym teacher is, of course, the instructor.
- Marbeline:
  Don't dilly dally, head for the alley. Marbles is the game to play and the Greaser determines the pay.
- Boardwalk Baseball:
  Root, root, root for the home team. . . . Take me out to the ball game. Hit a home run and reach fame. The umpire will be on hand to keep score.
- Round, Round, Get Around:
  Spin the hula hoop around and around, but if it falls, you lose. Look for the Girl Most Likely to Succeed.
- Penny Wise, Pound Foolish:
  Hang out with the gang in the alley for a good old penny toss. But never forget the leader of the pack is the Boss.
- Help Me, Honda:
  On your mark, get set, go . . . you're on the speedway for a lap around the track on your brand new 1955 Honda tricycle. The Flagman determines the winner at the finish line.
- American Graffiti:
  Write your graffiti on the wall. It's Win, Lose, or Draw for all. The high school principal will be the judge.
- We Go Together:
  Girls pin boys and boys pin girls at the prom. The mirror ball revolves, but you can't see it because you're blindfolded. Pin your date in the right spot and you'll win the game with a ticket that's hot. The prom queen is the host of this game.
- Spin the Bottle:
  Spin the bottle and seek your fortune. Guess the letters that spell 50's songs.
- Rough Stuff:
  Back 'em in and pile 'em up. Try to break the world record for the most people in the telephone booth. Two teams compete.

- Blast from the Past:
  Played like "Concentration." Try to match as many 45 record titles to the 50's as possible.
- Shoot the Hoops:
  Join in for a game of all can Horse. No dribbling allowed. Muffy, the head cheerleader, will keep score.
- The Putt Club:
  Tee off at an authentic three-hole miniature golf course. The golf pro is on hand to give you his tips.
- Flo's Beauty Parlor and Barber Shop:
  Stop in at Flo's where a little dab will do ya. Come as you are and we'll make you a star. Flo and her staff will design styles of the future.
- Enchantment Under the Sea Dance:
  Where better to meet the date of your dreams than at the high school dance? Stick around after the games close down for the Enchantment Under the Sea Dance. We'll be rockin'n'rollin' all night to the fantastic Papa Doo Run Run.

• • •

ENTERTAINMENT: Dr. Poindexter Nerdbaum, Professor of Zoology and Botany, on loan from the Smithsonian Institution, Washington, DC; International Fern Man of the Year, and renowned Beetle Authority, is often mistaken for Professor Julius J. Kelp, portrayed by Jerry Lewis in the movie, "The Nutty Professor." Poin will bring back or create memories of the fabulous 50's, which is even more enjoyable the second time around.

As in the movie, Professor Kelp evolves into a suave, charismatic entertainer named Buddy Love. Poin will also capture your imagination as the original teen idol with his portrayal of "Teenager in Love." His performance also includes: "My Prayer" and "You're Sixteen."

Elvis Presley and Poin were very close personal friends and, in fact, Elvis copied much of Poin's style early in his career. To prove this, Poin performs his Tribute to the King of Rock and Roll with "Can't Help Falling in Love," "Burning Love," "Don't Be Cruel," "The Wonder of You," "Suspicious Minds," and "I Want to Be Your Teddy Bear." His performance is indeed memorable.

Besides your band, juke box, and/or disc jockey, the High Energy Entertainers offer their 50's costumes in an original display of theatrics and dance. Costumed hamburgers, french fries, milk shake, and juke box mingle with guests while cheerleaders, nerds, greasers, greasettes, prom king and queen, and Elvis imitator dance with guests. Choreographed dance routines and dance contests such as hula hoop, the twist, hand jive, and the limbo are the specialties for this event. Consult with your catering executive for entertainment charges.

MUSIC: For dancing and background music pleasure we can offer a fabulous 50's/60's band. In addition to or instead of the live band, we will make arrangements for a Disc Jockey to provide the recorded sounds for the evening, as well as the Singing Machine.

Bet your guests have always dreamed of their chance to be a singing star! They can choose hit songs from Top 40, Country, 50's, 60's, 70's, Standards, Broadway Show Tunes, and more. It's the latest entertainment trend for the "closet crooner." For the first time ever, the average singer has an opportunity to take the spotlight on stage and act out his, or her, singing star fantasy.

It will allow your guests to sing their favorite songs with professional studio quality arrangements, minus the lead vocals, with added voice enhancements and lyrics provided. They will sound as if they've been in a Hollywood recording studio.

They can sing solo, duet, or as an entire group, and receive a free cassette of the experience.

We will alternate between the live DJ, the Singing Machine, and the live band, depending upon crowd acceptance and enthusiasm.

See your catering executive to discuss your music choices and expenses.

Please be advised, should the client make their own arrangements for a band or a D.J., they must instruct the band leader or D.J. that any and all equipment is to be unloaded and loaded at the back dock and that under no circumstances will they be allowed to bring their equipment in through any of the public entrances. It is of utmost importance that this information be relayed to the proper people, as failure to do so could delay the start of the function.

In the event the volume of the band or D.J. becomes too loud or bothersome to other groups, the Resort Management reserves the right to have the volume lowered to a reasonable level. The Resort Management will use good and fair judgment should this problem occur.

SETUP: We will provide various stations designed appropriately around all decor items. Some of the decor will be placed in the foyer. The exact locations of all decor and props will be under the complete control and direction of the Director of Catering. A bandstand will be provided for the D.J. and Singing Machine at least 12×16 feet, with an additional stage beside, measuring 18×24 feet, for the band and entertainment. In front of the stages, we will place a highly polished dance floor, as large as possible. Exact size of the dance floor will be determined on setup day, based on available space. We will provide an additional 6×8 foot stage for the spotlight. All buffet stations will be designed by the Banquet Maitre D'. There will be seating for guests at 8-foot rectangular tables of eight guests each, placed where space permits, and for no more than one-half of the total expected guests.

The Director of Catering will provide a complete diagram of the total room setup—beer, soft drinks, liquor, and specialty drink beverage stations will be appropriately located.

COSTUMES: Male servers to wear high school award sweaters, and female servers to wear hot pink poodle skirts with stretch belts, Peter Pan blouses, and hot pink ties in their hair.

IN CHARGE OF SERVICE: (Name Typed) _____

Banquet Maitre D'

(Name Typed) _____

Assistant Maitre D'

IN CHARGE OF FOOD PREPARATION: (Name Typed) _____

Executive Banquet Chef

PAYMENT ARRANGEMENTS: Bill to the_____

Master Account.

CONTACT ADDRESS: _____

_____

_____

_____

_____

ARRANGEMENTS BY:

The XYZ Resort & Spa
G. Eugene Wigger, CPCE
Executive Director of Catering
and Special Events

xxx/xxx
xxxxx
xx/xx/1997

Present Extraordinary, Fully Complete Proposals

When submitting a client proposal or prospectus, include everything you expect the client to accept, plus everything you would like him or her to accept. Never underestimate what your client will approve, if you are able to excite him or her with your proposal and its contents. Perfect your thematic experiences. By doing a few selected ones, doing them over and over until they are uniquely presented, they can become everything possible. Every time a theme party is presented, it should be better than every time it has been done before. Everyone must be committed to this goal!

Staff Involvement

If you want your staff involved and committed to the success of your business, you must make them a real part of everything you do (see photo on pages 63–68 and color insert). Involve them in the planning and development and make certain they are allowed to enjoy the party and get involved with the guests through interaction. That is the real reason I started doing the characterizations at my theme parties. When my staff saw me out there working that hard toward the success of the special event, it was a little hard for them not to be as committed to the success of that same affair. Plus, we all made sure we were having a good time and we made our work fun. If we were enjoying ourselves, it was easier to make certain our guests were also having fun.

It is my feeling that the person who gets ahead is the one who does more than is necessary—*and keeps on doing it*. A hotel or resort is like a human being, with its own personality and *every hotel or resort staff member* contributes to that personality. Everyone needs to get totally involved in the hotel's or resort's objectives if they hope to stand above the competition. My staff never knew which character I would assume next, since I set a high example for staff involvement.

Here is another outstanding example of a unique thematic experience proposal or prospectus. Yes, I created the first tacky tourist theme party.

THE SOUTH FLORIDA WACKY TACKY TOURIST BEACHLESS BEACH PARTY

(See Photo and Pages 63–68 and Color Insert)

Well, it's South Florida at its worst . . . tacky tourist capital of the Southeastern United States! Where hot pink flamingos and Bahama Mamas capture your eye and soothe your psyche.

Now this party may not be for every group, but if you're looking for a lot of laughs . . . this is the party for you! You'll never again see so many pink flamingos, alligators, or oranges in your life. Imagine yourself in the center of a souvenir shop . . . almost everywhere you look, you'll find something that is the height of tackiness.

Our staff will join in the fun by wearing some of their own tacky outfits. Your guests can look forward to meeting such memorable characters as Buddy Brew, Mortimer Toopes, Stan Studd, Bonni Body, and Harry Hannibacker. But your guests must rise to the challenge and show the Floridians what a Tacky Tourist really is! Hawaiian shirts, cameras, madras shorts, white socks, polyester . . . maybe that leisure suit you have been holding onto still fits (surely it will come back in style some day). Remember, this party is one where your guests can really make a "Fashion Statement!"

To insure your party reaches the ultimate level of tackiness, we can arrange for the Vern Applebee family from Union City, Indiana, to greet your guests as they arrive. Vern will be joined by various immediate family members, which could include his lovely wife, Mary Ethel, to whom he has been happily married for only two years (although they were married in 1957!); his son, Vern Junior (or VJ), who is the apple of his eye; his adopted son, Useless, who gives him a concern or two; his kid sister, Lena Wayback, who recently became a rich widow after the loss of her loving husband, Elmer, and who is already looking for a new man; and who could forget (even if you wanted to), Vern's Cousin Cora, who has an enormous . . . personality! **Price for these special appearances on request.**

We dare you to try this one!!

• • •

THE WACKY TACKY FLORIDIAN MENU

From the Surf Side Tackle House
Fresh from the Surf
Fresh Shucked Clams and Oysters (1 each per person)
Spiced Peel-and-Eat Shrimp (6 per person)
Shark Ceviche

From Vendor Carts on the Street
Junk Food Only
Soft Pretzels with Mustard
Boxes of Cracker Jacks
Bags of Potato Chips
Bags of Banana Chips

For Those Health Nuts
Oranges, Oranges, Oranges . . . only Florida Oranges,
of course
Topiaries of Fresh Veggies, with a Dip or Two
Petite Fresh Fruit Kabobs displayed from our
version of a Pineapple Tree

We'll Cut It for You
Whole Roast Steamship Round of Beef
Whole Roast Turkey
Whole Sugar-Cured Baked Ham
Including Miniature Rolls, Cocktail Rye, and
Pumpernickel
Accompanied by Mayonnaise and Mustard
(Chef Carvers Required, Complimentary)

From Zaharako's Gyro's Ethnic Zone (Well, or as
International as Fort Lauderdale Gets!)
Gyro's, Sliced Lamb, Shredded Lettuce,
Chopped Onions and Tomatoes, Served in Pita Bread
with a Cucumber-Yogurt Sauce
Pizza, Prepared by our Local Italian
Make-Your-Own-Taco Bar
Buffalo Wings with Celery Sticks
and Bleu Cheese Dressing

Over the Counter on a Stick
Cob of Corn on a Stick
Corn Dogs on a Stick

To Quench the Thirst
Florida Orange Juice, Fresh Squeezed
Assorted Soft Drink Bar
Coffee and Decaffeinated Coffee

From the Sweet Tooth on the Sweet Side of the Strip
Assorted Candy Bars
Key Lime Tarts
Orange Mousse in a Red Wine Glass
Carrot Cake Squares
Huge Chocolate Chip Cookies
Assorted Ice Cream Bars and Sandwiches
Florida Tacky Tourist Party Prices (include Food,
Decor, and Staff Costumes)

From 150 to 250 Guests	$ _____
From 251 to 350 Guests	$ _____
From 351 to 450 Guests	$ _____
From 451 to 550 Guests	$ _____
From 551 to 650 Guests	$ _____
From 651 to 750 Guests	$ _____
From 751 to 850 Guests	$ _____
From 851 to 950 Guests	$ _____
From 951 to 1,050 Guests	$ _____
From 1,051 to 1,150 Guests	$ _____
From 1,151 to 1,250 Guests	$ _____
Over 1,251 Guests	$ _____

• • •

EXTRA ITEMS AND ARRANGEMENTS:

Beverages: From _____ p.m. to _____ p.m. _____ Ballroom
_____ Hosted Bars, with _____ Bartenders, serving:
Premium Brands, Premium and Imported Beer, Domestic Beer, and Wine, along with Mineral Water
and Soft Drinks.
In addition, from _____ p.m. to _____ p.m., in the ballroom foyer, we will provide _____ Specialty Drink
Bars and _____ Bartenders, serving cooling, brightly colored, slightly silly, highly octaned concoctions
that you would drink only on retreat as a Tacky Tourist. The specialty drinks will include:

Hurricane Vern
A drink that you can cry for . . . or cry over.
Amber Rum, Coconut Rum, Orange Juice, and a splash of Grenadine.

T T's Bahama Mama

Bright Orange/Yellow with a swirl of Scarlet, this refreshing drink will bring the tackiness out in every tourist.
White Rum, Rum Liqueur, Pineapple Juice, Orange Juice, and a splash of Grenadine.

The Applebee Surf Sider

You'll feel as if you're riding the waves after trying this drink.
White Rum, Blue Curaçao, Pineapple Juice, Lemon Juice, and Simple Syrup.

Goomba Boomba

We don't know what it means, but you'll love it.
Coco Lopez Coconut Cream, White Rum, Mango Juice, and a splash of Chambord.

Green Coral

This frosty potion will make others green with envy.
Myer's Dark Rum and Midori.

Sharkbite

This is one drink that you'll get a real "bite" out of!
Myer's Dark Rum, Orange Juice, and a splash of Grenadine.

Special Tacky Garnishes, such as Parasols and Suction Cup Animals, will be placed on each of the drink glasses.
A total flat rate charge for six hours of open premium brand beverage service and the specialty bar will be $ _____ per person, including the bartenders. The amount charged is based on the food, function guarantee, or the number in attendance, whichever is greater.
Note to Client: **The Flat Rate Bar opens and closes promptly at the given times.**
If alcoholic beverages are to be served on the Hotel premises (or elsewhere under the Hotel's alcoholic beverage license), the Hotel will require that beverages be dispensed only by Hotel servers and bartenders. The Hotel's alcoholic beverage license requires the Hotel to (1) request proper identification (photo ID) of any person of questionable age and to refuse alcoholic beverage service if the person is either underage or if proper identification cannot be produced, and (2) refuse alcoholic beverage service to any person who, in the Hotel's judgment, appears intoxicated.

Service Charge: _____% Service Charge on all Food and Beverages, added to the account.

State Sales Tax: _____% Florida State Sales Tax on all Food and Beverages, added to the account. By State Law, the 18% Service Charge is taxed.

Linen/Skirting: We will use less than deluxe brightly colored beach towels for linen, as well as skirting. All choices will be appropriately mismatched. For the tables, we will use the Tropical Parrot Tablecloths, and other selected tablecloths, included in the decor price.

Decorations: We will provide elaborate three dimensional props to include: a Two-Story Key West Style Bed and Breakfast Home, a Tackle House, and an elevated Specialty Drink Bar. Additional props will include a tall lifeguard chair, a whale, a porpoise, a Tacky Tourist frog, a Tacky Tourist gator, and a Tacky Tourist shark. Additionally, we will provide many other less than deluxe tabletop size decor to include, but not be limited to: outdoor coolers, some pool lounges, palm tree umbrellas, and a wind surfer. Inflatables will include a Giant Lobster, Flamingos, a Giant Blue Whale, a Giant Sea Turtle, a Killer Whale, a Huge Tiger Shark, Seals, Giant Alligators, Palm Trees, and Beach Balls. Also, various souvenir gift items such as plastic flowers, Florida beach balls, Florida snowmen, and tourist attraction brochures to be scattered about the Buffet Tables.
Also included will be additional three-dimensional props including two vendor shacks: Sunny's Souvenir Shop; a T-Shirt hut, Teddy's T's; and two Eateries: Zaharako's Gyro's and The Sweet Tooth, as well as various vendor carts.

Additional props included in the package are: airbrushed art works, an unbelievable amount of tabletop decor; Orange Sculpture; and many, many Souvenir Shop items. This tacky party wouldn't be so memorable without inflatables . . . boy, do we have inflatables.

"Two Lives Are Worth Saving"

A 6-foot tall, well-developed Lifeguard holding a nearly drowned boy in one hand and a girl in the other. In the background will be a tall Lifeguard stand.

"Prime Florida Real Estate"

A slick-dressed, deed-holding, fast-talking super-salesman knee deep in Florida swamp land with an open-mouthed, realistic, fully dimensional 8-foot long Florida Alligator about ready to "close the deal."

"Guess Who's Coming to Dinner"

A real shark attack by a Huge Shark Diner with Bib about to partake of his Human Prey. This will be displayed near the Tackle House where we will be serving what else but . . . shark!

And for that crowning innovative touch we will add the following realistic but humorous Fiberglass Sculptures, nearly life size. These Sculptures are fully dimensional or relief:

"Happiness Comes in the Form of a Wet T"

No contest proves to be as much fun for everyone as a Wet T-Shirt and Wet Swimsuit Contest. Our male and two female contestants bring a whole new meaning to the saying, "You're all wet!"

"Have I Got a T-riffic Deal for You"

T-shirts galore and all for such a deal. Our wheeling-dealing T-shirt vendors make an unforgettable sacrifice in their dealings with three out-of-state tourists.

The above decorations are included
in the per-person price

• • •

OPTIONS: HERE ARE SOME ADDITIONAL DECOR CONCEPTS AND OTHER SUGGESTIONS.

Additional Decorations, Activities, and Entertainment Available at an Additional Expense:

Additional perimeter and entrance decor will include signage, "The Florida Tacky Tourist Beachless Beach Party," clusters of natural palm trees with jumbo jade tops in hot tree bases with beach paraphernalia such as giant beach balls, surfboards, towels, thongs, sand pails (no sand), giant umbrellas, wind surfing sails, lifeguard stand, wave cut-outs. Neon flamingos and neon palm trees will also add to the tackiness, along with 8-foot three-dimensional Coca-Cola bottles. Items will also be displayed as part of the souvenir shop and food stations.

Miami Vice's Elvis the Alligator

This thatched-roof chickee hut-like area will be freestanding, surrounded by natural palms, and used to house our live "Elvis the Alligator" from the television production, Miami Vice, and his two trainers. This will be a great photo opportunity. The group will be available from _____ p.m. to _____ p.m.

Tikki Bird Village

In this hut area our loudly and tackily dressed bird trainer will display brightly colored exotic birds to be placed on the guests' shoulders . . . also great for photos. He will be available from _____ p.m. to _____ p.m.

Roving Photographers

We will arrange for three Polaroid photographers to take approximately _____ photographs with corporate logoed covers for each photograph at various photo opportunities from _____ p.m. to _____ p.m.

Teddy's T's

Two airbrush artists will airbrush the guest's name, along with a palm tree or a sailboat, on the shirt pocket area of the silk screen shirts, provided in a choice of two colors. The artists will be placed in a tacky chickee hut with T-Shirt decor. The airbrush artists will be available from _____ p.m. to _____ p.m.

Beefcake and Cheesecake

We will make arrangements for one sun-tanned, oiled, well-developed male body builder, as well as one voluptuous, well-developed female body builder, to stroll around the beach from _____ p.m. to _____ p.m., while comparing their physiques with the guests'. This should indeed present some impressive photo opportunities.

Caricaturists

We will arrange for three talented caricaturists to capture the essence of our Tacky Tourist guests for posterity from _____ p.m. to _____ p.m.

Theme Augmentation:

Wake Up to Make Up

(Placed on hotel risers, number to be advised.) Six makeup artists and six beauticians will be positioned in an old-fashioned barbershop environment. Guests will take turns sitting in chairs to have their hair styled as well as their faces painted with unusual and creative makeup.

Tattoo Parlor

Here guests can choose from water-based and stick on tattoo designs to be placed on any exposed part of their body. (Two staff will be dressed as leather bikers.)

Boardwalk Buttons

In this booth, guests will have their photos taken through video and placed on a 3-inch button that will double as a key chain, mirror, or magnet souvenir. A creative Florida environment will be produced as a backdrop for this setting. (Two sets of equipment will operate simultaneously.)

Hot Shots Costumes

This section will offer guests attending not in costume the opportunity to accessorize their outfits with a multitude of paraphernalia (costumes, hats, beads, boas, jewelry, and so on).
Hot Shots Costumes are only loaned to guests and must be returned upon their departure from the photo booth. Guests slip costumes over existing clothes with velcro or drawstrings rather than changing. It is primarily an accessory.

"Singing in Toon"

This area will offer guests the opportunity to enter a mini recording studio where they can sing along with prerecorded popular sound tracks. Their singing will be recorded for life on a cassette with background music.

Goofy Golf

Here we recommend three to six miniature golf putt greens (more available upon request and spacing) complete with balls and clubs.

Shuffleboard

One or two authentic Miami Beach shuffleboard courts will allow guests to participate in one of Florida's oldest pastimes for the old at heart.

Help Me, Honda

On your mark, get set, go. . . . You're on the speedway for a lap around the track (side of room or lobby with road cones) on your brand new Honda tricycle. The flagman determines the winner at the finish line.

Round, Round Get Around

Spin the hula hoop round and round but if it falls you lose. Three people compete simultaneously; the last one remaining wins.

Participation Games: Game Booths (12 Booths):

1.   Each booth will be an 8 × 8 foot freestanding white miniature tent.

2.   Each tent will be decorated with prizes (similar to fair prizes) ranging from tacky bracelets and sunglasses to stuffed animals.

3.   Props and game supplies will be provided.

4.   Appropriate signage will identify the booth by name.

5.   Tacky Tourist costumed operators will conduct the games.

6.   Appropriate lighting for visibility will be provided.

Price per booth ($ _____ each), inclusive of all accessories. Game booths include:

- Close Shave:
  Barber Bob foams up the balloon heads as each contestant tries for the closest shave without nicking the balloon. First one finished "shaves face." Carnival prizes.
- Beach Blanket Bingo:
  Players are given ten balls to throw into bingo box. Five balls in a row wins. Carnival prizes.
- Beach Balloonacy:
  Players are given three darts to throw at balloons. Two popped balloons wins. Carnival prizes.
- Sun Showers:
  Players shoot at lit candles with water pistols and are given 15 seconds to douse the flame. Carnival prizes.
- Catch of the Day:
  A small pond is filled with floating fish. Participants receive a prize based upon the marking on the belly of the fish they reel in. Carnival prizes.
- Dime Store:
  Guests are given dimes to pitch on top of a variety of dishes. If a dime remains on a dish, it makes you a winner. Carnival prizes.
- Ring Fling:
  Guests toss the rings onto the necks of Coke bottles. One out of three makes a winner. Carnival prizes.
- Can It:
  An array of garbage cans with partially open lids challenges guests' skills at tossing bean bags into the cans. Three out of four makes a winner. Carnival prizes.
- Twist and Shout:
  Four participants at a time compete on an 8 × 8 foot giant Twister board. The last person standing wins the battle. Carnival prizes.

- Battle of the Bulge:
  Two contestants stand on a platform and compete against the clock to fill their clothes with as much stuffing as possible. The stuffiest wins. Carnival prizes.
- Tuff Tourists:
  Players are given three whiffle balls to knock over silhouettes of tourists. Two out of three wins. Carnival prizes.
- Hats Ahoy:
  Step up to Miami Beach's tackiest Hat Shop and select three hats. Toss them onto the tourist's head. Two out of three makes a winner. Carnival prizes.

ENTERTAINMENT: From _____ p.m. to _____ p.m., we will present the ultimate in entertainment, **High Energy Entertainers,** eight dancers, three full hours of entertainment spanning a Tropical Heat Wave to a 50's/60's Review.

MUSIC: We have made arrangements for a live D.J. to provide the recorded sounds for the evening, as well as the Singing Machine.

Bet your guests have always dreamed of their chance to be singing stars! They can choose hit songs from Top 40, Country, 50's, 60's, 70's, Standards, Broadway Show Tunes, and more. It's the latest entertainment trend for the "closet crooner."

For the first time ever, the average singer has an opportunity to take the spotlight on stage and act out his, or her, singing star fantasy.

The Singing Machine will allow your guests to sing their favorite songs with professional studio quality arrangements, minus the lead vocals, with added voice enhancements and lyrics provided. They'll sound as if they've been in a Hollywood recording studio.

They can sing solo, duet, or as an entire group and **receive a free cassette of the experience.** We will alternate between the live D.J. and the Singing Machine, depending upon crowd acceptance and enthusiasm.

The total cost of this service is $ _____, to be added to the Master Account.

• • •

SETUP: We will provide various stations designed appropriately around all decor items. Some of the decor will be placed in the _____ Ballroom Foyer, as well as in the foyer on the North end of the _____ Ballroom. The exact location of all decor and props will be under the complete control and direction of the Director of Catering.

A bandstand will be provided for the D.J. and a dance floor will be immediately in front of the bandstand and will measure *at least* 12 × 15 feet—larger if at all possible. Exact size of the dance floor will be determined on setup day, based on available space. We will provide an additional 6 × 8 foot stage for the spotlight.

The Banquet Maitre D' will design all Buffet Stations. There will be seating for half the total number of guests expected, at 8 foot rectangular tables of eight guests each, placed where space permits.

CUSTOM SHIRTS: Arrangements have been made for special golf shirts, in various colors and sizes, to be custom-printed for the occasion. On the backs of the shirts will be printed our specially designed Wacky Tacky Beach Bum imprinting and guests may have their name and simple decorations added by the airbrush artist, if they so choose.

Exact cost of these golf shirts, as well as the design has yet to be determined. As soon as an exact price has been determined, this amount will be added to the Master Account.

AUDIOVISUAL: We will provide an ultra-quartz Trouperette follow spot at $ _____ and an operator at $ _____ per hour from _____ p.m. to _____ p.m. The spotlight will be used for the entertainment.

COSTUMES: All servers to be attired in Tacky Tourist attire, with the compliments of the Resort.

GUESTS' ATTIRE: Here are some "Nerdy Beachy" fashion tips to help your guests dress to make just the right statement.

- Wear your pants too high, with the length too short, and white-creamed schnoozes.
- Hawaiian shirts, jams, and clip-on sunglasses are Hot!
- White socks with sandals and button those top buttons!
- Hushpuppies make a real statement, especially with Polyester!
- A little toilet tissue stuck on the heel of your shoe is a nice touch.
- Geeky glasses, wide ties, and pens in your pocket.

- Definitely mix plaids with florals; dress sloppy.
- A little food in the corners of your mouth and on your clothes is just right.
- Madras shorts and one or more cameras are a Must!

• • •

SUGGESTED ATTIRE ACCESSORIES: Calculator or slide rule on the belt, slip hanging below your dress, decorated bathing cap with chin strap, broken zipper, zit medicine on face, gold medallion, I.D. bracelet, cardigan worn over the shoulder with a sweater guard chain, pink spongy hair rollers, ukulele, bongos, pooka shell necklace, hibiscus flower behind the ear, bows and boufants are the look for your hair, heavy eyeliner, major lips, and plenty of false eyelashes. Lots of blue hair with rubber flower bonnets and Nikon necklaces.

So use your imagination, creativity, and enthusiasm. Close your eyes and imagine that exotic feeling of sand in the soles of your Hushpuppies, fondling the keys of your calculator while nibbling the corner off a fresh "Little Debbie" snack cake. The beach is packed, littered with sun-worshippers, sand-goddesses, and skin cancer candidates. Half-baked Chiquitas in G-strings that resemble the floss you threaded through your teeth this morning. Or was it last week? Well-oiled aging bronze gods with loincloths on their hips and lust on their minds. And those vacationing snowbirds who baste their buns on the beach . . . our tacky tourists and what a sad lot they are. Gee Whiz, South Florida is Great!!

• • •

SPECIAL APPEARANCES: Vern Applebee, Tacky Tourist from Union City, Indiana, and his entire family will greet your guests upon their arrival at the party.

After meeting Vern Applebee, you'll know why Vern can show the Floridians what a tacky tourist really is all about.

We dare you to get to know Vern!!

Poindexter Nerdbaum, Professor of Zoology and Botany at South Florida High and first declared candidate for President of the United States Nerdocrat Party, will make a special appearance, dance and sing "Teenager in Love." His performance includes other hits of the original teen idols, as well as his very special tribute to the King of Rock and Roll. His performance is indeed memorable!

Prices for these special appearances upon request.

IN CHARGE OF SERVICE: (Name Typed)

Banquet Maitre D'

(Name Typed)

Assistant Maitre D'

IN CHARGE OF FOOD PREPARATION: (Name Typed)

Executive Banquet Chef

PAYMENT ARRANGEMENTS: Bill to the_____

Master Account.

CONTACT ADDRESS:_____

_____

_____

_____

_____

ARRANGEMENTS BY:

The XYZ Resort & Spa

G. Eugene Wigger, CPCE
Executive Director of Catering
and Special Events

xxx/xxx
xxxxx
xx/xx/1997

Use Descriptive Proposal Terms

Paint word pictures with your proposal terms. Make everything special by describing not only the food but even the equipment and setup requests in narrative and pictorial terms. Here are some examples of embellishment terms and/or descriptions:

- Circulate with Mobile Butler Carts (instead of rolling room service tables).
- Appropriate colored linen selection.
- From an attractively decorated Buffet Table, we will present and serve the following:
- Bars will be placed at strategic locations.
- Prepared tableside by selected waiter attendants.
- From a serpentine-shaped Buffet Table.
- To serve a complete selection of Highballs and Cocktails.
- From specially designed skirted Buffet Tables, we will present a culinary display to include:
- We will serve the following selection of Hot Hors d' Oeuvres and Cold Canapés:
- Presented in Gleaming Silver Chafing Dishes:
- Multipresentations of mirrored International and Domestic Cheese Displays.

- Elevated Head Table.
- Seating according to a diagram.
- A highly polished dance floor.
- We will create a specially designed Ice Carving for the occasion.
- Groupings of cocktail tables and chairs around the perimeter of the room.
- Guests will be seated at round tables of _____ guests each.

Develop Unique Concepts

Don't offer the same old tired theme parties that every other hotel and resort is offering. Instead, work at the development of unique theme concepts. Creativity—in my opinion—is the key to survival in this industry. You need new ideas, better ideas, ideas to wake people and get them involved, more involved than they have ever been before. Every single theme party requires us to dig down deep and pull out even more fabulous ways to motivate, reward, and entertain. It's an exhilarating challenge, and an exhausting one.

Here is a unique thematic experience that will get your attendees involved in a special affair for the corporate outings or employee picnics festivities.

"A Family A-Fair"

Join us at this celebration of family festivities, where husbands and wives, sons and daughters, aunts and uncles, and even grandparents can participate at the "Family A-Fair." All family members are encouraged to stroll along the midway and partake in the various activities, either alone or as a family team. Every winning family or family member will receive a coupon for their efforts. The family with the most coupons at the end of the fair will be our grand prize winner.

In a tribute to some of America's most popular families, we present our family festivities:

The Flintstones'® Bedrock Boulder Building:	In this prehistoric event, the Flintstones and the Rubbles compete against the hour glass. Each team is given piles of Bedrock Boulders. The family that stacks the tallest pile of lightweight boulders wins. The caveman judges the competition. A prehistoric game booth is constructed with stones, tree stumps, and animal skins.
The Partridge Family® Sing-Along Studio:	Every family can take their turn singing a song in harmony, just like the Partridges. These memorable sounds will be recorded on cassettes as souvenir gifts. Each family receives a coupon just for participating. A freestanding 6 × 6 foot recording booth is used with a flashing "On Air" sign.
The Cunninghams' Happy Days® Hula Hoop Hop:	This recreation of an authentic 50's diner will put every family in the hopping spirit. Just try on your hoop and start spinning. The family member with the last hoop spinning is the winner. Now, no cheating, because the Fonz is the boss.
Our Nation's First Family Political Pull:	Uncle Sam Wants You!!! And your entire family too. Democrats on the left and Republicans on the right. On your mark . . . get set . . . pull! It's a tug-of-war! Red, white, and blue bunting and balloons section off this area.
The Jetsons'® Video Starcade:	Enter the world of technology and video games. Here's where you can test your skills against the wizardry of video mania and George Jetson. Set in a futuristic space design, the Starcade is 24 feet long.
The Swiss Family Robinson® Rifle Range:	This adventure lets four (4) people participate using dart guns. Aim carefully at the target and the closest to the bullseye wins. A large treehouse (ground level) is used as decor for this section.

The Hatfields and the McCoys Battle It Out in . . . Family Feud:	Just like on the TV show, the Hatfields and the McCoys challenge each other's knowledge to come up with the most complete answers. Two (2) families compete: the Hatfields wear straw hats and the McCoys wear hunting hats. It's a battle to the finish. TV studio, game show, and set are recreated.
The Addams Family® Portraits:	They're creepy and they're hokey . . . mysterious and spooky . . . they're altogether kooky . . . it's your own family. Choose from an array of costumes that fit over your clothes, as well as accessories and wigs. Once dressed, family portraits are immortalized with an instant photograph, framed as a souvenir. Coupons are given to all the participating families. Set in front of a haunted house.
The Ingalls' Horseshoe Shuffle:	Welcome to the Little House on the Prairie® where Pa is stacking up the horseshoes while two (2) families stack up the points. Each horseshoe on a ring is worth a point. Every family member gets one (1) turn and the team with the most points wins. This design is created around a little log cabin house.
Pop-A-Smurf® and Family:	Enchanted by the colorful flowers and trees from the land of the Smurfs, you're invited to "Pop-A-Smurf." This is done by throwing darts at the Smurf balloons. Two out of three is a winner. Smurfette will keep you in line.
Hollywood Squares® Salutes the Brady Bunch®:	Marsha, Jan, and Cindy are the left squares. Greg, Peter, and Bobby are the right squares. Mom and Dad are the top and bottom middle squares, and Alice is the center square. Two (2) family teams compete to form Ticktacktoe with X's and O's by choosing squares and selecting the right answers. TV studio, game show, and set are recreated.
The Beverly Hillbillies'® Possum Pitch:	Join the Clampetts and take your turn tossing possum into the barrel. Two (2) teams compete, one with Ellie May and the other with Jethro. When Granny says "Go" start pitching them possum. The family with the most possum in their stew, wins.

Options: Choose from caricaturists, face painters, clowns, mimes, jugglers, or balloon sculptors to entertain family members in this area. Costumed characters can also walk around and mingle. Decor can consist of a castle entrance designed to resemble The Magic Kingdom®.

To take out some of your competitive frustrations along the midway, all are invited to join in a favorite family pastime . . . eating. Food stations, as well as a bar and beverage services, will be positioned throughout the fairgrounds, each designated with themed food supplied by a caterer, as well as with decor.

Station Name	Decor	Suggested Food Service
The Jetsons'® Lunching Pad	Outer space scenery	Sub sandwiches
The Munsters'® Cheeses	Candelabras and Cobwebs	Assorted cheeses, fruits, and crudités
Swiss Family Robinson's® Tree House Treats	Trees and foliage	Fried chicken, corn-on-the-cob
Cunninghams' Happy Days® Diner	Diner, counter, stools, and props	Hot dogs and baked beans
The Flintstones'® Bronto Burgers	Animal skins skirting	Hamburgers and french fries
Ewings' Southfork Salads	Split rail fencing, western wagon, and gear	Tuna, chicken, and potato salads
Walton's Mountain	Bales of hay, barrels, crates, and related props	Ice cream/make-your-own sundae bar
Disney's Delights	Balloons	Popcorn, cotton candy
Uncle Sam's Apple Pie	Red, white, and blue bunting	Apple pie and pastries
The Partridge Family® Punch	Musical notes and records	Fruit punch

Each station is complete with signage and should be placed close to appropriate participation booth for maximum impact of decor.

Chapter 4

Creative Thematic Meeting Breaks

Death of a Salesman Meeting Break

(See Color Insert)
(Minimum 100 Guests)
(Maximum Service Time: 20 Minutes)

It's close to midnight; something evil is lurking in the dark. In the moonlight you see a sight that almost stops your heart. You try to scream but terror takes the sound before you make it. You start to freeze and so it looks you right between the eyes . . . you're paralyzed. You feel the door slam and you realize there's no place to run. You feel the cold and you wonder if you'll ever see the sun. You close your eyes and you hope that it is just your imagination but all the while you hear a creature creeping up behind.

What you're experiencing is the nightmare of every salesman who hasn't met his goals and who is terrorized by his own shortcomings and fear of failure. In his own hounded mind, his territory is always the poorest and he feels no mere mortal could do a better job—he has an excuse for every failure. The darkness of his career falls across the land as the midnight hour closes in.

This frightening glimpse of the terror of failure is better viewed than lived. This Meeting Break will let you experience the seal of doom and scare you into realizing that whosoever shall be found, without the soul for getting down, must stand and face the hounds of hell, and feel as if you're inside a corpse's shell.

We will create the terror of a graveyard at midnight, and you won't need your imagination to frighten you into improved performance.

Don't venture alone!

· · ·

**From an appropriate Buffet arrangement,
Including a wooden coffin on display,
we will serve the following:**

A variety of Special Petite Poltergeist Pastries that are only Black & White in color

· · ·

Petite White and Milk Chocolate Drop
Dead Delicacies

· · ·

Double Rich Chocolate Fudge Brownies

· · ·

Meringue Spook Cookies
Choco Ghoul Macaroons
White Coconut Phantom Cookies
Black Magic Licorice Sticks

· · ·

Knudsen's All Natural Fruit Juices
Assorted Soft Drinks, including Diet and Caffeine-free
Perrier Mineral Water

· · ·

Hot Cider in a Large Kettle,
served over an open flame by an appropriately attired
server

· · ·

Freshly Brewed Devil's Coffee
Freshly Brewed Decaffeinated Coffee
Boiling Hot Water with Mausoleum
Tea Selection

· · ·

Music: Audio tapes will be played, included in the per-person cost.

Costumes: All servers will wear ripped and shredded attire and appropriate haunted makeup, at no additional expense.

The After School Mickey Mouse Club
Matinee Meeting Break

(See Photo on Page 69)
(Minimum 100 Guests)
(Maximum Service Time: 20 Minutes)

Remember the Fabulous '50s? Remember piling into the family station wagon with our parents for a drive-in movie? Remember white socks and pegged pants, pony tails and poodle skirts? Remember early television, with the tiny black and white screen? How about blue suede shoes and, of course, Elvis? How about the Howdy Doody Show®, slicked back DA's, and Frankie Avalon? And who could fail to remember—The Mickey Mouse Club®? Every young boy from that time will remember his "crush" on Annette! Well, we have re-created those days in our After School Mickey Mouse Club Matinee.

To ensure your attendees' involvement, we suggest that we arrange for a special appearance by Doctor Poindexter Nerdbaum, the Professor of Zoology and Botany on loan from the Smithsonian Institution, who will exhibit some prized specimens for discussion. Price for this special appearance on request.

Our specially designed Buffet Tables will be covered with "50's Rock'n'Roll" tablecloths where we will present our afternoon favorites, as well as a realistic, fully dimensional foam sculpture, covered in fiberglass cloth and resin with an airbrushed enamel finish, of who else but—Annette. Also, we will have a Wurtlizer juke box, school zone signs, a flashing stoplight, and other 50's decor.

Put on your mouse ears and join us as we relive those special times.

Rock, Roll, and Eat will include:

Popcorn, popped in the room
Cotton Candy, prepared for the guests
Sno-Cones, Shaved Ice with a variety of flavors
• • •

The Soda Fountain

Your favorite Float or even a Cherry Coke
• • •

Lunch Box Favorites

Sno Balls
Cupcakes
Twinkies
• • •

Live from the Neighborhood Street

A Goodies Ice Cream Cart
serving all those great Ice Cream Bars
and Sandwich Treats
• • •

For the Adults

Fresh Brewed Decaffeinated Coffee,
Hot Water with Tea Selection, Fresh Brewed Coffee

Music: We will spin the 1950's sounds throughout the break, included in the per-person cost.

Costumes: All servers will be attired within the proper 50's dress code, at no additional cost.

It's a Jungle Out There Meeting Break

(See Color Insert)
(Minimum 100 Guests)
(Maximum Service Time: 20 Minutes)

The business world . . . what a competitive jungle, where we have to prove our worth every day or risk losing our share of the shrinking marketplace. We have to match wits with our competition each and every day, or we may lose our edge. Our competitive spirit allows us to continue to be successful, as we shape our futures and make realities happen, by dedication to our endeavors.

Our decor will include buffet tables covered with camouflage linen, a steamer trunk, the front end of a broken down jeep, grass mats, netting, and layered palm trees, placed in front of a city skyline with a jungle in the foreground.

As a focal point, we will present a realistic but humorous sculpture of foam, covered in fiberglass cloth and resin with an airbrushed enamel finish, and nearly lifesize, of a well-suited businessman, with briefcase, in a large boiling pot over flames; a lifelike Gorilla, a Black Rhinoceros, a Giraffe, a Toucan and a Parrot, and an 8-foot pair of Elephant tusks.

You are right . . . it's a jungle out there!

In the jungle we will serve the following:

Chocolate-Covered Bananas on a stick,
Rolled in Crushed Peanuts

• • •

Fresh Fruit Display with
Fresh Chunked Coconut
and a selection of Dips

• • •

Fried Elephant Ears, dusted with Powdered Sugar

• • •

Deep-Fried Plantains

• • •

An elevated Specialty Bar serving
a nonalcoholic Jungle Juice Banana Flip,
which will bring the Tarzan out
in everyone!

• • •

Knudsen's All Natural Fruit Juices
Assorted Soft Drinks, including Diet and Caffeine-free

• • •

Fresh Brewed Decaffeinated Coffee
Hot Water with Shrunken Head Selection of Teas
Fresh Brewed Coffee

Music: Recorded sounds of the jungle will be present and included in the per-person cost.

Costumes: All servers will be attired in Safari clothes with Safari Hats or in camouflage gear, at no additional expense.

Special Appearance: Request, at your own risk, our on-property gorilla, at an additional charge.

The Temptin' Temptations Meeting Break

(See Color Insert)
(Minimum 50 Guests)
(Maximum Service Time: 20 Minutes)

The basis for all chocolate, and ultimately all delicious chocolate desserts, is the cocoa bean. The bean comes from the seed pods of the tropical cacao tree, also known as *Theobroma cacao*, "the food of the gods."

More pronouncements have been made about chocolate than about any other food. They run the gamut from chocolate being proclaimed as "heaven sent" to "the devil's do." These utterances have included: "If it isn't chocolate, it isn't dessert!" "When in doubt, serve chocolate!" And "Chocolate is Black Magic!"

Chocolate is an obsession with an affinity for evil. There is a decadence with chocolate that makes it seem practically obscene. This demoniac obsession has lured us into a cult of chocoholic sinners.

So give your evil spirits a lift and go forth and create a chocolate sin with this meeting break . . . and to the devil with sinning no more!

With the decor we will create a chocoholic hell that will entice you with the following sinfully rich and so chocolaty delicacies:

**Elevated in the center of the break
will be a Neon Hershey Chocolate Bar Sculpture**

• • •

Petite White Chocolate Mousse Tarts
Chocolate-Covered Strawberries

• • •

Little Devils
A chewy Chocolate Fudge Brownie topped with Vanilla
Ice Cream and rich Chocolate Sauce

• • •

Double Chocolate Drop Cookies with Chocolate Glaze
and Chopped Pistachios
White and Milk Chocolate Peanut and Raisin Nuggets
Chocolate Innocence Nut Dainties
Choco Macaroons

• • •

Knudsen's All Natural Fruit Juices
Assorted Soft Drinks, including Diet and Caffeine-free
Perrier Mineral Water

• • •

Viennese Coffee
Kona Coffee
Fresh Brewed Decaffeinated Coffee
Hot Chocolate

• • •

Assorted Herbal Teas

Music: We will provide recorded music, to include Charlie Daniels' "Fiddling Duet with the Devil," included in the per-person cost.

Costumes: One of our staff will be attired in a bright red Devil's costume, and all other staff will be attired in long black robes, at no additional expense.

The Florida Wacky Tacky Tourist Meeting Break

(See Color Insert)
(Minimum 100 Guests)
(Maximum Service Time: 20 Minutes)

Now this may not be for every group, but if you're looking for a lot of laughs . . . this is the meeting break for you. You'll never see so many pink flamingos, alligators, or oranges in your life. Imagine yourself in the center of a souvenir shop. Almost everywhere you look, you'll find something that is the height of tackiness. Our staff will join in the fun by wearing some of their own tacky outfits.

Included in the tacky decor will be an elevated Bahama Mama Specialty Bar, some airbrushed art works, less than deluxe tacky nautical props, outdoor coolers, and some inflatables.

And for the crowning innovative touch, we will highlight realistic but humorous sculptures of foam, covered in fiberglass cloth and resin with an airbrushed enamel finish, and nearly lifesize. The fully dimensional and relief sculptures will be as follows:

"Prime Florida Real Estate" — A slick-dressed, deed-holding, fast-talking super-salesman waist deep in Florida swampland with an open-mouthed realistic fully dimensional 8-foot long Florida Alligator about ready to "close the deal."

"Have I Got a T-rrific Deal for You" — T-shirts galore and all for such a deal. Our wheeling-dealing T-shirt vendor makes an unforgettable sacrifice in his deal with two out-of-state tourists.

Special Appearance: To ensure the meeting break reaches the ultimate level of tackiness, we can arrange for the Vern Applebee family, from Union City, Indiana, to greet your guests. Price for this special appearance on request.

We dare you to try this one!

Tropical Storm Vern
A nonalcoholic Strawberry-Orange Froster, which seems like quite a threat, but does little damage.

• • •

Fresh Squeezed Florida Orange Juice, displayed in Plastic Gallon Jugs

• • •

Knudsen's All Natural Fruit Juices
Assorted Soft Drinks, including Diet and Caffeine-free

• • •

Tacky Assorted Fancy Finger Sandwiches,
Ham, Turkey, Cheese, Tuna, and Watercress

• • •

Florida Key Lime Tarts

• • •

Fresh Brewed Decaffeinated Coffee,
Hot Water with Tea Selection, Fresh Brewed Coffee

Music: We will arrange for appropriate "Tacky" music to include: Miami Sound Machine, Jimmy Buffet, and others, included in the per-person cost.

Costumes: All servers will be attired in Tacky Tourist attire, at no additional cost.

The Sports Penalty Meeting Break

(See Color Insert)
(Minimum 50 Guests)
(Maximum Service Time: 20 Minutes)

Even though sports professionals and amateurs follow a sports chemistry diet, many people may not be aware that nutritional advice is for nonathletic people as well. You don't have to be a Wimbledon Tennis Champion or a Boston Marathoner to enjoy the benefits of maximum performance.

Most of us know nothing about the relatively new and highly specialized science of sports nutrition. You can discover the secret of achieving peak performance and endurance in training and competition, the seemingly endless energy and stamina levels that can help you through your professional season.

Locker-room lore should be replaced with the facts. Different sports make different demands on your body. Jogging, skiing, swimming, and aerobic dancing are endurance sports that require aerobic metabolism. Running, swimming, cycling, martial arts, and prolonged meetings call for high-energy anaerobic activity; many sports demand both types of metabolism.

Would you like to eat your way to success in business? Staying fit for the office means performing at your highest level of creativity and work output, regardless of your corporate position or responsibilities. It can boost your energy during board meetings, sales conferences, presentations and during stressful periods of both mental and physical labor. Most office workers almost instinctively reach for sugar-laden foods and coffee to boost their sagging energy. This is precisely what they should not do for more energy. In the end, sugar and caffeine will increase fatigue and inefficiency.

This eat-to-win break is for all active people, from Weekend Warriors to potential Olympic Decathlon Champions. Indeed, every active American stands to benefit from it.

At a given time our Chief Referee will barge into the meeting room blowing his whistle, throwing the penalty flag and imposing a 20-minute penalty for "prolonged sitting!" All sports fans will be ushered into the locker room for some "Thirst-Aid!!"

So be a good sport and give yourself a healthy break that will make your feel like a real winner!

In the center of the Locker Room, will be displayed a collage of giant-sized Big League Sport Sculptures for Big victories, extra efforts, and small consolations. The sculptures will include a giant-sized Louisville Slugger Baseball Bat, a huge "Annie" Smith Golf Ball, an immense Ace Pitcher Baseball, a colossal Fearless Goalie Soccer Ball, a Big Foot-sized Winner Sneaker, a Goliath-sized Game Hero Football, an enormous Tourney Champ Tennis Racquet with Tennis Ball, and some mountainous Diehard Supporter Sport Caps!

Also, from various vendor carts, our staff will "hawk" the following:

Soft Pretzels with Mustard
Cracker Jacks
Fresh Fruit in a Plastic Cup
Individual-size packages of Peanuts
Huge Chocolate Chip Cookies

• • •

Assorted Ice Cream Bars and Sandwiches

• • •

Sno-Cones,
Shaved Ice with a variety of Flavors
Popcorn, popped in the locker room

• • •

Knudsen's All Natural Fruit Juices
Assorted Soft Drinks, including Diet and Caffeine-free
Flavored Gatorade, all served in waxed cups

• • •

Fresh Brewed Decaffeinated Coffee
Hot Water with Tea Selection
Fresh Brewed Coffee

Video: "The All New Not-So-Great Moments in Sports" video will be played from television monitors, included in the per-person cost.

Uniforms: The entire staff will be dressed as referees or in sport uniforms, included in the per-person cost.

The America Is a Great Country Meeting Break

(See Photo on Page 70)
(Minimum 50 Guests)
(Maximum Service Time: 20 Minutes)

Leave it to us to rouse your patriotic spirit by celebrating America in a glorious splash of color and sound. Whether you're a Yankee Doodle Dandy or a Johnny Reb—we've got the meeting break for you!

A backdrop of Americana and a collage of flags, stars, and red, white, and blue bunting represent the states of the Union. As in Lee Greenwood's song, "God Bless the USA," you'll be "proud to be an American, where at least I know I'm free. And I won't forget the men who died, who gave that right to me. And I'd gladly stand up next to you and defend her still today. 'Cause there ain't no doubt I love this land. God Bless the USA."

America is a holiday that works!

In front of a large American flag, waving with assistance from a fan, we will present and serve:

Boxes of Cracker Jacks
Sliced Apple Pie à la Mode
Sliced Cherry Pie à la Mode
Frozen Milky Way and Snickers Bars

• • •

Knudsen's All Natural Fruit Juices
Assorted Soft Drinks, including Diet and Caffeine-free

• • •

Fresh Brewed Decaffeinated Coffee
Fresh Brewed Coffee
Hot Water with Tea Selection

• • •

Music: Recorded music to include: Shades of Ray Charles' "America," Lee Greenwood's "God Bless the USA," and other patriotic tributes, included in the per-person cost.

Costumes: All servers will be attired in Red and White Striped Jackets with Top Hats or Skimmers, at no additional expense.

The Business 'Robics for Health's Sake
Meeting Break

(See Color Insert)
(Minimum 50 Guests)
(Maximum Service Time: 20 Minutes)

At the very moment you're reading this sentence, there is a world revolution going on. No governments will topple, no wars will be declared and not a single shot will be fired. I'm speaking of the nutrition revolution. You can join our peak performance team as a world class member. This change in attitude toward food can be linked to an awareness among Americans about health. Everyone is becoming more weight and health conscious.

America is currently experiencing a fitness and health revolution that will eventually lead it to dominate world athletics and help all Americans achieve optimal health and fitness.

Once you've adopted a peak performance program you'll discover how to reach new heights of energy, stamina, and endurance. You can eat the very foods you used to avoid—foods that you can enjoy—while still achieving your peak performance levels of energy and endurance, on the job or on the playing field.

So let's get started with a healthy break, as well as some Business 'Robics or Soft Aerobics for conditioning your cardiovascular system. Get ready for a gentler aerobic workout that is safe, effective, and, best of all, fun!

We will arrange for a ten-minute Stretch Lesson to be conducted by an Aerobics Instructor, at an additional charge.

No, we're not serving pine cones, twigs, weeds, and acorns . . . but Euell Gibbons would be proud just the same.

As a focal point, our healthy and natural break includes: a huge Whole Fruit Display, presented around a realistic sculpture of foam, covered in fiberglass cloth and resin with an airbrushed enamel finish, and nearly lifesize, of Carmen Miranda. She emerges from the middle of the fruit display, also surrounded with bite-size pieces of Fresh Fruit. We also will present:

Individual containers of Assorted Yogurt

• • •

Our Special Blend of Tropical Granola,
Banana Chips, Coconut, and Raisins

• • •

Carrot Bread
Bran and Blueberry Muffins
Zucchini Bread
Whole Wheat and Banana Bread
Butter, Honey, and Cream Cheese

• • •

Skim Milk
Knudsen's All Natural Fruit Juices
Assorted Soft Drinks, including Diet and Caffeine-Free
Perrier Mineral Water

• • •

Fresh Brewed Coffee
Fresh Brewed Decaffeinated Coffee
Hot Water with Herbal Tea Selection

• • •

Music: A selection of popular music will get your heart beating and your feet tapping as you enjoy a healthy natural break, at no additional cost.

Uniforms: All servers will wear gym or health club attire, included in the per-person cost.

Special Appearances: If requested, we can arrange an appearance of Petie Pipsqueak, Mr. Florida 1987, to provide a special "Championship Posing" routine to the music of "Rocky." Also, additional male and female bodybuilders can be secured. Special appearance prices, on request.

The Beachless Beach Meeting Break

(See Color Insert)
(Minimum 100 Guests)
(Maximum Service Time: 20 Minutes)

The sun's out, surf's up and you're set for that legendary Fort Lauderdale Beach Party meeting break. All that's missing is the crystal white sandy beach, and with your imagination—you'll never miss it. You bring the beachgoers, and we bring the rest.

Included in the beach decor will be a Sand Castle Buffet

Table Sculpture, less than deluxe nautical props, pool loungers, palm tree umbrellas, beach balls, some airbrushed art works, outdoor coolers, some inflatables, and vendor carts "peddling" the food selections.

And for the crowning innovative touch, we will highlight realistic but humorous sculptures of foam, covered in fiberglass cloth and resin, with an airbrushed enamel finish, and nearly lifesize. The fully dimensional and relief sculptures will be as follows:

"Two Lives Are Worth Saving" — A 6-foot tall, well-developed Lifeguard holding a nearly drowned boy in one hand and a girl in the other. In the background will be a tall Lifeguard tower from which a small, soft sculpture boy with goggles, fins, and an innertube, is about to dive into a 5-foot inflated Flamingo Swimming Pool.

"Happiness Comes in the Form of a Wet T" — No contest proves to be as much fun for everyone as a Wet T-Shirt and Wet Swimsuit Contest. Our male and two female contestants bring a whole new meaning to the saying "You're all wet!"

To add fun under the sun, why not consider professional skateboarders? Or male and female body builders who will cruise the "beach" displaying their deltoids? Prices on request.

Eat your hearts out, Frankie and Annette!

Served from Various Vendor Carts

Soft Pretzels with Mustard
Fresh Fruit in a Plastic Cup
Huge Chocolate Chip Cookies
Assorted Ice Cream Bars and Sandwiches

• • •

Sno-Cones
Shaved Ice with a variety of Flavors

• • •

Knudsen's All Natural Fruit Juices
Assorted Soft Drinks, including Diet and Caffeine-free

• • •

Fresh Brewed Decaffeinated Coffee
Fresh Brewed Coffee
Hot Water with Tea Selection

Music: We will arrange for appropriate "Beachy" music to include the Beach Boys, Jan and Dean, The Kinks, and the Safaris, which will ring through the air, recreating the days on the beach. Included in the per-person cost.

Costumes: All servers will be attired in beach attire, at no additional cost.

The Give Me a Break Intermission Meeting Break

(See Color Insert)
(Minimum 50 Guests)
(Maximum Service Time: 20 Minutes)

We have recreated the lobby of your favorite movie theater for our Intermission Break. Nowhere else do these special treats taste so good. You'll see the ticket booth, the ushers, the counters, and smell the freshly popped popcorn as it pops while you order. Most of the time, these intermissions were more memorable than the flicks!

So step right up and place your order.

Displayed and Served from Counter-like displays:

Popcorn
Popped in the theater lobby

Sno-Cones
Shaved Ice with a variety of Flavors

M & M's
With and without Peanuts

• • •

A variety of Candy Bars
Nachos and Cheddar Cheese Spread

• • •

Assorted Soft Drinks, including Diet and Caffeine-free
A & W Root Beer and Orange Soda

• • •

Fresh Brewed Decaffeinated Coffee
Hot Water with Tea Selection
Fresh Brewed Coffee

Music: Recorded music will be played through the sound system. Included in the per-person cost.

Uniforms: All Theater staff will be attired in burgundy butler-style usher uniforms, at no additional expense.

The Strawberry Smoothie Smooth
Operator Meeting Break

(See Photo on Page 70)
(Minimum 50 Guests)
(Maximum Service Time: 20 Minutes)

As a dramatic, innovative focal point, we will feature a Giant Twin Strawberry Neon Sculpture with the music "Smooth Operator," as we present and serve the following robustious, wholesome, and vigorous break:

Strawberry Smoothies made in the room
and topped with a Fresh Strawberry

• • •

Fresh Fruit Display
including Pineapple cubes, Melon cubes,
Strawberries, and a selection of other Fruits,
accompanied by a Honey-Yogurt Dip

• • •

Knudsen's All Natural Fruit Juices
Chilled Perrier Mineral Water
Assorted Soft Drinks, including Diet and
Caffeine-free

• • •

Fresh Brewed Decaffeinated Coffee
Hot Water with Tea Selection
Fresh Brewed Coffee

Music: We will arrange for taped music to include "Smooth Operator" and "Strawberry Fields Forever." Included in the per-person cost.

The German Symphony Maestro
Musical Break

(See Color Insert)
(Minimum 100 Guests)
(Maximum Service Time: 20 Minutes)

In his brilliant musical compositions, Ludwig van Beethoven was a master of classical techniques. He also explored the new and more mysterious qualities of tone that attracted the romantic composers.

The three-dimensional Schwarzwald Hans building will serve as a backdrop, with a specially designed Serpentine Buffet Table in the foreground crowned with a fully dimensional bust of Beethoven on a pedestal. A series of small gold fountains will let water cascade down from varying levels, while a brass music stand, with conductor's baton poised on his sheet music, and layered live palms will add to the effect. Miniature white lights will highlight the edge of the buffet table as White-gloved servers, dressed formally in White Tie and Tails, also circulate, passing a selection of eatables from gleaming silver trays.

We will be privileged to serve:

Miniature Black Forest Tartlets
Buolow Nut Cake
Assorted German Breads and Butter
Assorted Finger Sandwiches
Deluxe Bonn Cookies and Chocolates

• • •

Assorted Teas
Fresh Brewed Jacobs Coffee
Fresh Brewed Decaffeinated Coffee
Hot Chocolate with Whipped Cream
Assorted Soft Drinks, including Diet and
Caffeine-free

Music: A selection of works from one of the greatest composers in musical history will be played, including Minuet in G, Moonlight Sonata, and the Fifth Symphony. Included in the per-person cost.

Attire: All servers will be in White Tie and Tails and White Gloves, at no additional cost.

The Bakery and Café Break

Suggested Foods

Croissants
Brioche
Fruit Strudels
Four-Foot Coffeecake
Miniature French Pastries
Fancy Cookies
Gugelhopf

• • •

Assorted Teas
Coffee
Cappuccino
Espresso

Suggested Decor: Bakery display counters with large food displays:

Wedding Cake
European Tortes

Servers will be in Chef's coats and ruffled aprons. Large strudel carved in room with classical music playing in the background.

Commentary: Vary foods depending on time of day. Same setup could be used several times. Hotel could often provide costumes at no charge.

The Western Campfire Morning Break

Suggested Foods

Biscuits
Cornbread
Whipped Butters
Honey
Preserves
Biscuits with Sausage Patties
Biscuits with Ham

• • •

Fruit

• • •

Coffee
Tea
Hot Chocolate

Suggested Decor: Chuck Wagons, Bandannas, Cowboy Hats, and Cactus in Pots. Servers will be dressed in Blue Jeans and Casual Shirts with checkered Linens on the tables. Soft recorded guitar music will be provided.

Commentary: Upgraded food could substitute for a full breakfast and reduce expense. Serving from stations in a stand-up mode would reduce length of sitting time.

The Dixieland–New Orleans Break

Suggested Foods

Hot Beignets
with Powdered Sugar

• • •

Spiced Coffee
Café au Lait
Tea

Suggested Decor: Dixieland Band and French Quarter Building.

Commentary: Simple food contrasted by lively entertainment. This can be easily built into other physical settings you may be creating.

The Healthy Jones Break

Suggested Foods

Whole Fresh Fruit
Sliced Fresh Fruit
Assorted Cups of Yogurt
Nuts
Raisins
Granola Bars
Fresh Vegetables

• • •

Fruit Juices
Iced Mineral Waters with Lime

Suggested Decor: Servers in jogging attire around a pool location.

Commentary: "Positive" food. People are very health conscious these days. Lighter foods are easier on your system—people stay awake.

The Oriental Break

Suggested Foods

Assorted Oolong Teas
Almond Cookies
Fortune Cookies
Mooncakes

Suggested Decor: Dramatic Linen Colors with Oriental Fans, Bonsai Trees, and flat wicker trays with tea mugs. Soft oriental string music in the background.

Commentary: Very light and simple foods. Sets a gentle mood. Good for lounge and/or hospitality area.

The Circus/Zoo Break

Suggested Foods

Chocolate-Dipped Bananas
Hot Dogs with Toppings
Freshly Popped Popcorn
Cotton Candy
Belgian Waffles with Berries and Whipped Cream

Suggested Decor: Striped tent backdrops with animal costumes, trees, organ grinder, fortune teller, portrait painter, and an animal act with a trainer.

Commentary: Strictly a fun break. Food items could vary tremendously, depending on how you want to use this break.

The Farmer in the Dell Break

Suggested Foods

Display of Fresh Vegetables on Crushed Ice with a Selection of Fresh Dips

VEGETABLE DRINKS:

Curly Carrot
Vanilla Ice Cream blended with Shaved Carrots and garnished with a Carrot Wave

Cucumber Calmer
Sour Cream blended with Cucumber and Poppy Seeds, Salt, Pepper, garnished with Lemon and Cucumber Wheels

Broccoli Bruiser
Plain Yogurt with Orange Juice and Puree of Broccoli, garnished with a Broccoli Flowerette

Tomato Tornado
Spiced Tomato Juice with a garnish of Cherry Tomato and Whole Mushroom

Suggested Decor: Servers in bib overalls with wheelbarrows for vegetables. Bales of straw instead of tables, with farm tools and equipment displayed throughout the room.

The Construction Site Break

Suggested Foods

Served in Individual Packages:
Danish
Raisins, Nuts and Such
Chips, Pretzels
Whole Fresh Fruits
Assorted Candy Bars

• • •

Coffee in Air Void Thermos
Portion Pack Sugar and Cream
Tea
Assorted Soft Drinks

Suggested Decor: Food displayed on boards on top of sawhorses. Framed windows used to display foods. Staff in T-shirts and jeans. Food could be prepackaged, "brown bags" for each guest. Wallpaper and material rules, tools. Disposable cups, plates, and glasses.

Commentary: Is your group building a new office? Have pictures and related models—this will set a nice casual atmosphere. Is the Hotel doing a renovation?

The Ice Cream Parlor Break

Suggested Foods

Assorted Flavors of Ice Cream
and Sugar Cones
Popsicles
Creamsicles
Ice Cream Sandwiches
Milk Shakes
Ice Cream Sodas
Assorted Soft Drinks

Suggested Decor: Café seating with servers in hats and striped jackets, calico aprons. Soda Bar. Caricaturist.

Commentary: Can be a fun pick-me-up without being too heavy. Could function as a hospitality lounge over several hours.

The Hostess & Co. Break

Suggested Foods

Twinkies
Hostess Cupcakes
Zingers
Crumb Cakes
Handi-Pies
• • •
Iced Cartons of Milk with Straws
Coffee
Tea

Suggested Decor: Checkered Linens.

Commentary: Fun-food break. A unique surprise.

The Military Break

Suggested Foods

Potato Skins and Toppings consisting of:
Sour Cream
Chives
Peanut Butter
Yogurt with Walnuts
Shredded Cheddar Cheese
• • •
Hershey Bars
• • •
Mint Ice Tea
Orange Ice Tea
Cinnamon Ice Tea

Suggested Decor: Fatigues, American flag, Red Cross nurse, camp-style equipment, metal coffee cups, ammunition box.

Commentary: Provides hearty food. Loud music is a good change of pace—wakes people up. Food can be carried into room and put on existing tables.

The Café-Espresso Bar Break

Suggested Foods

Demitasse Coffees

Cappuccino
Espresso
French Roast
Kona
Decaffeinated
• • •
Variety of Teas
Lemon Wheels
Cube Sugars
Unsweetened Whipped Cream
Lemon Twists
• • •
Miniature Pastries
Small Torte Squares
Cookies

Suggested Decor: Small café tables, colored linens, European backdrops. Can also be done outdoors.

Commentary: Good for heavy coffee drinker conventions. Allows for conversation areas between seminars.

The Give Me a Gorilla or King Kong Break

Suggested Foods

Frozen Bananas on a Stick
Dipped in Chocolate and Nuts

Suggested Decor: Gorilla Costume(s).

Commentary: Quickie-style break. Can be walked into meeting room and passed out, so time is minimal. Use at registration to relieve boredom in line. Gorilla provides an amusing diversion.

The Fun Kiddies-Only Break

Suggested Foods

Assorted Large Cookie Wheels Consisting of
Oatmeal Raisin
Chocolate Chip
Peanut Butter
Gingerbread Cake "Mud Pies"
• • •
Chocolate Milk
Whole Milk
Coffee
Tea

Suggested Decor: Little red wagons.

Commentary: We all like cookies!

The Baseball Break

Suggested Foods

Peanuts
Popcorn
Candy Bars
Boxes of Cracker Jacks
Ice Cream Sandwiches
• • •
Iced Soft Drinks

Suggested Decor: Baseball uniforms, hawkers with food trays.

Commentary: Food could be carried through the meeting room and passed down the aisles. Snack bar type setup could be used.

The Butler Break

Suggested Foods

Tea Sandwiches
Petite Muffins
Cookies
Miniature French Pastries
Chocolate Dipped Fruit Pieces
• • •
Assorted Teas
Lemon Wheels
Kona Coffee
Mineral Water

Suggested Decor: Servers in tuxedos and ruffled aprons. Crisp white linens, silver service, and stemmed glassware.

Commentary: Very formal. Best used for smaller groups such as Board of Directors Meetings, Executive Committee Meetings. Allows for "Roll-In" service.

The Vernor's Float (Boston Coolers) Break

Suggested Foods

Boston Coolers consisting of
Vernor's Ginger Ale Poured
over Vanilla Ice Cream

Commentary: A specialty product tied to the location. Use one item intrinsic to the area.

The Fruit and Juice Bars Break

Suggested Foods

Fresh Squeezed Juices

Orange—in Orange Shells
Grapefruit—in Grapefruit Shells
Cranberry
Apple
Spiced Tomato
• • •
Displays of Cubed Fresh Fruit
(No Coffee Should be Served)

Suggested Decor: Costumed "Fruit People," crates of fruit spaced around the room.

The Soda City (50's) Break

Suggested Foods

Mini Hot Dogs with Toppings
Freshly Popped Popcorn
Ice Cream Bars
Soda Fountain with "Jerk"
Bubble Gum
Other Delectable Junk
Assorted Soft Drinks

Suggested Decor: Juke box, motorcycle, soda fountain, hot dog cart, popcorn machine, and 50's background music.

Commentary: A good, fun, junk-food break. Have a dance contest.

The Always on Sundae Break

The opportunity of a lifetime! Create your wildest confection fantasy! Make your own sundae as gooey as you like, using one or all of the many toppings. Whatever strikes your fantasy!

Ice Cream
A Variety of Toppings
Hot Coffee

The Low-Cal Always on Sundae Break

You can slim down your fantasy by using frozen yogurt instead of ice cream! It's still a do-it-yourselfer! Also served with hot coffee.

The Euell Gibbons Break

No, we're not serving pine cones, twigs, weeds, and acorns. . . . Get Healthy.

A Selection of Bite-Sized Fresh Fruit and
Yogurt for Dipping
Iced Perrier with Lime
Coffee

Commentary: Lose weight the easy way. This break beats the heck out of jogging! Also, if you wish, we'll arrange for your guests to be served by a giant Chiquita Banana, a Bunch of Grapes, or other Fruit People, at an additional charge.

The Kookie Break

We won't drop your cookies. . . . Not these macho-sized cookies!

Chocolate Chip, Oatmeal,
Peanut Butter, or Sugar Cookies
Hot Coffee and Iced Cold Milk

This break is great in the morning. That's the way the cookie crumbles . . . .

The South of the Border Break

You'll adore this international break!

Beautifully prepared Sangria
Bite-sized Cubes of Fresh Fruit
Tostadas and Guacamole
Coffee

The Irving Kosher Deli Break

Hold the mayo on this afternoon delight!

Big Kosher Dills,
Mini-Reubens and, what else . . .
Cream Soda!!
Coffee included also

Ho-Hum Break

A typical a.m. coffee service. The only things that make this unique are:

Our Special Blend of Coffee
Our Homemade Hot Breads

The P.U.B. Break

Achtung! 'der pick up break or 'der *Pretzels und Beer* break. Pick up 'der meetink vis dis German Pub on Veels! Ve vill veel into 'der meetink around tree forty-five or four:

Dis Beer (two per person)
Pretzels

You vill be surprised how 'der meetink vill open up. Wunderbar!

The Give My Regards to Broadway Break

East Side, West Side, a great way to "beef" up an afternoon! We'll serve each of your guests:

One All-Beef Hot Dog With the Usual Condiments
A can of orange soda with a straw
Coffee included

Your guests will think they're on the sidewalks of New York!

Oh, Cheese Break

Domestic and Imported Cheeses
Garnished with Fresh Fruit and Lahvosh Crackers
Served with Hot Coffee and White Wine Spritzer

Humdrum Break

A so-so, everyday, "run-of-the-mill," meeting coffee service:

Coffee
Assorted Soft Drinks

You can always play it safe . . . .

The Health Food Store Counter Coffee Break

Staff in Old Fashioned Costumes to serve:

Juice Counter

Fresh Carrot Juice
Fresh Apple Juice
Display of Apples/Carrots
Two Juice Machines

Coffee Station

Coffee—Milk
Bags of Coffee Beans
Coffee Mill

Soft Drink Station

Assorted Soda Pop
Mineral Water

Tea Station

Rose Hip Tea
Camomile Tea
Red Ginger Tea

Health Food Store Counter

Four Types of Honey in Crocks
Swedish Dry Bread
Bran Muffins, Health Bread,
Date and Nut Bread
Half a Grapefruit with Plain Yogurt
Diced Fresh Fruits in Melon
Diced Dry Fruits in Copper Pans
Raisins, Eight types of Nuts, Sunflower Seeds
Seedless Grapes, Strawberries
Raw Vegetables Tray with Sour Cream,
Onion, Chives, Dill, and Cucumber Dips
Mint Molasses, Peanut Butter, Unsalted
Whipped Butter
Cottage Cheese, Plain and Mixed
Alpen Cereal, Bircher Muesli

Decor: Beehives, Honeycombs.

The Health and Fitness Break

A selection of popular music will get your heart beating and your feet tapping as you enjoy a Healthy Break.

Assorted Juices, Freshly Squeezed
while you wait
to include:
Orange
Grapefruit
Apple
Carrot
• • •
Fruit Delight
Melon Yogurt Board
Granola Bars
Assorted Sliced Fresh Fruits
• • •
Skim Milk
Coffee, Tea, Decaffeinated Coffee

The Butler Did It Meeting Break

English Butter Cookies Passed from Silver
Trays
• • •
Coffee, Tea, Decaffeinated Coffee,
Served Butler-style
By White-Gloved Waiters from Silver Trays
• • •
Also placed on an additional Buffet:
Assorted Herbal Teas
Freshly Brewed Regular and Decaffeinated
Coffee
• • •
Assorted Soft Drinks and Perrier will be
available

Music: Strauss music to be played on cassette tape.

Special Attire: Waiters to wear white gloves.

The English Tea Break

Scones with Devonshire Cream
Assorted Shortbreads, Cookies
Assorted Finger Sandwiches
English Cake
Fruit Tarts
Displayed on Silver Trays and
Compotieres
• • •
Assortment of Teas:
English Breakfast
Earl Gray
Darjeeling
Jasmine
• • •
Coffee, Decaffeinated Coffee

The Roman Break

Cappuccino
Cold Mineral Water
• • •
Pizza
Italian Cheese
• • •
Italian Ice Cream
Fruit Ices

The International Coffee Break

A variety of coffees will be offered, such as:

Turkish
Café au Lait
Italian
And so on

The Crêpes Break

Assorted Breakfast Pastries
• • •
Crêpes Made to Order
with Strawberry and Pineapple Filling
• • •
Special Presentation of
Baked Apples
and
Apples in Puff Pastry
with Vanilla Sauce
• • •
Coffee, Tea, Decaffeinated Coffee

The Old Mother Hubbard Break

Peach or Cherry Cobbler

• • •

Apple Strudel

• • •

Assorted Hot Breads and Coffee Cakes
Honey
and a Variety of Cookies

• • •

Coffee, Tea, Decaffeinated Coffee

The Seventh Inning Stretch

Hot Dog Chunks in Mustard Sauce

• • •

Popcorn Vendor
Peanut Vendor
Cracker Jacks

• • •

Gatorade
Lemonade
Ginger Ale

The Revival Break

Consommé

• • •

Miniature Open-Faced Sandwiches
Small Fresh Baked Rolls
Fresh Carrot Juice
Fresh Danish
Bran Muffins, Blueberry Muffins
Croissants

• • •

Coffee, Tea, Milk
Assorted Sodas, Perrier Water
Virgin Marys

Suggested Decor: Pharmacy Counter, Wheelchair and Stretcher, Blood Pressure Machine, Roll-Away Bed, Staff in Steward's Coats, I.V. Bottle.

Music: One-Man Band.

The Sophisticated Break

Fruit Chunks

• • •

Pound Cake Squares with
Chocolate
Caramel
Vanilla
and Butterscotch Sauces

• • •

Coffee, Tea, Decaffeinated Coffee

The Budget Break

If the subject of the meeting is money, why not make frugality the theme of the break?

Baked Beans and Sourdough Bread in
Blackened Pie Tins
and
Coffee in Tin Cups
Soft Drinks in Bottles or Cans

The Recovery Room Break

Instead of the usual morning Coffee, Tea, and Danish, why not minister to the needs of those who may be feeling the effects of too much of a good time the night before?

Set up a "recovery tent," staffed by a person dressed like a nurse. She can dispense Alka-Seltzer, Rolaids, Aspirin, and so on. Bloody Marys could be served from I.V. bottles.

The Golf Break

Drive a golf cart into the room with a professional model on back of the seat. She might pass out bags containing paper cups of coffee and doughnuts; cream, sugar, and so on to be available outside the meeting room. You might present this break as a morning session ends, before heading for the golf course. Model could be dressed in T-shirt with clever meeting-related and golf-oriented slogan on the front.

The Halloween Break

Hot Cider with Cinammon Sticks
Hot Chocolate
Halloween Candy, Toffee Apples
Mini Pumpkin or Mincemeat Tarts
Doughnuts, Pumpkin Bread, Zucchini Bread

Suggested Decor: Maybe a tub with apples in water so people can actually dunk for them. Styrofoam tombstones, fog machine, pulled apart gauze which has been dyed gray for cobwebs. Sound effects required as well as staff costumes. Witch should be stirring hot Apple Cider in large pot over flame effect.

The Old West Meeting Break

From an appropriately decorated Buffet, we will serve:

Miniature Chicken Fried Steak and Biscuit
Sandwich (Thin Medallions)
Country Sausage Patties and Biscuit Sandwich
• • •
Strawberry Shortcake
Pecan Tassies Tart
Apple Raisin Pie
Pecan-Stuffed Date Cookies
• • •
Assorted Soft Drinks, including Diet
Six Shooter Coffee, Tea, Decaffeinated Coffee

The Mummer's the Word Street Parade Meeting Break

Knudsen's All Natural Fruit Juices
Assorted Soft Drinks, including Diet
• • •
Hot Pretzels with Mustard
Miniature Hot Dogs with Condiments
• • •
Coffee, Tea, Brewed Decaffeinated Coffee

Music: Arrange for a Mummer's Band, complete with elaborate feathered and colored costumes, to march into and perform in the meeting break area.

The Island Break

From specially designed Buffet Tables, we will serve:

Knudsen's All Natural Fruit Juices
Additional Juices displayed on Ice including
Pomegranate, Mango, and Papaya Juices
• • •
Falafel
Vegetable Burger served in Quartered Pita
Bread garnished with Sesame Sauce,
Tomato, Parsley, and Radishes
• • •
Loukamades
Greek Honey Puffs
Prepared in the room,
served with
Honey, Walnut, and Cinnamon Sugar

The Give Me a Break Meeting Break

Eskimo Pies
Ice Cream Sandwiches
Popsicles
Nutty Buddy Drumsticks
• • •
Knudsen's All Natural Fruit Juices
Assorted Soft Drinks, including Diet
• • •
Coffee, Tea, and Freshly Brewed
Decaffeinated Coffee

Music: Arrange for a portable lighted disco dance floor and a four- or six-person Break-dancing group.

The Swiss Yodeler Break

Mountains of cubed Pound Cake and
Iced Fruits plunged into brimming pots
of Swiss Chocolate Fondue
Served with
Hot Swiss Mocha and imported
Mineral Waters

Island Paradise
(From Separate Stations)

Half Coconut filled with Vanilla Ice Cream flavored with Chartreuse, Topped with Crushed Pineapple and Brandied Bananas
• • •
Assorted Soft Drinks including Diet Coffee, Tea, Decaffeinated Coffee

Decor: We will provide tan linen and tan skirting with overlays of fishing nets. All tabletop nautical props. White Tivoli lights around the edge of the Buffet Table. Large wooden Pelican on pilings, large Sea Clams. Also available: palms, rowboat, plastic to cover floor and then covered with sand. Coffee Break Crew to make an erupting volcano filled with lava. A small island will also be constructed.

Music: Ocean sound tape to be played.

The French Palette Break

A civilized alternative to the "Coffee Break."

A selection of Rainbow Colored Sorbets, served in crystal sherry glasses
• • •
Demitasse, Espresso, and Perrier with a twist

The I Wish Every Day Was Sundae Break

Especially when you get to create your own with these Ice Creams:

(Choose Three Ice Creams)
Double Chocolate Ice Cream
Vanilla Bean Ice Cream
Rum Raisin Ice Cream
Natural Strawberry Ice Cream
Jamaican Coffee Ice Cream
With a luscious selection of Fruit and Chocolate Toppings
Novelty Candy Sprinkles
• • •
Hot Coffee on the side

The Cone-E Island Break

The same great selection of homemade ice creams, served in jumbo cones.

The All-American Hero Break

Six Feet Long and Cut to order!

Giant Sandwich features mounds of thinly sliced Deli Meats and imported Cheeses topped with Shredded Lettuce and a Special Dressing
Served with Ice Cold Cherry Coke

The Jamaican Adventure Break

An exotic assortment of Whole and Sliced Tropical Fruits displayed on Jungle Camouflage Cloths with Tropical Leaves and Macaw Mascot
Fruit Yogurts and Trail Mix
Natural Fruit Drinks on Ice and Jamaican Ginger Beer

The Cookie Stops Here Break

Chocolate Chip
Oatmeal Raisin and
Old-Fashioned Sugar Cookies
Hot Coffee and Cold Milk

Wonderful in the morning and even better in the afternoon.

The I've Got to Taco Break

Make your own . . . with hot crisp Mini Taco Shells, Spicy Beef and Refried Bean filling, fresh Lettuce, diced Onion and Tomato, shredded Cheddar, and hot Taco Sauce
Served with frosty Lemon-Lime-ade

French Musical Break

Claude Debussy (1862–1918): The symbolist poets and impressionist painters in Paris influenced Claude Debussy early in life. He set out to develop a similar style in music, and as a result, he composed sensitive works that led to the impressionistic style in music.

Explore the blending of the sensations of taste, touch, sight, sound, color, space, and movement in your French Coffee Break.

Sweet Vol Au Vent
Crêpes Roxanne
with different Fruit Fillings
Eclairs
Assorted Fresh Fruit Platter
Petite Croissant Sandwiches
filled with Brie and Camembert cheeses

• • •

Coffee, Tea, Decaffeinated Coffee
Perrier and Hot Chocolate

English Musical Break

Benjamin Britten (1913–1976): Britten, the leading British composer of the mid-twentieth century, was also an outstanding pianist and conductor. He won international acclaim for his instrumental work, and his operas are admired for their orchestral interludes as well as for their drama and depth of characterization.

Scones with Devonshire Cream
English Cake
Fruit Tarts
Assorted Shortbread Cookies
Assorted Finger Sandwiches

• • •

Assortment of teas to include:
English Breakfast
Darjeeling
Jasmine
Coffee, Decaffeinated Coffee

Austrian Musical Break

Johann Strauss, Jr. (1825–1899): The most talented and best-known member of the Strauss family, the Austrian musician became known as the "Waltz King." Johann Strauss, Jr. was a gifted writer of melodies and a brilliant orchestrator. His music will set the mood for the attractive Austrian Coffee Break.

Apple Strudel
Salsburg Nockel
Chocolate Fondue
Sacher Torte
Assorted Butter Bread Sandwiches

• • •

Coffee, Tea, Decaffeinated Coffee with
Whipped Cream
Hot Chocolate with Whipped Cream
Apple Juice and Assorted Sodas

Holiday Musical Break

Peter Ilyitch Tchaikovsky (1840–1893): Peter Ilyitch Tchaikovsky was a master of orchestration with a superb talent for blending instrumental sounds and writing melody. His lively ballet music from the Nutcracker Suite will add a holiday spirit to your coffee break.

Lacovmades
Butter Tarts
Fruit Tartlets
Gingerbread Cookies
Ice Cream
Christmas Log

• • •

Coffee, Tea, Decaffeinated Coffee
Egg Nog and Assorted Sodas

To enhance your musical break, we will provide a piano player, a string ensemble, or taped music, at an additional charge.

American Musical Break

Leonard Bernstein (1918–1990): Leonard Bernstein composed music in almost every form, including symphonies, ballets, Broadway musicals, and chamber music. The works of this American composer incorporate popular idioms and jazz rhythms, which will set the mood for your American coffee break.

Make your own Ice Cream Sundaes
with a variety of toppings
Deep Dish Apple Pie
Brownies
Chocolate Chip Cookies
Flavored Popcorn
Mini Hot Dogs
• • •
Coffee, Tea, Decaffeinated Coffee
Assorted Sodas

The Country Cousins Continental Express Buffet Breakfast Break

Fresh Squeezed Florida Orange Juice
Knudsen's All Natural Fruit Juices
• • •
Southern-Style Sausage Patties and
Buttermilk Biscuits
Grilled Ham and Buttermilk Biscuits
• • •
Petite Danish Pastries, Breakfast Bakeries,
and Breads
Marmalade, Fruit Preserves, and Butter
• • •
Freshly Brewed Coffee, Tea, Decaffeinated
Coffee

The Morning Eye-Opener Break

Freshly Brewed Coffee, Tea, Decaffeinated
Coffee
• • •
Petite Danish Pastries, Breakfast Bakeries,
and Breads
Marmalade, Fruit Preserves, and Butter

The Morning Grab a Biscuit and Run Break

Freshly Brewed Coffee, Tea, Decaffeinated
Coffee
• • •
Southern-Style Sausage Patties and
Buttermilk Biscuits
• • •
Petite Danish Pastries, Breakfast Bakeries,
and Breads
Marmalade, Fruit Preserves, and Butter

The All Health Is Breakin' Loose Break

Selection of Bite-Sized Fresh Fruit with
Yogurt for Dipping
• • •
Iced Mineral Water
• • •
Knudsen's All Natural Fruit Juices
• • •
Granola Bars and Macaroon Cookies
• • •
Freshly Brewed Coffee, Tea, Decaffeinated
Coffee

The Mid-Morning or Afternoon Bracing Break

Freshly Brewed Coffee, Tea, Decaffeinated
Coffee
• • •
Assorted Ice Cold Soft Drinks, including Diet
and Caffeine-free
Knudsen's All Natural Fruit Juices

A Basic A.M. Coffee Break

Display of Various Juices
to include
Orange, Grapefruit, Apple, Grape,
Cranapple, Tomato, Carrot,
Mango, and Guava
• • •
Sticky Buns
• • •
Coffee, Tea, Decaffeinated Coffee

A Basic P.M. Coffee Break

English Butter Cookies
passed on Silver Trays
• • •
Coffee, Tea, Decaffeinated Coffee
served Butler-Style

An Elaborate A.M. Coffee Break

Fresh Sliced Papaya
Freshly Squeezed Vegetable and Fruit Juices
• • •
Assorted Breads
Zucchini, Raisin,
Carrot,
Banana, and Date Nut
served from Wicker Baskets
• • •
Assorted Breakfast Pastries
displayed on silver trays
• • •
Coffee, Tea, Decaffeinated Coffee

An Elaborate P.M. Coffee Break

Assorted Juices Displayed on Ice
Including Pomegranate, Mango, and Papaya
• • •

Falafel
Vegetable Burger served in Pita Bread
garnished with Sesame Sauce,
Tomato, Parsley, and Radishes
• • •

Loukamades
Greek Honey Puffs
prepared in the room,
served with
Honey, Walnuts, and Cinnamon Sugar

The Giant Chocolate Chip Cookie Break

Freshly Brewed Coffee, Tea, Decaffeinated
Coffee
• • •
Huge Chocolate Chip Cookies
• • •
Assorted Ice Cold Soft Drinks, including Diet
and Caffeine-free
Knudsen's All Natural Fruit Juices

The Coffee and Tea Only Meeting Break

Freshly Brewed Coffee
Hot Water with Tea Selection
Fresh Brewed Decaffeinated Coffee

Additional Meeting Break Refreshments and Embellishments

Beverages by the Gallon

There is a minimum order of one gallon for all items sold by the gallon (approximately 20 cups or servings per gallon).

Hot Fresh Brewed Coffee
Hot Water, with Tea Selection
Hot Fresh Brewed Decaffeinated Coffee
Fresh Squeezed Orange Juice
Tomato, Grapefruit, Apple, V-8, and Cranberry
  Juices
Fresh Tropical Fruit Punch
Refreshing Iced Tea
Iced Natural Lemonade
Hot Chocolate

Other Refreshing à la Carte Ideas

Assorted Soft Drinks, including Diet and Caffeine-free

Knudsen's All Natural Fruit Juices

Milk, Skim Milk, Buttermilk, by the carton

Chilled Mineral Water with Lemon and Lime Wedges

Ice Cream Novelties, Consisting of Ice Cream Bars, Sandwiches, Nutty Buddies, and so on

Sin on a Stick: Häagen-Daazs Ice Cream Bars in a Variety of Flavors

Giant Assorted Chocolate Chip, Peanut Butter, Oatmeal, *or* Sugar Cookies

Assorted Petite Danish Pastries

Assorted Regular Size Danish Pastries

Beignets or Brioches

Petite Croissants

Oatmeal, Bran, Blueberry, or Corn Muffins

Banana, Zucchini or Orange Macadamia Nut Breads

Sliced Bagels with Cream Cheese

Brownies or Blondies

Southern-Style Sausage Patties and Buttermilk Biscuits

Grilled Ham and Buttermilk Biscuits

Strudels: Apple, Cherry, or Cheese

Assorted Fancy Petits Fours

Assorted Fancy Petite French Pastries

White and Dark Chocolate

Peanut and Raisin Nuggets

Individual Fruit-Flavored Yogurts on Ice

Assortment of Whole Fresh Fruits

Assorted Fancy Finger Sandwiches: Ham, Turkey, Cheese, Tuna, and Watercress

Granola Bars

Assorted Candy Bars

Frozen Fruit Bars

Chocolate-Covered Bananas on a Stick, Rolled in Peanuts

White and Dark Chocolate-Covered Strawberries

Here is the Vern Applebee family at the Tacky Tourist Party. Vern is joined by his wife, Mary Ethel, their son, Vern Jr., their adopted son, Useless, and Vern's kid sister, Lena Wayback.
Tiffany Photo.

This is "Prime Florida Real Estate," a slick-dressed, deed-holding, fast-talking, super-salesman waist-deep in Florida swamp land. You can always trust a man with a smile like that!
Tiffany Photo.

One of the major Tacky Tourist props is "Have I Got a T-rrific Deal for You," with T-shirts galore and all for such a deal.
Tiffany Photo.

"The Sweet Tooth" prop at the Wacky Tacky Tourist thematic experience. Note that the table is *not* skirted nor is the linen straight.
Tiffany Photo.

This tacky food presentation includes an old row boat with a hole in the bottom, an inflatable alligator, neon sculpture, beach balls, and beach towels instead of buffet table linens and skirting.
Tiffany Photo.

Neon carrot sculpture identifies the crudités displayed appropriately . . . tacky.
Tiffany Photo.

"Sunny's Souvenir Shop" is open for business with an unbelievable assortment of wacky, tacky Florida souvenir items "for sale."
Tiffany Photo.

Create a fun, tacky atmosphere with this eight-foot white parrot. When this birdy is hungry—you better feed him!
Tiffany Photo.

Don Johnson even drops by to give a ride to Baby Shamu, which makes a big splash!
Tiffany Photo.

Zaharako's Gyro's provide a real ethnic zone—well, as international as Fort Lauderdale gets!
Tiffany Photo.

Time for a pit stop for some refreshments before the big race. This sleek race car is sure to be a winner!
Tiffany Photo.

One of the guests, looking very patriotic and showing his "muscle." It would appear that she will be able to defend herself!
Tiffany Photo.

Barber Bob foams up the balloon heads as each contestant tries for the closest shave without nicking the balloon.
Tiffany Photo.

Golly gee, even "Elvis the alligator" showed up to strut his stuff.
Tiffany Photo.

What beach scene would be complete without a "Miami Vice" car? Vern is getting his car buffed just right.
Tiffany Photo.

This is one party that will long be remembered because all guests are asked to provide their own creativity, in the way of their own wacky tacky tourist attire.
Tiffany Photo.

Greek delicacies are served up at Zaharako's and will remind you of the picturesque islands.
Tiffany Photo.

Guests express themselves through their own creativity. They came with the thought that they were going to have a good time.
Tiffany Photo.

The Tacky Tiki Bird Village provides a bird of another feather for guests who want to pose holding one of these graceful and majestic creatures.
Tiffany Photo.

When you ask your staff to become involved by developing their own characters, you allow them to share their commitment.
Tiffany Photo.

In addition to elaborate three-dimensional props, add simple tabletop decor.
Tiffany Photo.

This three-dimensional prop of a Mexican Cantina helps re-create the hot-blooded, colorful image of Mexico. It surrounds you as you feast in the Spanish tradition of an old-age ceremony.
Tiffany Photo.

Having live monkeys, birds and alligators there for attendees to touch, hold, and pose with provides involvements that really add fun and make their party so wacky and tacky.
Tiffany Photo.

Make the luncheon buffet station look like something special when in fact it is only strawberries, blueberries, and kiwi with a dash of liqueur, topped with whipped cream, and served in a giant martini glass.
Tiffany Photo.

This life-size fiberglass fisherman in yellow slicker stands tall in his rowboat showing off his prize catch. You create an island fantasy with this one.
Tiffany Photo.

This three-dimensional prop provides a backdrop for cannolis, filled to order at the buffet. This same prop was designed with interchangeable signage, so this European building can be converted to give an impression of convey Italy, Germany, or France.
Tiffany Photo.

Tropical Fest is created by huge three-dimensional props of a two-story Key West–style house, a Surf Side Tackle House, and an elevated Bahama Mama Specialty Bar.
Tiffany Photo.

At "The After School Mickey Mouse Club® Matinee Break," you will remember the Fabulous 50's. Jiminy Cricket, it's going to be fun! Join us as we relive those special times.
Joe Saget Photo.

Leave it to us to rouse your patriotic spirit by celebrating America in a glorious splash of color and sound. Whether you're a Yankee Doodle Dandy or a Johnny Reb . . . we've got the meeting break for you—the "America Is a Great Country Break!"
Joe Saget Photo.

"The Strawberry Smoothie Smooth Operator Break."
As a dramatic, innovative focal point, we feature a giant twin strawberry neon sculpture.
Joe Saget Photo.

Chapter 5

Breakfast Appetizers

Chilled Indian River Citrus Sections

Fresh Squeezed Florida Orange Juice

Chilled Melon Wedge, in season, with Lime Garnish

Fresh Florida Grapefruit Juice

Chilled Cranberry Juice

Select Florida Orange and Grapefruit Sections

Broiled or Chilled Half Grapefruit

Fresh Pineapple with Kirsch

Coupe of Fresh Melon

Compote of Kadota Figs, Prunes, and Apples

Raspberry Champagne Cocktail

Peaches and Bing Cherries au Kirsch

Cranberry Shrub: Cranberry Juice Laced with Orange Sherbet

Florida Smoothie: A Blending of Juices, Yogurt, and Fresh Fruits

Skewered Fresh Pineapple and Strawberries

Fresh Yogurt with Granola Sprinkled on Top

Fresh Strawberries with Brown Sugar and Heavy Cream

Chilled Fresh Tropical Fruit Cup

Papaya, in Season, with Fresh Strawberries

A Mélange of Fresh Fruit Blended with Nuts and Banana Chips

Fresh Strawberries in Pink Champagne

Crescents of Fresh Melon with Seasonal Berries

Chapter 6

Lunch/Dinner Appetizers

Chilled Melon with Lime Wedge

Coupe of Melon with Anisette and Mint

Medley of Fresh Fruits au Kirsch

Minted Fresh Pineapple Chunks

Fresh Orange Shrub

Fresh Melon Slices with Port Wine

Fillet of Sole Walewska

Papaya filled with Seafood Salad

Chilled Vegetable Juice, Celery Stick Garniture

Suprême of Fresh Fruit Segments Ambrosia

Sliced Tomatoes and Onions Vinaigrette

Assorted Melon Wedges, in Season

Orange and Grapefruit Slices

Chilled V-8 Juice with Lemon Wedges

Citrus Fruit Cocktail

Pineapple Chunks with Kirsch

Macédoine of Fresh Fruits

Chilled Vegetable Juice with Zucchini Sticks

Assorted Melon Balls, in Season

Cottage Cheese with Fruits

Waldorf Salad

Antipasto: Assorted Meats and Cheeses on a Salad Bed Garnished with Fresh Vegetables

Seafood en Terrine

Chef's Country Pâté with Red Onions and Sliced Egg, with Cumberland Sauce

Crab Cardinal: Lump Crabmeat Glazed with Rich Seafood Sauce with a Herb Crouton

Conch Chowder: A Florida Specialty of Conch, Cream, Herbs, and Brandy

Quenelles of Pompano: Poached Dumplings of Florida Pompano in Cream and Wine Sauce

Langoustine Bouchées: Individual Puff Pastries, filled with Regional Delicacies

Ceviche Acapulco: Marinated Seafood with Tomatoes, Avocado, Olives, and Crisp Vegetables

Collection of Fresh Fruit Plate

Cheddar Cheese Beer Soup with Sliced Pepperoni

Shrimp Rémoulade: Bouquet of Four Jumbo Shrimp, Garni

Seafood Market Chowder

Prosciutto and Melon, in Season

Hearts of Artichoke, Marinated with Sliced Tomato and Hearts of Palm

Cantaloupe Wedge with Fresh Strawberries, au Porto

Shrimp Bisque au Cognac

Fillet of Dover Sole, stuffed with Shrimp and Crab

Paupiettes of Boston Sole Kennebec with Mousse of Salmon, Sauce Véronique

Lobster Crêpe Nantua

Fillet of Sole Véronique

Coquille St. Jacques: Scallops, nested in White Wine and Cream Sauce

Fresh Mushrooms and Bay Shrimp, Sweet and Sour, on a Bed of Bibb Lettuce

Lobster Nantua St. Jacques

Smoked Trout with Fresh Horseradish Dressing

Danish Lobster Tail, Stuffed with Lobster Thermidor

Seafood Cocktail with Lobster Medallion, Sauce Aurora

Bay Shrimp and Sliced Scallops Salad, Avocado and Yogurt Dressing

Gratin of Sea Scallops and Bay Shrimp, with Corn Coulis

Rolled Fillet of Sole, with Salmon Mousseline, and Noilly Chive Sauce

Assorted Seafood Plate, Red Pepper and Basil Sauces

Assortment of Pâtés and Terrines, Rhubarb Compote

Bay Shrimp Cocktail in a Coconut Shell, Marie Rose

Assortment of Three Smoked Fish with Dill Sauce

Mousseline of Lobster with Tiny Vegetables

Gratin of Oysters, Smoked Salmon and Heart of Palm

Terrine of Smoked Salmon, with Gravlax and Watercress Sauce

Roulade of Salmon and Spinach in Pernod Sauce

Chapter 8

Salads

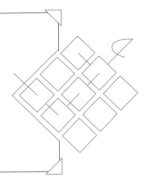

Suncoast Salad: A blending of seasonal melon, citrus, pecans, and almonds, topped with poppy seed dressing.

Tossed Green Salad: Greens tossed with cherry tomatoes and sliced radishes, served with French dressing.

Pasta Salad: Marinated vermicelli on a bed of fresh spinach.

Esquire Salad: Hearts of romaine and spinach leaves with tomato wedges, bacon bits, egg slices, and croutons, with warm bacon dressing.

Spinach and Mushroom Salad: Spinach leaves and mushrooms with pepper dressing and bacon bits.

Eastern Market Salad: Green pepper, olives, cherry tomatoes, Bermuda onions, radish and feta cheese on a bed of iceburg and romaine lettuce, topped with vinaigrette dressing.

Boston Bibb Lettuce: Bibb lettuce with red pimientos, vinaigrette dressing.

Salad Las Olas: Bibb lettuce, fresh sliced mushrooms, alfalfa sprouts, tomato and cucumber wedges, with peppercorn dressing.

Fresh Spinach and Romaine Lettuce: Spinach and romaine lettuce with sweet vinaigrette dressing.

Spinach Salad: Cherry tomatoes, fresh sliced mushrooms, hard-cooked egg, sliced and shredded Monterey Jack cheese, with hot bacon dressing.

Salade Maison: A symphony of garden greens, endive, tomato and cucumber wedges, olives, and Swiss cheese, with peppercream dressing.

Salade au Suisse: Mixed green salad with julienne of Swiss cheese, with oil and vinegar dressing.

Mixed Garden Greens: Mixed greens with bouquet of watercress, julienne of carrot, and fresh sliced mushrooms, served with creamy Italian dressing.

Salad Caesar Style: Selection of crisp romaine, parmesan cheese, and toasted croutons, with Caesar dressing.

Sliced Tomatoes and Cucumbers: Sliced tomatoes and cucumbers served on a bed of Boston lettuce, with oil and vinegar dressing.

Mixed Green Salad Printanier: Garden greens with sliced mushrooms, julienne of carrots, tomato wedges, and bouquet of watercress, with Italian dressing.

Rainbow Salad: Iceberg and romaine lettuce, carrots, zucchini, red cabbage, cherry tomatoes, and sprouts, with creamy Italian dressing.

Salad Rosemarie: Orange and grapefruit sections with sliced avocado, laced with vinaigrette dressing.

Salad of Kentucky Bibb: Kentucky bibb, radicchio, hearts of palm, avocado, and red onion, with Dijonaise dressing.

Hearts of Romaine: Hearts of romaine with sliced tomatoes and mustard vinaigrette.

Empress Salad: A mixture of Far East herbs and spices with bean sprouts, water chestnuts, carrots, green peppers, and sesame seed dressing.

Key West Salad: Crisp lettuce with baby shrimps, garnished with fresh vegetables, oil and lemon dressing.

Salade Gasconne: Endive and watercress with julienne of pascal celery and oil and vinegar dressing.

Italian Salad: Selection of lettuce with anchovies, oregano, chopped onions, peppers, crushed olives, parmesan cheese, and Italian dressing.

Oriental Noodle Salad: Oriental noodles blended with peanut and cucumber dressing tossed with carrots, snow peas, sprouts, peppers, and fried wontons.

Watercress and Endive Julienne: Julienne of watercress and endive with lemon oil dressing.

Romaine and Bibb Lettuce Salad: Romaine and bibb lettuce with sliced hearts of palm, julienne of carrots, and lemon oil dressing, garnished with chopped parsley.

Princess Salad: Julienne of watermelon, honeydew, cantaloupe, turkey, and egg, presented on Bibb lettuce with poppy seed dressing.

Salade Normande: Salad of endive, watercress, lettuce, hearts of palm, sliced fresh mushrooms, and toasted croutons, with oil and vinegar dressing.

Composed Vegetable Salad: Mixed vegetables with tarragon dressing.

Maine Lobster Salad: Salad of Maine lobster with shallot vinaigrette and basil sauce.

Smoked Breast of Duck: Smoked breast of duck served with fine green bean salad.

Colorful Garden Diggin's Salad: Mixed garden greens with shredded vegetables.

Tour of the Garden Salad: Crisp seasonal greens and vegetables with celery seed dressing.

Pinenut Spinach Salad: Spinach leaves and pinenuts served with herbed croutons, sliced mushrooms, chopped eggs, and hot bacon dressing.

Salad Julienne: Thinly sliced pea pods and carrots with enoki mushrooms on a bed of chicory, garnished with oriental noodles, champagne dressing.

Chapter 9

A Guide to Vegetable Dishes

Artichokes

(French: Artichauts)

All year round; best in March, April, May, October, November

Artichoke (Whole Fresh): Whole fresh artichoke, top trimmed, boiled in lemon water, choke and first leaves removed. Served with melted butter (as appetizer).

Artichoke Hollandaise: Prepared as above, served hot with Hollandaise sauce (as appetizer).

Artichoke Bonne Femme: Prepared as above, served hot with brown butter (as appetizer).

Artichoke Mousseline: Prepared as above, served hot with mixture of Hollandaise and whipped cream (as Appetizer).

Artichoke Cavour: Prepared as above, cut in quarters, glazed with grated parmesan cheese, topped with chopped egg, anchovy fillets in butter, and parsley.

Artichoke Italienne: Artichoke, top trimmed, choke and first leaves removed, cut in quarters and braised with bacon, white wine, and brown veal stock.

Artichoke Paysanne: Prepared as for Italienne, braised with bacon, pearl onions, Chateau potatoes,* beef stock.

Artichoke with Mushrooms: Prepared as for Italienne, braised with fresh mushrooms and crushed coriander in olive oil and beef stock.

Artichoke à la Polita: Artichoke, braised with pearl onions, carrots, potatoes,** and fresh dill in olive oil and chicken stock.

Artichoke Bottoms: Artichoke bottoms filled with cauliflower flowerettes.

* Chateau Potato: Potato cut in the shape of large olives, sautéed in clarified butter until golden brown.
** Carrots and potatoes are cut in ball shapes or half-inch cubes.

Artichoke Clamart: Artichoke bottoms filled with buttered green peas or artichoke bottoms filled with French peas or with puree of peas.

Artichoke Brussels: Artichoke bottoms filled with Brussels sprouts and julienne of ham.

Artichoke Diable: Artichoke bottoms sautéed with garlic, capers, bread crumbs, and parsley.

Artichoke Parisienne: Hearts of artichoke sautéed with shallots in half olive oil and half butter and sprinkled with seasoned bread crumbs.

Artichoke Vinaigrette: Hearts of artichoke served with vinaigrette sauce.

Asparagus

(French: Asperge)

March–June only for fresh asparagus

Fresh Asparagus with Butter: Asparagus cleaned, trimmed, and boiled or steamed, served with butter.

Fresh Asparagus Polonaise: Asparagus cleaned, trimmed, boiled, topped with chopped egg, parsley, and bread crumbs with butter.

Fresh Asparagus Flamande: Asparagus cleaned, trimmed, boiled, topped with chopped egg yolk and butter, seasoned with nutmeg.

Fresh Asparagus Hollandaise: Asparagus cleaned, trimmed, boiled, served with Hollandaise sauce.

Fresh Asparagus Mornay: Asparagus cleaned, trimmed, boiled, topped with light cheese sauce, and glazed.

Fresh Asparagus Milanaise: Asparagus cleaned, trimmed, boiled, topped with parmesan cheese, and glazed.

Fresh Asparagus Maltaise: Asparagus cleaned, trimmed, boiled, served with mixture of Hollandaise sauce and orange juice.

Fresh Asparagus Française: Asparagus cleaned,

trimmed, boiled, dipped in egg wash, then in flour, and deep fried.

Fresh Asparagus German Style: Asparagus cleaned, trimmed, boiled, topped with bread crumbs and melted butter.

Fresh Asparagus with Chervil: Asparagus cleaned, trimmed, boiled, cut into 2-inch pieces, mixed with light cream sauce and fresh chopped chervil.

Beans

Green Beans
(French: Haricots Verts)

All year round; height of season is April–October

Buttered Fresh Green Beans: Beans cleaned, boiled, buttered, and seasoned.

Buttered Fresh or Frozen French Cut Green Beans: Beans lengthwise cut into julienne, boiled, buttered, and seasoned.

Buttered Fresh or Frozen Cut Green Beans: Beans cut into 1-inch pieces, boiled, buttered, and seasoned.

Green Beans with Cheddar Cheese: Beans boiled, mixed with cheese sauce, topped with bread and cheese crumbs, and baked in oven.

Dutch Green Beans: Beans cleaned, boiled, mixed with bacon, vinegar-mustard sauce, flour, and onion.

Southern Green Beans: Beans braised with salt pork.

Western Beans: Green beans simmered with kidney beans, bacon, and onions.

Green Beans Amandine: Beans boiled, buttered, topped with toasted sliced almonds.

Green Beans with Water Chestnuts: Beans cleaned, boiled, buttered, and served with water chestnuts.

Green Beans Lyonnaise: Beans boiled, buttered, and mixed with sautéed onions.

Green Beans with Mushrooms: Beans boiled, buttered, and mixed with sautéed, sliced mushrooms.

Green Beans with Lemon Butter: Beans steamed or boiled, sautéed in lemon butter.

Green Beans with Walnut Butter: Beans steamed or boiled, sautéed in walnut butter.

Green Beans with Maître d'Hôtel Butter: Beans steamed or boiled, sautéed in Maître d'Hôtel butter.*

Green Beans with Tomato: Beans boiled, sautéed

* Maître d'Hôtel Butter: Mixture of butter, lemon juice, chopped parsley, salt, and pepper.

with fresh tomato that has been peeled, seeded, and chopped.

Green Beans with Bacon: Beans simmered with bacon and onions.

Green Beans Provençale: Beans boiled, sautéed with oil, garlic, and parsley.

Green Beans Polonaise: Beans boiled, sautéed with butter and bread crumbs.

Green Beans Normande: Beans boiled, blended with heavy cream or cream sauce and egg yolk.

Green Beans with Paprika Sauce: Beans boiled, blended with paprika sauce.

Green Beans Française: Beans braised with pearl onions, julienne of lettuce, and blended with beurre manie.**

Green Beans and Carrots: Beans boiled, buttered, mixed with steamed carrots.

Green Beans and Flageolets: Beans boiled, buttered, mixed with cooked white beans.

Green Beans Bouquet: Beans boiled, wrapped in blanched bacon strips, and braised.

Princess Beans† in Lemon Sauce: Beans boiled, mixed with slightly lemon-flavored Hollandaise sauce.

Princess Beans† in Dill Sauce: Beans boiled, mixed with light cream sauce and fresh chopped dill.

Princess Beans† with Sofrito Sauce: Beans boiled, mixed with a sauce of tomato, capers, oregano, olive oil, parsley, and savory.

Note: All preparations for green beans are interchangeable with Princess beans or yellow wax beans.

Dried Beans

Beans (dried) Haricots Blanc: Baked beans with pork, onions, celery, brown sugar, baked in chicken broth.

Southern Baked Lima Beans: Lima beans baked with salt pork, onion, tomatoes, and green peppers, seasoned with dry mustard and sugar.

Chili Beans: Kidney beans with onion, tomato and Enchilada sauce.††

Beans Creole: Kidney beans with green pepper, onions, mushrooms, and tomatoes.

Lima Beans: Boiled and served with butter.

Refried Beans: Pinto beans simmered with salt pork, cumin powder, bay leaf and garlic, fried in bacon fat, and refried again in bacon fat.

Bean Sprouts (fresh only): Should be only served when they can be prepared to order. Best when stir-fried with combination of other stir-fry vegetables.

**Beurre manie: Equal parts of butter and flour.
†Princess Beans are young and very tender green beans.
††Enchilada Sauce: Yellow onions, serrano chili, paprika, chili powder, garlic, oregano, and tomato in cream sauce.

Beets

(French: Betteraves)

All year round; peak June–October

Buttered Beets: Cooked, peeled, sliced beets, buttered and seasoned with salt, pepper, and sugar.

Minted Buttered Beets: Cooked, peeled, sliced beets, buttered, seasoned, and mixed with chopped fresh mint.

Harvard Beets: Cooked, peeled, sliced beets, buttered and seasoned with sugar, cider vinegar, bay leaves, cloves, salt, and pepper.

Hot Spiced Beets: Cooked, peeled, sliced beets simmered with onions, celery, coarse ground pepper, cider vinegar, and sugar.

Broccoli

All year round; peak October–April

Buttered Fresh Broccoli: Broccoli, boiled in seasoned water and served with butter.

Broccoli Italienne: Broccoli, boiled in seasoned water, and served with olive oil and lemon juice.

Broccoli Hollandaise: Broccoli, boiled in seasoned water, topped with Hollandaise sauce.

Broccoli Orly: Broccoli, blanched, dipped in beer batter, deep fried.

French Fried Broccoli: Broccoli, breaded and deep fried.

Creamed Broccoli: Broccoli, boiled, mixed with medium cream sauce, sprinkled with butter crumb topping, and lightly browned.

Broccoli Mimosa: Broccoli, boiled, topped with chopped boiled egg yolk, melted butter.

Broccoli Polonaise: Broccoli, boiled, served with topping of bread crumbs, chopped egg, parsley, melted butter.

Broccoli Milanaise: Broccoli, boiled, topped with shredded cheese and brown butter, and glazed.

Broccoli Mornay: Broccoli, boiled, topped with chopped cheese sauce, and glazed.

Broccoli à la Grecque: Broccoli, boiled, sautéed with mushrooms in olive oil, lemon juice, and oregano.

Broccoli with Lemon Butter: Broccoli boiled in seasoned water, served with lemon butter.

Broccoli with Pimiento Butter: Broccoli, boiled in seasoned water, served with Pimiento butter.*

*Pimiento butter: Butter, chopped pimiento, and chopped parsley.

Brussels Sprouts

(French: Choux de Bruxelles)

Best October–March; peak season October–December

Buttered Fresh Brussels Sprouts: Brussels sprouts, boiled, buttered and seasoned.

Fresh Brussels Sprouts Amandine: Brussels sprouts, boiled, buttered, topped with toasted almonds.

Fresh Brussels Sprouts with Poppy Seeds: Brussels sprouts, boiled, sautéed with butter and poppy seeds.

Fresh Brussels Sprouts with Chestnuts: Brussels sprouts, boiled, sautéed with glazed chestnuts and butter.

Fresh Brussels Sprouts Italienne: Brussels sprouts, boiled, sautéed in butter, topped with anchovy fillets and parmesan.

Fresh Brussels Sprouts Farmer Style: Brussels sprouts, boiled, sautéed with chopped onions, bacon or ham strips, seasoned with nutmeg.

Fresh Brussels Sprouts à la Crème: Brussels sprouts, boiled, served in light cream sauce.

Fresh Brussels Sprouts Polonaise: Brussels sprouts, boiled, topped with butter and bread crumbs.

Cabbage

(French: Choux)

All year round

Buttered Cabbage: Green cabbage, boiled, buttered, and seasoned.

Buttered Celery Cabbage: Celery cabbage, boiled, buttered, and seasoned.

Cabbage au Gratin: Green cabbage, boiled, mixed with medium cheese sauce, glazed with cheese crumb and bread crumb topping.

Hot Green Cabbage Slaw: Green cabbage, shredded, boiled and seasoned with onion, mustard, sugar, salt, pepper, and cider vinegar, mixed with fried, diced bacon.

Hot Red Cabbage Slaw: Red cabbage shredded, simmered in butter, sugar, salt, and cider vinegar.

Red Cabbage Bavarian Style: Red cabbage, braised with bacon, onions, apples, vinegar, and sugar.

Braised Cabbage: Green cabbage, braised with salt pork, onions, caraway seeds, and vinegar.

Cabbage Wedge: Green cabbage wedge, boiled and seasoned.

Red Cabbage à la Borbon: Red cabbage simmered with ham and red burgundy, seasoned with bay leaf, vinegar, sugar, salt, and pepper.

Cabbage Puree: Green cabbage, pureed, mixed with cream and seasoned.

Red Cabbage: Red cabbage braised with bacon, onions, apples, red burgundy, and seasoned.

Braised Cabbage with Bacon: Green cabbage, braised with bacon and seasoned.

Braised Cabbage Balls: Green cabbage, blanched, shaped in small balls, braised with butter and seasoned.

Cabbage with Potatoes: Green cabbage, braised with potatoes, onions, marjoram, garlic, and sprinkled with chopped parsley.

Cabbage Polonaise: Green cabbage wedge, boiled, buttered, topped with buttered bread crumbs.

Stuffed Cabbage Provençale: Green cabbage leaf blanched, stuffed with rice, tomato, peas, onions, minced pork meat, braised in beef stock.

Stuffed Cabbage Rolls: Green cabbage leaf blanched, stuffed with minced, seasoned pork meat, braised with bacon, apples, and onions.

Cabbage Stuffed with Chestnuts: Green cabbage leaf, blanched, stuffed with chestnuts and braised.

Red Cabbage with Chestnuts: Red cabbage braised with bacon, onions, apples, red burgundy, vinegar, and sugar, served with glazed chestnuts.

Carrots

(French: Carottes)

All year round

Buttered Carrots: Peeled, cut, boiled in seasoned water (sugar, salt, pepper), and buttered.

Glazed Fresh Carrots: Peeled, cut, boiled in seasoned water, glazed with sugar and butter.

Parslied Fresh Carrots: Peeled, cut, boiled in seasoned water and butter, sprinkled with chopped parsley.

Creamed Fresh Carrots: Peeled, cut, boiled in seasoned water, and blended with medium cream sauce.

Fresh Carrots Lyonnaise: Peeled, cut, boiled in seasoned water, mixed with butter and sautéed diced onions.

Honey-Glazed Baby Carrots: Whole baby carrots glazed with honey.

Glazed Fresh Carrots: Boiled carrots, cut, and glazed with butter, sugar, sprinkled with chopped parsley.

Fresh Carrots Paysanne: Peeled, cut, braised with bacon and fresh pearl onions.

Fresh Carrots Maître d'Hôtel: Peeled, cut, boiled in seasoned water, and sautéed in Maître d'Hôtel butter.*

Cauliflower

(French: Chou-fleur)

The term Du Barry also means "with cauliflower."
All year round; height of season, September–January

Parslied Fresh Cauliflower: Cauliflower braised in butter with chopped parsley.

Cauliflower au Gratin: Cauliflower buds, boiled, gratinéed with medium cheese sauce, cheese crumb and bread topping.

Creamed Fresh Cauliflower: Cauliflower buds, boiled, in medium cream sauce and lightly browned with bread crumb topping.

French Fried Cauliflower: Cauliflower buds, breaded and deep fried.

Cauliflower Orly: Cauliflower buds, blanched, dipped in beer batter and deep fried.

Cauliflower English Style: Whole cauliflower, boiled, served with melted butter (good for center of bouquetiere of vegetables).

Cauliflower Florentine: Boiled cauliflower buds on spinach leaves, topped with cheese sauce, and glazed.

Cauliflower Mornay: Cauliflower buds, boiled, topped with medium cheese sauce and glazed with cheese crumbs.

Cauliflower Mimosa: Cauliflower buds, boiled, topped with chopped egg yolk and melted butter.

Cauliflower Polonaise: Cauliflower buds, boiled, topped with bread crumbs, chopped boiled egg, parsley, and melted butter.

Cauliflower Milanaise: Cauliflower buds, boiled, gratinéed with shredded cheese and brown butter.

Celery

(French: Céleri)

All year round

Buttered Diced Celery: Celery cut into half-inch pieces, boiled in seasoned water, and buttered.

Celery au Jus: Celery blanched in seasoned water, braised in a natural brown sauce.

Celery in Cream Sauce: Celery boiled in seasoned water, blended with light cream sauce.

Celery with Parmesan: Celery boiled in seasoned water, gratinéed with parmesan.

*Maître d'Hôtel Butter: Mixture of butter, lemon juice, chopped parsley, salt, and pepper.

Celery Bordelaise: Celery blanched in seasoned water, braised in Bordelaise sauce.

Celery Madeira: Celery boiled in seasoned water, blended with Madeira sauce.

Celery à la Grecque: Celery braised in tomato concasse,* with olive oil, lemon juice, bay leaves, coriander, and thyme.

Corn

All year round; best fresh May–September

Buttered Corn (Kernels): Corn boiled in water and served with butter.

Corn Fritters: Corn blended with batter of egg and flour, deep fried.

Corn Pudding: Corn blended with thin cream sauce and eggs, and baked.

Corn and Tomato: Braised corn with onion, celery, and chopped tomato.

Creamed Whole Kernel Corn: Boiled corn blended with medium cream sauce.

Creamed Corn Casserole: Corn braised with onions in a medium cream sauce, decorated with bacon bits.

Dixie Corn: Corn boiled with sautéed green pepper and yellow onions.

Spanish Corn or Corn O'Brien: Corn boiled with green pepper and pimiento peppers.

Corn on the Cob: Cleaned corn boiled in water, and served with butter.

Corn with Green Beans: Boiled and buttered corn with cut green beans.

Succotash: Corn and baby lima beans boiled and blended with cream.

Corn in Sour Cream: Corn blended with bacon fat, sautéed onions, sour cream, diced pimiento, and garnished with bacon bits.

Cucumbers

(French: Concombres)

Cucumber Andalouse: Peeled, seedless half cucumber, braised in tomato sauce, topped with parmesan cheese, and glazed.

Cucumber Clermont: Peeled, seedless sliced cucumber braised with artichoke bottom in butter, garnished with chopped parsley.

Cucumber with Fennel: Peeled, seedless, sliced cucumber braised in light cream sauce with fresh chopped fennel and parsley.

Cucumber in Dill: Peeled, seedless, sliced cucumber braised in light cream sauce with chopped fresh dill.

Eggplant

(French: Aubergine)

Best August–September

French Fried Eggplant: Eggplant peeled and cut into strips, breaded, and deep fried.

Fried Eggplant: Eggplant cut in thin round slices, seasoned, floured, and fried.

Eggplant Napolitaine: Eggplant cut into thick slices, seasoned, dipped in flour, and fried. Covered with tomato sauce and parmesan cheese and gratinéed.

Eggplant Provençale: Eggplant baked with onions and tomato, bread crumbs, garlic, and chopped parsley, served with tomato sauce.

Deep Fried Eggplant: Sliced eggplant, seasoned, dipped in beer batter, deep fried, and served with tomato sauce.

Eggplant Capri: Eggplant peeled, cubed, floured, sautéed, and topped with mozzarella and spaghetti meat sauce,** glazed with Capriccio cheese mixture.†

Eggplant Parmesan: Sautéed eggplant slices on Capriccio sauce,†† sprinkled with Capriccio cheese mixture,† topped with grated mozzarella, and glazed.

Eggplant Andalouse: Eggplant baked, topped with peeled, seedless, chopped tomato, mushroom, and bell pepper.

Fennel

(French: Fenouil)

Fennel is not very well known in the United States and seldom served. It can be braised, steamed, and boiled in any of the ways celery can.

Kale

Best throughout winter

Fresh Kale: Picked, cleaned and washed, boiled in seasoned water, buttered.

*Concasse: Tomato peeled, seeded, and chopped.
**Spaghetti meat sauce: Fresh ground beef, paprika, flour, onions, celery, green pepper, garlic, tomato, and seasoning.
†Capriccio cheese mixture: Equal parts of romano and parmesan cheese.
††Capriccio sauce: Tomato sauce made from veal bones (no meat), seasoned with olive oil, onion, parsley, garlic, pepper, rosemary, oregano, sweet basil, bay leaf, and allspice.

Braised Kale: Picked, cleaned and washed, blanched, braised with bacon and carrots.

Mushrooms

(French: Champignons)

All year

Sautéed Sliced Mushrooms: Mushroom slices, sprinkled with lemon juice, sautéed in butter.

French Fried Mushrooms: Breaded whole mushrooms, deep fried.

Sautéed Mushrooms with Sherry: Mushrooms, sprinkled with lemon juice, chopped green pepper and onions, sautéed in butter and sherry wine.

Sautéed Mushrooms with Madeira: Whole mushrooms, sprinkled with lemon juice, sautéed in butter and madeira wine.

Sautéed Mushroom Caps: Mushroom caps, sprinkled with lemon juice, sautéed in butter.

Creamed Mushrooms: Sliced mushrooms, sautéed in butter, blended with heavy cream sauce.

Sautéed Mushrooms Maître d'Hôtel: Mushrooms, sprinkled with lemon juice, sautéed in Maître d'Hôtel butter.*

Mushrooms in Fresh Cream: Mushroom slices, sprinkled with lemon juice, sautéed with shallots, and simmered in fresh heavy cream, seasoned with cayenne and chopped chives.

Sautéed Mushrooms Fines Herbes: Mushroom slices, sprinkled with lemon juice, sautéed in butter with chopped shallots and herbs.

Mushrooms and Artichokes: Mushrooms, sprinkled with lemon juice, sautéed in butter with artichoke hearts.

Mushrooms with Cilantro: Mushrooms, sprinkled with lemon juice, sautéed with shallots, garlic, and crushed cilantro.

Onions

(French: Oignons)

All year

Boiled Fresh Silverskin Onions: Cleaned onions, boiled in salt water.

Buttered Fresh Silverskin Onions: Cleaned onions, boiled in salt water, buttered.

Pan Fried or Roasted Onions (silverskin): Blanched, cleaned onions, sautéed in butter.

*Maître d'Hôtel Butter: Mixture of butter, lemon juice, chopped parsley, salt, and pepper.

Onions with Cheese: Peeled yellow onions, boiled in salt water and butter, blended with medium cheese sauce.

Creamed Onions: Fresh, peeled, silverskin onions, boiled in salt water, topped with heavy cream sauce.

Au Gratin Onions: Fresh, peeled, silverskin onions, boiled in salt water, mixed with medium cheese sauce, and gratinéed with cheese crumb topping with bread.

French Fried Onion Rings: Onion rings breaded in egg wash, flour, egg wash, and bread crumbs, deep fried.

Glazed Silverskin Onions: Peeled, fresh silverskin onions, boiled in salt water, glazed with sugar (syrup).

Sautéed or Smothered Onions: Cleaned yellow onions, sliced, soaked in cold water to sweeten, sautéed in butter.

Sauterne-Glazed Onions: Fresh, peeled, silverskin onions, boiled in salt water, glazed with sauterne white wine, sugar water, and butter.

Okra

May–September

Boiled Fresh Okra: Cleaned fresh okra, preboiled in salt water, simmered with onions and butter in beef broth.

Okra Creole: Cleaned fresh okra, boiled, sautéed in butter, seasoned.

Fresh Okra with Tomato: Cleaned fresh okra, preboiled in salt water, simmered in peeled, seeded, chopped tomatoes.

Fresh Okra Oriental: Cleaned fresh okra, preboiled in salt water, simmered with fresh tomato, garlic, and seasoned with cloves, salt, and pepper.

Note: Okra is used primarily in soups, stews, and creole cookery. It may be boiled, baked or fried. Combines well with other vegetables, especially with tomatoes.

Peas

(French: Petit Pois)

January–July

Buttered Peas: Peas gently boiled in water with salt, pepper, and butter until just tender.

Peas and Mushrooms: Peas gently boiled in water with salt, pepper, and butter until just tender, then blended with sautéed mushroom slices.

Creamed Peas: Peas gently boiled in water with salt, pepper, then blended with medium cream sauce.

Buttered Peas and Carrots: Diced carrots, boiled in seasoned water and butter until just done, peas added.

Buttered Peas and Celery: Sliced, cleaned celery, Chinese style, boiled in seasoned water and butter until just done, peas added.

Buttered Peas Amandine: Peas gently boiled in water with salt, pepper, and butter until just tender, topped with toasted almond slices.

Buttered Peas with Water Chestnuts: Peas gently boiled in water with salt, pepper, and butter until just tender, sliced water chestnuts added.

Buttered Peas and Pearl Onions: Peas and pearl onions, gently boiled in water with salt, pepper, and butter.

Creamed Peas and Pearl Onions: Peas and pearl onions, gently boiled in water with salt, pepper, and butter, blended with medium cream sauce.

Buttered Peas with Mint: Peas gently boiled in water with salt, pepper, and butter until just tender, sprinkled with chopped mint.

Buttered Peas Française: Peas and pearl onions gently boiled in water with salt, pepper, and butter until just tender, julienne of lettuce added.

Buttered Peas Anna: Same as Française, plus chopped mint.

Buttered Peas Paysanne: Same as Française, plus medium cream sauce.

Snow Pea Pods with Water Chestnuts: Pea pods stir-fried with water chestnuts, seasonings, sherry wine, and bound with corn starch.

Peppers

All year

Bell pepper is mostly used for combinations, stuffed, and for stir-fried vegetables.

Potatoes

(French: Pommes)

Brabant Potatoes: Baking potatoes, peeled, cut into half-inch cubes, blanched, and sautéed with garlic butter, sprinkled with chopped parsley.

Potato Puffs Dauphine: Boiled, dry, mashed potatoes combined with a batter of water, flour, eggs, nutmeg, salt, and pepper, then formed into small balls, lightly rolled in bread crumbs, and deep fried.

Potato Croquettes (Baked): Whipped potatoes blended with eggs, salt, pepper, nutmeg, and chopped parsley, shaped into cylinders, rolled in crushed potato chips or corn flakes, and baked in the oven.

Potatoes Suzette: Baked potatoes cut open and pulp removed. Pulp pureed and blended with egg yolks, cream, chopped parsley, nutmeg, salt, and pepper. Piped into potato skins, sprinkled with parmesan cheese, and baked.

Baked Stuffed Potato Specialty: Baked potatoes cut in half and pulp removed. Pulp pureed and mixed with chopped ham, bacon bits, sour cream, chopped parsley, nutmeg, salt, and pepper. Piped into potato shells, sprinkled with parmesan cheese, and baked.

Potato Pancakes*: Grated raw potatoes and onions mixed with eggs, salt and pepper, flour, and garlic, scooped into thin patties and fried in bacon fat.

Au Gratin Potatoes: Diced or sliced potatoes, boiled and mixed with medium cheese sauce. Covered with cheese and bread crumb topping and baked.

Baked Potatoes: Baking potatoes, plain or wrapped in aluminum and oven-baked. *Note:* Can be served with butter, sour cream, chives, or bacon bits.

Salt Baked Potatoes: Baking potatoes, rolled in Kosher salt and oven-baked.

Baked Potatoes, Cheese Stuffed: Baked potatoes cut open, pulp removed. Pulp whipped and blended with milk, sharp cheddar cheese, salt, and pepper. Piped into potato skins, sprinkled with sharp cheddar cheese, and baked.

Home Fried Potatoes: Boiled sliced potatoes browned in butter with finely chopped onions and seasoned with salt, pepper, and paprika, garnished with chopped parsley.

Whipped Potatoes: Boiled potatoes whipped, and blended with milk, butter, salt, and pepper.

Anna Potatoes I: Sliced potatoes arranged shingle style into pan layered with butter and baked until brown on both sides.

Anna Potatoes II: Sliced potatoes arranged shingle style. Chicken stock flavored with onion and curry added, baked in the oven, and glazed with butter.

Creamed Potatoes and Peas: Boiled potato cubes blended with creamed pea sauce.**

Baked Sweet Potatoes: Sweet potatoes, baked.

Browned Potatoes: Small potatoes, peeled, boiled, and deep fried.

Candied Sweet Potatoes: Sweet potatoes glazed with sugar and butter.

*Small party or ethnic food and theme party.
** Pea sauce: Peas blended with thin cream sauce.

Creamed New Potatoes: Small new potatoes, boiled, blended with medium cream sauce.

Delmonico Potatoes: Diced potatoes boiled, and blended with thin cream sauce and smothered onions.

Escalloped Potatoes: Sliced potatoes, blanched and baked in thin cream sauce and smothered onions.

French Fried Potatoes: Potatoes that have been cut into thick to thin strips, soaked in cold water, blotted dry, then deep fried until crisp and golden brown.

Hash Brown Potatoes: Finely chopped, cooked potatoes that are fried (often in bacon fat) until well browned.

Lyonnaise Potatoes: Boiled, sliced potatoes sautéed in butter with sliced onions.

Lyonnaise Potatoes, Shredded: Shredded potatoes mixed with sautéed onions, flattened on grill, and browned on both sides.

Lyonnaise Potatoes, Baked: Shredded, baked potatoes mixed with sautéed onions, flattened on grill, and browned on both sides.

Oven Browned Potatoes: Small, seasoned potatoes placed in a baking pan with butter and browned in the oven.

Parslied New Potatoes: Boiled new potatoes, coated with butter, and sprinkled with chopped parsley.

Boiled Potatoes: Small, whole, peeled potatoes boiled in salt water.

Dill Boiled Potatoes: Small, boiled potatoes coated with butter, and sprinkled with freshly chopped dill.

Pittsburgh Potatoes: Diced or julienned potatoes, boiled and blended with medium cheese sauce, sautéed onions and diced pimientos, baked in the oven until brown.

Potatoes Hashed in Cream: Diced, boiled potatoes blended with hot heavy cream and cooked until cream is almost absorbed, sprinkled with buttered crumb topping, and browned.

Potatoes Parisienne*: Potatoes scooped into small balls, blanched, and browned in butter.

Oven Grilled Sweet Potatoes: Sweet potato chunks topped with a mixture of butter, sugar, nutmeg, and salt and baked in the oven.

Cooked Sweet Potatoes: Sweet potatoes sautéed in Maître d'Hôtel Butter,** topped with grated Swiss cheese and oven baked.

Potatoes Boulangere: Sliced potato and onions, mixed with white beef stock, and oven-baked.

*Due to the excessive labor involved in the preparation of these potatoes, they should only be served to small parties.
**Maître d'Hôtel Butter: Mixture of butter, lemon juice, chopped parsley, salt, and pepper.

Potatoes Paysanne: Cubed potatoes sautéed with fresh pearl onions and julienne of bacon.

Potatoes Biarritz: Whipped potatoes with chopped ham, bell pepper, and parsley.

Potatoes à la Bordelaise: Cubed potatoes sautéed in butter with chopped garlic and parsley.

Potatoes Ambassadeur: Anna potatoes with grated parmesan cheese added.

Potatoes Colbert: Cubed potatoes sautéed in butter, glazed with brown veal stock, and sprinkled with chopped parsley.

Potatoes Elizabeth: Potato puffs dauphine with chopped spinach added.

Potatoes à la Flamande: Cubed potatoes, boiled in chicken stock with fresh pearl onions and olive shaped carrots.

German Fried Potatoes: Boiled, sliced potatoes sautéed in butter.

Duchess Potatoes: Boiled, dried, mashed potatoes mixed with egg yolk, butter, and seasoning, and piped into a cone shape, brushed with whipped egg yolk, and oven-baked.

Potatoes Pont Neuf: Like steak fried potatoes, thumb-shaped potatoes, deep fried.

Potatoes à la Favorite: Boiled potatoes, blended with butter, fresh herbs (parsley, chive, etc.), and green beans.

Potatoes Marquise: Duchess potatoes with tomato paste added.

Potatoes à la Normande: Sliced potatoes sautéed with butter, onions, and leek, blended with chopped parsley, chives, thin cream sauce, and gratinéed.

Potatoes O'Brien: Boiled potatoes, chopped and sautéed in butter with chopped pimientos and green pepper added.

Potatoes Parmentier: Cubed potatoes sautéed in butter, sprinkled with chopped chives.

Potatoes Chateau: Olive-shaped potatoes blanched and sautéed in butter, sprinkled with chopped parsley.

Potatoes Fondantes: Large olive-shaped potatoes, blanched and baked with butter and a small amount of white stock.

Potatoes Amandine: Potato croquettes with sliced almonds added to the potatoes, rolled in sliced almonds, and deep fried.

Potatoes Berny: Potato croquettes with truffle, rolled in sliced almonds and deep fried. (For lower cost, eliminate truffle.)

Potatoes Macaire: Pulp from baked potatoes removed, mashed, and blended with butter and seasoning, formed into patties, and browned on both sides.

Potato Gratin Dauphinoise: Sliced potatoes mixed with milk, onions, and parmesan cheese, and then baked. *Note:* Minced garlic is optional.

Ratatouille

Ratatouille Niçoise: Sautéed zucchini squash, green pepper, red pepper, eggplant, onion, and tomatoes seasoned with thyme, garlic, salt and pepper, and bay leaf.

Spinach

(French: Epinards)

All year

Buttered Fresh Spinach: Cleaned spinach, boiled in seasoned water, and buttered.

Creamed Fresh Spinach: Buttered fresh spinach, drained, combined with medium cream sauce.

Creamed Spinach Special: Cleaned, boiled, and ground spinach, blended with Supreme sauce seasoned with salt and pepper, minced garlic, and ground nutmeg, with cream added.

Sautéed Fresh Spinach: Cleaned spinach, boiled in seasoned water, sautéed in butter with finely chopped onions, seasoned with salt and pepper, minced garlic, ground nutmeg.

Squash

(French: Courgettes, Courges)

Baked Acorn Squash: Acorn squash cut into halves, thirds, or quarters, seeds removed, and baked, sprinkled with sugar, orange rind, orange juice, and glazed.

Baked Acorn Squash Slices: Acorn squash baked as above, sliced and glazed.

Buttered Butternut Squash: Cleaned, washed, peeled, and seeded squash, cut into slices, boiled in seasoned water, and buttered.

Buttered Yellow Squash: Peeled and seeded squash, cut into slices, boiled in seasoned water, and buttered.

Lyonnaise Yellow Squash: Squash cooked as in previous entry, mixed with smothered onions.

French Fried Zucchini Squash: Trimmed and sliced zucchini, breaded and deep fried.

Buttered Zucchini Squash: Trimmed and sliced zucchini, boiled in seasoned water, and buttered.

Zucchini Squash Italienne: Trimmed and sliced zucchini, sautéed with onions and tomatoes, baked with grated sharp cheddar cheese.

Sautéed Zucchini in Cream: Trimmed and sliced zucchini, sautéed in butter, seasoned with salt, pepper, and nutmeg, cream added, sprinkled with snipped dill.

Lyonnaise Zucchini Squash: Trimmed and sliced zucchini, boiled in seasoned water, buttered, and mixed with smothered onions.

Tomatoes

(French: Tomates)

Stuffed Tomatoes Clamart: Tomato halves seeded, filled with buttered peas, creamed peas, or pureed peas.

Stuffed Tomatoes with Cauliflower Buds: Tomato halves seeded, filled with cauliflower buds.

Stuffed Tomatoes with Broccoli Buds: Tomato halves seeded, filled with broccoli buds.

Stuffed Tomatoes with Sautéed Sliced Mushrooms or Creamed Mushrooms: Tomato halves seeded, filled with sautéed or creamed mushrooms.

Stuffed Tomatoes Florentine: Tomato halves seeded, filled with buttered spinach or creamed spinach.

Stuffed Tomatoes Provençale: Tomato halves seeded, topped with bread crumbs, parsley, and clarified butter.

Note: Tomatoes are used year round for garnishing or filled with other complementing vegetables; they can also be topped with bread crumbs and herbs.

Chapter 10

Desserts

Growing up, I was always urged to eat sparingly of the main course so as to leave a little room for the "hereafter."

Dieters often get tired of living by a list of desserts that should be avoided. However, fruit is a natural dessert that everyone should eat more often. Fresh fruit and unsweetened fruit juice can be used in many recipes to replace some, if not all, of the sugar. When using recipes that call for fresh fruit, remember that, usually, the riper the fruit, the sweeter the flavor.

Taste-tempting desserts should always be considered the visual climax to any dining experience.

Mud Pie
Caramel Ice Cream and Meringue
Banana Cake
Pineapple Sorbet and Hot Chocolate Sauce
Chocolate Brownie Chantilly
Caramelized Ginger Cream
Lemon Chiffon Pie
Trio of Fresh Fruit Sorbets
German Black Forest Cake
Almond Pear Tart, Whipped Cream
Crown of Orange Sherbet au Cointreau with a Butter Cookie
Frozen Raspberry Soufflé
Chocolate Cream Pie
Blueberry Sorbet
Key Lime Pie
Melon Sorbet
Italian Rum Cake
Caramelized Orange Cream
Fresh Fruit Flan
Pineapple Tart with Minted Lemon Cream
Fruit Cheesecake
Savarin of Fresh Fruit
Pecan Pie
Hazelnut Ice Cream
Orange Flavored Chocolate Mousse
Raspberry Bavarian
Kahlua Parfait Glacé
Viennese Apple Strudel and Hot Cinnamon Sauce
Crème de Menthe Parfait
Almond Ice Cream Bombe
Lemon Mousse Torte

Sherbet Delight: Lime Sherbet with Crème de Menthe
French Apple Strudel with Whipped Cinnamon Cream
Chocolate Eclair with Chocolate Rum Sauce
Assorted Fruit Pies
Carrot Cake
Ice Cream Roll with Melba Sauce
Crème Caramel
Strawberry, Chocolate, or Lemon Mousse
Cheesecake with Crushed Strawberry Sauce
Coupe Kahlua
Grand Marnier Parfait
Chocolate Almond Mousse
Amaretto Coupe
Mandarin Orange Ice with Orange Twist
Apple Strudel, Vanilla Sauce
Rum Cream Pie
Amaretto Mousse
Florida Orange Bombe with Grand Marnier
Neapolitan Bombe with Crème de Menthe
Crown of Raspberry Sherbet, Sauce Framboise, and a Chocolate Cookie
Coupe of Lemon Sherbet, Sauce à la Menthe
Hazelnut Cheesecake
Pear Belle Helene
Raspberry Cheesecake
Frozen Ice Cream Log with Crushed Strawberry Sauce
Assorted French Pastries
Sacher Torte
Savarin of Lime Parfait

Wigger's Ice Cream Bombes

An ice cream bombe is a frozen dessert consisting of layers of ice cream or sherbet. The ice cream is softened and spread, one layer at a time, in a mold. Each layer is hardened before the next one is added. The center of a bombe is often custard laced with fruit. After it's frozen solid, the bombe is unmolded and often served with a dessert sauce. The original bombe molds were spherical; however, any shape mold may be used today.

Napoleon's Defeat: A bombe of chocolate and brandy-flavored coffee ice creams, topped with crushed roasted almonds. Chocolate fudge sauce passed.

Bombe Carioca: Rum and chocolate ice creams, with crushed pineapple sauce passed.

Bombe Glacé Praline: Praline ice cream topped with selected fruits and sauce passed.

Hawaiian Sunset: Pineapple and lemon sherbet bombe with chilled Crème de Menthe sauce passed.

Bombe Manhattan: Vanilla ice cream and raspberry sherbet with blueberry Melba sauce passed.

The Aristocrat: Pistachio and vanilla ice cream bombe with strawberry sauce passed.

Bombe Glacé Corey: Vanilla ice cream bombe topped with California peaches flambé.

Bombe Coppelia: Praline and coffee ice creams, served with warm chocolate sauce passed.

Bombe Mousseline: Strawberry ice cream with whipped cream and chopped fresh strawberries passed.

Bombe Americana: Strawberry and vanilla ice creams topped with fresh orange sections and served with Melba sauce passed.

Bombe Nabob: Brandy-flavored praline ice cream topped with candied fruits and served with chocolate sauce passed.

Bombe Fleurettes: Lemon sherbet topped with sliced peaches and strawberries and served with Melba sauce passed.

Bombe Othello: Vanilla-flavored praline ice cream topped with sliced peaches and served with sabayon sauce passed.

Bombe Grand Duc: Orange sherbet flavored with Benedictine liqueur and served with raspberry sauce passed.

Pistachio and Chocolate Bombe: Pistachio and chocolate ice creams with chocolate almond sauce passed.

Bombe Andalouse: Yellow cake with cherry vanilla ice cream and lemon sherbet, sauce melba passed.

Bombe Cardinal: Vanilla ice cream and raspberry sherbet, sauce melba passed.

The American Dream: Bombe of strawberry and vanilla ice creams on a bed of white cake, blueberry melba sauce passed.

Bombe Glacé: Rum-flavored ice cream with sliced bananas flambé au cognac.

Bombe Sacher: Chocolate and coffee ice creams, chocolate cake, and chocolate icing, served with rich chocolate sauce.

Pear Helena Bombe: Pear ice with poached pears on a slice of chocolate torte with chocolate sauce and shaved milk chocolate.

Fried Almond Ice Cream Bombe: Almond ice cream with mandarin liqueur flambé.

Savarin Ring Desserts

Vanilla Savarin #1: Vanilla savarin with cherries flambé passed.

Vanilla Savarin #2: Vanilla savarin with marinated strawberries passed.

Chocolate and Vanilla Savarin: Chocolate and vanilla savarin with warm chocolate sauce passed.

Pistachio Savarin: Pistachio savarin with mandarin oranges passed.

Desserts at an Additional Charge

Strawberry Shortcake

Baked Alaska Flambé

Cherries Jubilee Flambé en Parade

Las Bananas Flambés: Sliced bananas flamed in sugar and brandy over ice cream.

Strawberry Glacé en Corbeille au Chocolat: Strawberry ice cream in a semisweet chocolate cup topped with whipped cream and a cherry.

Lime Sherbet Hawaiian en Corbeille au Chocolat: Lime sherbet in a semisweet chocolate cup topped with crushed pineapple and whipped cream.

Soufflé Glacé Grand Duc: Vanilla ice cream topped with brandied bananas.

Vacherin Glacé: Sponge cake base with raspberry and vanilla ice creams, meringue, and blueberry melba sauce.

Soufflé Grand Marnier: Ice cream soufflé with orange-flavored cognac.

Fraise Rafraîchie au Champagne Rosé: Brandy snifter filled with strawberries over raspberry sherbet, laced with pink champagne.

Plombiere au Chartreuse: Apricots laced with chartreuse.

Orange Chantilly: Scooped whole orange filled with frozen sabayon-rouge.

Samoan Enchantment: Tiny scoops of Chartreuse-flavored vanilla ice cream, arranged in a pyramid in a half coconut, topped with toasted grated coconut and sliced brandied bananas flambé.

South Seas Paradise: Half coconut filled with vanilla ice cream flavored with Chartreuse, topped with crushed pineapple and brandied bananas.

Croquembouche: A pyramid effect of mini cream puffs glazed with a clear sugar coating.

Tropical Delight: Whole papaya scooped and filled with fresh diced papaya and pineapple, marinated in Triple Sec (orange peel-flavored liqueur), topped with a rosette of lime sherbet and a sprig of mint.

Häagen Daaz: Rum raisin ice cream, milk chocolate garniture.

Poached Pear Symphony, au Chocolat: Whole pear poached in applejack brandy and dipped in chocolate, floating in zabaglione sauce.

Mocha Mousse: In semisweet chocolate shell, topped with whipped cream, decorated with sprinkles of milk chocolate with cookie served on the side.

Raspberry Ice with Fresh Kiwi Medallion: Raspberry-flavored ice and sliced kiwi served in a silver suprême.

If you wish to create a signature dessert for your hotel, resort, or an event, the pièce de résistance of desserts can be created with the use of high quality chocolate couverture from Chocolates à la Carte, which is a unique specialty chocolate company recognized by the country's best chefs and catering executives for premium quality, design creativity, exacting production controls, and exceptional customer service. The possibilities are sensational!

West Coast Telephone: (818) 364–6777
East Coast Telephone: (407) 332–0059

Chapter 11

Breakfast Entrées

Eggs

Eggs Cordon Bleu (Maximum 250 Guests): Breaded and fried ham and cheese, topped with poached eggs and Marchand de Vin Sauce. Served with a grilled tomato half.

Eggs Yvette: Fluffy scrambled eggs served in tartlets with asparagus tips and bay shrimp. Served with a baked apple half.

Eggs St. Corey: Two poached eggs on fresh crouton, topped with Seafood Mornay and Hollandaise Sauce. Served with a broiled tomato and fresh fruit garnish.

Roulade of Ham and Spinach Basquaise: Thinly sliced ham stuffed with spinach, served with scrambled eggs

Collops of Beef Tenderloin in Horseradish: Tenderloin of beef in horseradish served with mustard sauce, cajun potatoes, stuffed mushrooms, and scrambled eggs.

Croustade of Poached Eggs and Smoked Salmon: Poached eggs and smoked salmon in a pastry shell served with sun-dried tomato Béarnaise Sauce.

Scrambled Eggs Vol-au-Vent: Puff pastry shells filled with eggs scrambled with your choice of the following: cheddar cheese, Swiss cheese, mushrooms, green peppers, diced ham, onions.

Eggs Astor: Scrambled eggs, Gruyère cheese, diced ham, and bacon, baked in a potato shell, glazed with Béchamel Sauce.

English Eggs: Scrambled eggs over Canadian bacon and biscuit, smothered with Cheese Sauce.

Eggs Hussard: Scooped tomatoes filled with diced ham, mushrooms, scrambled eggs, glazed with Cheese Sauce.

Peppered Scrambled Eggs: Scrambled eggs with scallions, pepperoni, and cheese.

Eggs à la Reine en Croustade: Poached egg, creamed chicken, and Hollandaise Sauce in a pastry shell.

Crêpes Filled with Scrambled Eggs: Crêpes stuffed with scrambled eggs, topped with Cheese Sauce.

Country-Style Scrambled Eggs: Fluffy scrambled eggs with onions, tomato, and green pepper.

Benedict Twins: Two poached eggs—one with ham, the other with sautéed mushrooms, both with Hollandaise Sauce. Served with fresh fruit skewer.

Chipped Beef, Broiled Egg: Chipped beef and a broiled egg served with Cheddar Sauce on a toasted English muffin.

English Hunt Breakfast: Lamb chop, sausage, bacon, scrambled eggs, and tomato.

Farm Fresh Scrambled Eggs: Scrambled eggs served with a potato shell, stuffed with Louisiana spicy hash.

Eggs Wigger: An English muffin, sausage patties, and poached eggs covered with our Mushroom Sherry Sauce and served with potato pancakes.

Kosher Salami with Scrambled Eggs "Oven Baked": Baked kosher salami and scrambled eggs, served with three potato pancakes.

Waffles

Fresh Strawberry Waffles: Waffles topped with whipped cream or ice cream and strawberries. Dusted with powdered sugar and served with strawberry syrup.

Apple Waffles: Fresh diced apples baked in waffle batter and seasoned with Saigon cinnamon. Served with apple nectar.

Pecan Waffles: Waffles made with fresh toasted Georgia pecans, dusted with powdered sugar.

Blueberry Waffles: Waffles made with plump fresh blueberries, served with blueberry compote and powdered sugar.

Bacon Waffles: Crisp bits of real bacon in our waffle batter.

Coconut Waffles: Waffles made with toasted coconut, served with tropical syrup and dusted with powdered sugar.

Crêpes

French Pancakes: Crêpes rolled with fresh strawberries or preserves, dusted with powdered sugar, and served with strawberry syrup.

Palastine Pancakes: Crêpes rolled with sour cream and Cointreau, a gourmet's delight. Dusted with powdered sugar and served with tropical syrup.

Kijafa Cherry Crêpes: A Danish favorite, crêpes filled with red sour pitted cherries simmered in Kijafa wine, dusted with powdered sugar.

Mandarin Pancakes: The Crêpes Suzette of the Orient. Crêpes served with mandarin orange segments, mandarin syrup, and powdered sugar.

Apple Crêpes: Crêpes made with diced apples, pecans, sour cream, Cointreau, and cinnamon sugar. Served with warm apple nectar. (Due to the ingredients of the product, it must be served at room temperature.)

Pancakes

Blueberry Pancakes: Blueberry pancakes dusted with powdered sugar, served with fresh, warm blueberry compote.

Swedish Pancakes: Pancakes with imported lingonberries and butter.

Hawaiian Pancakes: Pancakes with chunks of pineapple, dusted with powdered sugar, served with tropical syrup.

Pecan Pancakes: Pancakes made with pecans, dusted with powdered sugar. The Southland's favorite.

Coconut Pancakes: Pancakes made with toasted coconut flakes dusted with powdered sugar and served with tropical syrup.

49'er Flapjacks: Three large chewy-gooey thin pancakes.

Sourdough Pancakes: Pancakes made from old-fashioned yeasty sourdough, dusted with powdered sugar.

Buttermilk Pancakes: Pancakes made with buttermilk, served with whipped butter, hot syrup.

Potato Pancakes: Pancakes made from grated potatoes, served with applesauce or sour cream.

Cakes of the Sea: Whole baby clams in crêpe-like batter.

Wheat Germ Pancakes: Pancakes made with wheat germ and enhanced with sour cream.

Bacon Pancakes: Pancakes with crisp bits of real bacon.

Yeasty Old-Fashioned Buckwheat Pancakes: Buckwheat pancakes served with whipped butter, hot syrup.

Banana Pancakes: Banana pancakes dusted with powdered sugar, served with tropical sauce.

Chapter 12

Seated Breakfast Menus

The Celebration Breakfast

Upon the guests' arrival, they will be offered champagne and orange juice cocktails, served from a silver tray by a white-gloved waiter.

An Individual Plate Presentation of:
Iced Fresh Fruit to include Papaya, Mangoes, Bananas, Strawberries, etc.

• • •

Casserole Eggs à la Florentine

• • •

Assorted Breakfast Rolls to include:
Petite Danish, Croissants, Breakfast Bakeries, and Blueberry Muffins
Marmalade, Fruit
Preserves, and Swan-Molded Butter

• • •

Coffee, Tea, Decaffeinated Coffee

The Crêpe for You Breakfast

Melon Wedge filled with Yogurt Mousse

• • •

Kijafa Cherry Crêpes
A Danish favorite, filled with Red Sour, Pitted Cherries
simmered in Kijafa Wine, Dusted with Powdered Sugar,
Extra Kijafa Sauce passed

• • •

Assorted Breakfast Pastries and Danish passed on Silver Trays by Waiters

• • •

Coffee, Tea, Decaffeinated Coffee

• • •

The Beat Your Eggs a Different Way Breakfast

V-8 Juice Cocktail, each glass garnished with Celery Stick, Zucchini Spear, and Scallion
Juice poured by Servers from Pitchers in room
Tabasco and Lea & Perrins Sauce on each Table

• • •

Eggs Beatrix
Crêpe Stuffed with Scrambled Eggs and Diced Ham, served atop Holland Rusk with Sauce Mousseline with Watercress and Parsley

• • •

Rudy's Farm Sausage Patties,
Farmers Potatoes

• • •

Homemade Cracked Wheat Bread,
wide sliced and served in a wicker basket
Molded Butter and Individual Jars of Strawberry Preserves

• • •

Coffee, Tea, Decaffeinated Coffee

The Frenchie Breakfast

Fresh Fruit Cup in Silver Suprême

• • •

French Toast with Blueberry Butter
Hot Maple Syrup placed on each table in the Mrs. Butterworth's Bottle
Canadian Bacon Slices, Dried Peach and Prune Garnish

• • •

Coffee, Tea, Decaffeinated Coffee

The Cereal-Go-Round Breakfast

The following items will be displayed as an edible centerpiece, on a Lazy Susan in the center of each round table:

Glass Bowl of Carafes in Shaved Ice
containing:
Freshly Squeezed Orange Juice, Grapefruit
Juice, and Milk

• • •

Individual Cereal: Raisin Bran, Wheaties,
Rice Krispies, and Bran Flakes

• • •

Individual Glass Bowls filled with:
Cubed Honeydew Melon,
Sliced Peaches, Fresh Strawberries, Dry
Raisins, Dates, Apricots, Walnuts,
Honey, Granola

• • •

Wicker Baskets of Assorted Breakfast Breads
and Creamery Butter

• • •

Individual Room Service Jars of Honey,
Jellies, and Marmalade
at each place setting

• • •

Coffee, Tea, Decaffeinated Coffee

The Dukes of Dixieland Family-Style Breakfast

Southern decor juice bar serving
presentations of:
Fresh Fruit Juices, Fresh Cut Fruit of Mango,
Peach, Papaya, Orange, Grapefruit, Melons,
Casaba, Strawberries

• • •

Southern-Style Scrambled Eggs, Smithfield
Ham, Sausage Patties, Hominy Grits, Red
Eye Gravy

• • •

Selection of Pecan Sticky Buns, Muffins,
Beignets, Buttermilk Biscuits
Calloway Brand Peach and Muscadine
Preserves, Whipped Butter
Small Basket with Honey and Preserves

• • •

Coffee, Chicory Coffee, Café au Lait

Music: Dukes of Dixieland.

Special Requirements: Hostesses in Antebellum Costumes, Waitresses in Gingham Checked Aprons. Azalea plants on each table, camelia blossom on each napkin, floral decor of dogwood, azaleas, and magnolia. Appropriate serving vessels for family-style service.

• • •

The Honorable Benedict Breakfast

Fresh Orange Juice en Supreme

• • •

Eggs Benedict
Diced Farmers Potatoes Sautéed with
Scallions
Garni of Papaya with Kiwi

• • •

Croissants, Brioche, Petite Danish
Bread Baskets made of Homemade Bread
Preserves and Molded Butter
Individual Jelly Jars

• • •

Apple Snow
Served in Fresh Apple, placed on a
Glass Plate

• • •

Coffee, Tea, Decaffeinated Coffee

The Sardi Side Up Breakfast

Seasonal Melon with Mélange of Berries

• • •

Eggs Sardi
Tomato Stuffed with Poached Eggs,
Sauce Hollandaise,
Fresh Asparagus,

Veal Gruillade
Veal Sautéed with Mushrooms

• • •

Croissants and Muffins
Preserves and Butter

• • •

Coffee, Tea, Decaffeinated Coffee

The Don't Reine on My Parade Breakfast

Grapefruit Basket with Mélange of
Fresh Fruits

• • •

Eggs à la Reine
Poached Egg and Chicken à la Reine,
Presented in a Puff Pastry, Sauce Hollandaise
Fresh Asparagus, Cinnamon Apple Slices

• • •

Coffee, Tea, Decaffeinated Coffee

The Everything Is Bigger in Texas Breakfast

Chilled Freshly Squeezed Orange Juice,
garnished with a Strawberry

• • •

Texas Golden Buck Eggs with Canadian Bacon
Poached Eggs on Pastry Shell with
Cheese Topping, Hash Brown Potatoes

• • •

Assorted Breakfast Bakeries
Marmalade, Fruit Preserves, and Butter

• • •

Coffee, Tea, Decaffeinated Coffee

The Tater Cakes and Eggs on Apple Breakfast

Tropical Fruit Cup served in
Silver Suprême, Garnished with Fresh
Strawberry

• • •

Eggs à la Wigger
Potato Pancakes, Sliced Apple, Poached Egg
Sauce Hollandaise, Sausage Patties, Papaya
with Kiwi Garnish

• • •

Pastry Baskets of:
Brioche, Croissants, Petite Danish
Butter Molds and Assorted Fruit Preserves

• • •

Coffee, Tea, Decaffeinated Coffee

The Savory in the Morning Breakfast

Chilled Melon Wedge (in season), with
Lime Garnish

• • •

Eggs Savory en Croustade
Fluffy Eggs in Pastry Shell, Cream Glazed
and
Accompanied with Ham Steak and Grilled
Tomato

• • •

Assorted Breakfast Bakeries
Marmalade, Fruit Preserves, and Butter

• • •

Coffee, Tea, Decaffeinated Coffee

The Shroomies and Eggs Breakfast

Fresh Berries in Season, with Heavy Cream

• • •

Fluffy Scrambled Eggs with Fresh Sliced
Sautéed Mushrooms,
Home Fried Potatoes, and
Grilled Hickory Ham

• • •

Petite Danish Pastry, Breakfast Bakeries
Marmalade, Fruit Preserves, and Butter

• • •

Coffee, Tea, Decaffeinated Coffee

The Hash and Dash Breakfast

Fresh Florida Orange Sections

• • •

Roast Beef Hash with Poached Egg
Grilled Tomato

• • •

Basket of Danish Pastries and Muffins
Jelly, Marmalade, and Butter

• • •

Coffee, Tea, Sanka, Milk

The Duchesse Under the Arch Breakfast

Select Orange and Grapefruit Sections
• • •

Eggs Archiduchesse
Fluffy Scrambled Eggs with Diced Ham and
Mushrooms, Topped with an Asparagus Tip
Potatoes O'Brien
Seasonal Fresh Stewed Fruits
• • •

Assorted Breakfast Bakeries
Marmalade, Fruit Preserves, and Butter
• • •

Coffee, Tea, Decaffeinated Coffee

The Countrytime Breakfast

Fresh Carrot or Orange Juice at Each
Place Setting
• • •

Country Scrambled Eggs
Combination of Diced Ham, Sausage, Pepper,
and Onions
Hot Grits in Pastry Shells
• • •

Lovely Female Attendants passing Baskets of
Fresh Pastries, English Muffins, Rum Buns,
Toast, and Homemade Biscuits with Crocks
of Jams, Jellies, Honey, and Butter
• • •

Coffee, Tea, Decaffeinated Coffee

The Lorraine, I Love You Breakfast

Slice of Seasonal Melon with Lime Wedge
• • •

Nouvelle Quiche Lorraine
Broiled Tomato
• • •

Home Baked Coffee Cake
• • •

Coffee, Tea, Sanka, Milk

The Popeye's® Spinach Breakfast

From an attractively decorated buffet table, we
will serve a mirrored display of fruits to
include:
Fresh Pineapple, Bananas, Melon, Pears,
Grapes, and Strawberries
To complement the fruit, Honey, Fresh
Cream, and Sour Cream
• • •

Served at the Table:
Freshly Squeezed Orange Juice
• • •

Eggs Florentine
Poached Eggs with Spinach and
Hollandaise Sauce
Canadian Bacon, Link Sausages, Hash Brown
Potatoes, Broiled Tomatoes
• • •

Assorted Breakfast Bakeries and Pastries,
Creamery Butter, Jam, and Marmalade
• • •

Coffee, Tea, Decaffeinated Coffee

The Dice with No Gamble Breakfast

Fresh Florida Grapefruit Half
• • •

Diced Ham Scramble Forestiere
Cubed Country Ham and Sautéed
Mushrooms with Scrambled Eggs
Golden Brown Lyonnaise Potatoes
Broiled Half Tomato
• • •

Hot Homemade Corn Muffins,
Banana Bread
Butter, Jam, Jelly, and Marmalade
• • •

Coffee, Tea, Sanka, Milk

The Not with My Eggs You Don't Breakfast

Florida Orange Juice or
Skewered Fresh Pineapple and Strawberries

• • •

Three-Egg Omelettes
Choice of Western, Mushroom, or Cheese
Crisp Bacon
Home Fried Potatoes

• • •

Toast and Assorted Muffins
Jelly, Jam, Marmalade, and Butter

• • •

Coffee, Tea, Sanka, Milk

The Smooth Scramble Breakfast

Florida Smoothie
A Blending of Juices, Yogurts, and Fresh
Fruit

• • •

Country Fresh Scrambled Eggs with Crisp
Smoked Bacon or Link Sausage, Hash Brown
Potatoes or Buttered Hominy Grits, Sun-
Dried Fruit Garnish

• • •

Petite Pastries, Breakfast Bakeries
Marmalade, Fruit Preserves, and Butter

• • •

Coffee, Tea, Decaffeinated Coffee, or Milk

The Move Over Chicks, This Is Cattle Country Breakfast

Indian River Grapefruit Sections

• • •

Breakfast Sirloin Steak
with Soft Scrambled Eggs
Home Fried Potatoes

• • •

Home Baked English Muffins
and Danish
Marmalade and Butter

• • •

Coffee, Tea, Sanka, Milk

The Lox, Lox, and More Lox Breakfast

Fresh Strawberries with Brown Sugar and
Heavy Cream

• • •

Lox of Lox
With Fluffy Scrambled Eggs and Onions
Spooned over a Toasted Bagel
Fiesta Potatoes, Fresh Fruit Garnish

• • •

Petite Pastries, Breakfast Bakeries
Marmalade, Fruit Preserves, and Butter

• • •

Decaffeinated Coffee, Tea, Coffee, Milk

The Ranch Breakfast

Fresh Yogurt with Granola Sprinkled on Top

• • •

6-ounce Grilled Petite Filet Mignon on Toast
with Scrambled Ranch Eggs
Golden Brown Fried Potatoes, Sun-Dried
Fruit Garnish

• • •

Coffee, Tea, Decaffeinated Coffee, or Milk

The Filet and Cheese Omelet Breakfast

Melon Crown with Strawberries and Honey
Yogurt Sauce

• • •

Petite Cheese Omelettes, Petite Filet Mignon
Lyonnaise Potatoes

• • •

Fresh Blueberry Muffins, Fresh Bran Muffins

• • •

Beverage

The Mariner Breakfast

Papaya Half with Fresh Strawberries

• • •

Eggs Mariner
Two Poached Eggs on Fresh Crouton,
Laced with Béchamel Sauce and
Lump Crabmeat
Broiled Tomato Half

• • •

Breakfast Bakeries, Petite Pastries
Marmalade, Fruit Preserves, and Butter

• • •

Coffee, Tea, Decaffeinated Coffee, Milk

The Port of Portugal Breakfast

Baked Honey-Glazed Florida Grapefruit Half

• • •

Eggs Portuguese
Poached Eggs in Puff Pastry Shell
with Portuguese Sauce, Crisp Smoked Bacon,
Sun-Dried Fruit Garnish

• • •

Petite Pastries, Breakfast Bakeries,
Marmalade, Fruit Preserves, and Butter

• • •

Coffee, Tea, Decaffeinated Coffee, Milk

The Cajun Breakfast

A Mélange of Fresh Fruit Blended with Nuts
and Banana Chips

• • •

Eggs New Orleans
Farm Fresh Scrambled Eggs in a
Potato Shell Stuffed with Louisiana Spicy
Hash, Sliced Tomato
Buttered Hominy Grits

• • •

Petite Pastries, Breakfast Bakeries,
Marmalade, Fruit Preserves, and Butter

• • •

Coffee, Tea, Decaffeinated Coffee, or Milk

The Love Me Tenderloin Breakfast

Crescents of Fresh Melon with
Seasonal Berries

• • •

Eggs Tenderloin
Poached Eggs served on Thinly Sliced
Tenderloin and Toasted English Muffin with
Sauce Béarnaise

• • •

Warm Cinnamon Apple Slices

• • •

Coffee, Tea, Decaffeinated Coffee

The Mornay on My Eggs Breakfast

Fresh Berries with Fresh Cream

• • •

Poached Eggs Mornay on Artichoke Bottom
Sausage, Potato Pancakes

• • •

Country Biscuits, Nut Breads,
Freshly Baked Danish, Pecan Rolls

• • •

Beverage

The Spotlight on Excellence Breakfast

Raspberry Champagne Cocktail

• • •

Early Elegance
A Vol-au-Vent Shell filled with Scrambled
Eggs and Garnished with Caviar and a Dollop
of Sour Cream
Link Sausage and Crisp Bacon Strips

• • •

Baskets of Fresh Baked Banana, Date, and
Pumpkin Breads
Butter Molds

• • •

Coffee, Tea, Decaffeinated Coffee

Chapter 13

Buffet Breakfast Menus

The Up and at 'Em Buffet Breakfast

From various stations, we will serve the following:

• • •

Omelette Stations

Omelettes or Scrambled Eggs made to order in the room by four Chefs from various stations.

The following condiments will be displayed in glass bowls in glow-ice pans:

Sliced Mushrooms, Chopped Green Onions, Chopped Green Peppers, Diced Tomatoes, Diced Ham, Diced Bacon, Shredded Cheddar, Shredded Swiss Cheese, Sauce for Western Omelette

• • •

Assorted Whole Fresh Fruit displayed in a basket as an edible centerpiece in the center of each round table

• • •

Assorted Breakfast Pastries and Breads served in wicker baskets to include:

Blueberry Muffins, Corn Muffins, and Biscuits
Butter, Preserves, and Honey

• • •

Fresh Fruit Juice Station

Chilled Oranges and Grapefruit will be squeezed to order from a juice machine by a Waiter Attendant

• • •

Coffee, Tea, Decaffeinated Coffee

The Around-the-World Buffet Breakfast

Country Kitchen
Sausage Biscuits, Country Ham Biscuits
Red-eye Gravy, Hominy Grits
Corn Bread with Honey Butter

• • •

French Farmhouse
Quiche Lorraine
Fruit Crêpes, Croissants, and Brioches
Scrambled Eggs Bouchées
Lyonnaise Potatoes

• • •

Polynesian
Fresh Tropical Fruits
Fresh Melon Wedges
Broiled Grapefruit
Coconut Bread and Banana Nut Bread

• • •

Mexican Fiesta
Sopaipillas
Huevos Rancheros in Tortillas
Tropical Fruit Salad
Fried Plantains

• • •

Manhattan Morning
Fresh Fruit Salad
Smoked Salmon, Bagels with Cream Cheese and Appropriate Condiments
Cheese Blintzes
Coffee, Tea, Decaffeinated Coffee

The This Buffet Has It All Buffet Breakfast

Carafes of Chilled Fruit Juices
To Include: Freshly Squeezed Orange Juice,
Grapefruit Juice, V-8, and Apple Juice on
Crushed Ice

• • •

Tropical Fruit Selection and Seasonal Berries
Sprinkled with Shredded Coconut

• • •

Assortment of Fruity Yogurts
Assorted toppings to include Granola,
Plantain Chips, Chopped Nuts, Wheat Germ,
and Sliced Cling Peaches

• • •

Eggs Scrambled with Ribbons of
Smoked Salmon
Fluffy Scrambled Eggs with Fines Herbes
Hickory Bacon, Hot Cajun Sausage
Cinnamon French Toast, Pineapple Beignets
Choice of Boysenberry and Maple Syrup

• • •

Cranberry Nut Bread, Assorted Muffins,
Danish, and Toasted Bagels
Cream Cheese, Butter, Marmalade,
and Honey

• • •

Coffee, Herbal and Regular Teas,
Brewed Decaffeinated Coffee, and Milk

The Basic with a Little More Buffet Breakfast

Assorted Chilled Juices:
Orange, Grapefruit, Tomato, and Apple

• • •

Fresh Seasonal Fruits

• • •

Assorted Cold Cereals and Farm Fresh
Cream

• • •

Freshly Scrambled Country Eggs Fines
Herbes

• • •

Thick French Toast, Dusted with Powdered
Sugar and served with Whipped Butter,
Maple-Flavored Syrup
Rashers of Crisp Bacon and Country Sausage
Links
Cottage Fried Potatoes

• • •

Petite Danish Pastries, Breakfast Bakeries,
and Bread
Marmalade, Fruit Preserves, and Butter

• • •

Coffee, Tea, Decaffeinated Coffee, or Milk

The Basic Buffet Breakfast

Assorted Chilled Juices:
Orange, Grapefruit, and Tomato

• • •

Fresh Seasonal Fruits

• • •

Assorted Cold Cereals and
Farm Fresh Cream

• • •

Fluffy Scrambled Eggs
Crisp Bacon Strips, Country Sausage Links
Fiesta Potatoes or Buttered Hominy Grits

• • •

Petite Danish Pastries, Breakfast Bakeries,
and Breads
Marmalade, Fruit Preserves, and Butter

• • •

Coffee, Tea, Decaffeinated Coffee, or Milk

The Bavarian and Eggs Buffet Breakfast

Half Pineapple Filled with Fresh Fruits of the
Season (Preset)

• • •

Chilled Orange Juice (Preset)

• • •

Bavarian Pancakes filled with Wild
Lingonberries

• • •

Eggs Prepared to Order in the room by a Chef
in White Uniform
Link Sausage, Crisp Bacon, Smithfield Ham
Home Fried Potatoes

• • •

Blueberry and Corn Muffins, Assorted Rolls,
Butter and Jelly to be placed on tables, Warm
Danish Pastries to be Passed

• • •

Coffee, Tea, or Decaffeinated Coffee

The Complete and Healthy Buffet Breakfast

Assorted Chilled Juices to Include:
Freshly Squeezed Orange and
Grapefruit Juice,
Tomato and Apple Juice

• • •

A Variety of Fresh Sliced Fruits, on Ice
Warm Poppy Seed Dressing

• • •

Yogurt in Assorted Flavors with a Variety of
Toppings to include: Chopped Dates, Prunes,
Nuts, Wheat Germ, Granola, and Dried
Fruits

• • •

100% Natural Cereal, Granola Bars,
Macaroons, Assorted Seeds

• • •

Peppered Scrambled Eggs with Scallions,
Pepperoni, and Cheese
Crispy Bacon and Smoked Sausage

• • •

Walnut and Bran Muffins
Toasted Raisin Bread, Cinnamon Danish
Hot Bread Selections to include:
Banana Nut, Carrot, Zucchini
Butter, Honey, and Cream Cheese

• • •

Whole Milk, Skim Milk, Buttermilk
Assorted Teas, Coffee, Decaffeinated Coffee,
Mineral Water

The All-American Country-Style Buffet Breakfast

From an appropriately decorated Buffet Table,
we will serve the following:
Freshly Squeezed Orange Juice

• • •

Texas Golden Buck Eggs with Canadian
Bacon

• • •

Eggs Wigger
An English Muffin, Sausage Patties, and
Poached Eggs covered with Our Mushroom
Sherry Sauce,
Potato Pancakes with Applesauce on the side

• • •

Cottage Fried Potatoes, Grits with Red Eye
Gravy
Country Ham, Crisp Bacon

• • •

Biscuits with Country-style Gravy

• • •

Hot Biscuits, Corn Bread, Breakfast Pastries
Creamery Butter, Honey, Jam, and
Marmalade

• • •

Coffee, Tea, Decaffeinated Coffee

The New York-Style Buffet Breakfast

Fresh Orange Juice, Fresh Apple Juice

• • •

Dairy Platter of Cheese Blintzes, Nova
Salmon, Whitefish Salad, Smoked Sturgeon,
and Cheese Omelettes

• • •

Attractive Baskets of Challah, Kaiser Rolls,
Assorted Danish, Bagels, Bear Claws, Babka
Pastry, Rye Toast, Bialys, "Mohn" Poppy
Seed Turnovers, and Butter

• • •

Coffee, Tea, Decaffeinated Coffee

The Miniature Puff Pastries Buffet Breakfast

Chilled Fruit Juices: Orange, Tomato, Apple,
Grapefruit
Fresh Sliced Seasonal Fruits with Yogurt Dips

• • •

Miniature Puff Pastries with
Scrambled Eggs and Bacon Garnish
Country-Style Biscuits with Sausage
Beignets with Powdered Sugar
Apple and Banana Fritters

• • •

Assorted Croissants
Fruit Breads to include: Banana Nut and
Zucchini
Butter, Honey, Cream Cheese

• • •

Coffee, Sanka, Milk or Skim Milk

The Get Cracking Buffet Breakfast

Juice Station
With Two Juice Machines:
One Orange Juice Machine, One Tomato
Juice Machine
Banquet Servers to Operate

Condiments
Worcestershire Sauce, Tabasco,
Lemon Wedges
• • •
Bread Display on Each Table with Butter and
Three Jams
• • •
A Poached Egg on Pancakes and Apple Rings
Tomato Stuffed with Spinach,
Hollandaise Sauce
Sausage Patties
• • •
Coffee, Tea, Decaffeinated Coffee
(Overhead mirror for cooking demonstration)

The American Buffet Breakfast

From an attractively decorated buffet table we
will serve:
Vermont Baked Apples with Brown Sugar and
Cinnamon Sticks, served with Cream
• • •
New Hampshire Egg Pie
Garnished with Sliced Tomatoes
• • •
Maryland Cheese Rarebit served with
Toast Points
Sliced Virginia Ham, West Virginia
Sausage Patties
• • •
South Carolina Spoon Bread, Georgia
Country Biscuits,
Johnny Cakes, Hot Cross Buns
North Carolina Moravian Sugar Cake
• • •
Coffee or Tea
• • •
Beverages: From hosted Bars, serve Bloody
Marys and Screwdrivers

The Separate Stations Buffet Breakfast

Station 1
Governor's Smiles prepared with Orange
Juice, Egg White, and Vodka, Fresh Orange
Slice Garnish
• • •

Station 2
Ice Gondola Filled with Watermelon,
Cantaloupe, Honeydew, Strawberries,
Pineapple, and Papaya
Iced Juices from Decanters (Orange,
Cranberry, Apple)
• • •

Station 3
Crêpes prepared to order, filled with
Fresh Fruits and Whipped Cream
• • •

Station 4
Smoked Salmon Display Garni
Bagels and Cream Cheese
Eggs Benedict, Mushroom Omelette
Canadian Bacon, Sausage Patties, Crisp Bacon
Potatoes Lyonnaise
• • •

Station 5
Danish, Croissants, Muffins, Hard Rolls
Jams, Preserves, Butter
Coffee, Tea, Sanka, Milk

The Mesquite Steaks and Cakes Buffet Breakfast

Fresh Squeezed Orange Juice
• • •
Buttermilk Pancakes
Ham Steaks Grilled over Mesquite Charcoal
Biscuits and Gravy, Sausage Links
Fresh Sliced Fruits
• • •
Baskets of Freshly Baked Muffins
• • •
Coffee, Tea, Decaffeinated Coffee

The Lox of Lox Buffet Breakfast

Freshly Squeezed Orange and Grapefruit
Juices to be served in frozen scooped-out
oranges

• • •

Fresh Strawberries and Raspberries to be
served in
Ice Socles with Fresh Cream

• • •

Decorated Mirrors of Papayas, Mangoes,
Assorted Melon, Pineapple, Grapes

• • •

Watermelon Boats filled with Macédoine of
Fresh Fruit

• • •

Chef to Carve Lox to be served with
Appropriate Condiments
Bagels and Cream Cheese

• • •

From a separate Buffet Table, we will serve
the following items freshly cooked and served
at the buffet by Chefs:
Large Spanish Omelette
Bauern Omelette
Kaiser Schmarn
Crêpes filled with Lingonberries

• • •

Assorted Pastries and Rolls

• • •

Beverages

The Lamb Chops for Breakfast Buffet

From Silver Chafing Dishes:
Choice of Irish Bacon or Canadian Bacon
Link Sausage and Sausage Patties
Whole Baked Virginia Ham carved by Chef
Baby Lamb Chops
Cream of Wheat, Southern Hominy Grits,
Home Fried Potatoes

• • •

Hot Homemade Biscuits
Homemade Corn Bread and
Blueberry Muffins
Croissants, Assorted Hard Rolls, and
Zopf Breads
Coffee Cake, Streusel Kuchen, Petite Danish

• • •

Decorations: Blue checkered tablecloths.
Buffets to be made up from old hay wagons
filled with crates of fruits, vegetables, etc. Also,
cages filled with live chickens and bunny
rabbits. Hostesses at entrance dressed in long
gingham dresses with aprons to serve juices as
guests arrive. Waiters to wear bib overalls,
flannel shirts, bandanas, and farmer straw hats.

The Farm Fresh Eggs Buffet Breakfast

Fresh Squeezed Orange Juice, Sliced
Fresh Fruits

• • •

Farm Fresh Scrambled Eggs,
Ranch Fried Potatoes
Sausage Links and Grilled Medallions of Beef

• • •

Homemade Biscuits with Apple-Cinnamon
Butter, Blueberry Muffins

• • •

Natural Cereals with Farm Fresh Cream

• • •

Beverages

The European Buffet Breakfast

Impressive Butter Sculptures

• • •

Fresh Juices of: Orange, Grapefruit, Tomato,
Cranberry, Papaya, Grape, Apple, and Prune

• • •

Pastry Fruit Strips, Mini Doughnuts
Chocolate, Almond, Regular Croissants
Bear Claws, Nut Coffee Cake, Gugelhopf
Decorated Breads, Tea Rings
Scandinavian Flat Breads

• • •

Salted and Unsalted Butter, Flavored Butters
Selection of Preserves in Jars

• • •

Varieties of Yogurt
Port Salut, Belle Paese, Gourmondese Cheeses
Shaved Ham

• • •

Coffee, Tea, Sanka, or Milk

The Poolside Buffet Breakfast

From two stations poolside, we will serve the following:

Fresh Florida Orange Juice served from Two
Sculptured Ice Casks
From Glass Decanters, displayed in crushed
ice, we will serve the following
additional juices:
Fresh Grapefruit, Apple, Cranberry,
Pineapple

• • •

Fresh Fruit Fantasy
A variety of Elegantly Displayed Assorted
Fruits and Freshly Made Fruit Yogurt

• • •

From the Bakery
Freshly Baked Couronnes au Amandes
Palmiers Glacé
Flaky Croissants, Danish Pastries,
Blueberry Muffins
Brioche à Tete, French Crispy Rolls
Bagels, Fruit Breads
Roses of Honey Butter, Strawberry Butter,
and Sweet Butter

• • •

Silver Service of
Coffee, Herbal Teas, Hot Chocolate, and
Decaffeinated Coffee

The Cheesecakes and Beefcakes Training Table Buffet Breakfast

Freshly Squeezed Florida Orange Juice
Knudsen's All Natural Fruit Juices

• • •

Fresh Seasonal Fruits
Assorted Cold Cereals and Farm
Fresh Cream

• • •

Thick French Toast, Dusted with Powdered
Sugar and served with Whipped Butter and
Maple Syrup
Country Scrambled Eggs Fines Herbes
Rashers of Crisp Bacon and Country
Sausage Links
Scalloped Potatoes

• • •

Petite Danish Pastries, Breakfast Bakeries,
and Bread
Marmalade, Fruit Preserves, and Butter

• • •

Coffee, Tea, Brewed Decaffeinated Coffee,
Skim and Whole Milk

Bodybuilders: Make arrangements for three
male and three female bodybuilders who will
present a posing routine to music, during
Training Table Buffet Breakfast service.

The Normandy Invasion Buffet Breakfast

Chilled Orange Juice
Tomato, Grape, and Grapefruit Juices
Fresh Pineapple and Melon

• • •

Natural Cereals and Cream

• • •

Fresh Scrambled Eggs with Chives
Crêpes Normandy
Bacon Strips and Sausage Links
French Toast with Maple Syrup
Fiesta Fried Potatoes

• • •

Coffee Cake, Muffins, and Danish
Sweet Butter and Preserves

• • •

Coffee, Tea, Decaffeinated Coffee

The Benedict Just the Way I Like It Buffet Breakfast

Chilled Tropical Juices
Fresh Orange and Grapefruit Slices

• • •

Eggs Benedict
Scrambled Eggs with Mushrooms
Grilled Hickory Smoked Ham, Sausage,
and Bacon
Creamed Chicken over Biscuits
Cheese Blintzes with Fruit Sauce
Potato Pancakes

• • •

Pecan Rolls, Coffee Cake, Danish, and
Muffins
Butter and Preserves

• • •

Beverages

The Hush It's Hash Buffet Breakfast

Selection of Chilled Fruit Juices
Orange and Grapefruit Segments
Compote of Kadota Figs, Prunes, and Apples
Variety of Fresh Melon and Pineapple
in Season
Assorted Cold Cereals with Berries and Milk
or Cream
• • •
Corned Beef Hash
Poached Eggs Florentine
Ham, Bacon, and Link Sausages
Griddle Cakes with Hot Maple Syrup,
Blueberry Sauce, and Sour Cream
• • •
Banana Bread, Danish, Walnut Muffins, and
Croissants
Sweet Butter and Preserves
• • •
Coffee, Brewed Decaffeinated Coffee,
Selection of Imported Teas, or Milk

The Eggs Toppings Bar Buffet Breakfast

Bing Cherries and Southern Peaches au
Kirsch
An Assortment of Fruit Juices Royale
Decorated Mirror of Sliced Fresh Melons
Compote of Whole Fresh Fruits
• • •
Freshly Scrambled Eggs with Toppings Bar
of:
Sautéed Mushrooms, Sweet Peppers, Cheddar
Cheese, Diced Ham, Onions, and Freshly
Ground Pepper
Bacon Strips, Pork Sausage Links, Home
Fried Potatoes
Assorted Danish Pastries, Buttermilk Biscuits
Fruit Muffins, Bagels and Cream Cheese
Butter and Jellies
• • •
Coffee, Tea, Decaffeinated Coffee, Milk

The Oscar and Much More Buffet Breakfast

Selection of Sliced Fruit, Melon and Berries,
in Season
• • •
Assorted Cold Cereals and Farm Fresh
Cream
• • •
From Gleaming Silver Chafing Dishes:
Freshly Made
Scrambled Eggs with Chives, Eggs Benedict
on English Muffins
• • •
Hickory Smoked Ham, Rashers of Crisp
Grilled Bacon
Country Link Sausage, Fiesta Potatoes
Pancakes Oscar with Hot Strawberry Sauce
and Marshmallow
• • •
Petite Danish Pastries, Breakfast Bakeries,
Breads, and Hot Biscuits
Marmalade, Fruit Preserves, Honey,
and Butter
• • •
Coffee, Tea, Decaffeinated Coffee, or Milk

The Schroomie and Eggs Buffet Breakfast

Selection of Chilled Fruit Juices on Ice
Freshly Squeezed Orange, Grapefruit,
Pineapple, and Tomato Juice
• • •
Mirrors of Whole and Sliced Fresh Tropical
Fruits Decorated with Ribbons of Seasonal
Berries, Brown Sugar, and Crème Fraîche
• • •
Selected Dry Cereals and Granola
Pitchers of Whole Milk
• • •
From Silver Chafing Dishes:
Fluffy Scrambled Eggs with
Sautéed Mushrooms
Cheese Blintzes with Blueberry Sauce and
Sour Cream
Grilled Canadian Bacon and Spicy
Link Sausages
Cottage Fried Potatoes
• • •
Hazelnut Coffee Cake, Selection of Danish
Pastries, Muffins, and Breakfast Rolls
• • •
Coffee, Herbal and Regular Tea, Brewed
Decaffeinated Coffee, and Milk

The Fruity Blintzes Buffet Breakfast

Choice of Three Juices
Platters of Fresh Pineapple, Strawberries,
Papaya, Melons, Bananas
(some items are seasonal)

• • •

Assorted Dry Cereal
Stewed Prunes, Kadota Figs
Fruit Blintzes
Scrambled Eggs
Eggs Cooked to Order
Omelettes made to Order

• • •

Canadian Bacon, Corned Beef Hash,
Country Sausage

• • •

Assorted Fruit Muffins and Danish Croissants
Butter and Preserves

• • •

Beverages
Chefs to cook to order at an additional charge

The Texascapes Buffet Breakfast

(See Color Insert)

Fresh Hand-Squeezed Orange Juice
Chilled Tomato and Grapefruit Juices

• • •

Scrambled Texas Golden Buck Eggs
Canadian Bacon, Cottage Fried Potatoes
with Onions

• • •

Miniature Chicken Fried Steak and Biscuit
Sandwiches (Thin Medallions)
Country Sausage Patties and
Biscuit Sandwiches

• • •

Hot Biscuits, Corn Bread, Breakfast Pastries,
Creamery Butter, Honey, Jams, Apple Butter,
and Marmalade

• • •

Six Shooter Coffee, Tea, Fresh Brewed
Decaffeinated Coffee
White Milk and Chocolate Milk

Flowers: Arrange a cowboy hat turned up-
side down with a potted cactus inside wrapped
with a red or blue bandanna.

Costumes: Staff to be attired in Western
style, including cowboy hats and shirts, blue-
jeans, and red and blue bandannas.

Special Appearance: Also, complimentary
special appearance of International Chili Champion, Lone Star Chili Willi, a crotchety old
chuck wagon cook from Lizard Tail, Texas, is
guaranteed to get the morning off with a
"Bang."

Music: Arrange for a five-piece country band
and one female singer in costume.

The Chef, Prepare It My Way Buffet Breakfast

Iced Carafes of Selected Juices
Fresh Squeezed Orange Juice, Pear Nectar,
Cranapple, Tomato Cocktail

• • •

Mirrors of Sliced Tropical Fruits including:
Papaya, Mango, Kiwi, Pineapple, Passion
Fruit, Star Fruit, and Banana with bowls of
Whipped Cream, Brown Sugar, and Toasted
Coconut

• • •

Hearty Granola and Bran Cereals
Whole and Skim Milk

• • •

Vanilla Yogurt on Ice
with Assorted Dried Fruit and Nut Toppings

• • •

Chefs* in White Uniforms will prepare Eggs
and Omelettes to order
Variety of Fillings to include: Diced Ham,
Shredded Cheddar, Mushroom,
Spinach, and Western
From Silver Chafing Dishes:

Eggs Nouveaux
Poached Eggs on Canadian Bacon Topped
with a Brandied Cream Sauce, Asparagus
Tips, and Baby Shrimp
Crisp Hickory Bacon and Sautéed Ham
Silver Dollar Pancakes
Strawberry Compote and Whipped Butter
O'Brien Potatoes

• • •

Chef's Finest Selection of Breakfast Bakeries

• • •

Coffee, Herbal and Regular Tea,
Brewed Decaffeinated Coffee, and Milk

• • •

*One Chef required for each 50 guests guaranteed,
at an additional charge.

The Aloha Lagoon Poolside Buffet Breakfast

Pool Cart by Entrance
Fresh Pineapple Juice served in Half Pineapple
(mixed with Coconut Milk)
Fresh Mango Juice in single old-fashioned glass,
coconut rim with lime wedge
Fresh Orange Juice in scooped-out oranges
(Each item to be identified with signs on fruits; use two juice machines;
pineapple juice to be made in advance)
• • •

Buffet with Thatched Roof
Fresh Fruit Cocktail in Watermelon
Poached Eggs in Half Coconut
Fried Eggs made to order on Flambé Wagon
Scrambled Eggs, Back Bacon, Sausage
Home Fried Potatoes, Fruit Garnish with Fried Eggs
Smoked Cooked Ham, Red Snapper, and Hot Sliced Fruits
Crêpes with Mango or Banana Rum and Vanilla Sauce
Assorted Cereals with Cream and Diced Fresh Fruits
• • •

Turtle and Crocodile Bread Display
Assorted Rolls, Ginger Bread, Banana and Coconut Bread
Fresh Toast, Whipped Butter, Assorted Jams in a Half Coconut

Decor: Tea and palm leaves, two ice carvings, jumping fish fruit display with dry ice.

Serve at Tables: Coffee, Tea, Sanka, and Milk.

The Three-Theme Buffet Breakfast

Juice Bar to Serve: Fresh Orange, Grapefruit, Apple, Berry, Cranberry, and Pineapple Juices
• • •

Southern American Station
Corn Muffins with Diced Ham
Corn Muffins with Ground Sausage
• • •

Petite Pecan Rolls and Biscuits
Honey, Peach Preserves, and Marmalade
• • •

Apple Turnovers
• • •

Coffee, Tea, Sanka, Cut Fresh Fruit
• • •

European Station
Croissant, Brioche, Tea Rings
Ham Loaf with Hard-Boiled Egg in Center
• • •

Sliced Long Broiled Coffee Rings with Assorted Toppings
Marmalade, Butter, Currant Jelly
• • •

Coffee, Tea, Sanka, Hot Chocolate
Cut Fresh Fruit
• • •

Chinese Station
Hombau
• • •

Danish with Oriental Fillings
• • •

Steamed Dumplings
Tofu with Ginger Sauce
Rice Puddings with Dried Fruits
Chicken Broth with Hard-Boiled Egg and Cubed Duck
• • •

Tea Selections, Coffee, Sanka, and Fresh Fruit

Chapter 14

Buffet Bruncheon Menus

Buffet Bruncheon # 1

Freshly Squeezed Orange Juice
Apple, Tomato, and Grapefruit Juices

• • •

Fresh Sliced Fruits
Berries in Season with Cream

• • •

International Selection of Cheeses
with Lahvosh

• • •

Smoked Salmon, with Appropriate Garnishes

• • •

Omelettes made to order
(Ham, Cheese, Spanish, Chicken Liver)

• • •

Cheese Blintzes
with Strawberry and Blueberry Sauces
Boneless Breast of Chicken Calvados
Crabmeat Newburg
Beef Stroganoff
Rice and Peas
Stir-Fried Vegetables

• • •

Assortment of Muffins, Bagels, Coffee Cake,
Hard Rolls, and Croissants
Butter, Preserves, and Honey

• • •

White Chocolate Mousse
Strawberry Bavarois
Fresh Fruit Tarts, Tortes

• • •

Coffee, Tea, and Brewed Decaffeinated Coffee

Buffet Bruncheon # 2

From a Crystal Ice Carving, Selected Fruits to include:
Fresh Pineapple Cubes, Cantaloupe, Honeydew, and
Watermelon Cubes, Strawberries and a selection of other
Fruits of the Season

• • •

Freshly Squeezed Orange Juice,
Apple, Cranberry, and Pineapple Juices

• • •

Display of Fresh Whitefish
International Selection of Cheeses, Garni
with Lahvosh and Wafers

• • •

From Gleaming Silver Chafing Dishes:
Crabmeat Newburg in Pastry Shells
Boneless Petite Breast of Chicken, Sauce Chasseur
Whole Tomato with Ratatouille
Garden Fresh Vegetables
Potatoes O'Brien

• • •

A Variety of Omelettes, made to order
Sausage Links
Belgian Waffles with Blueberry Compote,
Sliced Bananas and Fresh Whipped Cream

• • •

Pancakes Oscar with Fresh Strawberry Compote

• • •

Assortment of Muffins, Bagels, Petite Danish, Croissants,
and Hard Rolls with Sweet Butter, Marmalade, Honey,
Preserves, and Jams

• • •

Mousse au Chocolat
Strawberry Bavarois, Chantilly
Marzipan Torte, Fresh Fruit Tarts
Assorted French Pastries
Crème Caramel

• • •

Coffee, Tea, Decaffeinated Coffee, or Milk

Buffet Bruncheon # 3

Assorted Chilled Juices
Fresh Melon in Season
Orange and Grapefruit Segments
Fresh Cut Fruit

• • •

Scrambled Eggs
Bacon, Ham, and Link Sausages
Cottage Fried Potatoes
Smithfield Eggs with Artichoke
Béarnaise Sauce
Strips of Chicken Breast in
Lemon-Lime Sauce
Rice Pilaf

• • •

Danish Pastries, Apple Turnovers, Bran and
Blueberry Muffins,
Sweet Butter and Preserves

• • •

Assortment of Domestic and
Imported Cheeses

• • •

Coffee, Brewed Decaffeinated Coffee,
Selection of Imported Teas, or Milk

Buffet Bruncheon # 4

Fresh Berries in Season
Baked Cinnamon Raisin Stuffed Apples
Fresh Melon Compotes

• • •

Selection of Garden Fresh Salads
Smoked Salmon and Gravlax
Assortment of Cold Cuts, Pâtés, and
Terrines

• • •

Eggs Benedict and Florentine
Tenderloin of Beef in Green
Peppercorn Sauce
Cottage Fried Potatoes
Griddle Cakes with Cinnamon Sugar,
Blueberry Sauce, and Hot Maple Syrup

• • •

Scottish Trifle, Assorted Fresh Fruit Flans
Danish, Bran and Blueberry Muffins
Banana and Walnut Breads
Sweet Butter and Preserves

• • •

Coffee, Brewed Decaffeinated Coffee,
Selection of Imported Teas, or Milk

Buffet Bruncheon # 5

Selection of Tropical Juices
Chilled Melon, Fresh Berries in Season
Potpourri of Fruit Compotes

• • •

Selection of European Breakfast Breads,
Pastries, Bagels, and Croissants
Continental Preserves and Sweet Butter

• • •

Matjes Herring in Wine Sauce
Smoked Salmon with Cream Cheese
Crisp Garden Salads with Choice of Dressings
Sliced Beefsteak Tomatoes, Sauce Vinaigrette
Chicken Liver Mousse

• • •

International Cheese Board and Charcuterie

• • •

Eggs Florentine
French Omelettes
Hash Brown Potatoes
Cheese Blintzes with Fruit Topping

• • •

Quiche Lorraine
Bouchées Cardinal

• • •

Medley of Fresh Vegetables

• • •

Selection Finest French Pastries

• • •

Coffee, Tea, Sanka, Milk

Buffet Bruncheon # 6

Choice of Three Juices
Seasonal Sliced Fresh Fruit Platter

• • •

Scrambled Eggs
Sausage, Bacon
Quiche Wedges
Chicken Livers with Mushrooms in Red
Wine Sauce

• • •

Carved Top Round of Beef or Glazed Ham
Carved to Order or Presliced

• • •

Sliced Tomatoes
Lyonnaise Potatoes
Sautéed Zucchini and Yellow Squash
Danish, Muffins, Sliced Breads
Jellies, Butter Curls

• • •

Beverages

Buffet Bruncheon # 7

Fresh Fruit in a Watermelon Boat
Strawberries with Brown Sugar and
Heavy Cream
Assorted Florida Citrus Juices

• • •

Eggs Benedict on English Muffin
with Canadian Bacon and Hollandaise Sauce
Scrambled Eggs with Fresh Sliced
Mushrooms
Quiche Lorraine

• • •

Grilled Link Sausage, Crisp Bacon
Lyonnaise Potatoes
Cheese Blintzes with Hot Strawberry Sauce
Banana Fritters with Stewed Blueberries
Crêpes Normande

• • •

Hot Biscuits, Croissants, Sweet Rolls, and
Fruit Muffins

• • •

Beverages

Buffet Bruncheon # 9

Choice of Three Juices
Seasonal Sliced Fresh Fruit Platter
Sliced Smoked Salmon with Onions
and Capers

• • •

Eggs Cooked to Order
Baron of Beef Carved to Order
Sausage, Bacon, Ham (Choice of Two)
Beef Hash
Quiche Wedges
Home Fried Potatoes
Mixed Fresh Vegetables
Sliced Tomatoes
Cream Cheese

• • •

Danish, Bagels, Muffins, Sliced Breads
Jellies, Butter Curls

• • •

Beverages

Buffet Bruncheon # 8

Assorted Chilled Juices
Fresh Seasonal Fruits

• • •

Scrambled Eggs with Condiments to Include
Salsa, Diced Ham, Mushrooms, Diced
Tomatoes, and Chives

• • •

Lox and Bagels with Cream Cheese

• • •

Bacon Strips and Sausage Links

• • •

Chicken Crêpes

• • •

Decorated International Cheese Tray

• • •

Carved Roast Beef
Veal Zurich with Rice

• • •

Marinated Vegetable Salad
Mediterranean Pasta Salad
Ambrosia Salad

• • •

Assorted Pies, Cakes, and Mousses

• • •

Beverages

Buffet Bruncheon # 10

Half Hawaiian Pineapple, with Fresh Fruits and Berries

• • •

Poached Eggs Florentine,
with Fresh Spinach and Sauce Supreme

• • •

Chilled Poached Salmon,
Parisienne, with Cucumber Baskets, Sauce Verte

• • •

Sliced Beefsteak Tomatoes, Hearts of Palm,
Served on Vine Cuttings, Sauce Vinaigrette

• • •

Seafood à la Newburg, Flavored with Sherry
Rice Pilaf

• • •

Breast of Maryland Capon,
Amandine,
Sauce Périgourdine

• • •

Traditional Quiche Lorraine, Cut into Wedges
Hot Pancakes Oscar, with Fresh Strawberries and Meringue,
Strawberry Sauce

• • •

Dessert Table to include:
French Pastries
Fresh Fruit Tarts
Crêpes Suzette

• • •

Beverages

Buffet Bruncheon # 11

Mimosa Royale
Fresh Orange Juice with Champagne and a
splash of Cointreau
• • •
Chef's Selection of Breakfast Bakeries,
Croissants, Bagels, Fruit Muffins
Preserves and Butter
• • •
Iced Carafes of Selected Juices
• • •
Seasonal Fruit Display,
Ribbons of Fresh Berries
• • •
Fruit Yogurts on Ice,
Dried Fruit and Nut Toppings
• • •
Smoked Fish Display Featuring:
Salmon, Sable, Kingfish
Mini Bagels, Pumpernickel and Rye Rounds
Cream Cheese, Capers, and Onions
• • •
Sliced Beefsteak Tomato, Onion, and Endive,
Vinaigrette
Marinated Button Mushrooms with Pimiento
Matjes Herring in Wine Sauce
Cucumber and Dill Salad
Marinated Baby Shrimp and Sweet Corn
Chicken Liver Mousse with Onion Straws
Eggs Florentine
• • •
Soft Scrambled Eggs
Grilled Canadian Bacon
Bouchées aux Fruits de Mer
Medallions of Chicken Mandarin
Rosti Potatoes
Snow Peas, Carrots, and Water Chestnuts
Medley
• • •
Viennese Pastry Display
• • •
Freshly Brewed Colombian Coffee
Selected Herbal Teas

Buffet Bruncheon # 12

Mimosa Royale
Fresh Orange Juice with Champagne and a
splash of Cointreau
• • •
Selection of Chilled Juices
• • •
Mirrors of Whole and Sliced
Fresh Tropical Fruits,
Whipped Cream and Brown Sugar
• • •
Hearty Granola and Fruit Yogurts,
on Ice with Milk, Cream, and Honey
• • •
From Silver Chafing Dishes:
Eggs Benedict,
Truffle garni
• • •
Fluffy Scrambled Eggs,
Ribbons of Smoked Salmon
• • •
Chicken Liver and Button Mushroom Sauté
Grilled Sweet Sausage
• • •
Cheese Blintzes,
Sour Cream and Blueberry Topping
• • •
Crisp Fried Potatoes
• • •
Cheese Danish, Toasted Bagels,
Assorted Muffins and Croissants
Butter, Marmalade, Cream Cheese
• • •
Blended Coffee
Selection of Herbal Teas

To complement any of the Bruncheons, we suggest serving free-flowing House-Selected Champagne at a special per bottle price or Mimosas, Fresh Orange Juice with Champagne, charged as served, by the glass or by the gallon.

Chapter 15

Luncheon Entrées

Chicken Luncheons

Supreme of Capon Mandarin: Capon flavored with mandarin oranges served on oriental rice.

Chicken à la Reine in a Patty Shell: Diced chicken in a creamy white wine–mushroom sauce, served in a pastry shell.

Half Pineapple Boat with Curried Chicken: Curried chicken garnished with raisins, coconut, and toasted almonds, served in a half pineapple and accompanied by cream cheese finger sandwiches, fresh cold vegetables en bouquet.

Roasted Half Spring Chicken: Roasted spring chicken basted with tarragon butter.

Boneless Breast of Chicken Sauté au Chablis: Boneless chicken breast laced with a light white wine sauce.

Vol-au-Vent of Curried Chicken and Pineapple: Puff pastry stuffed with curried chicken and pineapple with saffron rice, topped with toasted coconut.

Breast of Chicken Chasseur: Hunter's style chicken with plum tomatoes and fresh mushrooms, Sauce Madeira.

Breast of Chicken Oriental: Chicken breast with Chef Chow's fried rice.

Breast of Chicken Apricotine: Chicken breast with a pilaf of white and wild rice.

Breast of Chicken à la Normande: Chicken breast stuffed with apples and almonds, Sauce Calvados.

Breast of Chicken Valadier: Boneless chicken breast with watercress sauce.

Breast of Chicken Hawaiian: Boneless chicken breast with pineapple.

Breast of Chicken Burgundy: Boneless chicken breast with a red wine sauce.

Breast of Chicken Smitane: Sautéed boneless breast of chicken in a sour cream sauce with paprika.

Chicken Tarragon: Boneless breast of chicken with a julienne of pea pods and enoki mushrooms and tarragon sauce.

Chicken Calvados: Boneless breast of chicken crowned with thinly sliced apples and a lightly flavored sauce.

Piccata of Chicken #1: Thin chicken cutlets in a rosemary-lime sauce.

Escalopes of Chicken: Thinly sliced chicken with mushrooms and pecans.

Breast of Chicken: Chicken breast with ginger and peppered apples.

Boneless Breast of Chicken Bercy: Boneless chicken breast served with spiced apple.

Sauté of Breast of Chicken and Virginia Ham: Sautéed breast of chicken and Virginia ham served on a toasted English muffin, with red wine sauce.

Old-Fashioned Chicken Shortcake: Plantation-style chicken and mushrooms in a fricassee sauce, served on a baking powder biscuit.

Chicken Véronique: Whole fresh chicken breast coated with a white wine sauce and garnished with white seedless grapes.

Chicken Luncheons (continued)

Chicken Calcutta: Tender pieces of chicken in a light curry sauce ladled into a pastry shell and topped with shredded coconut and raisins.

Chicken Jerusalem: Full boneless breast of chicken, lightly floured, browned, and served with a white Supreme Sauce, garnished with artichoke hearts.

Oriental Chicken: Full chicken breast marinated in a Teriyaki Sauce, garnished with a grilled pineapple wedge.

Papaya Filled with Hawaiian Chicken Salad: Chicken salad in a hollowed-out papaya served with banana nut bread and whipped butter, assorted garden vegetables, and deviled eggs.

Breast of Chicken New Englander: Filled with a Stuffing of apples, onions, butter, bread crumbs, and selected seasonings.

Stuffed Chicken Breast Hawaiian: Chicken breast stuffed with diced pineapples, walnuts, pimientos.

Stuffed Chicken Breast Apple-Almond: Chicken breast stuffed with apple pieces, slivered almonds, plump raisins, and brown sugar.

Chicken Breast Marsala: Tender boneless chicken breast served in a wine and mushroom sauce.

Dragon Silk Chicken: Strips of chicken breasts cooked with oriental vegetables.

Chicken Oscar: Chicken breast with crabmeat, asparagus spears, and Sauce Béarnaise.

Breast of Chicken Nancy: Boneless breast of chicken smothered with a sauce of apples, cinnamon, and almonds.

Chicken Florida: Boneless chicken breast, baked and topped with cheese, sliced avocado, and fresh tomato sauce.

Chicken Guido Bleu: Boneless chicken breast stuffed with provolone cheese, prosciutto ham, and heaped with Marinara Sauce.

Chicken Amaretto: Breast of chicken marinated in an Amaretto sauce, grilled to perfection and covered with slivered almonds.

Chicken Oriental: Stuffed chicken breast with Chinese vegetables.

Piccata of Chicken #2: Thin chicken cutlets sautéed in lemon butter with capers.

Chicken Scampi: Sliced chicken breast sautéed in olive oil and garlic.

Chicken Dijonnaise: Tender young chicken rubbed with cracked pepper, spiced, roasted, and served by the half with Dijonnaise Sauce.

Poulet à la Madame Pompadour: Chicken cutlet with peaches and topped with sautéed sweet green peppers on rice pilaf.

Breast of Chicken Cordon Bleu: Chicken breast filled with layers of ham and cheese, dipped in egg and lightly breaded, sautéed and served with Sauce Madeira.

Breast of Chicken Teriyaki: Breast of chicken in teriyaki sauce, traditionally served with stir-fry vegetables.

Chicken Marengo en Croûte: Breast of chicken with tomato, green peppers, mushrooms, provolone cheese, onions, and olives wrapped in puff pastry.

Savory Crêpes à la Reine: Chicken and mushrooms in a delicate cream sauce.

Roast Lemon Chicken: Half chicken rubbed with herbs and lemon butter.

Chicken Baton Rouge: Boneless breast of chicken marinated in creole mustard with chopped pecans, spicy tomato sauce with juniper berries.

Cold Roast Half Chicken Rosemary: Cold roast half chicken cooked with rosemary, served with German potato salad, slices of tomato, and cucumber.

Suprême of Chicken Niagara: Roast breast of chicken laced with Cointreau-flavored peach sauce.

Ballotine of Chicken Chasseur: Boned chicken filled with mushrooms, rice, and chicken liver, with a red wine sauce.

Crêpe à la Reine: Diced chicken in a creamy white wine-mushroom sauce, wrapped in a crêpe.

Chicken Breast à la Orange: Chicken breast flavored with fresh oranges.

Chicken Delmonico: Breast of chicken filled with ham and broccoli, draped with Sauce Mornay.

Boneless Breast of Capon Szechuan: Capon laced with a fruit teriyaki sauce, served with fried Chinese rice and stir-fried vegetables.

Fresh Breast of Chicken Montmorency: Breast of chicken with bing cherries in red wine sauce.

Turkey Luncheons

Turkey Ambassador: Sliced turkey breast with tomato sauce and sliced avocado and topped with melted Swiss cheese.

Breast of Turkey on Broccoli: Turkey breast on broccoli laced with a light Sauce Supreme.

Roast Stuffed Turkey Breast: Roast turkey breast stuffed with spinach, cheddar cheese, and pinenuts.

Tivoli Grill: A large baking powder biscuit, topped with sliced tomatoes, breast of turkey and laced with Welsh Rarebit Sauce, crisp bacon strips, and slivered almonds.

Cold Turkey Salad, Princess: Cold turkey salad garnished with white asparagus tips, hard-boiled eggs, and pineapple wedge.

Breast of Turkey Parmesan: Sautéed breast of turkey with cheese, mushrooms, Capricio.

Turkey and Dressing: Tender turkey breast and corn bread dressing.

Turkey Piccata: Tender medallions of turkey breast dipped in egg batter, sautéed in lemon butter.

Turkey Breast Divan: Turkey scallopini, topped with creamed mushrooms and broccoli spears served on toast with Rissolé Potatoes.

Turkey Charlene: Roulade of turkey stuffed with sausage, spinach, feta cheese, and sage, topped with Béchamel Sauce flavored with rosemary, basil, and lemon.

Turkey Schnitzel: Sautéed turkey breast with a lemon-caper sauce.

Turkey Marco Polo: Broccoli on a slice of ham topped with sliced turkey breast, Mornay Sauce glaze.

Turkey and Wild Rice en Croûte: Turkey and wild rice baked in a crust, served with Sauce Périgueux.

Beef Luncheons

Beef Tips Sautéed in Peanut Oil: Beef tips sautéed in peanut oil served with teriyaki steamed rice.

Petite Filet Mignon: Petite filet mignon wrapped in bacon served with Sauce Périgourdine.

Braised Swiss Steak: Round steak smothered with chopped tomatoes, onions, carrots, celery, and beef broth and braised.

Roast Prime Rib of Beef: Beef prime rib in our natural Au Jus, luncheon cut.

Broiled Ground Sirloin Steak Forestiere: Ground sirloin steak topped with a mushroom sauce.

Sliced Top Sirloin of Beef (Maximum 250 Guests): Sliced top sirloin served with a sherry, shallots, and mushroom sauce and potato pancakes.

New York Sirloin Steak: Sirloin steak served on sliced French bread, garni.

Sliced New York Sirloin: Sliced sirloin with Sauce Bordelaise.

Beef Tips Hunan: Beef tips with asparagus and oriental stir-fried rice.

Boeuf à la Mode: Beef classically prepared in the provincial French manner.

Sirloin Steak Café de Paris: Sirloin steak with herb butter.

Teriyaki Steak: Strip steak marinated and broiled with a special teriyaki sauce.

Braised Brisket: Braised brisket served with fresh vegetables.

Beef Luncheons (continued)

Marinated London Broil (Maximum 250 Guests): — Marinated London broil with sherry-mushroom sauce.

Roast Sirloin of Beef: — Roast sirloin of beef in a Zinfandel sauce.

Braised Beef: — Braised beef in a bacon, mushroom, and green peppercorn sauce.

Escalopes of Beef Tenderloin: — Thinly sliced beef tenderloin in a Pinot Noir sauce with mushrooms and artichokes.

Beef Roulade Flamande: — Sliced beef laced with mustard and fine herbs and a mild duxelle, braised in a red wine sauce, served with red cabbage.

English Roast Sliced Sirloin, Marchand de Vin: — Roast sliced sirloin laced with a red wine sauce.

Braised Yankee Pot Roast (Maximum 250 Guests): — Pot roast with red wine gravy.

Tender Beef Tips Stroganoff: — Beef tips stroganoff served with buttered egg noodles.

Sirloin and Pasta Salad: — Lean slices of roast sirloin and a marinated tortellini salad on a bed of greens.

Brochette of Beef: — Skewered beef with onions, green pepper, mushroom caps, Sauce Demi-Glace, served with saffron rice pilaf.

Beef Carbonnade: — Beef braised in wine with mushrooms.

Chilled Prime Rib, English Cut: — Prime rib with mustard sauce, white horseradish, marinated mushrooms, and artichoke hearts à la grecque.

Oriental Pepper Steak: — Steak stir-fried in our wok with soya and oriental vegetables, served with wild rice.

Country-Fried Steak: — Fried steak served with black skillet cream gravy.

Barbecued Cheese Steak: — Grilled chopped sirloin topped with barbecue sauce, grated cheddar cheese, crispy onion rings, and bacon.

Beef Stroganoff: — Strips of beef sautéed with mushrooms in a red wine sauce.

Medallions of Beef Blanc et Noir: — Twin filets mignons sautéed with shallots and served with Sauces Béarnaise and Périgourdine, passed.

Beef Kabob: — Beef kabob with Sauce Piquante.

Broiled Salisbury Steak Diablo: — Salisbury steak served with a mustard sauce.

Roast Sirloin of Beef: — Roast beef sirloin served with Scotch green peppercorn sauce.

Sliced Tenderloin of Beef Bordelaise: — Sliced beef tenderloin served with Bordelaise sauce.

Veal Luncheons

Veal Scaloppine, Marsala: — Thin veal cutlets, Marsala, with a medley of wild and brown rice.

Veal Cacciatore: — Veal cacciatore with Fettucini Milanaise.

Sautéed Veal Medallions: — Sautéed veal medallions with Sauce Morille.

Roast Milk-Fed White Veal: — Milk-fed veal with sherry sauce.

Veal Piccata: — Sautéed veal cutlets with lemon butter and capers.

Medallions of Veal: — Veal medallions with sun-dried tomato and basil sauce, saffron risotto.

Escalopes of Veal Breaded: — Thinly sliced veal breaded with almonds and herbs.

Fricassee of Milk-Fed Veal: — Veal fricassee served on a turban of rice pilaf.

Veal Zurich: — Tender pieces of veal served in a light cream sauce over blended rice.

Escalopes of White Veal à la Crème: — Thinly sliced veal with white Pennsylvania mushrooms.

Veal Scaloppine: — Veal with mustard sauce.

Veal Parmigiana: — Veal with tomato sauce, mozzarella and parmesan cheeses.

Scaloppine of Veal Anglaise: Veal lightly sautéed in egg batter and served with a sweet butter.

Veal Cordon Bleu: Veal filled with layers of ham and cheese, dipped in egg, lightly breaded, and sautéed in butter.

Roast Leg of Veal: Roast leg of veal served with Risi Bisi and glazed carrots.

Escalope of Veal Normande: Thinly sliced veal garnished with mushrooms and served with Calvados-flavored cream sauce.

Veal Marengo: Veal sautéed in olive oil, then braised with tomatoes, onions, olives, garlic, white wine, and seasonings.

Pork Luncheons

Baked Sugar-Cured Ham: Baked sugar-cured ham topped with a delicate Champagne sauce and seedless white grapes.

Roast Pork Loin Polynesian: Roast pork loin with Chef Chow's fried rice, snow peas, and water chestnuts.

Grilled Pork Tenderloin with Fruit Chutney: Pork tenderloin, marinated in seasoned oil and vinegar, grilled, then sliced and served with special fruit chutney sauce.

Gingered Pork Tenderloin Salad: Thinly sliced pork tenderloin, marinated in ginger, cilantro, Teriyaki Sauce, and pepper, then tossed with potatoes, artichokes, and onions in a special dressing.

Jamaican Pork Tenderloin: Pork tenderloin, marinated in coconut milk and vegetables, then roasted, sliced, and napped with boiled sauce.

Tomato-Basil Pork Scaloppine: Pork tenderloin medallions, gently flattened and sautéed with shallots and garlic, then simmered in seasoning, served over rice or linguine.

Herbed Pork Chops Trattoria: Boneless pork loin chops, coated with herbs and olive oil, then browned over medium-high heat, and finished over low heat.

Roast Pork Loin Normandy: Roast pork loin served with applesauce.

Sweet and Sour Pork: Pork with a sweet and pungent sauce.

Smoked Pork Loin: Smoked pork loin with braised onions and cabbage.

Pork Chops Sauté: Sautéed pork chops with glazed apples, Sauce Piquante.

Loin of Pork: Pork loin in a sweet and sour sauce.

Broiled Double Pork Chops: Broiled double pork chops served with applesauce and red cabbage.

Crown Roast of Pork: Crown pork roast marinated with Dijon mustard, soy sauce, garlic, sage, marjoram, served with Madeira Sauce.

Stuffed Pork Chop au Poivre: Pork chop stuffed with a savory stuffing.

Roast Loin of Pork Stockholm: Roast loin of pork filled with apple and prune dressing.

Lamb Luncheons

Roast Leg of Lamb: Roast leg of lamb with herbed Meaux Mustard Sauce.

Roast Shoulder of Lamb Provençale: Roast shoulder of lamb served with a red wine sauce.

Seafood/Fish Luncheons

Seafood Crêpes Française: Crêpes filled with fresh Florida seafoods, Sauce Nantua.

Chilled Seafood Delight (Maximum 250 Guests): Brioche ring topped with thinly sliced Swiss cheese and filled with crisp greens, marinated fresh vegetables, and Florida seafood salad, topped with fresh fruit garnish.

Fresh Garden Greens with Tuna Chunks: Greens and tuna chunks with alfalfa sprouts, sliced fresh mushrooms, deviled egg, and quartered tomato.

Grilled Fresh Salmon Steak: Grilled salmon steak with Béarnaise Sauce.

Seafood/Fish Luncheons (continued)

Broiled Fillet of Fresh Florida Red Snapper: Broiled fillet of red snapper with lemon butter.

Fresh Super Grouper: Fresh grouper fillet, broiled or sautéed in lemon butter or poached in rosé wine.

Avocado Pear with Seafood Salad: Avocado pear and seafood salad with asparagus tips.

Baked Fillet of Fresh Florida Red Snapper: Baked fillet of red snapper with white wine, shallots, and mushrooms.

Baked Stuffed Shrimp Imperiale: Baked stuffed shrimp with Scampi Butter and tomato rice pilaf.

Cold Poached Salmon Medallions: Poached salmon medallions with yogurt-cucumber sauce, hard-cooked eggs, ripe and green olives, watercress, and hearts of palm.

Crab and Spinach Quiche: Crab and spinach quiche served with half peach filled with lingonberries, fried zucchini sticks, parmesan cheese.

Vol-Au-Vent Newburg: Patty shell filled with Seafood Newburg.

Shrimp Salad: Shrimp salad served on a tomato crown, with asparagus spears, and a hard-cooked egg.

Fillet of Sole Meunière: Fillet of sole sautéed in butter and finished with lemon and parsley.

Artichoke Neptune: Shrimp salad in whole chilled artichoke, served with sliced tomato, deviled egg halves, and vinaigrette dressing.

Twin Avocados Filled with Seafood Salad: Avocados stuffed with seafood salad served on a bed of lettuce with sliced tomato, cucumbers, and olives.

Cold Seafood Plate: Cold plate of poached salmon, gravlax, shrimp, crab claw, and marinated scallops, with watercress mayonnaise and bell pepper coulis.

Roulade of Sole and Seafood Forcemeat: Sole stuffed with seafood served with red pepper coulis.

Grilled Salmon: Grilled salmon with balsamic vinegar, Béarnaise Sauce.

Poached Snapper: Poached snapper in a spinach, parsley, and apple sauce.

Croustade of Scallops: Scallops in puff pastry with crab coulis.

Avocado and Florida Seafood Salad: Avocado and seafood salad with asparagus tips.

Poached Fillet of Sole Véronique: Poached fillet of sole complemented with a delicate lobster sauce and a white sauce with white seedless grapes.

Swordfish: Swordfish with herb butter.

Baked Flounder: Baked flounder with fresh spinach and fennel.

Cajun Barbecued Shrimp: Barbecued shrimp served in the traditional New Orleans style.

Baked Red Snapper: Baked red snapper fresh from the sea with herbed bread crumbs.

Salmon Steak Doria: Salmon steak with cucumber.

Broiled Red Snapper: Broiled red snapper served on a bed of watercress, with ginger sauce.

Feuillette of Salmon: Layers of puff pastry filled with spinach and salmon mousse, served with Chardonnay wine sauce.

Seafood Pasta: Large pasta shells stuffed with a blend of mushrooms, crabmeat, and spinach with Marinara Sauce.

Fillet of Sole Bonne Femme: Fillet of sole in a white wine sauce with mushrooms and shallots.

Hot Shredded Lobster in Brioche: Lobster flavored with soy sauce and fresh ginger, served in a sherry sauce in a brioche presentation.

Lightly Sautéed River Trout: Sautéed river trout served with a Swedish dill sauce.

Seafood Quiche Nantua: Crusty pie shell filled with egg, baby shrimps, scallops, and mushrooms, with broccoli and lemon butter.

Supreme of Salmon: Salmon with Sauce Mousseline, poached in a herbed vegetable bouillon.

Poached Paupiette of Sole, Sauce Véronique: Rolled poached sole with white wine sauce, garnished with white grapes.

Mixed Grill Luncheons

Philadelphia Mixed Grill: Second joint of capon, bacon, link sausage, mushroom caps, served with hash brown potatoes and tiny green peas.

Mixed Grill London Style: Broiled lamb chop, broiled sausage, mushroom caps, strip of bacon, and broiled half tomato, chicken, with small roasted potatoes.

Sandwich Luncheons

The Traditional Club, Garni: Club sandwich garnished with marinated fresh vegetables.

Croissant Filled with Chicken Cashew Salad: Chicken cashew salad on a croissant with fresh fruit garnish and deviled egg.

Deli Sliced Ham and Cheese on French Bread: Ham and cheese on French bread served with Bavarian potato salad.

Philly Cheese Steak Sandwich: Thinly sliced sirloin and onions sautéed, served on a French roll with our special cheese sauce, accompanied by hot German potato salad and sliced tomato to garnish.

The Perfect Pocket: Deli-sliced roast beef, ham, turkey, and Swiss cheese in a pocket of pita bread with potato salad, dill pickle spear and a fruit garnish.

The French Connection: Sliced roast beef and Brie cheese on a flaky croissant spread with a special herb butter, garnished with fresh fruit.

The Muffaletta: Deli sliced ham, Genoa salami, and Swiss cheese topped with chopped olive dressing on baked sourdough loaf, served with assorted relishes, potato salad, and condiments.

New York Sirloin Steak Sandwich: 8-ounce Maître d'Hôtel served on sliced French bread, with fresh vegetable du jour.

Open-Faced Reuben Sandwich: Corned beef on Bavarian rye bread, with hot German potato salad and half broiled tomato.

Prime Dip: Mounds of thickly sliced prime rib on French bread with onion au jus for dipping.

Pelican's Pouch: Pita bread stuffed with tuna, ham, *or* chicken salad, served with potato salad.

56th Street Special: Freshly sliced French roll filled with sliced ham, turkey, salami, American, and Swiss cheeses, surrounded with shredded lettuce and sliced tomatoes, accompanied with potato salad on a crisp lettuce cup.

The Deli Twins: One corned beef and one pastrami on twin rolls, with sliced dill pickles and cole slaw.

Broiled Tenderloin Steak: Broiled beef tenderloin on a toasted roll with Sauce Béarnaise.

Rib Eye Steak Sandwich: Rib eye steak served on a slice of grilled pumpernickel and garnished with crispy onions.

Georgia Grill Sandwich: Turkey and beef served open faced on swirl rye with a cheese sauce and marinated vegetables.

Pack a Pita: Pita bread stuffed with a mixture of shaved ham, turkey, roast beef, and salami, combined with peppers, Swiss cheese, tomato, onion, and shaved lettuce, garnished with fresh fruits and relishes.

Other Luncheon Choices

Assorted Open-Faced Sandwiches: Smoked salmon, baby shrimp, smoked chicken breast, pastrami, ham, and roast beef on a variety of breads.

Quiche, Quiche, Quiche: Quiche of mushrooms, broccoli, green onions, and goat cheese.

Other Luncheon Choices (continued)

Salad of Fresh Fruit and Vegetables: Fresh fruit and vegetables with honey-yogurt and anisette dressings.

Painter's Palette: Platter of cottage cheese or sherbet surrounded with orange and grapefruit sections and fresh fruit in season.

Avocado Acapulco: Avocado with baby shrimp Rémoulade, accompanied with melon slice, ripe olives, lemon wedge, grapefruit sections, and Boston lettuce.

Stuffed Papaya Delight: Chicken in tomato crown and albacore salad, surrounded with ripe papaya, garnished with cheese wedge, asparagus spears, green and black olives, served with banana nut bread.

Tomato Surprise Twins: Half tomato with tuna salad and half tomato with egg salad, served with Waldorf salad garni.

Sea and Citrus Platter: Platter featuring chunk gulf shrimp, citrus fruit, cole slaw, egg wedges, and olives, Sauce Neptune or Gourmet Rémoulade Sauce passed.

Vol-au-Vent Varieties: Twin pastry shells filled with tasty mixtures of Chicken à la Reine, Beef Stroganoff, or Seafood Newburg (choice of two selections).

The Dynamic Duo: From atop twin crowns of tomato are served curried chicken salad and tuna salad, with fresh vegetables.

Country Wellington: Fresh seasonal vegetables and grated parmesan cheese wrapped in puff pastry, with Marinara Sauce.

Grant Avenue Salad: Chilled seasonal greenery served with ribbons of beef, water chestnuts, sliced Swiss cheese, asparagus spears, croutons, and grated cheese. Roquefort and Thousand Island Dressings passed.

Wedge of Quiche Lorraine à la Française: Crusty pie shell filled with a blend of egg, ham, and diced onions.

Delicatessen Platter: Slices of roast beef, turkey breast, ham, kosher-style salami, corned beef, American and Swiss cheeses, garnished with cold English potato salad, tomato wedges, slices of hard-boiled egg, cucumbers, and olives, on a bed of romaine, with fresh melon wedge, in season, Garni. Accompanied by baskets of rye and pumpernickel bread on the table, with appropriate condiments.

Fruit Plate Extravaganza: Assorted fresh tropical fruits, in season, on a wedge of fresh pineapple with cottage cheese and honey-lemon dressing, accompanied with date nut bread and cream cheese.

Primavera Salad: Salad of spinach rotelli, pasta shells, zucchini, broccoli buds, cherry tomatoes, black olives, and red pepper garni, served on a glass plate on a bed of lettuce, parmesan cheese passed.

Twin Miniature Patty Shells Filled with Chicken à la Reine and Seafood Newburg: Pastry shells of Chicken à la Reine and Seafood Newburg served with broiled tomato parmesan.

Cold English Plate: Platter of roast beef, country pâté, smoked loin of pork, and roast turkey, with aged cheddar and salad of marinated vegetables.

Vegetable Wellington: Vegetable Wellington with sorrel sauce.

Tarragon Chicken Salad: Tarragon chicken salad on a bed of lettuce garnished with tomato and egg.

Poached Brook Trout: Poached brook trout with champagne sauce.

Chef's Salad Julienne: Chef's salad of ham, turkey, and Swiss cheese, decorated with tomato, egg, and Thousand Island Dressing.

Cobb Salad: Crisp greens selection topped with diced ingredients arranged in rows to include: hard-cooked egg, tomato, turkey, crisp bacon, bleu cheese crumbles, and avocado, with peppercorn dressing.

Chapter 16

Seated Luncheon Menus

Chicken Seated Luncheons

Chicken #1

Bibb Lettuce with Pimiento, Chopped Egg
Yolk, and a Hot Shrimp Hazelnut Dressing,
Tossed in the Ballroom

• • •

Ginger Sorbet served in
unique glass flower presentation

• • •

10-ounce Roasted Chicken Breast filled with
Black Mushrooms, presented in a Fan Shape,
on a Bed of Butternut Squash Sauce
Stir-Fried Leaf Spinach

• • •

Petite Luncheon Rolls and Butter

• • •

Double Chocolate Mousse Cake Roll
with Chocolate Sauce, passed

• • •

Coffee, Tea, Sanka

Chicken #2

Wonton Soup

• • •

Chicken Teriyaki, Chinese Fried Rice
Stir-Fried Vegetables with Snow Pea Pods
Kumquat Garnish

• • •

Mandarin Ice with Fortune Cookie

• • •

Coffee, Tea, Sanka, or Milk

Chicken #3

Coquille of Alaskan Shrimp,
Brandied Seafood Sauce

• • •

Double Breast of Boneless Chicken,
Mustard Dill Sauce

• • •

Baby Carrots and Green Grape Sauté
Panache of White and Wild Rice

• • •

Baskets of Warm Croissants, Creamery Butter

• • •

Coconut Snowball, Hot Chocolate Sauce

• • •

Beverage

Chicken #4

Cold Cucumber Soup

• • •

Chicken Pontabla
Thinly Sliced Chicken Breast on
a Bed of Hash Brown Potatoes,
Sautéed with Minced Ham
Served with Sauce Hollandaise
Broccoli au Beurre
Tomato Provençale

• • •

Ice Cream Cake, Raspberry Sauce, passed

• • •

Coffee

Chicken #5   Hawaiian Luncheon

Sautéed Plantain with
Fried Swiss Cheese, Polynesian style,
served on a Bed of Island Greens

• • •

Polynesian Chicken Salad Fantasy
Served in Half Coconut,
garnished with Fresh Fruit

• • •

A Colorful Selection of Fresh Fruits to
include:
Papayas, Mangoes, Kiwi, Pineapples,
Blueberries, Sprinkled with Brown Sugar and
Accompanied with Sour Cream,
served à la carte,
presented on a Bed of Emerald Leaves

• • •

Kona Coffee

Chicken #7

Chilled Gazpacho, garnished with Chopped
Celery and Green Peppers, Croutons to be
passed separately on each table

• • •

Boneless Breast of Chicken Montmorency,
With Black Oregon Cherries in
Port Wine Sauce
Spiced Peach Half
Rissolé Potatoes, Petits Pois Parisienne

• • •

Frozen Ice Cream Log, Strawberry Sauce

• • •

Coffee

Chicken #6

Fusilli Pasta Salad Primavera,
Garnished with Vegetable Flowerettes
in a Light Vinaigrette

• • •

Sautéed Medallions of Chicken,
Armangnac Sauce with Shiitake Mushrooms

• • •

String Beans Wrapped in Crisp Bacon
Jardiniere of Yellow Squash and
Fresh Carrots

• • •

Warm Croissants
Butter

• • •

Individual Fruit Tartlets

• • •

Beverage

Chicken #8

Salad Mimosa Orientale
Mixed Green Salad, Sliced Fresh Mushrooms,
Topped with Chopped Egg Yolk,
Sesame Dressing

• • •

Whole Boneless Breast of Chicken,
Sweet and Sour
Oriental Fried Rice
Oriental Vegetable Sauté, to include:
Bean Sprouts, Water Chestnuts, and
Snow Peas

• • •

Individual Pineapple Cheesecake, with
Lemon Cream
Crushed Strawberry Sauce, passed

• • •

Coffee, Tea, Sanka

Chicken #9

Wonton Soup

• • •

Sesame Chicken Breast, Oriental Glaze
atop Fried Rice
Broccoli Szechuan, Stir-Fry Vegetables

• • •

Pear Bombe Litchi
Pear Ice, White Cake, Litchi Sauce

• • •

Coffee, Tea, Sanka
Another possible dessert: Green Tea Sorbet

Chicken #10

Melon Ring with Orange and Grapefruit
Sections, Poppy Seed Dressing

• • •

Chicken Delmonico
Breast of Chicken Filled with Ham and
Broccoli, Draped with Sauce Mornay
Spiced Peach Filled with Cranberries

• • •

Assorted Rolls and Butter

• • •

Fresh Fruit Tart with Whipped Cream

• • •

Coffee

Chicken #11

Iceberg Lettuce with Tomato, Bean Sprouts,
Scallions, on Leaf Lettuce,
Chef's Dressing

• • •

Boneless Breast of Capon Szechuan
Capon Laced with a Fruit Teriyaki Sauce
Fried Chinese Rice, Stir-Fried Vegetables

• • •

Assorted Rolls and Butter

• • •

Mandarin Chiffon Pie

• • •

Coffee

Chicken #12

Hearts of Palm with Cherry Tomatoes,
Artichoke Hearts, Boston Lettuce,
Wedge of Brie Cheese, Raw Sliced
Mushrooms, and Pimiento
Light Mustard Vinaigrette passed by waiters

• • •

Breast of Chicken Amandine, Sauce
Périgourdine
With Tomato filled with Broccoli and
Cauliflower Flowerettes with
Sauce Mornay Glaze, Continental Rice Pilaf

• • •

One Croissant on each bread and butter plate,
plus one basket on each table with
extra Croissants and an assortment of
Luncheon Rolls and Butter

• • •

Thickly Sliced Double Chocolate Ice Cream
Cake Roll, Beautifully decorated and
garnished with Walnut Pieces, Chocolate
Fudge Sauce and Whipped Cream passed

• • •

Coffee, Tea, Sanka

Chicken #13

Fresh Fruit Plate consisting of:
Melon Slices, Pineapple Wedge, Fresh
Strawberries, Litchi Nuts,
on a Bed of Bibb Lettuce,
Topped with Shredded Coconut and Slivered
Almonds, Honey-Lime Dressing to be passed

• • •

Breast of Chicken Tananarive
Boneless Chicken Breasts Sautéed and Braised
in a Madagascar Sauce Garni with
Chanterelle Mushrooms
Artichoke filled with a Medley of
Fresh Vegetables
Pilaf of Wild Rice

• • •

Praline Soufflé Swan, Filled with Frozen
Praline Soufflé nestled in a Bed of Chocolate
Fudge Sauce, Topped with Shaved Chocolate,
a Dollop of Fresh Whipped Cream, and
Dusted with Powdered Sugar

• • •

Coffee, Tea, Sanka, or Milk

Chicken #14

Seasonal Melon Spears Wrapped in
Prosciutto, on a Bed of Red Leaf Lettuce

• • •

Chicken Piccata, Lemon Butter and
Caper Sauce
Carrot Mousse, in an Artichoke Bottom
Spinach Tortellini

• • •

Frozen Raspberry Soufflé Chantilly,
Chocolate Cup Presentation, Sauce Anglaise

• • •

Beverage

Turkey Seated Luncheon

Turkey #1

Tossed Garden Salad with
Sliced Radishes and Tomatoes,
French Dressing

• • •

Turkey Ambassador
Turkey, Tomato Sauce, Avocado,
Melted Cheese
Bouquetierre of Vegetables

• • •

Rolls and Butter

• • •

Vanilla Ice Cream, Strawberry Sauce

• • •

Coffee, Tea, Sanka, or Milk

Beef Seated Luncheons

Beef #1

Gold Coast Salad
Jumbo Shrimp, Lobster Chunks, Sliced Papaya and Avocado,
Greek Olives, arranged elegantly on a Bed of Colorful Greens,
accompanied with Rémoulade and Cocktail Sauces

• • •

Filet Mignon Classic
Tender Fillet of Beef, Lightly Cooked, served on a
Zucchini Crouton with Béarnaise Sauce, passed
Tomato Basket Filled with Cauliflower
French Green Beans
Julienne of Carrots

• • •

Bread Service to Include:
Miniature Baguettes of Sourdough, Saltsticks, Lahvosh,
Banana Bread, and Elegant Butter Roses

• • •

Le Pâté de Chocolat
An elegance of White, Milk, and Cadbury Chocolates,
all blended together and served on a unique sauce

• • •

Coffee, Herbal Teas, and Decaffeinated Coffee

Beef #2

Deluxe Shrimp Salad Plate
Selection of Fresh Garden Greens, Topped
with Fresh Jumbo Shrimp,
Appropriately Garnished with
Tomato Rosette
Lemon Star Filled with Cocktail
Sauce—Chef's Selection—and Rémoulade
Sauce

• • •

Medallions of Beef Tenderloin,
Sauce—Chef's Choice
Two Fresh Vegetables,
Potato—Chef's Choice

• • •

Fresh Rolls and Butter

• • •

Chocolate Cheesecake

• • •

Coffee or Tea

Beef #3

Consommé Celestine

• • •

Beef Bourguignonne, Noodles à la Crème,
Fines Herbes, String Beans aux Echalotes

• • •

Assorted French Pastries

• • •

Coffee, Tea, Sanka, or Milk

Beef #4

Sweet and Sour Lentil Soup with Ham

• • •

Braised Sauerbraten
Potato Pancakes, Red Cabbage with Apples

• • •

Black Forest Cake

• • •

Coffee, Tea, Sanka, or Milk

Beef #5

Consommé du Jour,
Paillettes

• • •

Shrimp Creole, Rice Pilaf

• • •

Minute Steak with Mushrooms,
Sautéed in Butter
Spinach Italian

• • •

Boston Lettuce, Cherry Tomatoes,
Vinaigrette Dressing

• • •

Cheesecake with Fresh Blueberry Sauce,
passed

• • •

Coffee

Beef #6

Spinach Salad Mimosa, Bacon Bits, Shredded Egg,
Toasted Croutons, Sweet and Sour Dressing

• • •

Sliced London Broil,
Chasseur Sauce or Barbecue Sauce
Bâtonnets of Carrot and Zucchini
Small Roasted Potatoes

• • •

Selected Breads, Creamery Butter

• • •

Cherry Strudel, Chantilly

• • •

Beverage

Beef #7

Hearty Soup du Jour or Selected Salads

• • •

Cold Prime Rib Plate, Creamy Horseradish Sauce

• • •

Russian Vegetable Salad, served in a Tomato Crown

• • •

French Rolls, Whipped Butter

• • •

Boysenberry and Lemon Sorbet, Served in a Chocolate Cup,
Lemon Cream Sauce

• • •

Beverage

Beef #8

Salad Acapulco
Avocado, Bibb Lettuce, Bay Shrimps, Orange
Sections, Louis Dressing

• • •

Sliced Beef Tenderloin,
Sauce Marchand de Vin
Pommes Chateau
Bouquetierre of Vegetables

• • •

Fresh Rolls and Butter

• • •

Strawberries Romanoff

• • •

Coffee or Tea

Beef #9

Cold Creamed Senegelaise,
Grated Toasted Coconut

• • •

Chinese Pepper Steak
Pilaf of White Rice
Broccoli with Herbed Bread Crumbs

• • •

Bombe of Strawberry and Coffee Ice Creams,
Chocolate Sauce

• • •

Coffee

Beef #10

Tossed Watercress, Bermuda Onion, and
Navel Orange Salad,
Sprinkled with Sunflower Seeds,
Orange Vinaigrette

• • •

Individually Grilled Filet Mignon, 6 ounces,
Béarnaise Sauce
Sugar Snap Pea Pods, Sautéed with Diced
Sweet Red Peppers
Parisienne Potatoes

• • •

Salt Sticks and Lahvosh
Butter

• • •

Classical Crème Caramel

• • •

Beverage

Beef #11

Chilled Cream of Broccoli Soup

• • •

Cold English Cut, Prime Rib Plate, Mild
Horseradish Sauce
Marinated Vegetable Salad, Carrot and
Raisin Salad
Sliced Eggs, Fruit Garniture

• • •

Date Nut Bread, Cream Cheese and Butter

• • •

Coffee, Tea, Sanka

Beef #12

A variety of Fabulous Salads,
to be displayed in the center of each table,
three separate groupings, to include:
Wurst Salad with Emmenthaler
Seafood Salad
Marinated Vegetables in Tomato Sauce
Tomato and Onion Salad
Cucumber and Potato Salad

• • •

Giant Hamburger Magilla
Fried Onions and Watercress
Cone of Fresh French Fried Steak Cut
Potatoes, garnished appropriately and with
the proper condiments

• • •

Fabulous Strawberry Shortcake,
made from Giant Homemade Biscuits,
Fresh Strawberries, Fresh Ice Cream,
Chocolate Curls, and Topped with
Fresh Whipped Cream

• • •

Coffee, Iced Tea, Sanka, and
Assorted Soft Drinks

Beef #13

Deluxe Shrimp Salad Plate
Selection of Fresh Garden Greens,
topped with Fresh Jumbo Shrimp,
appropriately garnished with a
Tomato Rosette, Lemon Star filled
with Cocktail Sauce

• • •

Medallions of Beef Tenderloin,
Sauce Bordelaise
Fresh Seasonal Vegetables,
Selected by the Executive Banquet Chef
Pommes Croquette

• • •

Fresh Rolls and Butter

• • •

Chocolate Cheesecake,
topped with grated Bavarian Chocolate

• • •

Coffee or Tea

Beef #14   Maxim's versus Mac-Scenes
Luncheon

The Reception area should resemble the French restaurant, Maxim's. The Maître d'Hôtel should be properly attired and standing behind a podium. Large arrangements of flowers in urns should flank the entrance. Under a large crystal chandelier, the reception service staff, clad in Tuxedos and White Gloves, should serve Perrier water, imported premium beers, and nonalcoholic champagne from gleaming silver trays. Violinists should play in the Reception Area.

When the doors leading to the Luncheon area open, they should reveal a Dixieland-type (upbeat) setting complete with a gazebo. Staff and band should be dressed in Striped Vests and Straw Hats, Tables should be set with checkered Linens, balloons should serve as Centerpieces on the tables for eight, and a sign should read: "Welcome to Mac-Scenes—Home of the Magnificent Hamburger."

Small printed menus should be on each table as follows:

Vegetable Soup in Acorn Squash

• • •

Pepper Burger
Green Peppercorn Sauce

• • •

Pita Burger
Slices of Bean Sprouts, Shrimps, Leeks, Onion, and Celery

• • •

Reuben Burger
With Sauerkraut and Swiss Cheese

• • •

French Connection Burger
Baked in Casava Shell, Topped with Ratatouille

• • •

Apple Tart with Caramel Sauce

• • •

Coffee, Tea, Assorted Soft Drinks

The Service Staff should take burger orders before serving the homemade vegetable soup in an acorn squash.

Veal Seated Luncheons

Veal # 1

Red Snapper Chowder,
Golden Fleuron

• • •

Medallions of Veal Madagascar
Tender Medallions of Veal in a Mild
Green Peppercorn Sauce

• • •

Selected Rolls and Butter

• • •

Marble Cheesecake, Sauce Anglaise

• • •

Beverage

Veal #2

Summer Salad
Selections of Boston Bibb Lettuce,
Crowned with Marinated Artichokes,
Vinaigrette Dressing

• • •

Medallions of Veal Marsala
Wild Rice
Tomato Bouquetiere

• • •

Fresh Rolls and Butter

• • •

Strawberries Romanoff

• • •

Coffee or Tea

Veal #3 Recognition Luncheon

Deluxe Cold Jumbo Shrimp Cocktail, with
Cocktail Sauce
in a Cucumber Cup and a Lemon Crown

• • •

Sautéed Veal Medallions,
Sauce Morille
Bouquetiere of Baby Vegetables
Potatoes Berny

• • •

Assorted Petite Luncheon Rolls and Butter

• • •

Special Presentation

Savarin Grand Duc
Savarin of Orange Sherbet flavored with
Benedictine Liqueur, served with
Fresh Raspberry Sauce, passed, and a
Macaroon Cookie

• • •

Coffee, Tea, Decaffeinated Coffee

Veal #4

Pacesetter Salad
Bibb Lettuce, Belgian Endive,
Tomato Rosette, Watercress, Eden Rock
Dressing, Served on a chilled clear
crystal plate

• • •

Veal Piccata
Medallions of Veal, Lemon and Butter Sauce
Vermicelli Savarin with Ratatouille
Braised Celery with Mornay Sauce, passed

• • •

Croissants and Butter

• • •

Amaretto Parfait
Vanilla Ice Cream and Amaretto,
garnished with Rock Candy and Topped with
Fresh Strawberry and Amaretto Cookies,
served on the side

• • •

Coffee and Tea

Veal #5

Minestrone Soup with Parmesan Cheese

• • •

Veal Cacciatore
Fettucini Milanaise, Baked Zucchini

• • •

Neapolitan Ice Cream Cake

• • •

Coffee, Tea, Sanka, or Milk

Pork Seated Luncheon

Pork #1

A Waioahi Seafood Salad
With Crab and Shrimp, served in a half
Pineapple, presented on special matting, with
Banana, Poppy Seed, and Honey Dressing

• • •

Kahuna Roast Pig
For presentation and display,
a Suckling Pig, wrapped in Banana Leaves,
presented on a stretcher by four (4) captains,
with Whole Fruit Garnish and Island Leaves

• • •

Whole Smoked Pork Roast,
Rubbed in Garlic and wrapped in Banana
Leaves, Lean Slices served on Banana Leaf,
accented with Hawaiian Salt,
Garnished with Crabapple
Layers of Banana, Pineapples, Litchi Nuts
Baked in Bubbling Brown Sugar
Hawaiian Fried Celery with Water Chestnuts,
Pea Pods and Bamboo Shoots

• • •

Fresh Luncheon Rolls and Butter

• • •

Coconut Coma
Blend of Rich Ice Creams,
Toasted Fresh Coconut, Chopped Macadamia
Nuts, and Passion Fruit, served in a
Coconut Shell, garnished with Sticks of
Sugar Cane and Fresh Vanda Orchids

• • •

Coffee or Tea

Lamb Seated Luncheons

Lamb #1

Fresh Fillet of Snapper,
Sauté Beurre Blanc au Fennieul

• • •

Noisettes of Lamb served with
Minted Demi-Glace
Boiled Turned New Potatoes
Fresh Baby Carrots
Whole Green Beans wrapped in Red
Pepper Strip
Banana Nut Bread and Lahvosh
Molded Butter

• • •

Hot Marble Soufflé with
Vanilla and Chocolate Sauces

• • •

Coffee, Tea, Sanka

Lamb #2

Chilled Melon Soup,
Garnished with Sliced Almonds

• • •

Broiled Lamb Steak
Tarragon Butter
Broccoli Flowers
Tomato Crown
Filled with Saffron Rice and White Raisins

• • •

French Apple Tart,
Crème Anglaise,
Flavored with Calvados

• • •

Beverage

Seafood/Fish Seated Luncheons

Seafood #1

Salad Exceptionale
Fresh Spinach, Watercress, Cherry Tomatoes,
Hearts of Palm, and White Asparagus,
Eden Rock Dressing

• • •

Fresh Seafood Crêpe
Scallops, Shrimp, and Mushrooms in a White
Wine Sauce
Tiny Belgian Carrots
Fresh Garden Green Peas

• • •

Croissants and Butter

• • •

Croquant Parfait
Garnished with Rock Candy and Fresh
Strawberry

• • •

Coffee or Tea

Seafood #2

Boston Bibb, Radicchio, and Romaine,
Tossed with Enoki Mushrooms, grated
Carrots, and Artichoke Hearts,
Vinaigrette Dressing

• • •

Grilled Pompano *or* Red Snapper Fillet,
Maître d'Hôtel Butter

• • •

Selected Seasonal Vegetables

• • •

Freshly Baked Breads
Whipped Butter

• • •

Cream Puff Swan,
Filled with White Chocolate Mousse,
Raspberry Melba Sauce

• • •

Beverage

Seafood #3

Turtle Soup, Cajun Style

• • •

Papaya Stuffed with Seafood Salad,
Sauce Aurora, Garnished with Strawberry,
Kiwi, Grapes, and Orange Slices on a Bed of
Spinach and Bibb Lettuce
Baguettes and Butter

• • •

Mocha Mousse in a Chocolate Shell

• • •

Coffee, Tea, Sanka, or Milk

Seafood #4

Chicken Egg Drop Soup

• • •

Avocado Pear, Filled with Shrimp, Crab,
and Scallop Salad, Bengal Sauce
Asparagus Spears
Carrot Ribbon

• • •

Baskets of Mixed Miniature Rolls
Butter Rosettes

• • •

Profiterole Mexicaine, Filled with
Kahlua Ice Cream, Hot Fudge Sauce

• • •

Beverage

Seafood #5

French Onion Soup with Parmesan Croutons

• • •

Assorted Cold Seafood Platter,
which will consist of the following:
Chunked Crabmeat, Two Small Crab Claws,
Two Jumbo Shrimp, Two Freshly Shucked
Oysters, and Two Freshly Shucked Clams

• • •

Fresh Rolls and Butter

• • •

Strawberries Romanoff

• • •

Coffee, Tea, or Sanka

Seafood #6

New England Clam Chowder

• • •

Fresh Poached Fillet of Sole, Shrimp Sauce
Buttered Parsley Potatoes
Garden Peas with Mushrooms

• • •

Strawberry Shortcake

• • •

Coffee, Tea, Sanka, or Milk

Seafood #7

Tossed Bibb and Romaine Lettuce,
Hearts of Palm, Grated Carrot, and Toasted
Croutons, Creamy Dijon Vinaigrette

• • •

Fillet of Coho Salmon à la Russe, Herb Butter
Sautéed Cucumbers with Walnuts
Baby Belgian Carrots

• • •

Petit Pain and Lahvosh, Butter Rosettes

• • •

Key Lime Pie
Coconut Macaroon

• • •

Beverage

Seafood #8

Suprême of Fresh Fruits

• • •

Seafood Medley, Selected Cold Seafoods:
Oysters, Clams, Shrimp, Crabmeat and Claws,
Fillet of Fish, and Scallops, Garnished with
Lettuce Leaves, Sliced Cucumbers,
Cherry Tomatoes, White Asparagus Spears,
and Lemon Wedge,
Louis Dressing

• • •

German Black Forest Cake

• • •

With Luncheon
Offer guests Coffee, Hot Tea, Iced Tea,
Decaffeinated Coffee, or Milk

Mixed Seated Luncheons

Mixed #1

Chilled Peach Soup with Mint Garnish

• • •

Avocado Half with Seafood Salad and
Avocado Half with Chicken Walnut Salad
with Cascading Marinated Vegetables

• • •

Sliced French Bread and Butter

• • •

Apple Streusel with Cinnamon Cream

• • •

Coffee or Tea

Mixed #2

Florida Waldorf Salad
Fresh Pineapple, Apple, Orange, Celery,
Raisins, and Peanuts

• • •

Twin Crêpes, Filled with Seafood Newburg
and
Chicken à la Reine,
accompanied by Rice Pilaf
Tomato Stuffed with Broccoli Flowerettes

• • •

Petite Rolls and specially designed
Butter Swans

• • •

An Orange Basket,
filled with Lime Sherbet and garnished
with Mandarin Orange and Whipped Cream
Rosette and served in a Champagne glass

• • •

Coffee or Tea

Mixed #3   The Glass Fish Platter Luncheon

Presented on a large glass fish platter, we will
serve:
Jumbo Shrimp, Mussels, Salmon,
Pâté à la Maison, Smoked Duck Breast,
Oriental Pasta Salad, with Chicken
and Sesame

• • •

Assorted Fresh Fruits and International
Cheeses, displayed on silver trays and served
with French Bread and placed in the center of
each table
Display includes Fish Melon Carving and
Fresh Flowers

• • •

Cassata with Kiwi slices and
Fresh Strawberry Sauce, to be passed

• • •

Coffee, Tea, Decaffeinated Coffee,
Iced Tea and Assorted Soft Drinks

Mixed #4

Deluxe Antipasto
Selections of Provolone Cheese, Prosciutto
Ham, Salami, Sardines, Marinated Fresh
Vegetables, Tuna, Black Olives,
Vinaigrette Dressing

• • •

Sliced Tenderloins of Beef and Veal,
Sauces Morille and Béarnaise
Potato Basket
Fresh Sautéed Zucchini

• • •

Fresh Rolls and Butter

• • •

Kiwi with Raspberry Sauce
or
Poached Pear Symphony au Chocolat

• • •

Coffee or Tea

Mixed #5

Eden Rock Salad
Bibb Lettuce, Belgian Endive,
Tomato Rosette, and Watercress,
Eden Rock Dressing

• • •

A Traditional Mixed Grill
With a Medallion of Pork, Veal, Beef, Lamb,
Liver, and Kidney
Grilled Tomato Garnished with a
Strip of Bacon
Pommes Pailles
Fresh Braised Celery

• • •

Freshly Baked Rolls, of the Chef's Selection
with Butter Swans

• • •

French Raspberry Sorbet with Freshly
Peeled Kiwi

• • •

Demitasse and Imported Tea

Mixed #6

Chilled Melon Soup
or
Beef Consommé,
Sliced Pea Pods and Leeks

• • •

Salad Duo
Alaskan Shrimp and Scallion Salad
and Smoked Turkey Breast and Pecan Salad,
Fresh Fruit Garni

• • •

Baskets of Warm Croissants, Butter

• • •

Piña Colada Parfait,
Ladyfinger

• • •

Beverage

Mixed #7   Christmas Luncheon

Clear Oxtail Soup,
Warm Cheese Straws, passed

• • •

Medallions of Beef Tenderloin and Veal,
Sauces Béarnaise and Morille
Saffron Rice
Tomato Baskets Filled with Fiddleheads

• • •

Petite Luncheon Rolls and Butter

• • •

Individual Pastry Christmas Sled
with Parfait Grand Marnier

• • •

Demitasse

Mixed #8

Fresh Cucumber and Dill Salad

• • •

Sauté of Shrimp and Chipolata Sausages,
Provençale

• • •

Jardiniere of Yellow and Green Squash
Wild Rice Pilaf

• • •

Warm Apple Dumpling, Caramel Sauce

• • •

Beverage

Sandwich Seated Luncheons

Sandwich #1

Cold Cucumber Soup with Dill

• • •

Open-Faced Reuben Sandwich, on Bavarian
Rye Bread
Hot German Potato Salad
Sliced Tomato Garnish

• • •

Selection of Assorted Pastries

• • •

Coffee, Tea, Sanka

Sandwich #2

Caesar Style Salad,
Grated Parmesan, Toasted Croutons,
Caesar Dressing

• • •

Grilled Sirloin Sandwich Steak, on Toasted
Garlic Bread

• • •

Sautéed Onions, Red Peppers, and
Mushrooms
Croquette Potatoes

• • •

Layered Dark and White Chocolate Mousse,
Heart of Raspberry Puree,
Whipped Cream and Shaved Chocolate

• • •

Beverage

Sandwich #3

Chilled Cream Doria
Cream of Cucumber Soup

• • •

Presented on a Bed of Lettuce:
Grapefruit Basket with Mélange of Fresh
Fruit,
Poppy Seed Dressing
Surrounded by an Assortment of Finger
Sandwiches:
Turkey, Ham, Tuna, on Assorted Fruit
Breads, Appropriately Garnished

• • •

Watermelon Bombe,
Lime Ice outside, Watermelon Ice with
Chocolate Chips on inside

• • •

Coffee, Tea, Sanka

Chapter 17

Luncheon Buffet Menus

The Roll-In Luncheon Buffet

(Maximum 50 Guests)

For meetings with no time to break for lunch
Crisp Salad with Choice of Dressing
Fresh Seasonal Fruit
Pasta Salad

• • •

Platters of Assorted Finished
Open-Faced Sandwiches
Fresh Baked Breads and Rolls
Condiments and Crudités

• • •

An Array of Fresh Baked Pastries

• • •

Coffee, Tea, Decaffeinated Coffee, or Milk

The Delicatessen Buffet Luncheon

Watercress and Vegetable Salad, Sprinkled
with Walnuts
German-Style Potato Salad

• • •

Mounds of Shaved Pastrami, Corned Beef,
Salami, Roast Beef, Smoked Tongue,
Ham, and Turkey Breast
European and American Cheeses
Crocks of Pickles

• • •

Assorted Breads and Hearty Rolls
Condiments

• • •

A Selection of Fresh Sliced Fruits in Season
Chocolate and Macaroon Mousse

The Basic Luncheon Buffet

Fresh Sliced Fruits in a Watermelon Basket
Soup of the Day

• • •

Greengrocer's Salad Bar
Crisp Garden Greens with Choice of Dressings
Cold German-Style Potato Salad
Sliced Tomatoes and Cucumbers
Assorted Raw Vegetables, Pickled Beets
Vegetable Salad, Red Cabbage Slaw
Green Bean and Mushroom Salad

• • •

From Our Delicatessen Counter
Assorted Sausages, Salami, Corned Beef, Breast of Turkey,
Cooked Ham, Tuna Salad, Roast Beef, Pastrami, Pepperoni,
Provolone and Swiss Cheeses
Crocks of Pickles
Assorted Rolls, Breads, Butter, and Condiments

• • •

Our Sweet Table
Assortment of Daily Home Baked Pies and Layer Cakes,
English Trifle, and Cheesecake

• • •

Coffee, Tea, Decaffeinated Coffee, or Milk

• • •

Hot Selections Are in Addition:
Beef Bourguignonne with Egg Noodles
Broiled Red Snapper with Parsley Potatoes
Coq au Vin with Risi Bisi

Cold Selections Are in Addition:
Assorted Cheese Tray with Crackers
Steaks of Poached Salmon with Mayonnaise
Baby Shrimp Salad

The Deli-Style Buffet Luncheon

From Deli Style cases and counters, we will serve and prepare sandwiches to order using:
Corned Beef, Pastrami, Kosher Salami, Roast Beef, Turkey Breast, Swiss Cheese, Chopped Chicken Livers,
Tuna Fish Salad, Lox and Cream Cheese,
Herring in Sour Cream
Potato Salad, Cole Slaw, Fruit Salad
Pickled Eggs in Beet Juice
Red Horseradish
Bags of Potato Chips
Chicken Noodle Soup
Baked Beans with Molasses
Vlasic Hand-Picked Pickles
Varieties of Bread and Rolls
Mayonnaise, Mustard, Ketchup served in Jars or Pump Bottles

• • •

New York-Style Cheesecake
Chocolate-Covered Joya
Slim Jims
Lifesavers
Cartons of Milk
Coffee, Iced Tea
International and Domestic Beers
Dr. Brown's Celray Cream Soda
Diet Raspberry, Pepsi Cola, Perrier

Decorations

Paper napkins
Oilcloth tablecloths
Styrofoam plates
Blackboard menu
"Paper" ashtrays
Variety of shapes and sizes of tables and chairs
Large fan with streamers
Old registers
Clock (Pepsi, Coke, Beer-type)
Counters
Squeeze bottles for condiments
Plastic flowers in Perrier bottles
Paper "level" trays
Meat slicer(s)
Specialty breads
Bib aprons
Printed "Romance" cards to enlighten those not aware of "Deli"

The New York Deli Buffet Luncheon

Hot Pastrami
Rye and Pumpernickel Bread
Assorted Rolls
Appropriate Condiments

• • •

Hot Dog Cart
Appropriate Condiments

• • •

Hot Soft Pretzel Cart
Appropriate Condiments

• • •

Giant Italian Hero Sandwich:
Ham, Cold Roast Beef, Salami, Mortadella
Lettuce, Tomato, and Italian Dressing

• • •

Cheesecake
Giant Cookies
Italian Ice

• • •

Nonalcoholic Beer
Assorted Soft Drinks
Coffee, Tea, Decaffeinated Coffee

The Complete Deli Buffet Luncheon

Served from counters, shelves, and racks laden with a display of Sausages, Wurst, Salamis, Breads, and Crocks of Pickles

• • •

Roast Beef, Corned Beef, Salami, Pastrami,
Tongue, Cappacola, Pepperoni, Boiled Ham,
Provolone and Swiss Cheeses
Hard Rolls, Rye Swirl, Pumpernickel Breads
Mustards, Horseradish, Mayonnaise,
Thousand Island Dressing
Chicken Liver Pâté, Chicken Salad Spread,
Tuna Salad, Egg Salad, Pickled Eggs,
Shrimp Salad
Cole Slaw, Potato and Macaroni Salads

• • •

Kosher Spears, Sauerkraut, Pickled Tomatoes
Shredded Lettuce, Sliced Tomatoes

• • •

Potato Knishes with Ketchup

• • •

Cheesecake

• • •

Coffee

The Salads and Sliced Cold Deli Meats Buffet Luncheon

Array of Fresh Cut Florida Fruit
Chilled Pasta Salad
Fresh Seasonal Greens
Chicken Dijonnaise Salad
Marinated Cucumber and Tomato Salad
Deli Potato Salad
Creamy Vegetable Slaw

• • •

Deli Assortment of:
Sliced Roast Beef, Ham, Corned Beef,
Turkey Breast, Italian Salami,
Provolone and Swiss Cheeses
Accompanied by Sliced Tomatoes,
Shredded Lettuce, and Assorted Breads,
Onion and Kaiser Rolls, and a Selection of
Condiments

• • •

Chef's Selection of Sweets from Our Pastry
Shop

• • •

Coffee, Herbal Teas

The Sandwich Shop Buffet Luncheon

Cuban Black Bean Soup with
Chopped Onions
Deli Potato Salad, Creamy Vegetable Slaw
Marinated Cucumbers and Tomatoes

• • •

Your Selection of Three of the Following:
Deep Dish Pizza
The Reuben, King of Club Sandwiches
Six Foot Submarine Sandwich
"Philly" Cheese Steak Sandwich

• • •

Natural Potato Chips
Assorted Vegetables and Relishes
Mélange of Fresh Cut Florida Fruit
Brownies and Giant Cookies

• • •

Coffee and Herbal Tea

The Butcherblock Buffet Luncheon

Watercress and Vegetable Salad,
Sprinkled with Walnuts
Potato Salad

• • •

Mounds of Shaved Pastrami, Corned Beef,
Salami, Roast Beef, Smoked Tongue
European and American Cheeses

• • •

Crunchy Vegetables
Zippy Jicama Salad marinated in Lemon-
Lime Zest

• • •

Assorted Breads and Bulky Rolls
Condiments

• • •

A Selection of Fresh Sliced Fruit in Season

• • •

Chocolate and Macaroon Mousse

• • •

Beverage

The Make Your Own Sandwich Buffet Luncheon

Mandarin Waldorf Salad
Cole Slaw, Macaroni Salad
Sliced Beefsteak Tomatoes on Bibb Lettuce

• • •

Mirrors of Selected Cold Meats and Cheeses:
Roast Beef, Corned Beef, Pastrami, Turkey
Breast, Mortadella
Muenster, American, and Swiss Cheeses

• • •

White, Rye, and Pumpernickel Breads,
Kaiser Rolls
Mayonnaise, Horseradish, and
Imported Mustards

• • •

Assorted Whole and Sliced Fresh Fruits,
Decorated with Ribbons of Seasonal Berries
Bread Pudding
Whiskey Sauce
Black Forest Cake

• • •

Beverage

The Luncheon Italian Buffet

(See Color Insert)

In the foreground of the Ponte di Rialto Bridge, we will serve the following:

Pasta e Fagioli
Soup of White Beans and Pasta
• • •

A Selection of Large Pizzas
Toppings to include:
Pepperoni, Italian Sausage, Anchovies, Mushrooms, Onions, Green Peppers, Mozzarella Cheese, Homemade Sauce, and Spices and various combinations thereof
• • •

Calzone Ripieno
An inverted pizza filled with Shaved Ham, Mozzarella, and a touch of Tomato Oregano Sauce

From the Rolling Wooden Cart, with the canvas top, we will serve the following:

Antipasto Tray
Served on a Bed of Crisp Lettuce:
Marinated Cauliflower, Celery, Sweet Red Peppers, Black Olives, Artichoke Hearts, Mortadella, Hard-Cooked Eggs, Anchovies, Roasted Red Peppers in Olive Oil, Provolone Cheese
• • •

Italian Salad Bar
Make your own Fresh Vegetable Salad:
Lettuce, Carrots, Green Peppers, Cauliflower, Onions, Tomatoes, Mushrooms, Pickled Cucumber and Carrots, Hot Peppers
Shrimp Salad
Pasta Salad
Creamy Italian Dressing
Oil and Vinegar Dressing
• • •

Freshly Baked Italian Bread, Sliced Creamery Butter
• • •

From the foreground of the Casa Dolce Vita Building, we will serve:
Cannoli, filled to order by a Waiter Attendant, at the Buffet
• • •

Coffee, Soft Drinks (served tableside)

Suggested Flowers: A floral centerpiece imbedded in a large eggplant presented on crushed glass and topped with miniature Italian flags.

The Italian Buffet Luncheon

Hot Minestrone Soup
• • •

Five-Foot Super Submarine Sandwich
Mortadella, Salami, Provolone Cheese, garnished appropriately
• • •

Italian Antipasto on a Silver Platter
Italian Mushroom and Spinach Salad
Cheese Tray with Bel Paese, French Melba Toast and Fruit, Garnished
• • •

Tray of Cannolis

The American Harvest Buffet Luncheon

Tri-Color Vegetable Pâté, Dijon Sauce
White Beans Vinaigrette
Pickled Quail Eggs
Beefsteak Tomatoes and Red Onion Rings, Vinaigrette
Belgian Endive, Herb Mayonnaise
Marinated Shrimp, Sweet Corn and Scallion Salad served in a Large Natural Clam Shell
• • •

Barbecued Flank Steak Basted with Barbecue Sauce and carved at the Buffet
Rock Cornish Hens
Pan Gravy, Sausage and Apple Stuffing
Red Peppers Filled with Veal
Sugar Snap Peas with Grated Carrots and Cashew Nuts
Peaches in Brown Sugar and Butter
• • •

Hot Buttermilk Biscuits
Platters of Cranberry Nut Bread
• • •

Vermont Cheddar, Wisconsin Blue, Swiss, and Assorted New York State Cheeses
Apple and Pear Wedges
• • •

Ribier Grapes
Warm Indian Pudding, Chilled Cream
Seasonal Fruit Flans
Jumbo Oatmeal and Chocolate Chip Cookies
• • •

Blended Coffee, Selected Teas, and Mountain Spring Water

The Western Chuck Wagon Buffet Luncheon

(See Color Insert)

From various stations we will serve:

A preplated Taste of the West
Corn Bread Cake with Potato Border
filled with Baby Corn, Broccoli, Cauliflower,
Carrots, Green Beans,
topped with Butter Sauce

• • •

Sliced Smoked Barbecued Brisket of Beef
Barbecued Pork Rib
Sliced Country Ham
Barbecued Chicken Drumstick
Served to guests on a plate, with plate cover,
with a colorful napkin,
from cabinets disguised as buckboards

On each table, family-style, we will serve
Homemade Ranch Slaw
Barbecue Sauce
Fresh Lemonade
Fresh Fruit Presentation

Passed by Cowgirls from Large Baskets
Prepacked Cold Apple Pie Sliced

• • •

Coffee, Tea, Iced Tea, Milk

Decorations: All tables will be covered in terra-cotta skirts with blue denim overlays. Napkins will be multicolored bandannas. Chuckwagon facades to be constructed to conceal heated carts, which will hold the preplated food.

On each table will be a centerpiece of lasso, cactus, cowboy hat, and other western artifacts.

Various props to be placed about the room, such as bales of straw, split rail fence, wagon wheels, and large plywood cactus.

Waiters to wear western attire, bandannas and western hats.

Music: Western band to provide appropriate music.

The Salad Medley Buffet Luncheon

Hearty Minestrone with Parmesan Cheese
or
Spicy Gazpacho, on Ice

• • •

Chunky Pecan Chicken Salad,
with Seedless White Grapes and Pecans
California Bay Shrimp Salad with Scallions
Fusilli Pasta Salad
Tabbouleh Salad,
with Tomato, Onion, and Mint
Our Garden Salad
(choose three salads)

• • •

Baskets of Pumpernickel, Pita, and
Sliced French Bread

• • •

Swiss Carrot Cake
Chocolate Brownie Chantilly
Chocolate Mousse

• • •

Beverage

The Men Do Eat Quiche Buffet Luncheon

From an Attractive Buffet Table(s):
Assorted Cold Salads
Fresh Sliced Fruits

• • •

Four Types of Quiche to consist of:
Spinach
Mushroom
Lorraine
Walnut

• • •

Oriental Stir-Fry Vegetables
Broccoli Szechuan
Fried Rice

• • •

Sourdough Breads

• • •

Orange Ice, Served at the Buffet
with Mandarin Orange Sections
Almond Cookies
Ghiradelli Cookies

• • •

Beverages

The On the Lighter Side Buffet Luncheon

Assortment of Sandwiches:
Roast Beef, Ham and Cheese, Turkey,
Corned Beef, and Tuna Salad
Crunchy Relish Tray, Potato Chips,
Cole Slaw

• • •

Fudge Brownies

• • •

Beverage

The Eastern European Buffet Luncheon

Hungarian Beef Stroganoff
Polish Kielbasa
Buttered Noodles
Vegetables of Eastern Europe:
Carrots, Cabbage, Broccoli, Cauliflower
with Dill Sauce

• • •

Tossed Salad with Cherry Tomatoes
Russian Dressing

• • •

Cinnamon Apple Tarts (passed by Waiters)

• • •

Coffee, Tea, Sanka, or Milk

The Hawaiian Buffet Luncheon

Preset at Each Place Setting
Tossed Green Salad with Spinach,
Grapefruit Sections, Pineapple Chunks,
Chopped Nuts, Coconut Dressing

• • •

From Buffet Tables
Chicken Pieces, Hawaiian Baked Ham with
Ginger Sauce
Steamed White Rice
Oriental Vegetables
(Broccoli, Onion, Mushrooms, Snow Peas,
Bean Sprouts, Soy)

• • •

Mandarin Orange Cake (Passed by Waiters)

• • •

Coffee, Tea, Sanka, or Milk

The America the Bountiful Buffet Luncheon

From a unique buffet table, we will provide a
venison display with the following additional
items:

• • •

Cold Meats and Garnish

• • •

Pâté en Croûte
Mixed Green Salad,
prepared with Spinach and Romaine Lettuce,
Vegetable Garni,
Americus Dressing, Vinegar Dressing,
and French Dressing

• • •

Cheese Display with Garnish of Fruit Boat

• • •

Yellow Squash Pudding
Parsley Roasted Potatoes
Stuffed Tomato Victory

• • •

Sweet Breads and Pastry Shells

• • •

Breast of Duckling, with Honey-Almond
Sauce

• • •

Pâté Filet Rosine

• • •

Seafood Salad, Shrimp Salad, Marinated
Herring, Cucumber Salad, Crab Claws,
Smoked Salmon, Smoked Oysters, Smoked
Clams served in Scallop Shells with Garnishes

• • •

From a Separate Station We Will Serve
A beautifully created Centerpiece on a
Raised Pedestal
Fresh Raspberries with Sauce Zabaglione

From a Display of Fresh Apples
Home Baked Apple Strudel, French Pastries
and Fruit Tarts, Fancy Cookies, and Pralines
and additional specialties as designed by
Pastry Chef

• • •

Coffee

The Ho-Hum, Humdrum Soup and Salad Buffet Luncheon

(See Photo on Page 68)

From attractively decorated buffet stations, we will serve the following:

Station No. 1   International Salad Bar
(One Buffet with two lines)
(All served from large loaves of hollowed-out bread)
Tabbouleh Salad, Pasta Salad, Cold Beef Salad, Salmon Salad, Greek Salad, Oriental Salad

Station No. 2   Soup Bar
(One Buffet with two lines)
Conch Chowder
Old-Fashioned Vegetable Soup

Station No. 3   Dessert Station
Strawberries, Blueberries, and Kiwi with a Dash of Liqueur, topped with Whipped Cream,
served in a Giant Martini Glass
• • •
Coffee, Tea, Decaffeinated Coffee
Assorted Soft Drinks, including Diet

The Backyard Cookout Buffet Luncheon

Taco Salad
Hot Potato Salad
Colorful Tray of Iced Relishes and Fresh Vegetables
• • •
Mesquite-Broiled Hot Dogs, Bratwurst, Hamburgers, Cheeseburgers
Assorted Buns and Condiments
• • •
Fresh Sliced Fruit
Warm Cherry Turnovers
• • •
Beverages

The Tex-Mex Buffet Luncheon

From separate buffet lines we will serve:
Barbecued Sliced Beef
Southern Fried Chicken
Spanish Rice
Mexican-Style Corn
• • •
Tossed Salad with
Tomato Slices and Onions
Salsa and Guacamole Dressing
• • •
Flan Tarts (passed by waiters)
• • •
Coffee, Tea, Sanka, or Milk

The Caribbean Buffet Luncheon

Chilled Cream of Avocado Soup with Diced Tomato and Curry
or
Caribbean Fish Chowder
• • •

Tropical Fruit Display
Mangoes, Papayas, Pineapple, Bananas, Kumquats, Kiwi, and Orange on a Bed of Banana Leaves and laced with Shredded Coconut,
Yogurt Dips to be served from Half Coconuts
• • •

Platters of Tropical Salads
Hearts of Palm, Conch Meat Salad,
Shrimp and Bean Sprout Salad marinated in Ginger
• • •

From Silver Chafing Dishes:
Grilled Fish Kabob Antigua with Green Pepper and Sweet Onions
Jamaican Style BBQ Chicken
Baby Back Ribs
Fried Plantains
Sautéed Jardiniere of Native Squash
Pineapple Rice
• • •
Platters of Banana Bread, Corn Bread, Crusty French Bread
• • •
Coconut Cream Pie, Puerto Rican Caramel Flan
Jamaican Allspice Cake, Whipped Cream
Pineapple Mousse Topped with Shaved Chocolate
• • •
Blue Mountain Coffee, Herbal Teas

Chapter 18

Dinner Entrées

Chicken Dinners

Breast of Chicken Madeira: Chicken breast in Madeira wine with cinnamon, apple, and almond stuffing.

Breast of Chicken Eugenie: Chicken breast served on ham slice with cognac sauce.

Chicken Véronique: Boneless chicken breast sautéed in a white wine sauce with seedless grapes and rice pilaf.

Breast of Chicken Cordon Blue: Chicken Cordon Blue with Sauce Madeira.

Breast of Chicken Wellington, en Croûte: Breast of chicken Wellington in puff pastry with a duxelle of mushrooms, and a soubise of onions, Sauce Périgourdine.

Dragon Silk Chicken: Strips of chicken breasts, cooked with oriental vegetables.

Suprême of Chicken Venetian: Chicken filled with prosciutto and sun-dried tomatoes, served with four cheese cream sauce.

Suprême of Chicken Printaniere: Chicken with a julienne of vegetables and a natural tomato coulis.

Suprême of Chicken Oscar: Chicken with crabmeat and asparagus tips, topped with Hollandaise Sauce.

Suprême of Chicken Dijonnaise: Chicken sautéed and served with an herbed mustard sauce, flavored with Fumé Blanc wine.

Medallions of Chicken #1: Medallions of chicken served with mushroom sauce.

Medallions of Chicken #2: Medallions of chicken served with wild mushroom sauce.

Paillard of Chicken: Thinly pounded chicken with red and black currants and peppercorn sauce.

Piccata of Chicken: Thin chicken cutlets in walnut apple cream sauce.

Breast of Chicken: Breast of chicken with shiitake mushroom and spinach puree in filo, basil sauce.

Breast of Chicken au Champagne: Breast of chicken sautéed golden brown, with almonds, champagne sauce.

Chicken à la Kiev, Sauce Suprême: Chicken stuffed with garlic butter and fine herbs.

Boneless Breast of Chicken: Boneless breast of chicken stuffed with oysters and nut dressing, mango sauce.

Breast of Chicken Portuguese: Breast of chicken sautéed in olive oil with onion and sliced mushrooms, garnished with tomato filled with rice and a fresh vegetable jardiniere.

Breast of Chicken Nancy: Breast of chicken served with sauce of apples, cinnamon, raisins, and chopped almonds.

Breast of Chicken Bourguignonne: Boneless breast of chicken with a Bordelaise Sauce, bacon bits, and onions.

Boneless Breast of Chicken Waldostana: Boneless breast of chicken with sautéed cucumbers and mushrooms.

Chicken Breast Bressane: Boneless chicken breast filled with crabmeat and topped with tarragon sauce on a bed of spinach.

Coq au Vin de Chambertin: Disjointed chicken sautéed with red wine, mushrooms, and pearl onions, with continental rice pilaf.

Breast of Chicken Sauté Amandine: Breast of chicken sautéed with almonds served with Sauce Périgueux.

Chicken Dinners (continued)

Breast of Chicken Madagascar: Double breast of chicken, stuffed with spinach, tarragon, and pine nuts, simmered in a brandied green peppercorn sauce.

Breast of Chicken Forestiere: Tender chicken breast sautéed in wine, tomato, and mushroom sauce.

Suprême of Chicken Nouvelle: Chicken stuffed with mixed and wild rice and served with raspberry kiwi sauce.

Medallions of Chicken #3: Served with a three-mushroom sauce of Morels, chanterelles, and cèpes.

Chicken Cashew: Chicken breast sautéed in butter, accented with lemon and orange zests, cashews, and pea pods.

Chicken Souvaroff: Chicken with Sauce Madeira and ham, mushrooms, and truffles.

Suprême of Capon with Asparagus Mousse: Breast of capon covered with asparagus mousse, baked golden brown.

Double Breast of Chicken Normande: Double breast of chicken filled with sliced apples, calvados sauce.

Chicken Breast Marsala: Chicken breast in a Marsala wine sauce.

Breast of Chicken, Hungarian Style: Breast of chicken sautéed and served in paprika cream sauce with julienne of ham.

Double Breast of Chicken à la Forestiere: Double breast of chicken served with mushrooms.

Coq au Vin: Quartered chicken in red wine sauce, served with patma rice.

Breast of Chicken Elvira: Breast of chicken with Sauce Suprême and toasted almonds.

Breast of Chicken, Las Vegas: Breast of chicken with whiskey sauce and wrapped in bacon, served with wild rice mix.

Double Boned Breast of Capon, Sauce Bigarade: Breast of capon flavored with orange, lemon, and Grand Marnier served with Rice Valencia.

Breast of Capon, Sauce Cacciatore: Breast of capon topped with tomato sauce and parmesan cheese.

Chicken à la Grecque: Roasted chicken breast with lemon juice and oregano.

Roast Half Chicken Diavoco: Half chicken roasted with lemon juice and peppercorns.

Turkey Dinners

Roast Young Vermont Turkey: Roast young turkey with chestnut stuffing and pan gravy.

Roast Breast of Turkey: Roast turkey breast stuffed with sautéed spinach leaves, cheddar cheese, fine herbs, and pinenuts.

Poulet Piccata: Tenderloin of turkey, pounded thin and sautéed in lemon butter.

Roast Turkey and Dressing: Roast turkey stuffed with sage and onion dressing, served with cranberry sauce.

Boneless Breast of Turkey Marsala: Boneless turkey breast in a Marsala wine sauce.

Duck Dinners

Roast Long Island Duckling, Bigarade: Roast duckling flavored with orange, lemon, and Grand Marnier served with Minnesota herbed wild rice.

Boneless Breast of Duckling: Boneless breast of duckling in thyme, honey, and almond sauce, served with wild rice and papaya.

Duck in Cassis Vinegar Sauce: Duck in cassis vinegar sauce served with pear potatoes.

Half Boneless Roast Duck à l'Orange: Roast duck laced with orange sauce.

American Duckling with Glazed Apples: Duckling with glazed apples served with Minnesota wild rice.

Duck au Poivre: Half of a duck, with a spicy pepper sauce.

Roast Duckling Angelique: Duckling served with apricot sauce, flavored with cinnamon and apricot brandy.

Other Fowl Dinners

Rock Cornish Game Hen: Rock Cornish game hen stuffed with Wild Rice, Natural Sauce.

Boneless Rock Cornish Game Hens: Boneless Rock Cornish game hens served with long grain and wild rice.

Roast Stuffed Cornish Game Hen Forestiere: Stuffed Cornish game hen with wild rice filling and mushroom sauce.

Quail Stuffed with Goose Liver: Quail stuffed with goose liver served with truffle sauce.

Beef Dinners

Filet Mignon au Champignon: Filet mignon and mushrooms with Sauce Périgourdine.

Sliced Roast Tenderloin of Beef: Roast beef tenderloin with Sauce Bordelaise.

Tournedos of Beef, Rossini: Twin filets mignons, topped with pâté de foie gras, truffles, and laced with classical Madeira Sauce.

Whole Fillet of Beef Wellington, Périgourdine: Fillet of beef baked in pastry crust with pâté de foie gras, carved tableside.

Sliced Roast Top Sirloin of Beef (Maximum 250 guests): Roast top sirloin of beef with Sauce Bordelaise.

Roasted Prime Rib of Beef au Jus: Prime rib au jus served with horseradish cream, passed.

Ember Broiled New York Cut Strip Sirloin Steak: Broiled strip sirloin steak with sliced mushrooms, Sauce Forestiere.

Delmonico Steak, Maître d'Hôtel: Delmonico steak with Colbert Butter.

Grilled Filet Mignon: Grilled filet mignon with Sauce Béarnaise.

Roast Sliced Fillet of Beef: Sliced fillet of beef with Sauce Bordelaise.

Broiled Prime New York Sirloin Steak: Broiled sirloin steak with Colbert Butter.

Roast Rib of Western Beef au Jus: Roast rib of beef au jus served with Yorkshire popover.

Prime Roast Sirloin of Beef: Roast sirloin of beef with Sauce Madeira.

Tournedos Eugene: Tournedos sautéed in butter, garnished with Sauce Choron and chanterelle mushrooms.

Fillet of Beef, Pipérade: Fillet of beef with sweet peppers, served with Sauce Béarnaise.

Tournedos of Beef, Niçoise: Beef tournedos Niçoise with tomato demi-glace.

Filet Mignon au Champignon: Filet mignon and mushrooms with Sauce Madeira.

Tournedos of Beef Orlean: Beef tournedos with deviled crab.

Fillet of Beef, Sauce Lemon Sorrel: Beef fillet in lemon sorrel sauce with rose peppercorns.

Tournedos of Beef au Duxelle: Beef tournedos au duxelle with Sauce Béarnaise.

Sliced Tenderloin of Beef: Beef tenderloin with Sauce Curranaisse.

Sliced Tenderloin of Beef: Beef tenderloin with two-peppercorn sauce, a full bodied red wine sauce, with green and black peppercorns.

Sliced Roast Tenderloin: Roast tenderloin with Sauce Périgourdine, a classical sauce with truffles and Madeira wine.

Broiled New York Steak: Broiled New York steak with alpine herbed butter sauce.

Roast Tenderloin of Beef: Roast tenderloin of beef with Cabernet and mushroom sauce.

Escalope of Beef: Thinly sliced beef with stilton port wine sauce and pinenuts.

Roast Sirloin of Beef: Roast sirloin of beef with tarragon Meaux mustard sauce.

Beef Dinners (continued)

Roastbraten Count Esterhazy: Lightly grilled and braised sirloin steak in a rich sauce with celery-carrot julienne, onions and peppers, sour cream, laced with white wine.

English Roast Sirloin, Marchand de Vin: Sliced New York strip steak with red wine sauce.

Broiled New York Sirloin Steak Creole: Broiled sirloin steak covered with stewed peppers, onions, and sliced mushrooms.

Steak au Poivre: New York cut sirloin steak with cracked peppercorns and seasoned steak butter.

Larded Sirloin of Beef: Larded beef sirloin with Sauce Bordelaise.

Filet de Boeuf: Fillet of beef with Sauce Périgueux.

Prime Sliced Sirloin Tips: Prime sliced sirloin tips with Sauce Bordelaise.

Broiled Rib Eye Steak: Broiled rib eye steak with Maître d'Hôtel Butter.

Brisket of Beef Jardiniere: Tender beef with julienne of vegetables.

Swiss Steak: Tender braised beef, served with brown sauce with vegetable jardiniere.

Tournedos Douey: Tournedo medallion with deviled crabmeat and Sauce Béarnaise, along with a tournedo medallion with mushroom cap and Sauce Bordelaise.

Teriyaki Steak: Rib eye steak marinated in a teriyaki sauce and grilled.

Sirloin Steak: Sirloin steak with a sauce of green peppercorns, cognac, and cream.

Salisbury Steak Forestiere: Chopped sirloin steak with mushroom sauce.

Sliced Braised Beef Bourguignonne: Braised beef cooked in red wine with mushrooms.

Sliced Tenderloin of Beef: Sliced tenderloin of beef with fresh Madagascar pepper sauce.

Veal Dinners

Medallions of Veal, Marsala: Veal medallions in Marsala wine sauce with sliced mushrooms.

Veal Piccata, Lemon Sauce: Veal cutlets dipped in egg, sautéed to golden brown.

Roast Loin of Mature Veal: Roast loin of veal with fresh mushrooms, sherry sauce.

Medallions of Veal with Chanterelles: Veal medallions with mushrooms and sherry sauce.

Veal Nordic: Loin of veal stuffed with crab mousse.

Sliced Loin of Veal: Sliced loin of veal with lemon butter sauce.

Veal Loin Chop: Veal loin chop with a sauce of veal quenelles and kidneys with Madeira.

Medallions of Veal #1: Veal medallions with Sauce Morille.

Veal Chop aux Morilles: Veal chop with Sauce Morille.

Veal Wellington: Veal wrapped in mushroom puree and baked in fluffy puff pastry.

Roast Loin of Veal: Roast loin of veal with morel mushroom sauce.

Medallions of Veal Calvados: Veal medallions with thinly sliced apples and a light apple brandy cream sauce.

Veal Loin Steak: Veal loin steak with lemon-sage sauce.

Medallions of Veal #2: Veal medallions with artichoke and ginger sauce.

Piccata of Veal: Veal cutlets with terrine of wild mushrooms and basil-mustard sauce.

Medallions of Veal #3: Veal medallions stuffed with chicken and goose liver forcemeat, wrapped in leek, served with morel cream sauce.

Veal Medallions Normande: Sautéed veal medallions laced with a cream sauce, flavored with calvados and apple puree.

Veal Medallions à la Chasseur: Veal medallions laced with a classical Madeira Sauce, served alongside an artichoke bottom with goose liver pâté.

Escalope of Veal Parmigiana: Thinly sliced veal breaded, pan fried in butter, topped with stewed tomatoes, and glazed with mozzarella cheese.

Veal Louisianne: Tender veal loin sautéed in butter and smothered in a light white wine sauce, with pieces of lobster and crab.

Veal Crustacean: Sautéed veal loin served in a delicate cream sauce of mushrooms and green onions, garnished with shrimp.

Veal Cutlet Milanese: Veal cutlet with tomato sauce.

Veal Chop Oscar: Veal chop with deviled crabmeat, asparagus spears, and Sauce Béarnaise.

Rack of Veal: Rack of veal stuffed with seafood.

Veal Chasseur: Medallions of veal with Sauce Chasseur.

Roast Leg of Veal Forestiere: Escalope of veal tarragon, served with tarragon sauce and mixed wild rice with pinenuts.

Veal San Remo: Veal scallopine with prosciutto, asparagus, Gruyère cheese, and Sauce Marsala.

Pork Dinners

Medallions of Pork Hongroise: Pork medallions in light paprika sauce.

Roast Pork Loin: Sliced pork loin, served with apple and herb dressing.

Broiled Pork Chop.

Roast Loin of Fresh Pork: Roast pork loin with Cider Sauce.

Emince of Pork Loin Zurichoise: Sliced pork loin sautéed in sherry-flavored cream mushroom sauce.

Grilled Pork Tenderloin with Fruit Chutney: Pork tenderloin, marinated in seasoned oil and vinegar, grilled, then sliced and served with special fruit chutney sauce.

Gingered Pork Tenderloin Salad: Thinly sliced pork tenderloin, marinated in ginger, cilantro, Teriyaki, and pepper, then tossed with potatoes, artichokes, and onions in special dressing.

Jamaican Pork Tenderloin: Pork tenderloin, marinated in coconut milk and vegetables, then roasted, sliced, and napped with boiled sauce.

Tomato-Basil Pork Scaloppine: Pork tenderloin medallions, gently flattened and sautéed with shallots and garlic, then simmered in seasoning and served over rice or linguine.

Herbed Pork Chops Trattoria: Boneless pork loin chops, coated with herbs and olive oil, then browned over medium-high heat, and finished over low heat.

Lamb Dinners

Rack of Lamb, Polaise: Roast rack of lamb served with a minted Hollandaise Sauce.

Roast Rack of American Lamb: Roast rack of American lamb with natural sauce.

Fillet of Lamb Tenderloin: Fillet of lamb tenderloin with mint demi-glace.

Roast Rack of Lamb: Roast rack of lamb served with gratin of eggplant and a mint and green peppercorn sauce.

Rack of Lamb: Rack of lamb with wild mushroom and spinach puree in filo, tarragon Madeira sauce.

Rack of Lamb Dijonnaise: Roast rack of lamb with Dijon mustard mayonnaise sauce.

Medallions of Lamb Provençale: Boneless lamb loin sautéed, laced with diced tomatoes, fine herbs, cognac, and a light touch of garlic.

Twin Lamb Chops: Twin lamb chops with mint sauce.

Rack of Lamb Moutarde: Lamb rack seasoned with rosemary, thyme, and basil, accented with Dijon mustard.

Loin of Lamb en Croûte: Loin of lamb wrapped in spinach and baked in pastry crust, served with tarragon sauce.

Roast Leg of Spring Lamb Rosemarien: Roast leg of spring lamb with rosemary, served with mint jelly.

Seafood/Fish Dinners

Broiled Red Snapper: Broiled red snapper with fresh mushrooms, shallots, and white wine.

Fillet of Fresh Florida Sea Trout Sauté, Amandine: Fillet of sea trout sautéed with almonds.

Fillet of Sole, Shrimp Sauce: Fillet of sole with shrimp sauce.

Lobster Thermidor, in Season: Whole lobster presented in shell with a French mustard sauce au gratin.

Red Snapper Meunière: Red snapper cooked in butter, lemon, and parsley.

Poached Fresh Florida Grouper, Dugléré: Poached grouper glazed with a sauce of plum tomatoes, fine herbs, and cream.

Poached Salmon: Poached salmon with cider and leek sauce.

Suprême of Red Snapper: Red snapper braised in red wine and sun-dried tomato sauce.

Trio of Salmon, Scallops, and Shrimp: Salmon, scallops, and shrimp with mushroom duxelles in filo with a coulis of corn and chives.

Imported Cold Water Twin Lobster Tails: Imported lobster tails with lemon butter.

Poached Salmon Fillet Montpelliere: Poached salmon fillet with a white wine sauce enhanced with fine herbs.

Sautéed Fresh Fillet of Sole Française: Fillet of sole dipped in eggs, then sautéed with sweet butter, white wine, and lemon juice.

Salmon en Croûte, Sauce Mousseline: Fresh baked Kodiak salmon filled with spinach and fine herbs, wrapped in puff pastry.

Broiled Fresh Fillet of Florida Pompano, Amandine: Broiled fillet of pompano cooked with almonds.

Stuffed Lobster Tail: Succulent and tender lobster tail, stuffed with crabmeat.

Grilled Salmon Steak: Thick salmon steak with lemon-dill butter.

Flounder Stuffed with Crabmeat: Flounder stuffed with crabmeat served with Sauce Chablis.

Fillet of Sole Bonne Femme: Fillet of sole poached and served with a white wine sauce.

Baked Red Snapper: Baked red snapper with citrus butter and slivered almonds.

Paupiettes of Fillet of Sole: Rolled fillet of sole filled with crabmeat and topped with Sauce Mornay.

Baked Redfish: Baked redfish with creole sauce.

Seafood Brochette: Seafood brochette with light lobster sauce.

Poached Salmon with Leeks and Tomatoes: Poached salmon with leeks and tomatoes served with Fumé Blanc wine sauce.

Salmon Florentine: Fillet of salmon, stuffed with fresh sautéed spinach and topped with a Lime Hollandaise Sauce.

Fillet of Swordfish: Fillet of swordfish topped with almonds, served with dill sauce.

Fillet of Sole Donizetti: Fillet of sole served with mussels, olives, mushrooms, and capers, covered with white wine sauce.

Barbecued Salmon en Croûte: Barbecued salmon in puff pastry with sorrel sauce.

Poached Darne of Salmon: Poached darne of salmon with Sauce Mousseline.

Duo Entrée Dinners

Fillet of Beef and Scampi: Beef tenderloin steak with wine-laced mushrooms over an almond eggplant crouton, served with Sauce Béarnaise, passed, and four jumbo crabmeat-stuffed shrimp, cooked in Scampi Butter.

Filet Mignon and Lobster Tail: Full lobster tail served with drawn butter and a petite fillet of beef.

Breast of Quail and Petite Fillet of Beef: Breast of quail and petite fillet of beef garnished with pâté de foie gras, whole pear with guava jelly, and cinnamon stick.

Filet Mignon and Shrimp: Petite filet mignon and four broiled jumbo shrimp.

Filet Mignon and Duck: Quartered duckling and petite filet mignon, served with green peppercorn sauce.

Beef and Veal Medallions: Loin cuts of tender veal and beef perched atop vegetable croutons and served with Sauce Verte.

Chicken and Scallops: Breast of chicken accompanied by large tender scallops laced with a creamed wine sauce.

London Mixed Grill: Tender medallions of beef, veal, and lamb, served with Choron Sauce.

Tournedos Key West: Twin medallions of beef tenderloin garnished with baby lobster tails, served with Sauce Béarnaise.

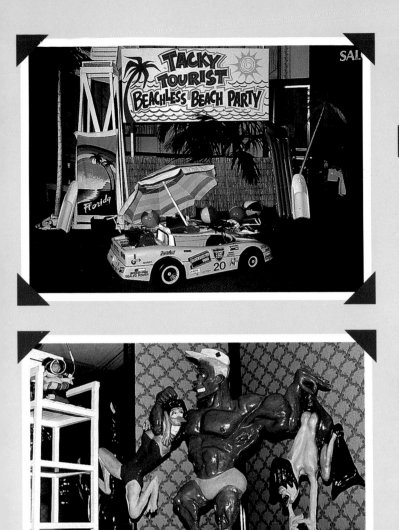

This unique thematic experience, created and designed by the author, is called "The Original Florida Wacky Tacky Tourist Beachless Beach Party." *Tiffany Photo.*

To ensure that this party reaches the ultimate level of tackiness, Vern Applebee (aka G. Eugene Wigger) from Union City, Indiana, along with his family, greets the guests upon arrival. *Tiffany Photo.*

This prop is called "Two Lives Are Worth Saving"—a 6-foot tall, well-developed lifeguard holding two nearly drowned kids. *Tiffany Photo.*

The success of the Tacky Tourist Party is assured by the staff involvement as the Applebee cousins, Buddy Brew, Mortimer Toopes, Stan Stud, Bonni Body, Harry Hannibacker, and Mrs. Mary Ethel Applebee. *Tiffany Photo.*

Help Me, Honda—on your mark, get set, go…around the road cones on your brand new Honda Tricycle. *Tiffany Photo.*

Here is the Tacky Strip Bed and Breakfast Inn, which will give you the kind of care you thought only your Mommy could provide! *Tiffany Photo.*

Letting guests pose with a baby alligator and giving them the picture will ensure that they will relive the experience and share it. *Tiffany Photo.*

Poindexter Nerdbaum, the Professor of Zoology and Botany (aka G. Eugene Wigger), doing the "Monster Mash" at the Fabulous 50's Hop. *Tiffany Photo.*

Memories of the Senior Class Sock Hop come alive tonight …when cool meant hot, hot meant stolen, and pimples were the end of the world. *Tiffany Photo.*

After the "Bunny Hop," "Stroll" on over to the Sweet Shoppe Soda Parlor for a soda or an ice cream sundae with the works. *Tiffany Photo.*

Pick a stool at Hamburger Haven for an A&W Root Beer Float and a burger with everything except onions. *Tiffany Photo.*

Under the large revolving pizza at Paisano's Pizzeria, grab a true slice or two of life and a "warm" coke. *Tiffany Photo.*

Teen Idol Poindexter Nerdbaum (aka G. Eugene Wigger) will capture your imagination and your heart with his portrayal of a "Teenager In Love." *Tiffany Photo.*

Elvis and Poin were close friends, so you won't want to miss his "Tribute to the King of Rock and Roll." *Tiffany Photo.*

Fiesta in any language means hearty merriment, and that's what you'll find inside the Mexican Cantina. *Tiffany Photo.*

Banquet staff in Mexican sombrero and attire will prove…when you're hot, you're hot! *Tiffany Photo.*

A resonant, ceremonial gong announces your arrival into the Far East, at Le Pavilion Chinoise, where the basic purity of the Orient creates food that stands apart from any other in the world. *Tiffany Photo.*

Mel Krumblum (aka G. Eugene Wigger), the proprietor of the Best of the Wurst Delicatessen, will appear with his rude, overbearing, and crude staff. *Tiffany Photo.*

The mission of every catering executive should be to perfect the art of the special event—from tabletop napery to decor. Hospitality expert G. Eugene Wigger (right) set the standard here with his dining experience, "Celebration." On the left is Banquet Maitre D' Bill Vaccaro. *Tiffany Photo.*

Enjoy Italy's old-world charm and passionate delights in front of the Ponte di Rialto Bridge, as gastronomical pleasures transport you to a land where every season speaks of romance. *Tiffany Photo.*

Stroll down the main street of of a 100-year-old western town and lasso the zest of the west in a wonderful array of tastes and aromas. Polish your boots and bring a ten-gallon-size appetite. *Tiffany Photo.*

Lone Star Chili Willi (aka G. Eugene Wigger) greets the guests as they arrive to the Texascapes special event. Here he bags a skunk for his Chili. How about a "special bowl of red?" Just hold your nose! *Tiffany Photo.*

This frightening glimpse of terror is a glimpse of a thematic meeting break called "Death of a Salesman—A 'Thriller' Break." A unique attraction is a walking gravedigger carrying a coffin with the top open to reveal a live Count Dracula (aka G. Eugene Wigger). *Joe Saget Photo.*

The business world… what a competitive jungle…in our "It's a Jungle Out There" meeting break. Among the animals is a walking gorilla carrying a steel cage with your live safari guide (aka G. Eugene Wigger) inside. *Joe Saget Photo.*

"The Temptin' Temptations Break" creates a chocoholic hell that will entice you with the sinfully rich and so chocolaty delicacies. The devil with sinning no more! *Joe Saget Photo.*

Now this may not be for every group, but if you're looking for a lot of laughs…"The Florida Wacky Tacky Tourist Break" is the meeting break for you. We dare you to try this one! *Joe Saget Photo.*

"The Sports Penalty Break" will prove you don't have to be a Wimbledon Tennis Champion or a Boston Marathoner to enjoy the benefits of maximum performance. That's Petie Pipsqueak, Mr. Florida (aka G. Eugene Wigger), who will usher the sports fans into the locker room for some "Thirst-Aid"! *Joe Saget Photo.*

"The Business-Robics for Health's Sake" Break will change your attitude toward food. This change can be linked to a new awareness among Americans about health. *Joe Saget Photo.*

The sun's out, surf's up, and you're set for that legendary "Beachless Beach Break." Eat your heart out, Frankie and Annette! *Joe Saget Photo.*

We re-created the lobby of your favorite movie theater, with our realistically painted backdrop, for our "Give Me a Break Intermission Break." So step right up and place your order. *Joe Saget Photo.*

At the "Strawberry Smoothie Smooth Operator Break" you can present and serve a robustious, wholesome, and vigorous break. *Joe Saget Photo.*

This elegant meeting break is entitled "The Germany Symphony Maestro Musical Break" and presents the brilliant musical compositions of Ludwig van Beethoven. We are privileged to serve! *Joe Saget Photo.*

Chapter 19

Seated Dinner Menus

Chicken Seated Dinners

Chicken #1

Scallops in Champagne Sauce and Julienne of
Vegetables, served in Pastry Shell

• • •

Bibb Lettuce with Marinated Artichokes and
Mushrooms, Herbed Vinaigrette, passed and
served with a Chilled Fork

• • •

Freshly Baked Rolls, Salt Sticks, Lahvosh,
Creamery Butter

• • •

Cassis Sorbet

• • •

Chicken Wellington
Chicken Breast Garnished with Mushrooms
Duxelles and Individually Encrusted in Puff
Pastry with Sauce Périgourdine, passed
Bouquetiere of Fresh Garden Vegetables

• • •

Frozen Tropical Beach Island Rum Cake
Rum-soaked Chocolate Cake and Vanilla Ice
Cream, Dusted with Cocoa Powder,
Chocolate Rum Sauce passed

• • •

Petits Fours and After Dinner Mints
Presentation

• • •

Coffee, Tea, Decaffeinated Coffee

Chicken #2

Celebration Ring
A Fan of Pineapple, filled with Tropical
Fruit, a Hint of Galliano, and Coconut Flakes

• • •

Salad Copacabana
Heart of Boston Bibb, Garnished with a
Tomato Decoration, Eden Rock Dressing and
served with a Chilled Fork

• • •

Freshly Baked Rolls, Salt Sticks, Lahvosh,
Creamery Butter

• • •

Le Poulet Oscar
Boned Breast of Chicken, Crowned with
Asparagus, Crabmeat, and Sauce Béarnaise
Fondant Potatoes
Bouquetiere of Fresh Vegetables

• • •

Vacherin Glacé
Sponge Cake Base with Raspberry and
Vanilla Ice Cream, Meringue,
and Blueberry Melba Sauce

• • •

Petits Fours and After Dinner Mints
Presentation

• • •

Coffee, Tea, Decaffeinated Coffee

Chicken #3

Seafood Vol-au-Vents
Crab, Shrimp, and other Seafood Delicacies,
Complemented by a Light, Creamy Coconut Sauce,
Ladled over a Puff Pastry Shell

• • •

Caesar Salad, Tossed Tableside, served with a Chilled Fork

• • •

Freshly Baked Rolls, Salt Sticks, Lahvosh, Creamery Butter

• • •

Le Poulet avec Chanterelles
Boneless Chicken Breast, Sautéed and Laced with a Sauce of
Cream and Chanterelles
Pommes Berny
Bouquetiere de Légumes

• • •

The Ultimate Chocoholic Celebration
An Ice Cream Truffle, specially blended and flavored mound,
smothered with Bittersweet Chocolate and decorated with Milk
Chocolate drizzles, presented in a Chocolate-Edged Wafer
Basket and floating in a Lake of Sabayon, artfully decorated
with Individual Designs of Milk Chocolate Sauce

• • •

Petits Fours and After Dinner Mints Presentation

• • •

Coffee, Tea, Decaffeinated Coffee

Chicken #4

Pâté Maison en Croûte, Cumberland Sauce

• • •

Tossed Bibb and Romaine Lettuce, with Hearts of Palm and
Pimiento, Garlic Croutons, Creamy Dijon Dressing

• • •

Chicken Piccata, with Lemon Butter and Capers
Tomato Florentine
Timbale of Wild Rice

• • •

Basket of French Bread and Dinner Rolls

• • •

Classic Crème Caramel

• • •

Blended Coffee, Selection of Teas

Chicken #5

Reception

Pupus
Polynesian Spare Ribs

• • •

Jumbo Tempura Shrimp with Coconut-
Orange Marmalade Dipping Sauce

• • •

Assorted Rumakis:
Prunes Wrapped in Bacon
Pineapple Wrapped in Bacon
Chicken Liver and Water Chestnuts
Wrapped in Bacon

• • •

Beef and Pineapple Yakatori on
Bamboo Skewer

• • •

Islander Baked Clams

• • •

Dinner Menu
Essence of Mahi Mahi with Dumpling

• • •

Kahala Salad of Hearts of Palm,
with Walnut Vinaigrette Dressing

• • •

Chicken Momi
Boneless Breast of Chicken Baked and Served
in a Pineapple, Secret Stuffing, Glazed with
Honey and Sesame Seeds
Mandarin Vegetables
Orange and Almond Fried Rice

• • •

Mango–Macadamia Nut Coupe, Fortune
Cookies

• • •

Kona Coffee

Duck Seated Dinners

Duck #1

Chicken Consommé
with Julienne of Sorrel

• • •

Lobster Nantua St. Jacques

• • •

French Haricots Verts, White Asparagus, on
a Bed of Bibb Lettuce, Vinaigrette, served
with a Chilled Fork

• • •

Freshly Baked Rolls, Salt Sticks, Lahvosh,
Creamery Butter

• • •

Boneless Breast of Duckling, Thyme, Honey,
and Almond Sauce
Wild Rice with Papaya
Bouquetiere of Fresh Garden Vegetables

• • •

Brie Cheese with Fresh Apple Slices

• • •

Petits Fours and After Dinner Mints
Presentation

• • •

Coffee, Tea, Decaffeinated Coffee

Duck #2

Double Consommé
Cheese Straws

• • •

Half Florida Lobster and Sautéed Sea
Scallops, in Lemon-Lime Butter

• • •

Champagne Sorbet

• • •

Boneless Breast of Crisp Duck, Cassis Sauce
Timbale of White and Wild Rice
Julienne of Fresh Seasonal Vegetables
Rosette of Chestnut Puree

• • •

Endive Salad,
Artichoke Hearts and Pimiento,
Sauce Vinaigrette

• • •

Selected Dinner Rolls, Creamery Butter

• • •

Layered Strawberries and Cream,
in Puff Pastry

• • •

Coffee, Herbal Teas

Other Fowl Seated Dinners

Fowl #1

Chesapeake Bay Crab Bisque au Cognac

• • •

Citrus Sorbet

• • •

Canard Roti with Lingonberry Sauce
Wild Rice à la Maison, Snow Peas
Salsify au Beurre Noisette
Tomato Du Barry

• • •

Breast of Maryland Quail, placed alongside a salad consisting
of Selected Lettuce and Watercress,
Olive Oil and Wine Vinegar Dressing

• • •

Selection of Fine Cheeses

• • •

Vacherin Glacé, Fresh Raspberries

• • •

Demitasse

Fowl #2

Artichoke Neptune
Fresh Artichoke filled with Shrimp, Scallops, and Mushrooms,
in a Brandy Sauce
or

Coquilles St. Jacques
Scallops and Mushrooms, Baked with Wine Sauce
• • •
Consommé Profiterole
• • •
Whole Boned Rock Cornish Hen, filled with Brown and Wild
Rice, Sauce Bigarade
Carrots Julienne, Zucchini Sticks
Broccoli Flowerettes
• • •
Bibb Lettuce, Oil and Vinegar Dressing, Tossed in Room
• • •
Camembert and Pont l'Evêque with Fresh Fruit,
French Baguette
• • •
Chocolate Mousse
• • •
Petits Fours
• • •
Coffee

Fowl #3

Hawaiian Papaya with Melon Pearls,
Marinated in Port Wine
• • •
Cream of Almond Soup,
Garnished with Sliced Roasted Almonds
• • •
Kentucky Bibb Lettuce,
Croutons, Vinaigrette Dressing
• • •
Rock Cornish Hen, Filled with White and
Wild Rice, Apple-Plum Sauce
Artichoke Bottom, Carrot Mousse
Sugar Snap Pea Pods with Pimiento
• • •
Petite Rolls, Butter
• • •
Bananas Foster Flambé,
Over Vanilla Ice Cream
• • •
Blended Coffee, Selected Teas

Wild Boar Seated Dinner

Wild Boar #1

Consommé Beaumont
Quenelles of Calves Brain
• • •
Vol-au-Vent of Langoustine
• • •
Calvados
Rack and Saddle of Wild Boar,
Chef's Special Game Sauce
Braised Endive
Baked Apple with Lingonberries glazed with
Caramel Sugar
Timbale of Chanterelles
• • •
Leaves of Boston Lettuce, Oil and Lemon
Dressing, Cold Fillet of Beef Strasbourgoise,
with Foie Gras and Truffles
• • •

Special Cheese Board
Brie de Meaux, Greek Goat Cheese, French
Grape Cheese, Italian Bel Paese, German
Munster, Dutch Edam, and Danish Bleu
Separate Flag of each Country to appear on the
top of each cheese.
Selection of French and German Breads
Fresh Red, White, and Black Grapes
• • •

Tropical Delight
Whole Papaya scooped and filled with Fresh
Diced Pineapple and Papaya, Marinated in
Triple Sec, Topped with a Rosette of Lime
Sherbet and a Sprig of Mint (served very cold)
• • •
Croquembouche
• • •
Demitasse (Medaglia d'Oro)

Venison Seated Dinner

Venison #1

Puree of Artichoke Soup

• • •

Paupiettes of Boston Sole, Kennebec, with Mousse of Salmon, Fresh Dill Sauce

• • •

Lemon Champagne Sorbet

• • •

Saddle of Venison, Juniper Sauce, Garni with Orange Basket Filled with Lingonberries
Glazed Acorn Squash Rings, filled with Toasted Chestnuts

Pommes Macaire
Brussels Sprouts au Beurre

Selected Lettuces, Sliced Mushrooms and Radishes, Vinaigrette Dressing

• • •

Savarin Ring au Rhum, filled with Fresh Fruit Salad, Sauce Sabayon

Demitasse

Beef Seated Dinners

Beef #1

Chicken Consommé
with Profiteroles

• • •

Romaine and Bibb Lettuce,
Sliced Hearts of Palm, Julienne of Carrots,
Lemon Oil Dressing with Chopped Parsley,
served with a Chilled Fork

• • •

Freshly Baked Rolls, Salt Sticks, Lahvosh,
Creamery Butter

• • •

Tournedos of Beef Orlean
with New Orleans-Style Crab Cake
and Sauce Piquante
Bouquetiere of Fresh Garden Vegetables

• • •

Bel Paese Cheese,
Seasonal Fruit, and Sliced French Bread

• • •

Poached Pear Symphony, au Chocolat
Whole Pear Poached in Applejack Brandy
and Dipped in Chocolate, Floating in a Lake
of Zabaglione Sauce

• • •

Petits Fours and After Dinner Mints
Presentation

• • •

Coffee, Tea, Decaffeinated Coffee

Beef #2

Galantine of Duck, Sauce Cumberland,
accompanied by Salad Waldorf and served with Toast Points

• • •

Billi Bi Soup
White Clam Bisque, topped with Whipped Cream and Curry,
Garnished with a Live Fresh Flower

• • •

Darne de Salmon Alexander, Sauce Nantua

• • •

Freshly Baked Rolls, Salt Sticks, Lahvosh, Creamery Butter

• • •

Beef Tenderloin Dorsey
Stuffed with Pheasant and Truffles,
Sauce Périgourdine
Bouquetiere of Fresh Garden Vegetables

• • •

Salad Copacabana
Hearts of Boston Bibb, Decorated with a Tomato Garnish
Eden Rock Dressing, passed,
served with a Chilled Fork

• • •

Souffle Bombe Glacé au Citron

• • •

Petits Fours and After Dinner Mints Presentation

• • •

Coffee, Tea, Decaffeinated Coffee

Beef #3

Clam and Mussel Consommé with Julienne of Leeks,
served Tableside from a Gleaming Silver Tureen

• • •

Broiled Semi-Boneless Quail, Pomegranate Glaze

• • •

Quest for Excellence Salad
Fresh Mushrooms, Bay Shrimp, and a Symphony of Garden
Greens, Presented and then Tossed Tableside by Service Staff
and accompanied with a Casablanca Dressing, served with a
Chilled Fork

• • •

Freshly Baked Rolls, Salt Sticks, Lahvosh, Creamery Butter

• • •

Filet Mignon
Sauce Lemon Sorrel with Rose Peppercorns
Bouquetiere of Fresh Garden Vegetables

• • •

Pear Helena Bombe
Pear Ice with Poached Pears on a Slice of Chocolate Torte with
Shaved Milk Chocolate, Chocolate Sauce, passed

• • •

Petits Fours and After Dinner Mints Presentation

• • •

Coffee, Tea, Decaffeinated Coffee

Beef #5

Cold Smoked Duck Breast, Garni,
Served on a Bed of Spinach

• • •

Chicken and Leek Consommé
Julienne of Chicken and Leek, Garni,
Served from Gleaming Silver Tureens

• • •

Freshly Baked Rolls, Salt Sticks, Lahvosh,
Creamery Butter

• • •

Fillet Oscar
With Crab Claw, Sauce Béarnaise
Bouquetiere of Fresh Garden Vegetables

• • •

The Prince Pückler Bombe, on Parade
Chocolate Cake, Vanilla Ice Cream
and Coffee Ice Cream,
Kirschwasser-Flavored Chocolate Sauce,
Shaved Milk Chocolate Decoration

• • •

Petits Fours and After Dinner Mints
Presentation

• • •

Coffee, Tea, Decaffeinated Coffee

Beef #4

Cream of Scallion Soup
Julienne of Pea Pods

• • •

Green Tea Sorbet in Ice Socle

• • •

Roast Tenderloin of Beef Curranaisse
Mélange of Mushrooms
Asparagus
Potato Lourette
Tomato Victory

• • •

Bibb Lettuce Salad, with Citrus Sections
and Honey and Lime Dressing

• • •

Pear Bombe Litchi

• • •

Selection of Teas to include: Ginseng, Jasmine, Oolong
Kona Coffee

Beef #6

Chicken Consommé with Profiteroles

• • •

Oysters Mosca

• • •

Lemon Sorbet, Laced with Champagne

• • •

Tournedos of Beef Orlean, with Deviled Crab
Pommes Lorette
Fresh Broccoli au Beurre
Tomato Du Barry

• • •

Romaine and Bibb Lettuce, Sliced Hearts of
Palm, Julienne of Carrots, Lemon Oil
Dressing with Chopped Parsley

• • •

Bel Paese Cheese
Seasonal Fruit and French Bread

• • •

Gooseberry Bavarois

• • •

Demitasse

Beef #7

Veal Tortellini, with Julienne of Pea Pods
and Prosciutto

• • •

Four Seasons Salad
Radicchio, Belgian Endive, and Spinach,
Artfully Arranged and Garnished with
Artichoke Bottoms, Tomato Wedge,
Tossed with a Cognac Vinaigrette Dressing,
served with a Chilled Fork

• • •

Freshly Baked Rolls, Salt Sticks, Lahvosh,
Creamery Butter

• • •

Tournedos Café de Paris
Beef Tenderloin Medallions, sautéed with
Café de Paris Butter,
Crowned with Truffle Decoration
Pommes Duchesse
Bouquetiere de Légumes

• • •

Soufflé Glacé Grand Marnier

• • •

Petits Fours and After Dinner Mints
Presentation

• • •

Coffee, Tea, Decaffeinated Coffee

Beef #8

Salmon Mousse, St. Patrick

• • •

Cocky Leeky Soup
Chicken and Leek Soup

• • •

Filet Mignon, Sauce Piquant
Bubble and Squeak
Zucchini Boat filled with Carrot Pudding
Fresh Green Beans

• • •

Spinach and Romaine Lettuce, Dill Dressing,
Wedge of Brie

• • •

Irish Whiskey Soufflé Glacé,
Oatmeal and Shortbread Cookies,
Chocolate Whiskey Sauce

• • •

Irish Tea and Coffee

Beef #9

Bisque de Homard
Lobster Bisque, Laced with Cognac
and Served with a Touch of Black Caviar and Cream

• • •

Buena Vista Salad, Supreme
Fresh Romaine, Palm Hearts, Mushrooms, Cherry Tomatoes,
Artichoke Hearts, Sliced Olives, and Tiny Bay Shrimp with a
Creamy Garlic Dressing, served with a Chilled Fork

• • •

Freshly Baked Rolls, Salt Sticks, Lahvosh, Creamery Butter

• • •

Filet Mignon, Sauce au Poivre
Beef Tenderloin Broiled to Perfection,
and Caressed with Peppercorn Sauce
Turned Potatoes
Bouquetiere de Légumes

• • •

Swan Lake
Swan-Shaped Profiterole Glazed with White and Dark
Chocolate, Filled with Vanilla White Chocolate Chunk Ice
Cream, Floating on a Lake of Fresh Raspberry Sauce

• • •

Petits Fours and After Dinner Mints Presentation

• • •

Coffee, Tea, Decaffeinated Coffee

Beef #10

Braised Dutch Mushroom Broth

• • •

Bay Shrimps and Sliced Scallops Salad,
Avocado and Yogurt Dressing

• • •

Fillet of Beef Pipérade, Sauce Béarnaise
Oven Roasted Potatoes
Broccoli au Beurre
Carrots in Dill Sauce

• • •

Fried Almond Ice Cream Bombe,
Mandarin Liqueur Flambé

• • •

Demitasse

Beef #11

Fish Broth with Red Snapper and Sorrel

• • •

Vegetable Greek Salad
Romaine, Cucumber with Dill, Greek Olives,
Quality Feta Cheese, Tomato Wedges, Dolmas,
Broccoli Flowerettes, Cauliflower Buds,
with a Greek Olive Oil Dressing

• • •

Grilled Steak, Greek Style
Marinated and Grilled Fillet
with a Light Lemon Demi Butter Sauce

• • •

Greek Orzo (Pasta), with Tomato, Onion, and Lamb Cheese

Peas Palita
Diced Onions, Peas, with Dill, Olive Oil, and a Cream Sauce,
Stuffed in an Artichoke Heart
and Topped with Braised Shredded Carrots
Braised Celery with Egg Lemon Sauce
Stuffed Baby Eggplant
With Onion and Cheese with Breadcrumbs

• • •

Mixed Bread Basket, with Quartered Pita Bread, Citrus and
Raisin Bread and Hard Rolls and Butter

• • •

Baklava with Orange Sections and Kirsch

• • •

Coffee, Decaffeinated Coffee, Tea

Beef #12

Chicken Consommé with Profiterole

• • •

Russian Salad with Lobster

• • •

Individual Fillet of Beef Wellington,
Sauce Périgourdine, Baked in Pastry Crust with Duxelles
Pommes Parisienne
Tomato Salsify
Green Beans wrapped with Bacon

• • •

Petite Rolls and Butter

• • •

Vanilla Ring Savarin, with Brandied Peaches, Flambé

• • •

Coffee

Beef #13

Essence of Wild Mushrooms
Julienne of Crêpe

• • •

Poached Fillet of Coho Salmon,
Two Caviars, Golden Fleuron

• • •

Green Apple Sorbet, Served in a hollowed
Apple, set on a bed of fresh leaves

• • •

Individual Beef Wellington,
Périgourdine Sauce
Sautéed Baby Vegetables, with Pimiento

• • •

Cheshire and Stilton Cheeses, with Carrs
Water Crackers and Toasted French Bread

• • •

Glass of Port Wine

• • •

Poached Pear Fan, on a bed of Raspberry
Coulis, Boulette of Almond Ice Cream, with
crystallized Violets

• • •

Chocolate-Dipped Fruits, Assorted Nuts

• • •

Coffee

Beef #14

Island Papaya and Italian Prosciutto

• • •

Bouchée of Baby Shrimp and Scallops,
In a Light Curry Sauce

• • •

Key Lime Sorbet

• • •

Sliced Roast Tenderloin of Beef,
Sauce Périgourdine or au Poivre
Bouquetiere of Fresh Vegetables
Small Roasted Potatoes

• • •

Limestone Lettuce and Radicchio, with
Hearts of Palm, Raspberry Vinaigrette
French Rolls, Butter Rosettes, on Lemon
Leaves

• • •

Baked Alaska, Topped with Chocolate
Meringue, Sauce Anglaise

• • •

Colombian Coffee, Selected Teas

Beef #15

Smoked Trout with Fresh Horseradish
Dressing
or
Danish Lobster Tail, Stuffed with Lobster
Thermidor

• • •

Princess Salad
Julienne of Watermelon, Honeydew,
Cantaloupe, Turkey, and Egg, Presented on
Bibb Lettuce, Poppy Seed Dressing

• • •

Raspberry Sorbet

• • •

Sliced Tenderloin of Beef, Sauce Curranaisse
Squash stuffed with Puree of Carrot
Braised Celery Hearts
Poached Straw Mushrooms
Rolls and Fruit Breads
Butter

• • •

Chocolate and Orange Mousse
with Rum Raisins
or
Soufflé Glacé au Citron

• • •

Demitasse

Beef #16

Avocado and Crabmeat Salad,
Served en coquille, Sauce Louis

• • •

Native Lettuce with Belgian Endive and
Watercress, Pimiento garni, Basil Vinaigrette

• • •

Sautéed Filet Mignon, Imported Foie Gras,
Sauce Périgourdine
Bâtonnets of Carrot and Zucchini
Compote of Wild Mushrooms
Chateau Potatoes

• • •

Petit Pain
Butter

• • •

Double Chocolate Terrine, Bed of Sabayon,
Mandarin Chantilly

• • •

Blended Coffee, Imported Teas

Beef #17

Coquilles St. Jacques
Tender Scallops in a White Wine and
Mushroom Sauce, served in a natural shell

• • •

Bibb, Radicchio, and Endive, Hearts of Palm
and Pimiento, Hazelnut Dressing

• • •

Broiled Sirloin Steak
Sauce Choron
Bouquetiere of Vegetables

• • •

Dinner Rolls
Butter

• • •

Brandied Peaches over Almond Ice Cream
Raspberry Sabayon, Petits Fours

• • •

Blended Coffee and Imported Teas

Beef #18

Consommé Celestine,
Julienne of Crêpe

• • •

Warm Scallop Mousse,
Delicate Orange Butter

• • •

Finlandia Vodka Sorbet

• • •

Filet Boursin au Poivre
Tender Filet Mignon filled with Boursin
Cheese, Rolled in crushed Black Peppercorns,
Brandied Cream Sauce
Julienne of Fresh Vegetables
Almond Soufflé Potatoes

• • •

Watercress, Bibb, and Romaine,
Enoki Mushrooms, Vinaigrette

• • •

Dinner Rolls, Butter

• • •

Fresh Strawberries and Pineapple, Marinated
in Grand Marnier, over Vanilla Ice Cream,
Pirouette Cookie

• • •

Blended Coffee, Herbal Teas

Beef #19

Kiwi Fruit, Mélange

• • •

Double Strength Pheasant Consommé,
Quenelles of Pheasant

• • •

Vol-au-Vent of Fresh Lobster in
Sauce Americaine

• • •

Champagne Sorbet

• • •

Filet Mignon, Rossini
Braised Endive
Tomato with Fresh Mushrooms

• • •

Pommes Soufflés

• • •

Hearts of Boston Lettuce,
Vinaigrette Dressing
Soufflé Glacé Anisette
Pralines, Cookies
Presented in Chocolate Box

• • •

Demitasse

Beef #20

Cantaloupe Crown,
Filled with Tropical Fruits,
topped with Fresh Strawberry

• • •

Coral Key Snapper Chowder,
Sesame Thins

• • •

Spinach Salad Mimosa
Sliced Mushrooms and Shredded Eggs,
Warm Bacon Dressing

• • •

Roast Prime Rib of Beef,
Creamy Horseradish Sauce
Bouquetiere of Vegetables
Anna Potatoes

• • •

Assorted Dinner Rolls, Butter

• • •

Kahlua Ice Cream Cake
Mocha Cream and Candied Coffee Beans,
Hot Chocolate Sauce

• • •

Blended Coffee, Herbal Teas

Beef #21

Cold Smoked Trout, Garni, Served on a Bed
of Spinach, Sweet Mustard Sauce

• • •

Consommé of Chicken and Leek Soup,
Julienne of Chicken and Leek, Garni

• • •

Rye and Pumpernickel Rolls
Unwrapped Butter

• • •

Filet Mignon, Mushroom Cap, Garni,
Sauce Venison
Finely Chopped Red Cabbage served in
a Poached Apple
Spaetzle
Whole Green Beans wrapped with
Thinly Sliced Westphalian Ham

• • •

The Prince Puckler Bombe, on Parade
Chocolate Cake, Vanilla Ice Cream and
Coffee Ice Cream, Kirschwasser-Flavored
Chocolate Sauce
Milk Chocolate Decoration

• • •

Demitasse

Beef #22

Clam and Mussel Consommé
with Julienne of Leeks

• • •

Broiled Boneless Quail, Pomegranate Glaze

• • •

Fresh Mushrooms and Bay Shrimps, Sweet
and Sour, on a Bed of Bibb Lettuce

• • •

Fillet Steak, Lemon Sorrel Sauce with Rose
Peppercorns
Pommes Amandine
Flageolets Provençale and Artichoke Bottom
Stuffed Red Pepper Florentine

• • •

Pear Helena Bombe
Pear Ice with Poached Pears on a Slice
of Chocolate Torte with
Chocolate Sauce and Shaved Milk Chocolate

• • •

Demitasse

Beef #23

Coquilles St. Jacques
Scallops nestled in White Wine and
Cream Sauce
• • •

Romaine and Bibb Lettuce Salad
Garni of Sliced Mushrooms, Hearts of Palm,
Cherry Tomatoes, Vinaigrette Dressing
• • •

Tournedos of Beef au Duxelle
Sauce Béarnaise
Fresh Green Beans wrapped in Bacon
Tomato Du Barry
• • •

Fresh Rolls and Butter
• • •

Bombe Sacher
Chocolate and Coffee Ice Cream,
Chocolate Cake, and Chocolate Icing,
Rich Chocolate Sauce
• • •

Demitasse

Beef #25

Mélange of Fresh Fruit
Presented in Champagne glass
and Topped with a
Fresh Silver Dollar Slice of Kiwi
• • •

Esquire Salad
Hearts of Romaine and Spinach Leaves,
Tomato Wedges, Bacon Bits, Egg Slice,
Toasted Croutons, Gourmet Dressing
• • •

Filet Mignon au Champignon
Sauce Périgourdine
Potatoes Lorette
Red Pepper stuffed with Mushrooms
Broccoli Polonaise
• • •

Mocha Mousse
in Semisweet Chocolate Shell,
topped with Whipped Cream,
decorated with sprinkles of Milk Chocolate,
with a cookie served on the side
• • •

Demitasse

Beef #24

Potage Parisienne, Leek and Potato Soup
• • •

Fresh Bibb Lettuce Salad,
with Tiny Bay Shrimp
• • •

Filet Oscar with Crab Claw, Sauce Béarnaise
Pommes Amandine
Fresh Broccoli au Beurre
Tomato Provençale
• • •

Fresh Petite Rolls and Butter
• • •

Bombe Sacher
Chocolate and Coffee Ice Cream,
Chocolate Cake and Chocolate Icing,
Rich Chocolate Sauce
• • •

Coffee

Beef #26

Consommé Double with Sherry,
Cheese Straws
• • •

Fillet of Sole, Dugléré
• • •

Key Lime Sorbet
• • •

Whole Roast Beef Tenderloin Forestiere,
with Sautéed Mixed Mushrooms
Bouquetiere of Vegetables
• • •

Spinach Salad with
Warm Bacon Dressing
• • •

Poached Pear with Rum Sabayon and
Chocolate Ice Cream, Petits Fours
• • •

Demitasse

Beef #27

Herbed Cream of Chestnut Soup

• • •

Esquire Salad
Symphony of Salad Greens to include:
Hearts of Romaine and Spinach Leaves,
Tomato Wedges, Bacon Bits, Egg Slices,
Toasted Croutons, Gourmet Dressing

• • •

Tournedos of Beef, Niçoise,
Tomato Demi-Glace
Buttered String Beans
Oven Roasted Potatoes
Artichoke Bottom with Gingered Carrots

• • •

Fresh Petite Rolls and Butter

• • •

Crown of Raspberry Sherbet, Sauce
Framboise, Fancy Cookies

• • •

Coffee

Beef #28

Chilled Cream of Avocado en Suprême

• • •

Shrimp, Scallops, and Lobster,
Vin Blanc

• • •

Passion Fruit Sorbet in Sherry Glass

• • •

Fillet of Prime Beef Wellington,
Sauce Périgourdine
Bouquetiere of Fresh Garden Vegetables

• • •

Petite Dinner Rolls, Passed
Butter Rosettes on Lemon Leaves

• • •

Small Hearts of Bibb Lettuce,
With Palm Hearts and Brie Cheese,
Creamy Tarragon Dressing

• • •

English Wafers,
Soufflé Glacé au Grand Marnier

• • •

Les Petits Fours

• • •

Blended Coffee

Beef #29

Lobster Bisque

• • •

Pâté Maison on Bed of Bibb Lettuce,
Cumberland Sauce

• • •

Filet Mignon au Champignon, Sauce Madeira
Pommes Lorette
Tomato Stuffed with Broccoli Flowerettes
Honey-Glazed Carrots

• • •

Fresh Petite Rolls and Butter

• • •

Baked Alaska, Chocolate Sauce

• • •

Coffee

Beef #30

Poached Fillet of Sole Véronique
With White Seedless Grapes,
Lobster Sauce, and White Sauce

• • •

Roast Sirloin of Beef
Sauce Bordelaise, Presented over Flames from
a Gueridon, and Carved in the Room
Baby Carrots
Buttered Fresh Asparagus Tips
Potatoes Anna

• • •

Radicchio Salad
Radicchio, Bibb Lettuce, Endive, Hearts of
Palm, and Tomato, Tossed in the Room with
Vinaigrette Dressing

• • •

Savarin of Vanilla Ice Cream,
with Fresh Berries in Melba Sauce,
Decorated with Whipped Cream
and Bitter Chocolate Shavings

• • •

Petits Fours and After Dinner Mints

• • •

Coffee, Tea, Decaffeinated Coffee

Beef #31

Hot and Sour Soup
· · ·
Orient Express Salad, Walnut Dressing
· · ·
Peacock Beef
Great Wall Shrimp
Dragon Silk Lemon Chicken
Autumn Wind Vegetables
Oriental Rice
· · ·
Ginger Mousse
· · ·
Fortune Cookies
· · ·
Tea

Special Beverages: In addition to an Open Bar, we would be delighted to arrange for the serving of Plum Wine, Kirin and Asahi Beers, Hot Sake and our Rising Sun Exotic Drink. Prices available upon request.

Music: Authentic entertainment is available to enhance the Oriental atmosphere where, delicate as the scent of Jasmine, musical notes drift from Oriental Strings. Prices available upon request.

Beef #32

Shrimp Cocktail with Spicy Cocktail Sauce
· · ·
Mixed Salad of Romaine, Bibb, and Watercress,
Raspberry Vinaigrette
· · ·
Filet Mignon, Sauce Tomato Béarnaise
Bouquetiere of Fresh Seasonal Vegetables
· · ·
Rolls, Breadsticks, Lahvosh
· · ·
Strawberries Romanoff
· · ·
Coffee, Tea, Decaffeinated Coffee

Beef #33

Scallops in Champagne Sauce
and Julienne of Vegetables,
Served in Pastry Shell
· · ·
Bibb Lettuce with Marinated Artichokes and
Mushrooms, Herbed Vinaigrette
· · ·
Roast Tenderloin of Beef,
Green Peppercorn Sauce
Bouquetiere of Fresh Seasonal Vegetables
· · ·
Rolls, Breadsticks, Lahvosh
· · ·

Savarin Montmorency
Vanilla Ice Cream with Hot Brandied
Cherries
· · ·
Coffee, Tea, Decaffeinated Coffee

Beef #34

Seafood Madras
Seafood with Light Curry Sauce in a Pastry
Shell
· · ·
Salad of Mache, Spinach, Artichoke Hearts,
Walnut Vinaigrette
· · ·
Roasted Sliced Strip Loin, Sauce Périgourdine
Bouquet of Fresh Seasonal Vegetables
· · ·
Rolls, Breadsticks, Lahvosh
· · ·
Rum Raisin Parfait, with Chocolate Sauce
· · ·
Coffee, Tea, Decaffeinated Coffee

Veal Seated Dinners

Veal #1

Florida Ceviche
A Chilled Blend of Mildly Marinated Scallops, Bay Shrimp,
and Florida Red Snapper, with Crisp Vegetables
• • •

Salade Fantaisie
Tender, Freshly picked Garden Greens to include Arugula,
Baby Romaine, Sucrine, Red Leaf Lettuce, Curly Endive,
and Radicchio, with Warm Baked Goat Cheese,
Coated with Black Sesame Seeds and Dressed by the Server
with Pear Vinaigrette, served with a Chilled Fork
• • •

Freshly Baked Rolls, Salt Sticks, Lahvosh, Creamery Butter
• • •

Champagne Sorbet
• • •

Broiled Veal Chop
Accented with Sauce Béarnaise, passed
Bouquetiere of Fresh Garden Vegetables
• • •

Assorted Seasonal Berries, Marinated in Asti Spumante,
Warm Zabaglione Sauce, passed
• • •

Petits Fours and After Dinner Mints Presentation
• • •

Coffee, Tea, Decaffeinated Coffee

Veal #2

Consommé Printanier, Golden Brown Cheese Straws
• • •

Galantine of Chicken, Sauce Tarragon Beurre Blanc
• • •

Freshly Baked Rolls, Salt Sticks, Lahvosh, Creamery Butter
• • •

Pear Sorbet, Pear-shaped atop Fresh Pear Base,
placed upon small Lemon Leaf
• • •

Veal Nordic stuffed with Crab Mousse, Sauce Venetian, passed
Bouquetiere of Fresh Garden Vegetables
• • •

Häagen-Dazs Rum Raisin Ice Cream,
Milk Chocolate Garniture
• • •

Petits Fours and After Dinner Mints Presentation
• • •

Coffee, Tea, Decaffeinated Coffee

Veal #3

Cream of Scallops Soup with
Julienne of Pea Pods
• • •

Paupiettes of Boston Sole Kennebec,
with Mousse of Salmon, Sauce Véronique
• • •

Freshly Baked Rolls, Salt Sticks, Lahvosh,
Creamery Butter
• • •

Raspberry Sorbet, served with Kiwi Pinwheels
• • •

Veal Chop aux Morilles,
Fennel Mornay Sauce, passed
Bouquetiere of Fresh Garden Vegetables
• • •

Salade Normande
Salad of Endive, Watercress, Lettuce, Hearts
of Palm, Sliced Fresh Mushrooms, Toasted
Croutons, Oil and Vinegar Dressing, served
with a Chilled Fork
• • •

Coupette of Fresh Fruit to include
Pineapple, Kiwi, Papaya, and Strawberries,
Laced with Cointreau
• • •

Petits Fours and After Dinner Mints
Presentation
• • •

Coffee, Tea, Decaffeinated Coffee

Veal #4

Crab Soup with Sherry
• • •

Salad of Bibb, Radicchio, Mushroom, and
Watercress, Tarragon Vinaigrette
• • •

Roast Loin of Veal,
Morel Mushroom Sauce
Bouquetiere of Fresh Seasonal Vegetables
• • •

Rolls, Breadsticks, Lahvosh
• • •

Old World Ice Cream Savarin
• • •

Coffee, Tea, Decaffeinated Coffee

Veal #5

Lobster Crêpe Cardinal

• • •

Fresh Belgian Endive, Selected Spinach
Leaves, Boston Bibb Lettuce, Arugula,
Tomato Decoration and Garnished with
Watercress and a Light Dijon Mustard
Dressing, passed, served with a Chilled Fork

• • •

Fresh Baked Rolls, Salt Sticks, Lahvosh,
Creamery Butter

• • •

Individual Veal Wellington,
Sauce Forestiere, passed
Bouquetiere of Fresh Garden Vegetables

• • •

Lemon Sorbet
with Fresh Strawberries and Kiwi Medallions

• • •

Petits Fours and After Dinner Mints
Presentation

• • •

Coffee, Tea, Decaffeinated Coffee

Veal #6

Consommé Printanier,
Golden Brown Cheese Straws

• • •

Spinach Salad with Bermuda Onion Rings,
Fresh Sliced Mushrooms, and Sauce
Vinaigrette

• • •

Medallions of Veal on Eggplant Crouton,
Sauce Curranaisse
Squash Stuffed with Puree of Carrots,
Asparagus with Butter, Braised Celery

• • •

Nut Breads, Rolls with Butter

• • •

Fresh Fruit Fantasy
From a hollowed Pineapple, we will serve
a selection of Fresh Fruits with
Meringue served with Chocolate Sauce

Veal #7

Scampi Nantua
Shrimp Sautéed and Baked in Puff Pastry
with Essence of Lobster

• • •

Butter Lettuce with Hearts of Palm, Dressed with a Creamy
Raspberry Vinaigrette, served with a Chilled Fork

• • •

Freshly Baked Rolls, Salt Sticks, Lahvosh, Creamery Butter

• • •

Veal Calvados
Milk-fed Veal Loin sautéed in Butter and Cream with Thinly
Sliced Green Apples, and Flavored with Apple Brandy
Pommes Berny
Bouquetiere of Fresh Vegetables

• • •

Macadamia Good Times Celebration Medley
Delicate Crêpes filled with Macadamia Nut Ice Cream,
Topped with Whipped Cream and Chopped Macadamia Nuts
and Hot Fudge Sauce, passed

• • •

Petits Fours and After Dinner Mints Presentation

• • •

Coffee, Tea, Decaffeinated Coffee

Veal #8

Seafood Antipasto with Fettucini
Presented on a Bed of Lettuce

• • •

Lemon Sorbet

• • •

Medallions of Veal, en Croûte,
Sauce Sorrel
Squash stuffed with Puree of Carrot
Braised Celery
Asparagus au Beurre

• • •

Rolls and Fruit Breads,
Butter

• • •

Individual Dessert Presentation to consist of:
Brie Cheese and Sharp Cheddar
Petits Fours
Strawberries, Kiwi, Papaya

• • •

Demitasse

Veal #9

Duck Galantine, Sauce Cumberland
• • •

Salade Méditerranéene
Mixed Green Salad Dressed with Artichoke Hearts, Carrots,
Mushrooms, Pimiento, Olives, Tiny Bay Shrimp,
and Feta Cheese with a Special Greek Dressing,
served with a Chilled Fork
• • •
Freshly Baked Rolls, Salt Sticks, Lahvosh, Creamery Butter
• • •

Veal Louisianne
Tender Veal Loin Sautéed in Butter
and Smothered in a Light White Wine Sauce with Pieces of
Lobster and Shrimp, Garnished with a Whole Crayfish
Bouquetiere of Fresh Vegetables
• • •
Assorted French Pastries, Passed on a Gleaming Silver Tray,
Petits Fours, Chocolate-Dipped Strawberries, Tarts, Tortes,
and Petite Eclairs
• • •
After Dinner Mints Presentation
• • •
Coffee, Tea, Decaffeinated Coffee

Veal #11

Key West Turtle Soup,
Flavored with Aged Sherry and Sorrell
• • •
Paupiettes of Boston Sole Kennebec, with
Mousse of Salmon, Sauce Véronique
• • •
Raspberry Sorbet served with Kiwi
• • •
Veal Chop aux Morilles, Fennel Mornay
Snow Peas
Fresh Leaf Spinach in Tomato Basket
Salsify au Beurre Noisette
Pommes Dauphine
• • •

Salade Normande
Salad of Endive, Watercress, Lettuce, Hearts
of Palm, Sliced Fresh Mushrooms, Toasted
Croutons, Oil and Vinegar Dressing
• • •
Coupette of Fresh Fruit
Pineapple, Kiwi, Papaya, and Strawberries,
Laced with Cointreau,
• • •
Demitasse

Veal #10

Lobster Crêpe Cardinal
• • •
Fresh Hot Butter Flake Rolls and Butter
Swans, Served with Salad Course
• • •
Fresh Belgian Endive, Selected Spinach
Leaves, Boston Bibb Lettuce, Arugula with a
Tomato Flower, Garnished with Watercress
and Dijon Mustard Dressing on the Tomato,
and Eden Rock Dressing on the Leaves
• • •
Individual Veal Wellington
with Fresh Snow Peas, Fresh Turned Carrots
and a Poached Pear in White Wine with
Chestnut Puree
• • •
Lemon Sorbet with Fresh Raspberries
and Kiwi Medallions
Assorted Fancy Fresh Fruit, Petits Fours
• • •
Kona Coffee

Veal #12

Vol-au-Vent of Fresh Lobster, Cardinale
• • •
Lemon Champagne Sorbet
• • •
Whole Roasted Racks of Veal, Calvados,
Garnished with the Sweetbreads and Kidneys,
Presented over Flames on a Gueridon and
Carved in the Room
Brussels Sprouts with Glazed Chestnuts
Tomato Duxelles
Baskets of Pommes Soufflé,
on each table
• • •
Salad of Belgian Endive and Watercress, on a
Bed of Boston Leaf, Vinaigrette Dressing
• • •
Pastry Christmas Sleigh, filled with Soufflé
Glacé Anisette, Decorated with Chocolate
Hemlock and Almond Christmas Package
• • •
Demitasse

Veal #13

Clear Oxtail Soup with Cheese Straws

• • •

Fillet of Sole, Waleska
Fillet of Dover Sole Stuffed with Shrimp
and Crab

• • •

A Collection of Raspberry Sherbet Balls and
Honeydew Melon Balls

• • •

Medallions of Veal, Sauce Morille
Vegetable Bouquetiere
Zucchini Florentine
Tomato Stuffed with Broccoli
Pommes Chateau

• • •

Regency Salad
Bibb Lettuce, Watercress, and Tomato
Rosette, Eden Rock Dressing

• • •

Poached Pear Symphony, au Chocolat
Whole Pear Poached in Applejack Brandy
and Dipped in Chocolate, Floating in
Zabaglione Sauce

• • •

Petits Fours

• • •

Demitasse

Veal #14

Cajun Seafood Boudin,
Orange Sauce, Crayfish Garni

• • •

Hearts of Bibb and Smoked Pheasant Salad,
Walnut Vinaigrette

• • •

Pink Grapefruit Sorbet

• • •

Medallions of Veal, Meaux Mustard Sauce
Bouquetiere of Seasonal Vegetables

• • •

Lahvosh and Petit Pain, Butter

• • •

Fresh Seasonal Berries, Rum Sabayon, Puff
Pastry Cup, Bed of Caramel Sauce

• • •

Coffee

Veal #15

Cream of Petits Pois with Curry

• • •

Fillet of Colorado River Trout, Sauté Amandine

• • •

Veal Scallopini au Marsala
Homemade Noodles
Zucchini au Gratin
Tomato Du Barry

• • •

Bibb Lettuce with Brie Cheese, Vinaigrette Sauce

• • •

Parfait Nougatine, Les Petits Fours

• • •

Demitasse

Veal #16

Key West Turtle Soup, Flavored with Aged Sherry and Sorrel

• • •

Paupiettes of Boston Sole Kennebec
with Mousse of Salmon, Sauce Véronique

• • •

Intermezzo
Raspberry Sorbet, Served in Kiwi

• • •

Saddle of Veal Orloff
Bouquetiere of Vegetables to include:
Tomato Du Barry
Salsify au Beurre Noisette
Snow Peas, Pommes Berny

• • •

Served as a separate course:

Salade Normande
Salad of Endive, Watercress, and Lettuce, Hearts of Palm, Sliced
Fresh Mushrooms, Toasted Croutons, Oil and Vinegar Dressing

• • •

Selection of After Dinner and Dessert Cheeses

• • •

Special Presentation
British Chocolate Teardrops Fantaisie,
served in a Silver Suprême over Dry Ice

• • •

Croquembouche

• • •

Demitasse

Veal #17

Angels' Hair Consommé

• • •

Bay Scallops with Vegetable Confetti,
In a Light Mushroom Sauce,
Puff Pastry cup presentation

• • •

Burgundy Sorbet

• • •

Roast Veal Loin,
Fine Stuffing of Spinach and Shrimp,
Sauce Naturelle
Bouquetiere of Fresh Vegetables

• • •

Dinner Rolls,
Butter Rosettes on Lemon Leaves

• • •

Bibb Lettuce with Fontina Cheese
and Seedless Grapes,
Water Crackers

• • •

Poached Pear on a Bed of Rum Sabayon,
Chocolate Ice Cream,
Amaretto Cookies

• • •

Espresso and Herbal Teas

Veal #19

Danish Mushroom Soup

• • •

Lobster Crêpe Nantua

• • •

Pear Sorbet, with appropriate Garnish

• • •

Sliced Loin of Veal,
Lemon Butter Sauce
Medley of Wild and Brown Rice
Tomato Stuffed with Ginger Carrots
Whole Fresh Green Beans,
with Red Bell Pepper Rings

• • •

Romaine and Bibb Lettuce, Sliced Hearts of
Palm, Julienne of Carrots, Lemon Oil
Dressing with Chopped Parsley

• • •

Bel Paese Cheese, Seasonal Fruit, and
French Bread

• • •

Gooseberry Bavarois

• • •

Demitasse

Veal #18

Herbed Cream of Chestnut Soup

• • •

Seafood Cocktail with Lobster Medallion,
Sauce Aurora,
served in a Champagne Glass

• • •

Watercress and Endive Julienne,
Lemon Oil Dressing

• • •

Veal Loin Chops,
Sauce of Veal Quenelles and Kidneys
with Madeira
Gingered Carrots in Romaine Braised
Pommes Lorette
Shirred Zucchini with Walnuts

• • •

Raspberry Ice with Fresh Kiwi Medallion,
served in a Silver Suprême

• • •

Demitasse

Veal #20

Silver Suprême of Seafood Salad,
Surrounded by Belgian Endive Leaves,
Topped with Glazed Lobster Medallion

• • •

Veal Nordic
Loin of Veal stuffed with Crab Mousse
Potatoes Lorette
Oriental Stir-Fry Vegetables
Fresh Green Beans

• • •

Bibb Lettuce Salad,
Mustard Vinaigrette Dressing

• • •

Brie Cheese,
Petite Salt Stick Baguettes

• • •

Häagen Dazs
Rum Raisin Ice Cream,
Milk Chocolate Garniture

• • •

Demitasse

Veal #21

Crab Cardinal
Lump Crabmeat glazed with rich Seafood
Sauce with a Herb Crouton
• • •

Salad Caesar Style
Selection of Crisp Romaine, Parmesan
Cheese, Toasted Croutons, Caesar Dressing
• • •

Medallions of Veal Marsala
With Sliced Mushrooms
Potatoes Lorette
Broccoli au Beurre
Yellow Squash with Carrot/Cauliflower
Mousse
• • •

Assorted Dinner Rolls, Bread Sticks,
Lahvosh, and Creamery Butter
• • •

Poached Pear Symphony
Whole Poached Pear in Applejack Brandy
stuffed with Zabaglione Sauce,
dipped in Milk Chocolate

After Dinner Mints Passed
• • •

Coffee, Tea, Decaffeinated Coffee, or Milk

Veal #22

Quenelles of Seafood, with Lobster Sauce
• • •

Grapefruit Sorbet, with Dry Vermouth
• • •

Tenderloin of Veal Florentine, wrapped in
Spinach in Puff Pastry, Sauce Morille
Bouquet of Fresh Vegetables
• • •

Bibb Lettuce with Julienne of Radish
Enoki Mushrooms,
Sherry Vinaigrette
• • •

Rolls, Breadsticks, Lahvosh
• • •

Coffee, Tea, Decaffeinated Coffee
• • •

Petits Fours

Veal #23

Seafood Trio
Maryland Lump Crab, Jumbo Shrimp, and
Alaskan Crab Claw presented in a coupe
glass, Sauce Lamase
• • •

Cassis Sorbet
• • •

Broiled Veal Chop,
Accented with Béarnaise Sauce
Twin Quenelles of Carrot and Turnip
Spinach Fettucini
• • •

Dinner Rolls
Butter Rosettes on Lemon Leaves
• • •

Bibb Lettuce with Hearts of Palm and
Pimientos, Toasted Almonds,
Vinaigrette Dressing
• • •

Assorted Seasonal Berries, Marinated in Asti
Spumante, Warm Zabaglione Sauce
• • •

Blended Coffee, Imported Teas

Veal #24

Buena Vista Salad, Supreme
Fresh Romaine, Palm Hearts, Mushrooms,
Cherry Tomatoes, Artichoke Hearts, Sliced
Olives, Avocado, and Shrimp, with a Creamy
Garlic Dressing
• • •

Clear Oxtail Soup with Sandelman Sherry,
Cheese Straws
• • •

Tender Steak of Milk-Fed Veal Sauté,
Morel Sauce
Buttered Homemade Noodles
Whole Tomato with French Peas
Green Asparagus Tips
• • •

Butter Rosettes on Lemon Leaves,
Small Dinner Rolls
• • •

Brie Cheese with a Bouquet of Fresh Fruits
Toasted French Bread
• • •

Ice Cream Pie with Brandied Strawberries
• • •

Beverage

Veal #25

Chilled Beef Consommé,
Mélange of Mushrooms,
Presented in glass tureens lined with Gelatin and decorated
(Bottoms of soup bowls decorated also)

• • •

Quenelles of Poultry, Sauce Terrapin,
Silver Trays and Sauce Boats

Pear Sorbet

Pear-Shaped atop Fresh Pear Base, placed upon small Lemon
Leaf, presented on individual Ice Leaf Socles

• • •

Veal Nordic

Stuffed with Crab Mousse, Sauce Venetian passed
Pommes Lorette
Fresh Green Asparagus wrapped in Red Bell Pepper Rings
(above preplated)
passed by waiters:
Stir-Fried Julienne of Carrots, Leeks, and Snow Pea Pods
Garni of Mushroom Slices

• • •

Special Dessert Creation

Lamb #2

Potage Boula Boula

• • •

Fillet of Dover Sole, Véronique

• • •

Champagne Sorbet,
Laced with Fine Champagne, tableside

• • •

Bibb Lettuce with Julienne Carrot and
Julienne Beets, Lemon-Oil Dressing

• • •

Fillet of Lamb Tenderloin, served with Mint
Demi-Glace
Plaza Rice
Tomato Florentine
Broccoli Flowerettes

• • •

Fresh Strawberries, served with warm
Sabayon

• • •

Demitasse

• • •

Petits Fours with Marzipan Decoration
Fancy Cookies
Mixed Nuts

Lamb Seated Dinners

Lamb #1

Double Consommé,
Garnished with a Jardiniere of Chinese Vegetables

• • •

Maine Lobster Strudel, Sauce Cardinal

• • •

Grapefruit Sorbet, Indian River, Splash of Mint Liqueur

• • •

Roast Rack of Baby Lamb, Plum Tomato and Basil Sauce
Zucchini Boat Filled with Carrot Puree
String Beans Wrapped in Crisp Bacon
Panache of White and Wild Rice, with Minced Apricots

• • •

Artichoke Hearts and Limestone Lettuce, Wedge of Brie,
Vinaigrette Dressing

• • •

Petite Soft Rolls
Butter Rosettes

• • •

Tarte Tatin

• • •

Imported Coffee, Herbal Teas

Lamb #3

Terrine of Vegetables, in Port Wine Aspic

• • •

Suprême of Salmon, with Two Caviars

• • •

Champagne Sorbet

• • •

Twin Lamb Medallions,
Lingonberry Sauce
Crisp Snow Peas
Sautéed Chanterelles
Berny Potatoes

• • •

French Rolls and Butter

• • •

Tender Bibb Lettuce, with Hearts of Palm
and Pimiento, Tarragon Vinaigrette

• • •

Gâteau St. Honoré

• • •

Imported Coffee, Selected Teas

Seafood/Fish Seated Dinners

Seafood #1

Hawaiian Papaya with Melon Pearls,
Marinated in Port Wine

• • •

Bibb, Radicchio, and Endive, Hearts of Palm
and Pimiento with a Hazelnut Dressing,
Presented and then Tossed Tableside, served
with a Chilled Fork

• • •

Freshly Baked Rolls, Salt Sticks, Lahvosh,
Creamery Butter

• • •

Salmon Florentine
Fillet of Salmon Stuffed with
Fresh Sautéed Spinach and Topped
with Sauce Tarragon
Bouquetiere of Fresh Garden Vegetables

• • •

Pineapple Celebration
Baby Pineapple Half filled with Chartreuse-
Flavored Vanilla Ice Cream, Topped with
Fresh Raspberries and Vanilla Sauce

• • •

Petits Fours and After Dinner Mints
Presentation

• • •

Coffee, Tea, Decaffeinated Coffee

Seafood #2

Consommé Florentine,
Shredded Spinach and Chicken Quenelles
with Curried Cream

• • •

Tender Bibb Lettuce in a Radicchio Cup,
Topped with a Julienne of Yellow Squash,
Toasted Almonds, Raspberry Vinaigrette

• • •

Poached Fillet of Salmon, Sauce Maltaise
Carrot Mousse, in Artichoke Bottom
Crisp Snow Peas
Red Jacket Potatoes

• • •

Lahvosh and Soft Dinner Rolls
Butter Rosettes

• • •

Amaretto Cheesecake, Chantilly

• • •

Colombian Coffee and Herbal Tea

Seafood #3

Cream of Asparagus Soup,
Sesame Sticks

• • •

Lemon Sorbet, in a Petite Lemon Basket

• • •

Grilled Swordfish Steak,
Coriander Butter
Buttered Leaf Spinach with Saffron Rice
Bâtonnets of Fresh Carrots

• • •

Soft Rolls and Cheese Bread
Toasted Pita

• • •

Endive and Bibb Salad with Artichoke Hearts,
Dijon Vinaigrette Dressing

• • •

Frozen Island Rum Cake
Rum-Soaked Chocolate Cake and Vanilla Ice
Cream, Dusted with Cocoa Powder, Served with
Chocolate Rum Sauce

• • •

Colombian Coffee, Selected Teas

Multiple-Entrées Seated Dinners

Multiple #1

Chilled Jumbo Shrimp,
Florida Lobster Chunks,
Ripe Papaya, and Avocado Wedges, Olives and
Parsley Garni
Rémoulade and Cocktail Sauces passed, served
with a Chilled Fork
• • •
Freshly Baked Rolls, Salt Sticks, Lahvosh,
Creamery Butter
• • •
Florida Classic Consommé with Veal and
Alligator, Garnished with Quenelles of Alligator
and Pastry Straws
• • •
Häagen Dazs Lemon Sorbet with a touch of
Cognac, Mint Leaves, and Lime
Pinwheels Garni
• • •

Poached Dolphin, Sauce Bonne Femme,
with Fleurons, Pastry Garni
and
Sautéed Filet Mignonette on Crouton
Champignon, Sauce Périgourdine passed
Bouquetiere of Fresh Garden Vegetables
• • •
A White Chocolate Conch Shell with Fresh
Blueberries, Kiwi, and Raspberries cascading
into a Lake of Caramel Sauce
• • •
Petits Fours and After Dinner Mints
Presentation
• • •
Coffee, Tea, Decaffeinated Coffee

Multiple #2

Fresh Florida Lobster Bisque au Cognac
• • •
Breast of Duckling Morocco, Toasted Almonds
and Shredded Coconut Garni
• • •
Hearts of Palm with Boston Lettuce, Pimiento Strip, Avocado,
Cherry Tomato, and Black Olives with a Light Creamy Fresh
Mustard Sauce passed, served with a Chilled Fork
• • •
Freshly Baked Rolls, Salt Sticks, Lahvosh, Creamery Butter
• • •
Medallion of Veal Loin with Lobster Decoration, Sauce Nantua
and
Tournedos of Filet Mignon, Sauce Périgourdine
Bouquetiere of Fresh Garden Vegetables
• • •

Savarin Montmerency
Vanilla Ice Cream with Hot Brandied Cherries
• • •
Petits Fours and After Dinner Mints Presentation
• • •
Coffee, Tea, Decaffeinated Coffee

Multiple #3

Coquille of Fresh Florida Fish
and Shellfish, Flavored with Saffron
• • •
Wedge of Iceberg Lettuce and Beefsteak
Tomato, Topped with Crunchy Croutons,
Creamy Herb Dressing,
served with a Chilled Fork
• • •
Freshly Baked Rolls, Salt Sticks, Lahvosh,
Creamery Butter
• • •
Poached Pompano, Topped with Large Twin
Shrimp, Glazed with Sauce Maltese
and
Tournedos of Beef on Crouton,
Sauce Demi-Glace
Bouquetiere of Fresh Garden Vegetables
• • •
Charlotte Russe with Strawberries and
Bananas
• • •
Coffee, Tea, Decaffeinated Coffee

Multiple #4

Tomato Bouillon with Mushrooms

• • •

Cold Jumbo Shrimp Cocktail,
Cocktail Sauce, Lemon Wedges

• • •

Veal Medallion atop Eggplant Crouton,
Sauce Béarnaise
and
Fillet of Beef Medallion atop Crouton,
Marchand de Vin
Pommes Berny
Green Beans Wrapped in Smoked Ham
Squash Stuffed with Puree of Carrot

• • •

Brie Cheese with Almonds,
Baguettes

• • •

Mandarine Bavarois, with Mandarin Liqueur
Sauce, Petits Fours

• • •

Demitasse

Multiple #5

Seasonal Melon Spears,
Wrapped in Westphalian Ham, Lime Garni

• • •

Quenelles of Sole and Salmon,
Sauce Vin Blanc and Sauce Newburg

• • •

Passion Fruit Sorbet

• • •

Medallions of Beef and Veal,
Morel and Cognac Sauce
Bouquetiere of Fresh Vegetables

• • •

Baguette, Butter Rosettes

• • •

Bibb and Radicchio Lettuce,
Wedge of Brie, and Seedless Grapes,
Sauce Vinaigrette, English Wafers

• • •

Frozen Crêpes,
Filled with Vanilla Ice Cream,
Hot Bananas Foster

• • •

Selected Coffee, Herbal Teas

Multiple #6

From the Florida Keys:
Succulent Giant Stone Crab Claws, in Season,
in an Individual Ice Socle and accompanied with Mustard Sauce

• • •

Hearts of Romaine and Beefsteak Tomato,
Topped with Crunchy Croutons, Fresh Parmesan Cheese,
Light Creamy Herb Dressing, served with a Chilled Fork

• • •

Freshly Baked Rolls, Salt Sticks, Lahvosh, Creamery Butter

• • •

Quail Ponce de Leon
Braised Quail with Wild Rice Pilaf and Quail Eggs,
Sauce Demi-Glace au Cognac
and

*Medallion of Veal Loin, Sauté with Twin Lobster
Decorations*
Sauce Nantua
Bouquetiere of Fresh Garden Vegetables

• • •

A Large Flamingo Ice Carving will be provided, for each Two
Hundred Guests, filled with Large Stemmed Strawberries
Sauce Sabayon, with a hint of Pernod, passed

• • •

Petits Fours and After Dinner Mints Presentation

• • •

Coffee, Tea, Decaffeinated Coffee

Multiple #7

Consommé Belmont with Asparagus and Diced Tomatoes

• • •

Salad of Bibb and Romaine Lettuce, Fresh Spinach,
Alfalfa Sprouts, and Walnuts, Walnut Vinaigrette

• • •

Medallions of Veal and Lamb,
with Fresh Blueberry Sauce and Chanterelles Sauce
Bouquetiere of Fresh Vegetables

• • •

Rolls, Breadsticks, Lahvosh

• • •

Pineapple Surprise
Baby Pineapple Filled with Ice Cream, Fresh Raspberries,
and Vanilla Sauce, Petits Fours

• • •

Coffee, Tea, Decaffeinated Coffee

Multiple #8

Carved Pineapple Boat
Filled with Exotic Fresh Fruits and
Garnished with Star Fruit and Shredded
Coconut
• • •

From Silver Tureens we will serve:
Cream of Scallop Soup with Julienne of
Pea Pods
• • •

Salade à la Suisse
Mixed Green Salad, with a Julienne of Swiss
Cheese, Oil and Vinegar Dressing
• • •

Campari and Grapefruit Sorbet
Presented in a Fresh Lime, in a Giant Martini
Glass, with a Fresh Flower Garnish
• • •

Medallion of Veal, Sauce Morille
and

*Medallion of Filet Mignon, Sauce
Périgourdine*
Pommes Duchesse
Green Beans Wrapped in Smoked Ham
Tomato Basket filled with Cauliflower
• • •

Fresh Dinner Rolls and Butter
• • •

Dark Semisweet Chocolate Shell, Filled with
White Chocolate Mousse, Floating on a Lake
of Fresh Berry and Grand Marnier Sauce,
with a Fresh Strawberry Garnish
• • •

Coffee, Tea, Decaffeinated Coffee

Multiple #9

Conch Chowder
A Florida Specialty of Conch, Cream, Herbs,
and Brandy
• • •

Florida Mushroom Vinaigrette
A Tender Head of Bibb Lettuce,
Complemented by Button Mushrooms,
Pimientos, Boiled Eggs, Served with Sliced
Beefsteak Tomatoes and Bermuda Onions,
Orange Vinaigrette Dressing passed, served
with a Chilled Fork
• • •

Freshly Baked Rolls, Salt Sticks, Lahvosh,
Creamery Butter
• • •

Grapefruit Sorbet
with Dry Vermouth
• • •

Chicken St. Jacques
Breast of Chicken Accompanied by
Large Tender Scallops Laced with
a Creamed Wine Sauce
Bouquetiere of Fresh Garden Vegetables
• • •

*Florida Toasted Coconut Snowball in a
Basket*
Ice Cream Snowball of Vanilla with White
Chocolate Chunks, Rolled in Toasted
Coconut and Presented in a Chocolate Edged
Wafer Basket with a Rich Crème de Cacao
Sauce, passed
• • •

Petits Fours and After Dinner Mints
Presentation
• • •

Coffee, Tea, Decaffeinated Coffee

Multiple #10

Carved Pineapple Boat
Filled with Exotic Fresh Fruits and
Garnished with Star Fruit and Shredded
Coconut

• • •

Danish Mushroom Soup
Served from Gleaming Silver Tureens,
Golden Brown Cheese Straws

• • •

Salade à la Suisse
Mixed Green Salad with a Julienne of Swiss
Cheese, Oil and Vinegar Dressing, served
with a Chilled Fork

• • •

Freshly Baked Rolls, Salt Sticks, Lahvosh,
Creamery Butter

• • •

Campari and Grapefruit Sorbet, in a Petite
Clam Shell, with a Live Fresh Flower Garnish

• • •

Medallion of Veal, Sauce Morille
and

*Medallion of Filet Mignon, Sauce
Périgourdine*
Bouquetiere of Fresh Garden Vegetables

• • •

Dark Semisweet Chocolate Shell
Filled with White Chocolate–Hazelnut
Mousse, Floating on a Lake of Fresh Berry
and Grand Marnier Sauce, with a Fresh
Strawberry Garnish

• • •

Petits Fours and After Dinner Mints
Presentation

• • •

Coffee, Tea, Decaffeinated Coffee

Multiple #11

Consommé Suzette
Consommé with Julienne of Celery, Garnished with Truffle
and Flavored with Dry Sherry, Served with Golden Brown
Cheese Straws

• • •

Salade de Californie
Green Salad Tossed with Tiny Bay Shrimp, Black Olives,
Alfalfa Sprouts, and Diced Avocado, then Dressed with
Peppercream, served with a Chilled Fork

• • •

Freshly Baked Rolls, Salt Sticks, Lahvosh, Creamery Butter

• • •

Petite Filet Mignon, Sauce Périgourdine
and
Petite Lobster Tail Thermidor

Bouquetiere of Fresh Vegetables

• • •

Bananas Foster Flambé
Sliced Bananas Sautéed in a Delicious Caramel Sauce and
Ladled over Vanilla Ice Cream

• • •

Petits Fours and After Dinner Mints Presentation

• • •

Coffee, Tea, Decaffeinated Coffee

Multiple #12

Avocado with Lump Crabmeat
One Quarter Avocado, Stuffed with All Lump Crabmeat,
in a Spicy Sauce Presented on Crisp Lettuce

• • •

Consommé Clear with Fine Vegetables, Cheese Straws

• • •

Bibb Lettuce with Palm Hearts, Cherry Tomatoes,
Sliced Mushrooms, Creamy Garlic Dressing

• • •

6-ounce Broiled Rock Lobster Tail, with Drawn Butter
4-ounce Broiled Filet Mignon, with Bordelaise Sauce

• • •

Buttered Broccoli
Roasted Potatoes

• • •

Assorted Dinner Rolls, Butter

• • •

Vanilla Ice Cream with Fresh Strawberries and Pineapple,
Grand Marnier, Coconut Macaroons

• • •

Beverage

Multiple #13

Glazed Isometric-cut Avocado,
Chilled Jumbo Coastal Shrimp, and Native
Stone Crab Claws, in season,
with Ravigote and Mustard Sauces
• • •

Salade Maison
A Symphony of Garden Greens, Cucumber
Wedges, Sliced Mushrooms, Artichoke
Hearts, Fresh Citrus Fruit, Cherry Tomato,
and Hearts of Palm, Light Creamy Tarragon
Dressing, served with Chilled Fork
• • •
Freshly Baked Rolls, Salt Sticks, Lahvosh,
Creamery Butter
• • •
Lime Sorbet with Lemon Pinwheels and
Mint Leaves Garni
• • •

Breast of Duckling St. Augustine
With Apricot Glaze, Coconut, Almonds, and
Dried Black Currants
and

Medallion of Veal Loin
Sauce Chanterelles, Flavored with Dry Sherry
Wine
Bouquetiere of Fresh Garden Vegetables
• • •

Cherries Jubilee
Vanilla Ice Cream, Smothered with a
Sweet Bing Cherry Sauce and Flamed
• • •

Petits Fours and After Dinner Mints
Presentation
• • •

Coffee, Tea, Decaffeinated Coffee

Multiple #14

Consommé Royale
Garnished with Custard Diamonds,
Served Tableside from a Gleaming
Silver Tureen
• • •

Semi-Boneless Quail
Served with Fois Gras, atop a
Seasoned Crouton
• • •

Salade Maison
A Symphony of Garden Greens, Diced
Cucumber, Sliced Mushrooms, Diced
Artichoke Hearts, Fresh Citrus Fruit, Diced
Tomato, and Hearts of Palm, with a Light
Creamy French Mustard Dressing, Presented
and Tossed Tableside, served with
a Chilled Fork
• • •
Freshly Baked Rolls, Salt Sticks, Lahvosh,
Creamery Butter
• • •

*Petite Fillets of Beef Tenderloin, Veal
Tenderloin, and Pork Tenderloin*
Presented with Sauce Chanterelles, passed
Bouquetiere of Fresh Garden Vegetables
• • •

Savarin of Vanilla Ice Cream
With Fresh Berries and Melba Sauce,
Decorated with Whipped Cream and Milk
Chocolate Shavings
• • •

Petits Fours and After Dinner Mints
Presentation
• • •

Coffee, Tea, Decaffeinated Coffee

Multiple #15

Black-Tie Pasta
A Large Black Bow Tie Pasta,
with Salmon and Black Caviar
and a Saffron Cream Sauce
• • •

Spinach Salad
Tossed Tableside with Hot Bacon Dressing,
Served with a Chilled Fork
• • •

Freshly Baked Rolls, Salt Sticks, Lahvosh,
Creamery Butter
• • •

Fillet of Beef and Scampi
Beef Tenderloin Steak and Wine-Laced
Mushrooms, Over an Almond Eggplant
Crouton, Served with Sauce Béarnaise, passed
and
Four Large Shrimp Stuffed with Crabmeat,
Cooked in Scampi Butter
Bouquetiere of Fresh Vegetables
• • •

Chocoholic Bubbly
A White Chocolate Champagne Glass, Filled
with Dark Milk Chocolate–Hazelnut Mousse,
Presented sitting in a Lake of Fresh
Raspberry Sauce, Artfully Decorated with
Individual Designs of Zabaglione
• • •

Petits Fours and After Dinner Mints
Presentation
• • •

Coffee, Tea, Decaffeinated Coffee

Multiple #16

Four Large Coastal Shrimp
Served with Cantaloupe and Honeydew
Melon, Spearmint Leaves Garni and Dressed
by the Server with Curry-Cream Dressing,
served with a Chilled Fork
• • •

Double Consommé
A Simmered Rich Beef Stock with Julienne of
Vegetables
• • •

Freshly Baked Rolls, Salt Sticks, Lahvosh,
Creamery Butter
• • •

Tournedos Key West
Twin Medallions of Beef Tenderloin
Garnished with Paired Baby Lobster Tails,
Served with Sauce Béarnaise, passed
Bouquetiere of Fresh Garden Vegetables
• • •

Fresh Florida Orange Bombe
with Grand Marnier Sauce, passed
• • •

Petits Fours and After Dinner Mints
Presentation
• • •

Coffee, Tea, Decaffeinated Coffee

Chapter 20

Buffet Dinner Menus

Thirty Various Buffet Dinner Menus

Buffet Dinner #1

Decorated Ham Pele-Mele
Whole Roast Turkey
Variety of Sliced Cold Cuts, Roast Beef, Ham,
and Prosciutto
• • •
Mixed Garden Greens, Choice of Dressings
Fancy Potato Salad, Relish Tray Fantasy
Chicken Salad Royale, Bean Salad Vinaigrette
Selected Sausage Charcuterie
Deviled Eggs, Assorted Cheese Tray
• • •

Choose Four Hot Entrées
Standing Roast Prime Beef
Fried Chicken Chez Soi
Sauté of Beef Burgundy
Glazed Buffet Ham
Coq au Vin
Scallopine of Veal Piccata
Bay Shrimp à l'Indienne in Fine Curry Sauce
String Beans Sauté with Almonds, Rice Pilaf
• • •

For the Sweet Tooth
Jellied Aspic Fruit Mold
Assortment from our Pastry Tray
• • •
Beverages

Buffet Dinner #2

Mixed Garden Green Salad Bowl,
Choice of Dressing
Tray of Sliced Tomatoes and Cucumbers
Creamy Cole Slaw with Raisins
Cottage Cheese
Chicken Salad Royale
Jellied Aspic Fruit Mold
Deviled Eggs
• • •
Variety of Cold Meats: Turkey, Ham, Roast
Beef, Salami
Assortment of Fine Cheeses
• • •

Hot Entrées
Fried Chicken
Beef Sauté Bourguignonne
Mixed Seafood Newburg
Baby Carrots with Green Peas Panache
String Beans Sauté
Rice Valentina
• • •
Rolls and Butter on your table
• • •
Assortment from our Pastry Tray
• • •
Beverages

Buffet Dinner #3

Relish Trays of Celery Sticks, Olives,
Radishes, Dill and Sweet Pickles
• • •
Chef's Mixed Green Salad, Selection of
Dressings
Cold Antipasto
Seafood Salad in Cocktail Sauce
Deviled Eggs Savoyarde
• • •
Platters of Assorted Cold Meats Including:
Brisket of Beef, Sliced Ham, Breast of Turkey
• • •
Top Sirloin of Beef,
Carved at Buffet by Chef in White Uniform
Seafood Newburg
Boneless Chicken Sauté in Wine and
Mushrooms
Rissolée Potatoes
Pilaf of Rice
Green Beans with Bacon and Onions
• • •
Fresh Rolls and Butter
• • •
An Assortment of Cheeses
Platters of Sliced Fresh Fruits of the Season
• • •
Pastries and Confections

Buffet Dinner #4

Relish Trays of Celery Sticks, Olives, Radishes,
Dill and Sweet Pickles
• • •
Mixed Garden Greens, Selection of Dressings
Pickled Beets with Chopped Onions
Three Bean Salad
Sliced Cucumbers and Tomatoes
Seafood Salad in Cocktail Sauce
• • •
Roast Baron of Beef, presliced
Barbecued Pork
Crispy Fried Chicken
Vegetable Medley
• • •
Fresh Rolls and Butter
• • •
An Assortment of Cheeses
Platters of Sliced Fresh Fruit of the Season
• • •
Pastries and Confections

Buffet Dinner #5

Orange and Grapefruit Sections
String Beans Vinaigrette
Russian Salad
Cole Slaw, Potato Salad
Cottage Cheese with Peaches
Four Seasons Salad Bowl,
French and Italian Dressing
• • •
Cold Meat Platter and Sliced Turkey,
Ham, Roast Beef, and Salami
Beef à la Deutsch
Scrod Amandine
Coq au Vin
Au Gratin Potatoes
Peas with Mushrooms
• • •
Assorted Pies and Cakes
Fruit Jello
Fresh Fruits

Buffet Dinner #6

Artistic Ice Carving,
Decorating the Buffet Table
• • •
Fresh Vegetable Salad
Caesar Salad Tossed at Buffet
Florida Waldorf Salad
• • •
Decorated Sliced Ham, Corned Beef,
and Turkey on Mirrors
Whole Decorated Salmon on Mirror
Top Sirloin of Beef, Sauce Bordelaise,
Carved at Buffet by Chef in White Uniform
Chicken Bavarian Style
Lobster Thermidor
Pommes Croquette
Green Asparagus with Butter Sauce
Pâté of Pheasant
• • •
Fresh Rolls and Butter
• • •
Assorted Cheeses with Fresh Fruit on Mirrors
• • •
Fantasies in Pastry

Buffet Dinner #7

Salads

Scallops, Mushrooms, and Mussels
à la Grecque
Fresh Vegetable Display with Flowering
Buds, With Favorite Dips
Baby Alaskan Shrimps, Served in a giant
natural shell with Brandied Cocktail Sauce
Traditional Antipasto Display,
Olive Oil and Red Wine Vinegar
Crisp Romaine Leaves, With Flavored
Croutons, Grated Cheese,
Creamy Garlic Dressing
Tiered Cheese Presentation,
Wafers and French Bread
Marinated Hearts of Palm with Pimiento

• • •

Cold Presentations

Columbia River Salmon, Glazed and Decorated
Seasonal Vegetables à la Russe
Selected Pâtés:
Pâté Maison, Pâté au Poivre, Pâté Campagne
Whole Roast Turkey,
Carved and Displayed
Prime Rib of Beef,
Slices of Rare Beef and Port Wine Aspic

• • •

Hot Entrées

Sirloin of Beef,
Carved to order, with Bordelaise Sauce
Boneless Breast of Chicken, Sauté,
Sauce Smitane
Tender Veal and Peppers
Baked Rice
Grilled Florida Fish,
Seedless Green Grapes and Walnuts

• • •

The Bread Basket

An Assortment of Home Baked Rolls and
Sliced Breads from Our Bakery, with Country
Butter

• • •

Desserts

Scalloped Melon Baskets,
Fresh Fruit, Whipped Cream, and Coconut
Chocolate Mousse, Chantilly
Assorted French and Italian Pastries,
Black Forest Cake, Tropical Fruit Flans,
Dobosh Torte, Linzer Torte, Tarte Tatin

• • •

Beverages

Buffet Dinner #8

Chef's Salad Bowl

Selections of Fresh Fruits of the Season
Relish and Fresh Vegetable Tray
Crisp Garden Greens, Choice of Dressings
Tomato and Cucumber Salad
Russian Vegetable Salad
Bavarian Potato Salad

• • •

From Our Delicatessen Counter

Array of Cold Meats, including Sliced Turkey, Cooked Ham,
Roast Beef, Pastrami, Pepperoni
Tuna Fish Salad
Crocks of Pickles
Assortment of Domestic and Imported Cheeses with Lahvosh,
Crackers, and Fresh Fruit

• • •

Hot Selections (Choice of Two)

Coq au Vin
Seafood in puree of Watercress and Wine Sauce
Braised Beef Tenderloin Tips, Bourguignonne
Curry of Chicken

• • •

Selection of Garden Vegetables and Patna Rice

• • •

Sweet Table

Chocolate Layer Cake, Assorted Fruit Gelatins,
Down Home Fruit Pies, Black Forest Cake, Chocolate Mousse

Buffet Dinner #9

Assorted Relishes
String Beans Vinaigrette
Cole Slaw
Four Season Salad Bowl
Italian and French Dressing

• • •

Assorted Cold Cuts
Pot Roast of Beef
Southern Fried Chicken
Pilaf of Rice
Corn O'Brien

• • •

Fruit Jello
Assorted Pies and Cakes
Coffee, Tea

Buffet Dinner #10

Selections of Fresh Fruits of the Season
Relish and Fresh Vegetable Tray
• • •

Chef's Salad Bowl
Crisp Garden Greens, Choice of Dressings
Bavarian Potato Salad
Mushrooms à la Grecque
Tomato and Cucumber Salad
Russian Vegetable Salad
Cucumber Llona
• • •

From the Delicatessen Counter
Turkey Salad Princess
Seafood Salad
Array of Cold Meats, including Sliced Turkey, Cooked Ham,
Roast Prime Rib, Pastrami, and Pepperoni
Salmon and Tuna Fish Salad
Crocks of Pickles
• • •
Assortment of Domestic and Imported Cheeses Served with
Crackers and Garnished with Fresh Fruit
• • •
Assortment of Fresh Rolls and Butter
• • •

Hot Selections (Choice of Two Entrées)
Braised Beef Tenderloin Tips Bourguignonne
Stir-Fried Seafood
Curry of Chicken Madras
Coq au Vin
• • •
Chef's Selection of Garden Vegetables and Patna Rice
• • •

Sweet Table
Viennese Pastries, Chocolate Layer Cake, English Trifle,
Assorted Fruit Gelatins, Home Baked Fruit Pies,
Chocolate Mousse, Crème Caramel
• • •
Coffee, Tea, Decaffeinated Coffee, or Milk
• • •

Other Hot Selections Are in Addition
Steamship Round of Beef (carved by Chef, at an additional
expense)
Roast Turkey (carved by Chef, at an additional expense)

Other Cold Selections Are in Addition
Golden Gulf Crab Claws, by the Hundred Pieces
Jumbo Shrimp Pyramid, by the Hundred Pieces

Buffet Dinner #11

Fresh Melon, in Season
Assorted Relishes
String Beans Vinaigrette
Asparagus Vinaigrette
Marinated Mushrooms and Cauliflower
Cucumber Salad
Assorted Garden Greens with Feta Cheese
• • •
Stuffed Tomato with Chicken Salad
Cold Sliced Turkey and Ham
Decorated Side of Nova Scotia Salmon
• • •
Seafood Newburg
Tenderloin of Beef Stroganoff
Baked Whole Ham in Pastry Shell
Pilaf of Rice
Au Gratin Potatoes
Peas with Mushrooms
Glazed Belgian Carrots
• • •
Assorted Cheeses and Crackers
French Pastries
Cakes
Chocolate and Strawberry Mousse

Buffet Dinner #12

Assorted Salad Bar with Choice of Dressings
Tuna Fish Salad
Fire and Ice Salad
Pasta Salad Bar
Domestic Cheese and Fruit Array with
Yogurt
Crudités on Ice with Dipping Sauces
• • •
Grouper Provençale
Chicken Risotto
Beef Bourguignonne with Buttered Noodles
Fresh Stir-Fried Vegetables
• • •
Assortment of Fresh Rolls and Butter
• • •
Assorted Home Baked Apple, Cherry,
and Key Lime Pies
Black Forest Cake
Carrot Cake
• • •
Coffee, Tea, Decaffeinated Coffee, or Milk

Buffet Dinner #13

Salads and Cold Presentations
Poached Fillet of Flounder,
With Cucumbers and Mayonnaise
Baby Alaskan Shrimp on Ice,
With Horseradish and Mustard Sauce
Sliced Smoked Kingfish,
With Marinated Onions and Mushroom
Buttons in White Wine
Russian Vegetable Salad
Avocado and Seafood Salad
Melon and Pineapple Spears and Strawberries,
With Yogurt Dip
Hearts of Bibb Lettuce, Palm Hearts, and
Pimiento, with Lemon Vinaigrette
Fresh Spinach Leaves, Bacon Bits,
Chopped Egg, and Minced Onions, with
Pernod Dressing
• • •
Whole Decorated Sugar-Cured Ham, Garni,
Presented on a Mirror with Portions of
Gallantine of Capon and Duckling
Sliced Wurst, Salami, Corned Beef,
and Pastrami
Favorite Condiments
• • •
Baskets of Assorted Homemade Breads,
Rolls, and Croissants
• • •

Hot Entrées
Shrimp and Chipolata Sausages, Provençale
Barbecued Cornish Game Hens
Baked Fillet of Grouper, with
Slivered Almonds
Roast Rounds of Beef, Carved to order, au Jus
or Béarnaise
Bouquetiere of Seasonal Vegetables
• • •

Desserts
Strawberries Romanoff,
Hot Banana Pudding, Band aux Fruits,
Chocolate Layer Cake, Strawberry
Cheesecake, Key Lime Pie, Rum Pie, Lemon
Meringue Pie, Cream Puff Swans
• • •
Beverages

Buffet #14

Selections of Fresh Florida Fruits of the Season
Relish and Fresh Vegetable Tray
• • •

Greens 'n' Things
Waldorf Salad
Bavarian Potato Salad
Asparagus Vinaigrette
Mushroom Salad à la Grecque
Spinach Leaf Salad, Choice of Dressings
Cucumber in Dilled Yogurt Dressing
• • •

Fish 'n' Fowl
Stuffed Eggs Moscovite
Jumbo Shrimp Pyramid (four pieces per person)
Pâté à la Maison
Smoked White and Kingfish
Curried Chicken Salad
Golden Gulf Crab Claws (four pieces per person)
Stuffed Artichoke Bottoms
Sauce Cumberland, Sauce Rémoulade,
Cocktail Sauce Napoleon, Sauce Vinaigrette
• • •

Our Pièces de Résistance
Decorated Whole Salmon Parisienne
Glazed Roast Prime Rib of Beef, Jardiniere
Decorated Baked Ham
Whole Roast Turkey Chaud-Froid
Hand-Carved Ice Sculpture Centerpiece
• • •

From the Hot Oven, Choice of Four Entrées
Roast Top Sirloin of Beef, carved by Chef
(Carver at an additional expense)
Fillet of Fresh Florida Fish Sauté, Amandine
Curried Chicken with Mango Chutney and Shredded Coconut
Prime Fillet of Beef Stroganoff
Stir-Fried Seafood with Long Grain and Wild Rice Mix
Baked Ham with Pineapple Sauce
Chicken Tsarine, Sauce Suprême, with Julienne of Fennel and
Cucumber
• • •
Chef's Garden Fresh Vegetables, Oven Roasted Potatoes
• • •
Assorted Rolls and Butter
• • •

Our Pastry Chef Creates for You
A Superb Selection of the Finest Pastries, Tortes, Mousses,
Cakes, Marinated Fruits, and Petits Fours
• • •
An International Assortment of Dessert Cheeses
• • •
Coffee, Tea, Decaffeinated Coffee, or Milk

Buffet #15

Decorated Mirrors of:
Sliced Ham, Turkey Breast, and Paprika Salami
• • •

Chef's Special Salad Selection
Tossed Green Salad, Potato Salad, Shrimp and Cucumber
Salad, Vegetable Garden Salad, Cherry Tomatoes, Relish Trays
• • •

Chafing Dishes of:
Beef Stroganoff, Seafood Newburg, Chicken Hawaiian,
Buttered Noodles, Vegetable Medley
• • •

Whole and Sliced Domestic and Imported Cheeses,
Decorated with Fresh Fruit
• • •

Selection of Assorted French Pastries, Pies, and Cakes
• • •

Beverages

Buffet Dinner #16

Artistic Carvings and Butter Sculptures
will Decorate the Buffet Table
• • •

Decorated and Sliced Ham, Corned Beef, and Turkey on
Mirrors
Whole Decorated Salmon on Mirrors
Sirloin of Beef, Sauce Bordelaise, to be carved at Buffet Table
Chicken Bavarian
Lobster Thermidor
• • •

Potato Croquettes
Fresh Green Asparagus, Butter Sauce
Additional Fresh Vegetables selected by Chef
• • •

Pâté of Pheasant
Fresh Vegetable Salad
Caesar Salad, Tossed at the Table
California Waldorf Salad
• • •

Assorted Cheeses with Fresh Fruits on Mirrors
Fancy Pastry Display
Sugar Modeling
• • •

Beverages

Buffet Dinner #17

Salads
Hearts of Artichoke, Vinaigrette
Mushrooms à la Grecque
Old-Fashioned Cucumber Salad
Hearts of Palm
Marinated Tomatoes
Curried Rice with Shrimp
Spinach with Mushrooms and Bacon
Bibb Lettuce
Belgian Endive
• • •

Assorted Bread and Cheese Display
• • •

Cold Presentations
Fillet of Beef Wellington
Smoked Pheasant
Decorated Silver Salmon
Virginia Country Ham, Sliced and Decorated
Roast Capon Medallion, Chaud-Froid
King Crab Bellevue
Lobster Parisienne
Vegetable Aspic
Duckling Galantine
• • •

Hot Entrées
Standing Prime Rib Roast of Beef,
carved to order,
Creamed Horseradish and au Jus
Seafood Newburg of Lobster,
Shrimp, and Scallops,
Served in Puff Pastry Shells
Paupiettes of Veal Forestiere, with
Mushrooms and Tomatoes
Curried Breast of Capon, Oriental Rice
Bouquetiere of Vegetables
• • •

Desserts
Cannoli
Fresh Fruit Tartlets
Sacher Torte with Whipped Cream
Cheesecake with Praline Sauce
French Apple Tart
Assorted French Pastries
Linzer Torte
Ice Cream Parlor with Assortment of
Toppings
• • •

Coffee, Tea, Sanka, Milk

Buffet #18

Appetizers
Assorted Relish Bowl
Russian Eggs, Sardines with Onion Rings
Antipasto with Tuna Fish
Curried Chicken Salad
Fruit Jello Molds

Salads
Chick Peas with Ham, Creamy Cole Slaw,
Pickled Beets, Potato Salad, Sliced Tomato,
Leaf Spinach with Sliced Mushrooms,
Mixed Garden Greens,
Dressings: French, Thousand Island,
and Vinaigrette

• • •

Cold Platters
Medallions of Florida Sea Trout,
Garnished with Asparagus
Roasted Cold Spring Chicken,
with Spiced Crab Apple
Assortment of Sliced Cold Meats, Salami,
and Mortadella

• • •

Sauces
Mayonnaise, Cocktail, Vert

• • •

Hot Dishes
Emince of Beef Stroganoff
Turkey à la King
Buttered Noodles or Rice Pilaf
Seasonal Fresh Vegetables
Rolls and Butter

• • •

Desserts
Assorted Cheeses with Fruit and Crackers
Apple Pie, Key Lime Pie
Savarin with Fruits, Strawberry Mousse
Coffee

Buffet Dinner #19

Tossed Garden Salad, Appropriate Garniture and Dressings
Imported Cheeses and Fruits of the World

• • •

Select Three
Curried Chicken and Almond Salad
Herring in Dill and Sour Cream
Chinese Noodle Salad
Vegetable Antipasto
Mustard-Marinated Tomato Wedges
Whole Baked Ham, Decorated and Displayed

• • •

Select Three Entrées
Whole Roast Prime Rib of Beef
Chicken Beaujolais
Fillet of Sole, with Salmon Mousse
Medallions of Veal, Sauce Champagne
Shrimp Marseille
Au Gratin Potatoes
Oriental Rice
Carrots Pernod
Seasonal Green Vegetables

• • •

Bakery Fresh Rolls and Loaves of Bread

• • •

Display of Rich Pastries and Desserts

• • •

Beverages

Buffet Dinner #20

A Selection of Imported and Domestic
Cheeses with English Tea Crackers and Fresh Fruit
Salad Fare
Bok Choy Salad
Marinated Vegetable Salad
Garden Salad with Dressings

• • •

Oriental Seafood
Steamship Round of Beef
Veal Marsala
Coq au Vin
Stir-Fried Vegetables
Roasted Potatoes, Herbed Rice
Zucchini Provençale

• • •

Assorted Cakes and Sweets

• • •

Oven Fresh Rolls and Butter

• • •

Coffee and Herbal Tea

Buffet Dinner #21

Appetizers
Bowl of Assorted Relishes
Cherry Tomatoes, Radish Roses, Carrot Curls, Cauliflower,
Broccoli, Celery Hearts
Stuffed and Ripe Olives
Alaskan Baby Shrimp in Giant Sea Shells
Marinated Artichoke Hearts
Mushrooms à la Grecque
Smoked White and Kingfish
Herring in Sour Cream with Sliced Apples
Watermelon Boat with Assortment of Fresh Fruits
Cantaloupe Melon with Prosciutto
• • •

Salads
Hearts of Lettuce with Orange Slices, Cream and Lemon
Dressing
Hearts of Palm with Pimiento, Grated Carrots, and Raisins
Watercress with Cherry Tomatoes
Celery and Beets, Lorette
Mixed Vegetables and Salami, Italienne
Mixed Garden Greens
• • •

Dressings
French, Thousand Island, and Bleu Cheese
• • •

Cold Decorated Pieces
Duck and Goose Liver Pâté,
Garnished with Stuffed Apples and Pears
Decorated Salmon, Moderne, Sauce Verte
Prime Rib of Beef, Jardiniere, with Slices of Cold Roast Sirloin
of Beef, Decorated with Vegetables and Meat Aspic
Roasted Whole Turkey Decorated with
Fruits and Sliced Breast of Turkey,
Creamed Horseradish, Cranberries, Cumberland Sauce
• • •

Hot Dishes
Curried Chicken with Mango Chutney and Shredded Coconut
Roasted Sirloin of Prime Beef, Mushroom Sauce
Fillet of Fresh Florida Fish Sauté, Amandine
Fresh Garden Vegetables, Savoyard Potatoes, Rice Pilaf
Assorted Rolls and Butter
• • •

Desserts
Display of Imported and Domestic Cheeses with Fresh Fruits,
Crackers, Pumpernickel and Rye Breads
Freshly Baked Cakes and Pies, Open Fruit Tarts
Chocolate Mousse, French Pastries
Cheesecake with Fruit Toppings
• • •

Coffee

Buffet Dinner #22

Appetizers
Relish Tray with Olives, Pickles, Celery
Sticks, Radishes, Scallions, and Carrot Sticks
Fresh Fruit Cocktail in a Watermelon Shell
Assorted Seafood Platters
Poached Eggs in Gelatin
• • •

Salads
Green Beans Niçoise, Waldorf Salad
German Potato Salad, Corn Mexicaine
Cucumber, Mixed Greens, Sliced Tomatoes
French, Thousand Island, or Bleu Cheese
Dressings

Mirrors
Decorated Whole Smoked Ham,
with Ham Roll and Slices
Whole Decorated Capon
with Breast of Chicken Jeanette
Fish Galantine,
with Scallops and Shrimp
Assortment of Sliced Cold Meats and Salami
• • •

Sauces
Mayonnaise, Cocktail
• • •

Hot Dishes
Fried Fillet of Boston Sole, Tartar Sauce
Whole Steamship Round of Beef, Carved at
the Buffet Table
Mixed Fresh Garden Vegetables
Lyonnaise Potatoes
• • •

Desserts
Display of Domestic Cheeses
with Fresh Fruits and Crackers
Freshly Baked Pies, Caramel Custard
Assorted Layer Cakes, Chocolate Eclairs,
Cheesecake, Fruit Tartlets
• • •

Coffee

Buffet Dinner #23

Presented on Decorated Mirrors
Sliced Corned Beef, Roast Beef, and
Turkey Breast
• • •

Presented on Silver Platters
Eggs à la Russe with Caviar
Roast Beef Rolls with Marinated Asparagus
Marinated Salmon with Cream Cheese
Artichoke Bottoms with Shrimp Mousse
• • •

From the Salad Bar
Seafood Salad
Sliced Beefsteak Tomatoes and Capers
Fresh Vegetable Salad
Caesar Salad
Salad à la Grecque with Diced Tomatoes,
Onions, Oregano, Feta Cheese, Ripe Olives,
and Lettuce
• • •

Presented in Chafing Dishes
Coq au Vin
Rice Imperial
Fillet of Sole Florentine
Roast Sirloin of Beef,
Carved by Chef at the Buffet Table
Fresh String Beans
Cauliflower au Gratin
Rissolée Potatoes
• • •

Mirrors of Whole and Sliced Imported and
Domestic Cheeses with Fresh Fruits
• • •

Pastry Display
Assorted French Pastries
Fruit Pies and Cakes
Chocolate Mousse with Whipped Cream
• • •
Beverages

Buffet Dinner #24

Iced Celery, Mixed Olives, Radish Roses, Carrot Curls

Decorated Culinary Pieces
Assorted Cold Cuts: Milano-Type Salami,
Roast Spring Chicken, Pickled Ox Tongue
Whole Decorated Salmon and Fillets
Tomato Stuffed with Russian Salad, Deviled Eggs

Salads
Mixed Greens, Selection of Dressings
French Pickled Beets, Potatoes Alsacienne
Cole Slaw, Sliced Tomatoes, Vinaigrette Italian Macaroni

Choice of Two of the Following Hot Dishes
Roast Duckling à l'Orange
Roast Prime Rib of Beef
Roast Sirloin of Beef
Fillet of Beef Wellington, Sauce Périgourdine
Potatoes and Vegetables
Rolls and Butter

Desserts
French Pastries, Assorted Cakes, English Trifle,
Fresh Fruit Salad
• • •
Coffee, Tea, Milk

Buffet Dinner #25

Garden Salad with Dressings
Marinated Seafood Salad
Tuna Antipasto
Florida Citrus Salad
Oysters on the Half Shell
Seafood Caribbean
Conch Chowder
• • •

Whole Roast Sirloin of Beef
Rice Pilaf
Vegetable Ensemble
Roast Duckling,
Your Choice of Black Cherry or Peppercorn Sauce
• • •

Assorted Cakes and Sweets to Include:
Key Lime Pie, Double Fudge Cake, Orange Mousse,
Banana Cream Pie, Fruit Tartlets, Lemon Torte,
Assorted Cheesecakes with Toppings
• • •

Oven Fresh Rolls and Butter
• • •

Coffee and Herbal Tea

Buffet Dinner #26

Whole Decorated Virginia Ham
Vermont Turkey—Decoupé et Remonté, Cranberry Molds

• • •

Fresh Shrimp Salad
German-Style Potato Salad
Sliced Beefsteak Tomatoes on Romaine

• • •

Assorted Relishes

• • •

Butter Rolls and Kaiser Rolls

• • •

From Chafing Dishes
Fillet of Beef à la Stroganoff, Minnesota Wild Rice
Coq au Vin de Chambertin, Fresh Green Broccoli
Paupiettes of Northern Sole, Walewska

• • •

Trays of Imported Cheeses, Fresh Fruit

• • •

Strawberry Tarts, Chocolate Mousse with Whipped Cream,
Viennese Pastries

• • •

Café

Buffet Dinner #27

Oysters Rockefeller and Clams Casino
Glazed Duckling Tidbits with Curaçao

• • •

Spiny Lobster en Bellevue, Attractively Decorated

• • •

Fresh Poached Salmon, Parisienne
Cucumber Salad with Dill

• • •

Sliced Beefsteak Tomatoes on Romaine
German-Style Potato Salad

• • •

Prime Larded Sirloin, Bordelaise, Carved to Order at Buffet
Potato Pancakes

• • •

Almond Chicken, with French Overtones
Zucchini Sauté
Paupiettes of Veal Madère, Risotto

• • •

Imported Cheeses, Fresh Fruit

• • •

Fancy Pastry Display
French Pastries, Mousses, and Fruit Tarts

• • •

Café

Buffet Dinner #28

Freshly Tossed Seasonal Greens
and Vegetables, with Choice of Dressings
Mirrors of Cheese and Fresh Fruits

• • •

Select Three Salads
Waldorf Salad, Vegetable Relish in Bloom
Fountain of Watercress, Tomato, and
Cucumber Salad
Assorted Chilled Sliced Meats

• • •

Select Three Entrées
Beef Tips with Mushrooms
Seafood Medley in Sherry Sauce
Chicken Teriyaki
Sliced Roast Loin of Pork
Baked Red Snapper Creole
Rice Pilaf, Vegetable Medley

• • •

Rolls and Butter

• • •

Assorted Cakes and Sweets

• • •

Beverages

Buffet Dinner #29

Silver Bowl of Fresh Fruit

• • •

Chef's Mixed Greens, Dressings Selection
Sliced Tomatoes with Onions
Cucumbers in Sour Cream and Dill
Waldorf Salad
Assorted Relishes

• • •

Homemade Pâté du Chef
Shrimp Salad, Herring and Sour Cream
Mushrooms and Artichokes à la Grecque

• • •

Roast Loin of Pork, Chicken Teriyaki,
Broiled Grouper, Seafood Newburg
Baron of Beef, Carved to Order
Rice Pilaf, Fresh Garden Vegetables

• • •

Assorted Breads and Rolls

• • •

International Cheeses, French Pastries

• • •

Friandises

• • •

Coffee

Buffet Dinner #30

Greens 'n' Things
Selections of Fresh Fruits of the Season
Relish and Fresh Vegetable Tray
Waldorf Salad
English Potato Salad
Marinated Bean Salad
Spinach Leaf Salad
Choice of Dressings
• • •

Fish 'n' Fowl
Jumbo Shrimp Pyramid (four pieces per person), Sauce Rémoulade
Curried Chicken Salad
Stuffed Eggs Moscovite

Our Pièce de Résistance
Whole Roast Turkey Chaud-Froid
Baked Ham
Hand-Carved Ice Sculpture Centerpiece
• • •

From the Hot Oven (Choice of Three)
Seafood in puree of Leeks and Wine Sauce
Roast Baron of Beef, carved by Chef
Roast Loin of Pork, Danoise
Chicken in Almond Sauce
• • •

Fresh Vegetable in Season
and Oven Roasted Potatoes
• • •

Pastry Display
Assorted French Pastries, Fruit Pies, and Cakes
Chocolate Mousse with Whipped Cream

Buffet Dinner Menus with a Theme

The Gastronomy Buffet Dinner

Minimum 250 Guests

Selection de Fruits de Mer
Huîtres du Point Bleu,
Petoncles de Cherrystone, Cuisses de Crabe
de l'Alaska, Homard d'Angleterre Nouveau

Seafood Bar
Blue Point Oysters, Cherrystone Clams,
Alaska King Crab Legs, New England Lobster
• • •

Salades
Salade Waldorf, Aspereges à la Vinaigrette,
Haricots verts du Lac Bleu, Champignons au Vinaigre,
Salades de Fruits de Mer, Salade Grecque

Salads
Waldorf Salad, Asparagus Vinaigrette, Blue Lake String Beans,
Pickled Mushrooms, Assorted Seafood Salads,
Mixed Garden Greens, Greek Salad
• • •

Selection Froide
Saumon Fumé de la Nova Scotia, Tranches de Bouef Froides,
Pâté Maison en Croûte, Harengs en Crème,
Oeufs Farcis au Caviar, Dinde de Vermont Decorée,
Jambon de Prosciutto avec Fruits, Pyramide de Crevettes,
Saumon Frais du Pacifique à la Parisienne, Pièce de Glace
Sculptée

Cold Selections
Smoked Nova Scotia Salmon, Cold Prime Sirloin of Beef,
Pâté Maison en Croûte, Herrings in Sour Cream,
Stuffed Eggs with Caviar, Decorated Vermont Turkey,
Prosciutto Ham with Fruits, Pyramid of Shrimps,
Fresh Pacific Salmon Parisienne, Hand-Carved Ice Sculpture

Selection Chaude
Côte de Boeuf Roti, Porcelet Hawaien, Homard ou Crevettes au
Curry, Saumon Entier Cuit au Four, Roulade de Veau

Hot Selections
Roast Prime Ribs of Beef, Suckling Pig, Hawaiian,
Curried Lobster or Shrimp, Whole Baked Salmon, Roulade of
Veal
• • •

Bouquetiere de Légumes, Bouquetiere of Vegetables
• • •

Desert
Pâtisseries Françaises, Gâteau St. Honoré, Mousse aux Fraises,
Croquembouches, Savarin Chantilly, Tarte aux Pêches,
Gâteau Forêt Noire, Eclairs au Moka

Dessert
French Pastries, Gâteau St. Honoré, Fresh Strawberry Mousse,
Croquembouche, Savarin Chantilly, Peach Tart,
Black Forest Cake, Mocha Eclairs
• • •

Selection de Fromages Decorés de Fruits Frais
Assorted Cheeses Decorated with Fresh Fruits
• • •

Café, Coffee

The Under the Southern Cross Buffet Dinner

Fruits of the Sea

A Presentation of Seafood to include:
Cold Jumbo Shrimps, Florida Stone Crabs, in Season,
Freshly Shucked Oysters and Clams, Ceviche,
Served with Cocktail Sauce, Mustard Sauce, and Lemon Stars
(Total Eight Pieces of Seafood per Person)

Florida's Bounty

Our Vegetable Cart Is Decorated with
an Assortment of Fresh Vegetables
and Tropical Fruits and offers the following:
Fresh Crudité Display, Attractively presented and
Accompanied by Assorted Dips including:
Cheese, Clam, and Dill
Presentations of International Cheeses,
with a Variety of Fancy Crackers, Bread Sticks,
and Sliced French Bread,
Garnished with Fresh Fruit

The Best in Beef

Whole Roast Steamship Round of Beef,
Served with Petite Rolls,
Accompanied by Creamy Horseradish Sauce
Carpaccio,
Thinly Shaved Raw Sirloin,
Topped with Finely Grated Parmesan Cheese,
and Ground Peppercorns,
Served with Mustard Mayonnaise Sauce, and Sliced Italian
Bread

Hors d'Oeuvres

Chinese Egg Rolls, with Sweet and Sour Sauce
Scallops wrapped in Bacon
Mushroom Caps filled with Crabmeat
Beef Tenderloin Brochettes
Melon and Prosciutto Ham on Mirror
(Eight Pieces per Person)

How Sweet It Is

For the Finishing Touch,
Numerous Delicacies of Special Palate Sweeteners, Tortes,
Mousses, Napoleons, Eclairs, French Pastries
Fresh Fruit and Fondue Display,
Fine Selections of Fresh Seasonal Fruit Accompanied by:
Brown Sugar, Sour Cream, Dark Chocolate Fondue,
Hazelnut-Flavored Whipped Cream

Beverages

In addition to the suggested Open Bar may we recommend
Our Tropical Specialty Drinks or choose from our Selection of
Nonalcoholic Drinks

The Come to the Carnival Dinner Buffet Stations

Let the games begin . . . !

Seafood Booth

Oyster and Clam Raw Bar
Boiled Shrimp in the Shell
Crab Soup with Sherry
• • •

Fun Foods

Relishes
Giant Submarine Sandwiches
Hot Dogs with all the Trimmings:
Mustard, Mayonnaise, Ketchup, Relish, and
Chopped Onions
Pizzas
Chili with Cheddar Cheese
Our Own Popcorn Machine
• • •

Barbecue and Salads

Barbecued Baby Pork Ribs
Barbecued Chicken with Miniature Rolls,
Horseradish, and Mustard
Corn on the Cob
Potato Salad
Tossed Salad,
Assortment of Dressings
• • •

Sweets

Giant Chocolate Chip Cookies
Make Your Own Ice Cream Sundae,
with a Variety of Toppings
Apple Turnovers
Deep Dish Blueberry Pie
Watermelon
• • •

Beverages

Coffee Station
Full Service Bar,
Soda Station, and Beer by the Keg,
Charges Additional

Decorations: Large circus side show signs flanked by multicolored balloon columns decorate the entrance while a calliope plays tunes. Cheerful red and white striped booths house games of fun and skill for your guests to play throughout the evening. Over two dozen games available. Circus performers interact with guests to provide juggling, magic, stilt-walking, unicycling, clowning, and so on. At the end of the evening, an auction can be held to cash in winners.

The Caribbean Island Adventure Buffet Dinner

(See Photo on Page 69)

If it's romance, swashbuckling, and buried treasure you seek . . . this theme is for you.

Fresh Oysters on the Half Shell, Crab Claws,
Cocktail Sauce and Mustard Mayonnaise
Black Bean Soup
with Chopped Onions
Salad Bar with Condiments
and Dressings
Variety of Island Specialty Salads

• • •

Jamaican Shrimp,
Marinated in Pineapple Juice, Brown Sugar,
and Rum
Boiled Lobster
Roast Jerk Pork Loin Calypso
Caribbean Jerk Chicken
Stir-Fried Vegetables
Rice with Red Peppers

• • •

Island Corn Bread with Chilies
Homemade Rolls

• • •

Fresh Tropical Fruit Display:
Melons, Pineapple, Kiwis, Mangoes, Papayas,
Star Fruit, and Bananas
Bananas Foster
Mango Mousse

• • •

Coffee, Tea, Freshly Brewed Decaffeinated
Coffee

Beverages

Exotic Drinks, such as Daiquiris and Piña
Coladas, add to the authenticity of this
evening.

Decorations: Pirates and treasure, lush foliage, sunken ships, exotic birds, and colorful fabrics combine to create an island atmosphere, reminding guests that South Florida had its beginnings in the days of the Spanish Galleon. Music from the islands is irresistible, and the steel drums will tempt your guests to get involved in the limbo dance. Incredible performers in colorful costumes will have everyone on their feet, joining the weaving line of dancers, before the evening ends.

The Best of the USA Stations Buffet Dinner

USA
Buffalo Chicken Wings
Mini Cheeseburgers
Chili Con Carne
Pizza Slices
Ice Cream with Toppings Bar

New Orleans
Barbecued Shrimp
Cajun Chicken Bites
Jambalaya
Mini Muffeletta Sandwiches
Creole Meatballs
Bourbon-Glazed Ham, Carved to Order,
Served with Silver Dollar Rolls, and Condiments

El Paso
Make-Your-Own Taco Bar
Matambre
Chocolate Chicken Bites
Mini Beef Enchiladas
Mini Barbecued Ribs
Flour Tortillas

Boston
Baked Scrod
Raw Bar Featuring: Oysters and Clams on Half Shell,
Lobster Bites
New England Clam Chowder

Charleston
Broiled Super Grouper
She-Crab Soup
Blue Crabs
Low-Country Shrimp
Daufuskie Crab Bites

New York
Mini Hero Sandwich
Foot Long Hot Dog
Manhattan Clam Chowder
Deli Station Featuring:
Top Round of Beef, Pastrami, Corned Beef, Turkey,
carved to order, Served with Silver Dollar Rolls and Condiments

Los Angeles
Lemon Chicken Bites
Teriyaki Steak
Chinese Noodle Salad
Rumaki
Fresh Vegetables with Dip
Domestic Cheeses

Beverage Stations

The Hawaiian Cookout Buffet Dinner

Roast Suckling Pig, Barbecued Beef Ribs
Fried Mahi Mahi, Oriental Chicken
Sweet Potatoes, Stir-Fried Vegetables
• • •
Salad Bar to Include:
Ceviche
Fruit Salad Mahi Tai
Chicken Salad with Coconut
Tossed Green Salad,
Selection of Dressings
• • •
Banana and Date Nut Bread
• • •
Pineapple Tree with Fresh Fruit
South Sea Sweet Table
• • •
Coffee

The Hawaiian Luau Buffet Dinner

Fried Mahi Mahi, Lemon Sauce
Sweet and Sour Pork
Sirloin Tips in Teriyaki Sauce
Fried Rice with Chicken
Oriental Vegetables
Sweet Potatoes Cut in Sticks, Hot Peanut
Sauce
• • •
Fresh Shrimp Salad in a Giant Sea Shell
Tomato Salad
Sliced Avocados and Onions, in Season
Creamy Cole Slaw
Tuna Salad
Bean Sprout Salad
Volcano Salad, Special Dressing
Assorted Relish Tray
• • •
Pineapple Spears, Grapes, Bananas
Jello Mold
Coconut Cake, Banana Pie
Fortune Cookies
• • •
Kona Coffee

The Four Corners of the Nation Buffet Dinner

South
Virginia Ham and Fresh Biscuits,
Chef to Carve
Freshwater Catfish Fried with Cornmeal
Braised Yellow Squash, Parsley Potatoes
Tossed Salad, Peppercorn Dressing
Cold Salmon Bellevue
Relishes
Key Lime Pie, Pecan Pie
Fresh Fruit

Midwest
Whole Roast Sirloin of Beef, Chef to Carve
Polish Sausage with Sauerkraut
Pan Fried Chicken
Brown Rice
Corn Fritters
Corn on the Cob
Salad Bar
Fried Bananas
Apple Pie and Ice Cream Sundaes

Northeast
New England Clam Chowder
Baked Stuffed Shrimp
Leg of Lamb, Chef to Carve
Fettucini with Clam Sauce
Fresh Vegetables, Eggplant Parmesan
Antipasto, Salad Bar
Rice Pudding, Cranberry Muffins

West
Roast of Pork, Chef to Carve
Barbecue Pork Ribs, Seafood Chow Mein
Stir-Fried Vegetables, Fried Rice Oriental
Oriental Salad Bar
Spinach Salad, Bacon Dressing
Crêpes Suzette, Pineapple Kirsch
Chinese Almond Cookies

The Bella Notte Italiana Buffet Dinner

Fettuccine Alfredo, Spaghetti Milanese
Scampi Marinera, Veal Piccata

• • •

Zucchini
Baked Eggplant

• • •

Italian Flag Antipasto Platter:
Salami, Pepperoni, Provolone Cheese, Olives,
Pickles
Giardiniera Italiana
Garden Fresh Salads and Condiments,
Italian and Creamy Dressings

• • •

Fresh Fruit
Pasticcinni
Spumoni Gelato

The Italian Festival Buffet Dinner

Antipasto alla Roma, Chicken Vesuvia
Pepper Steak al Dora, Lasagna al Forno
Spaghetti and Meatballs, Flagolet Beans
Napoli

• • •

Caesar Salad

• • •

Warm Italian Garlic Loaves and Butter

• • •

Roman Fruit Slices
Zuppa Inglese and Additional Pastries
Assorted Fresh Fruit Salad Bowl

• • •

Coffee

The Mardi Gras Buffet Dinner

Vegetable Crudité Display, with Variety of
Dips
Cucumber Salad with Fresh Mint
Marinated Cauliflower with Red Pepper
Marinated Leeks Vinaigrette
Sweet and Sour Cole Slaw
Cajun-Style Corn, Okra, and Pimiento Relish

• • •

French Quarter Creole Bouillabaisse,
Garlic Bread
Steamship Round of Beef
Cajun Barbecued Shrimp
Jambalaya
Spicy Sausage
Red Beans and Rice
Ratatouille

• • •

French Bread and Whipped Butter

• • •

Display of International Cheeses and Fruits

• • •

French Pastries
Pecan Pies
Strawberry Shortcake

• • •

Coffee, Tea, and Freshly Brewed
Decaffeinated Coffee

Chapter 21

Signature Line Gourmet Dinner Menus

Veal Gourmet Dinners

Veal #1

Consommé Double au Xérès
Beef Consommé with Sherry
• • •

Seafood Cocktail à la Moderne
• • •

*Salad d'Endive et Cresson
à l'Huile de Noix et d'Orange*
Belgian Endive and Watercress
with an Orange–Walnut Oil Dressing
• • •

Sorbet au Champagne
Champagne Sherbet
• • •

Grenadin de Veau aux Scampi
Medallion of Veal with Scampi
and Mushrooms

*Pommes Croquettes
Bouquetiere de Légumes*
• • •

Pêche Velvet
Alberta Peach Marinated in Apricot Brandy
• • •

Mignardises Maison
• • •
Café Kona

Veal #2

Consommé Double
A very strong Consommé flavored with
Sherry, served with Cheese Straws
• • •

Fruits de Mer Rémoulade
Pieces of Crab, Shrimp, and other Seafood,
in a mild Rémoulade Sauce
• • •

Galantine de Canard
Breast of Duck, served with
Cumberland Sauce
• • •

Veau aux Morilles
Milk-Fed Veal with a Sauce of
Morels and Sweet Cream

*Pommes Parisienne
Tomate Du Barry
Haricots Verts aux Champignons*
• • •

Coeurs de Romaine avec Brie
Hearts of Crisp Romaine Lettuce served with
a Lemon Dressing and a Wedge of
Brie Cheese
• • •

Crêpes Toque Noire Flambées
Delicate Crêpes Filled with Vanilla Ice Cream
and Ladled with Bing Cherries Jubilee

Veal #3

Première Assiette
La Ballottine de Caneton
Ballotine of Duckling, Cumberland Sauce

• • •

Mise en Bouche
L'Essence de Queue de Boeuf Claire au Madère
Clear Oxtail Broth laced with Madeira

• • •

Deuxième Assiette
La Timbale de Paupiettes de Sole Cardinal Sous Cloche
Poached Fillet of Sole with Lobster Sauce

• • •

Troisième Assiette
Le Jambonneau de Pardreau aux Pignon de Pin
Boneless Partridge Breast enhanced with Pinenuts

• • •

Pour se Rafraîchir
Le Sorbet au Fruit de la Passion
Passion Fruit Sorbet

• • •

Assiette Principale
Les Medallions de Veau Normande
Sautéed Veal Medallions laced with a
Cream Sauce, Flavored with Calvados and Apple Puree
Le Risotto aux Truffes
Risotto with Truffles
Le Fond d'Artichaut Crécy
Artichoke Bottoms filled with Puree of Carrots
Les Pointes d'Asperges Vertes au Beurre
Green Asparagus Spears with Butter

• • •

Issue de Table
La Salade Bibb de Boston à l'Huile Vierge et au Citron
Hearts of Boston Bibb with a light oil and lemon dressing
Le Fromage Brie de Meaux
La Ficelle Parisienne
Double Brie served with French Bread

• • •

Boutehors
Les Fraises Romanoff au Grand Marnier
Strawberries in Grand Marnier served in high goblets, topped
with Chantilly Cream
La Demitasse Colobien
Corbeille Fleurie de Friandises
Les Petits Fours et Chocolats
Les Liqueurs et Fines Champagnes Assorties

Veal #4

*Le Bouillon froid de Boeuf aux
Champignons Sauvages*
Chilled Beef Consommé with Mélange
of Mushrooms

• • •

Les Quenelles de Brochet, Nantua
Quenelles of Pike, Sauce Nantua

• • •

Le Sorbet de Poires
Pear Sorbet

• • •

*La Longe de Veau Nordique, Sauce
Venetienne*
Veal Nordic, Stuffed with Crab Mousse,
Sauce Venetian
Les Asperges en Poivron
Fresh Green Asparagus wrapped in Red Bell
Pepper Rings
Julienne de Legumes
Stir-Fried Julienne of Carrots, Leeks, and
Snow Pea Pods

• • •

Le Charlotte d'Ananas au Coulis de Fraise
Pineapple Charlotte with Strawberry Sauce

• • •

Demitasse

Veal #5

Cream of Petits Pois with Curry

• • •

Fillet of Colorado River Trout,
Sauté Amandine

• • •

Veal Scallopine au Marsala
Homemade Noodles
Zucchini au Gratin
Tomato Du Barry

• • •

Bibb Lettuce with Brie Cheese,
Vinaigrette Sauce

• • •

Parfait Nougatine
Les Petits Fours

• • •

Demitasse

Veal #6

Vol-au-Vent de Fruit de Mer
Seafood with Mushrooms served in a Pastry
Shell with a Lobster Sauce, topped with
Hollandaise Sauce

• • •

Consommé Suzette
Consommé with Julienne of Celery,
Garnished with Truffle and Flavored with
Dry Sherry, Served with Cheese Straws

• • •

Quenelles de Volaille d'Uzes
Petite Chicken Dumplings Garnished with
Truffle, Served with Aurore Sauce

• • •

Trou de Milieu
Champagne Sorbet

• • •

Filet de Veau Romanoff
Medallions of Veal served on a Canapé with
Puree of Mushrooms, covered with a Cream
Sauce, Flavored with Crayfish Butter
Braised Fennel and Parisienne Potatoes

• • •

Salade Isabelle
Finely Sliced Celery, Mushrooms, Artichoke
Bottoms, and Truffles, with
Oil and Vinegar Dressing
Chopped Chervil

• • •

Brie et Roquefort
Brie and Roquefort Cheese

• • •

Pêche Rose—Pompon
Fresh Peach Poached in Syrup
served with Raspberry and Vanilla Ice Cream,
covered with Chantilly Cream and Praline,
garnished with Pink Spun Sugar

• • •

Coffee

Veal #7

Première Assiette
Le Pâté de Campagne
Chef's Country Pâté with Lingonberry Sauce

• • •

Mise en Bouche
Le Consommé Double au Xérès, Les Bouchées de Brie
Consommé laced with Sherry, Bouchées of Brie

• • •

Deuxième Assiette
La Timbale de Homard du Maine, La Reine Anne
Maine Lobster Poached in Bourbon Sauce, served with a
Truffled Risotto

• • •

Troisième Assiette
La Paupiette de Veau Farcie au Basilic
Veal Medallion filled with Sweetbread Mousse Lightly Herbed,
laced with Basil Sauce

• • •

Pour se Rafraîchir
Le Granite à la Prunelle d'Alsace
Sorbet of Alsacian Prune Brandy

• • •

Assiette Principale
La Suprême de Faisan à la Sauce aux Morilles
Roast Breast of Pheasant, crowned with a Morel Sauce,
laced with Fine Herbs, Cognac, and White Wine
Le Panier de Pommes de Terre avec La Jardiniere de Légumes
Deep Fried Potato Basket with Fresh Vegetables of the Season

• • •

Issue de Table
La Salade d'Endive et Cresson,
avec l'Huile d'Abricots et Citron
Endive and Watercress with Apricot Dressing
Le Camembert au Noisettes, agrémenté de Toasts Croustillants
Camembert encrusted with Hazelnuts, Melba Toast

• • •

Boutehors
La Bombe Glacée Arlequin, agrémentée d'une Sauce
Sabayon au Marsala
Ice Bombe of Mint, Strawberry, and Vanilla Parfait, laced with
Sabayon Marsala Sauce
Le Café Anis
La Corbeille de Petits Fours aux Violettes
Les Liqueurs et Fines Eau de Vie

Veal #8

Buena Vista Salad Supreme
Fresh Romaine, Palm Hearts, Mushrooms, Cherry Tomatoes,
Artichoke Hearts, Sliced Olives, Avocado, and Shrimp,
with a Creamy Garlic Dressing

• • •

Clear Oxtail Soup with Sandelman Sherry, Cheese Straws

• • •

Tender Steak of Milk-Fed Veal Sauté, Morel Sauce
Buttered Homemade Noodles
Whole Tomato with French Peas
Green Asparagus Tips

• • •

Butter Rosettes on Lemon Leaves
Small Dinner Rolls

• • •

Brie Cheese with a Bouquet of Fresh Fruits,
Toasted French Bread

• • •

Ice Cream Pie, Brandied Strawberries

• • •

Beverage

Veal #9

Fruits de Mer Bombay
Crab, Shrimp, and other Seafood Delicacies, complemented by
a Sweet Curry Sauce, served in a Pastry Shell

• • •

Salade Maison
Sliced Tomatoes and Cucumbers, served on a Wedge of Bibb
Lettuce, Vinaigrette Dressing

• • •

Sorbet au Citron

• • •

Veau Calvados
Tender Veal sautéed in Butter, Cream, Apples,
and Apple Brandy

Pommes Rouge en Robe des Champs
Carottes Juliennes
Broccoli Polonaise

• • •

Crêpes des Anges
Vanilla Ice Cream, Banana, and Almond Slivers,
wrapped in a Crêpe, served with Hot Chocolate Sauce

• • •

Le Café

Veal #10

Faisan sur Canapé Titania
Pheasant Breast served on a Canapé with
Cognac, Garnished with Orange Segments

• • •

Soupe à l'Oseille
Sorrel Soup

• • •

Paupiette de Sole Sylvia
Dover Sole Fillet Stuffed with Fish Mousse
and Artichoke, Poached in White Wine,
served in Artichoke Bottom, covered
with a Light White Wine Sauce, Garnished
with Truffle

• • •

Trou de Milieu
Avocado Sorbet

Filet de Veau au Basilic
Légume Trois Mousquetaires
Veal Sautéed in Basil surrounded by Zucchini
Boats with
Puree of Carrots
Noisette Potatoes

• • •

Salade Nouvelle
Bibb Lettuce, Enoki Mushrooms, garnished
with Walnuts
Vinegar and Oil Dressing

• • •

Boucheron aux Mangues
Goat Cheese with Fresh Mango

• • •

Feuilletage aux Fraise, Sauce Caramel
Fresh Strawberries served in a Pastry Shell
with Caramel Sauce

• • •

Coffee

Beef Gourmet Dinners

Beef #1

Première Assiette
La Mousse de Saumon au Champagne
Sous Cloche
Salmon Mousse with Champagne Sauce
• • •

Mise en Bouche
Le Potage Froid au Concombre
Les Croutons de Saumon
Chilled Puree of Cucumber Soup served with
Salmon Croutons
• • •

Deuxième Assiette
La Selle de Lievre Dijonnaise
Marinated Saddle of Hare served with a Light
Mustard Sauce and Chestnut Puree
• • •

Pour se Rafraîchir
Le Sorbet au Vieux Calvados Normande
Sorbet of Aged Calvados
• • •

Assiette Principale
Le Filet de Boeuf Strasbourgoise
Sliced Roast Tenderloin of Beef Filled with
Goose Liver Pâté and Truffles,
Laced with Sauce Périgueux
Les Pommes de Terre Amandine
Croquette Potatoes, Breaded in Almonds
Les Haricots Verts au Jambon de Parme
Fresh String Beans blended with Fine Herbs,
Wrapped in Prosciutto
La Tomate de Printemps Farcie au Salsifis
Tomato Filled with Glazed Salsify
• • •

Issue de Table
La Salade d'Endives de Belgique, à l'Huile de
Noix et Citron
Belgian Endives with a Light Walnut-Lemon
Dressing
Le Fromage Montrachet
Les Toasts de Pain Français Croustillants
French Goat Cheese with Melba Toast
• • •

Boutehors
Le Soufflé Glacé aux Framboises, agrémenté
d'un Sabayon au Dom Perignon
Deep Chilled Raspberry Soufflé with
Champagne Sauce
• • •

Le Moka, Les Mignardises en Pastiage,
Les Liqueurs et Fines Eau de Vie

Beef #2

L'Essence de Queue de Boeuf Claire aux Vieux Sandelman
Clear Oxtail Soup with Sandelman Sherry
• • •

Le Feuilleté de Coquille St. Jacques aux Petits Légumes
Scallops with Small Vegetables in Pastry Shell
• • •

Le Sorbet au Vin Rouge
Red Wine Sorbet
• • •

Le Tournedo Farci, Cordon Rouge
Les Pommes Noisette
La Laitue Braise
La Tomate Princesse
Tournedo Stuffed with Goose Liver Mousse
Noisette Potatoes
Braised Romaine Lettuce
Tomato with White Asparagus Tips
• • •

Le Vacherin Glacé à la Chartreuse avec Compote de Fraises
Vacherin with Chartreuse Ice Cream and Strawberry Compote
• • •

Les Petits Fours
Le Café

Beef #3

Chilled Cream of Avocado en Supreme
• • •
Shrimp, Scallops, and Lobster, Vin Blanc
• • •
Passion Fruit Sorbet in Sherry Glass
• • •
Fillet of Prime Beef Wellington, Sauce Périgourdine
• • •
Bouquetiere of Fresh Garden Vegetables
Petite Dinner Rolls, Passed
Butter Rosettes on Lemon Leaves
• • •
Small Hearts of Bibb Lettuce, with Palm Hearts and Brie
Cheese, Creamy Tarragon Dressing
• • •
English Wafers, Soufflé Glacé au Grand Marnier
• • •
Les Petits Fours
• • •
Blended Coffee

Beef #4

Quenelles d'Opakapaka, Sauce Nantua
Poached Island Fish Dumplings with a Crayfish Butter Sauce

• • •

Consommé Diane, Paillettes au Fromage
Beef Consommé served with Cheesesticks

Salade de Saison
Seasonal Greens with Buttermilk-Dill Dressing

• • •

Tournedos Henry IV
Fillet of Beef served with Artichoke Hearts and Sauce Béarnaise

Pommes Chateau
Bouquetiere de Légumes

• • •

Soufflé Glacé au Grand Marnier
Ice Cream Soufflé with Essence of Grand Marnier Liqueur

• • •

Friandises

• • •

Café Kona

Beef #5

Bisque de Homard
Lobster Bisque Laced with Cognac and served with a Touch of
Caviar and Cream

• • •

Salade Méditerranéenne
Mixed Green Salad with Artichoke Hearts, Carrots,
Mushrooms, Pimiento, Olives, Bay Shrimp, and Feta Cheese

• • •

Le Sorbet au Calvados
Sorbet with Calvados

Le Filet de Boeuf, Duc de Wellington
Individual Fillets of Beef, Coated with Goose Liver Pâté and
Baked in Puff Pastry

Chou-Fleur au Beurre
Tomate Champignons
Asperges Hollandaise

• • •

Fruits Maison avec Crème d'Amandes
Fresh Seasonal Fruits, accented with Whipped Almond Cream

• • •

Le Café de Maison Spécial

Beef #6

Melon et Jambon Prosciutto
Melon wrapped in Prosciutto

• • •

Filet de Sole Véronique
Fillet of Sole with White Grapes

• • •

Le Sorbet de Fruit Frais
Fresh Fruit Sorbet

• • •

Filet de Boeuf Wellington, Sauce Périgueux
Prime Whole Fillet of Beef Wellington,
Sauce Périgueux

Chou-Fleur Polonaise
Cauliflower Polonaise

Carottes Nouvelles Glacées
Glazed Baby Carrots

Pommes de Terre à la Parisiennes
Parisienne Potatoes

• • •

Salade Pascaline, Sauce Vinaigrette
Salad Pascaline with Vinaigrette

• • •

Poire Maison, Quatre Saisons
Four Seasons Pear

• • •

Demitasse

Beef #7

Consommé Double with Sherry, Cheese Straws

• • •

Fillet of Boston Sole in White Wine, Dugléré

• • •

Key Lime Sorbet

• • •

Roasted Whole Beef Tenderloin,
Forestiere, With Sautéed Mixed Mushrooms
Bouquetiere of Vegetables

• • •

Spinach Salad with Warm Bacon Dressing

• • •

Poached Pear with Rum Sabayon
and Chocolate Ice Cream

• • •

Demitasse
Les Petits Fours

Beef #8

Consommé au Vermicelle
Clarified Broth with delicate Egg Noodles

• • •

Saumon Mousseline
Poached Salmon served with a Cream Sauce,
garnished with Red Caviar

• • •

Sorbet de Maison
Raspberry Sherbet garnished with a Kiwi
Wheel, Laced with Champagne

• • •

Filet de Boeuf
Roast Larded Tenderloin of Beef,
with Morel Sauce

*Fonds d'Artichauts, Pommes Berny,
Carottes Vichy*

• • •

Salade de Fraise
Fresh Sliced Strawberries and Feta Cheese
over Crisp Romaine with Lemon Dressing

• • •

Crêpe d'Avignon
A Crêpe Filled with Mocha Ice Cream,
served with Hot Fudge Sauce

• • •

Le Café

Beef #9

Clam and Mussel Consommé,
with Julienne of Leeks, served Tableside from a Silver Tureen

• • •

Broiled Boneless Quail, Pomegranate Glaze

• • •

Salade Maison
A Symphony of Garden Greens, Diced Cucumber,
Sliced Mushrooms, Diced Artichoke Hearts, Fresh Citrus
Fruit, Diced Tomato, and Hearts of Palm in a Light Creamy
French Mustard Dressing, and served with a Chilled Fork,
Presented and then Tossed Tableside

Roast Tenderloin of Beef, Carved in the Room by Chefs in
Crisp White Uniforms, with Bordelaise Sauce, passed
Pommes Lorette
Flageolets Provençale and Artichoke Bottom
Stuffed Red Pepper Florentine

• • •

Gold Coast Assortment of Warm Dinner Rolls
and Creamery Butter

• • •

Savarin of Vanilla Ice Cream with Fresh Berries in Melba
Sauce, Decorated with Whipped Cream,
and Milk Chocolate Shavings

Petits Fours and After Dinner Mints Presentation

• • •

Coffee, Tea, Decaffeinated Coffee

Chicken Gourmet Dinners

Chicken #1

Medallions de Homard Monaco
Lobster Medallions served with a Unique
Sauce, Garnished with Black Caviar, Dill, and
Lemon Wheel

• • •

Potage de Cresson
Cream of Watercress Soup served Chilled

• • •

Le Poulet avec Chanterelle
Boneless Chicken Breast, Sautéed and Laced
with a Sauce of Cream and
French Chanterelles

*Pommes Berny
Carottes Vichy
Asperges au Beurre*

• • •

Salade de Fraises
Fresh Sliced Strawberries and Feta Cheese,
over Crisp Romaine with Lemon Dressing

• • •

Pâtisseries Françaises Assorties
Assorted French Pastries

• • •

Le Café

Chicken #2

Salade d'Epinards
Fresh Spinach Salad tossed with Hot Bacon
Dressing, Fresh Mushrooms, Sour Cream,
and Flamed with Cognac
• • •

Le Sorbet au Champagne
• • •

Le Poulet Oscar
Boned Breast of Chicken Crowned with
Asparagus, King Crab Meat, and
Sauce Béarnaise

Tomate Clarmart
Ballottine d'Haricots Verts
Riz Maison
• • •

Fromages et Fruits
Platters of Cheese and Fresh Fruit
• • •

Crêpes Toque Noire Flambées
Delicate Crêpes filled with Vanilla Ice Cream
and Ladled with Bing Cherries Jubilee
• • •

Le Café

Other Fowl Gourmet Dinners

Other Fowl #1

Pâté à la Maison, Sauce Cumberland
Pâté with Red Currant Sauce
• • •

*Essence de Champignon, Paillettes au
Fromage*
Mushroom Consommé served with
Cheesesticks
• • •

*Salade de Feuilles Vertes de Manoa
au Juliennes de Canard,
Sauce Piquante au Poivre*
Manoa Lettuce garnished with Duck and a
Spicy Sauce
• • •

Granite de Kiwi
Kiwi Sherbet
• • •

Suprême de Volaille Monte Carlo
Scampi on Breast of Chicken

Riz Picasso, Bouquetiere de Légumes
• • •

Banane Fraise au Chantilly
Bananas and Strawberries in Whipped Cream
• • •

Friandises
• • •
Café Kona

Other Fowl #2

Consommé de Tortue Verte Amontillado
Green Turtle Soup Amontillado
• • •

*Suprême de Faisan Grand Veneur, Sauce
Périgourdine*
Suprême of Pheasant Grand Veneur,
Truffle Sauce

Riz Sauvage de Manitoba
Wild Rice

Morilles Sautées
Sautéed Morels

Coeurs d'Artichauts
Hearts of Artichoke

Tomate Du Barry
Tomato Du Barry
• • •

Salade Rosemarie, Sauce Vinaigrette
Salad Rosemarie, Vinaigrette

Fromage de Brie
Brie Cheese
• • •

Soufflé Glacé au Citron, Petits Fours
Lemon Soufflé Glacé, Petits Fours
• • •

Demitasse

Other Fowl #3

*La Salade Tiède de Langouste au Beurre
d'Orange*
Warm Lobster Salad with Orange Butter

• • •

La Soupe de Grenouille au Cresson
Frog Legs and Watercress Soup

• • •

*Le Suprême de Canard à la Fondue
d'Echalottes, Sauce Bercy
Les Pommes Fondantes
Les Navets Blancs*
Breast of Duckling, cooked pink, on a Bed of
Sautéed Shallots and Covered with Bercy
Sauce, Fondant Potatoes, and Parsnips

• • •

La Coeur du Palmier, Sauce aux Noix
Hearts of Palm with Hazelnut Dressing

• • •

*La Salade de Fruits du Temps au Coulis de
Fraise et la Glacé Vanille en Corolle*
Fresh Seasonal Fruit Salad with Strawberry
Sauce and Vanilla Ice Cream in Tulip

• • •

Les Petits Fours

• • •

Coffee

Lamb Gourmet Dinners

Lamb #1

Mise en Bouche
Le Consommé aux Truffes à la Paul Bocuse
Truffle Consommé, Overbaked with Puff Pastry

• • •

Première Assiette
Le Loup Braisé aux Feuilles de Laitues,
à la Mousse St. Jacques
Braised Striped Bass with Lettuce Leaves and
Scallop Mousse in White Wine Sauce

• • •

Deuxième Assiette
La Poitrine de Caneton Roti à la Rouennaise
Roast Breast of Duckling with Duck Liver
Pâté and Red Wine Sauce

• • •

Pour se Rafraîchir
Le Sorbet au Citron Vert
Key Lime Sorbet

• • •

Assiette Principale
La Selle d'Agneau Prince Noir
Roasted Saddle of Lamb with Fine Herbs and
Black Peppercorn Sauce au Cognac
Les Pommes Rissolées Noisette

Hazelnut-Shaped Potatoes, Sautéed with
Butter, Parsley
Les Choux de Bruxelles Limousine
Brussels Sprouts Tossed in Butter
with Chestnut Pieces, Sprinkled with Nutmeg
La Tomate Provençale
Sprinkled with Bread Crumbs, Cheese,
and Parsley

• • •

Issue de Table
La Salade de Chicorée Bien Blanche,
et de Cresson au Citron
Chicory Salad with Watercress, Lemon Dressing
Le Répertoire des Meilleurs Fromages de France
Les Toasts Croustillants
French Brie, Port Salut, and Boursin

• • •

Boutehors
Le Vacherin, Framboise
Meringue Ice Cream Cake,
Fresh Raspberry Sauce
Parfum aux Liqueurs
Le Moka Bresilien
Les Mignardises en Pastiage
Les Liqueurs et Fines Champagnes Assorties

Lamb #2

La Papaya de Hawaii aux Perles de Melon Mariné au Porto
Hawaiian Papaya with Pearls of Melon Marinated in Port Wine
• • •

La Mousse de Sole avec sa Sauce Verte et Broccoli
Mousse of Sole with Green Sauce and Broccoli
• • •

Le Sorbet au Calvados
• • •

Les Cotelettes d'Agneau Orientaux,
Les Pommes Croquettes, La Ratatouille Niçoise
Lamb Chops Oriental, Croquette Potatoes,
Zucchini and Eggplant Niçoise
• • •

Le Feuilleté de Poires, Sauce Caramel et la Glacé Vanille en
Corolle
Poached Pear with Puff Pastry, Caramel Sauce and Vanilla Ice
Cream in Tulip
• • •

Les Petits Fours
Le Café

Lamb #4

Consommé aux Truffes
Twice Clarified Broth with Truffles
• • •

Chevreuil Fumé
Smoked Venison, Garnished and Served Cold
• • •

Sorbet au Champagne
• • •

L'Agneau en Croûte
Individual Fillets of Lamb, wrapped in
Fresh Spinach, Ham, and Duxelles, then
Baked in Puff Pastry
Tomate Clarmart
Asperges Hollandaise, Chou-Fleur au Beurre
• • •

Fromages et Fruits
Mousse au Grand Marnier
• • •

Café avec Chantilly

Lamb #3

Coquilles St. Jacques en Croûte
Fresh Bay Scallops Served in a Sauce of Shallots,
White Wine, and Mushrooms, presented in a Seashell
• • •

Salade Caesar
Prepared in the room
• • •

Sorbet Maison
Raspberry Sherbet garnished with a Kiwi Wheel,
Laced with Champagne
• • •

L'Agneau Provençale
Roast Rack of Lamb prepared with Dijon Mustard, Parsley,
and Bread Crumbs

Pommes Parisiennes, Puree de Carottes,
Fonds d'Artichauts Florentines
• • •

Mousse de Citron
A Delicate Lemon Mousse
• • •

Le Café

Lamb #5

Quelques Coquillages dans leur Crème
Glacée
Mussels, Cockles, and Clams, in a Lightly
Creamed Sauce, with a Mousse of Sugar Peas
• • •

Escalope de Bar aux Figues
Sautéed Sea Bass with Figs, served in a Sherry
and Green Peppercorn Sauce
• • •

Selle d'Agneau Farcie, en Crépinette
Stuffed Saddle of Lamb

Courgette en Fleur
Young Zucchini

Gratin de Squash et Choux Verts
Cabbage and Squash Gratin
• • •

Nos Deux Gâteaux au Chocolat; Succès et
Fondant aux Poires
Our Two Chocolate Cakes with Pear Fondant
• • •

Tuiles et Mignardises
Coffee

Lamb #6

Petite Marmite Henry IV
Double Consommé with Diced Beef
and Vegetables

• • •

**Coquille Nantua—Homard, Crevettes,
Crabe, et Huitres Cuits en Coquille**
Coquille Nantua—Lobster, Shrimp,
Crabmeat, and Oysters, Baked in Seashell

• • •

Le Sorbet de Fruit Frais
Fresh Fruit Sorbet

• • •

Carré d'Agneau Roti à la Richelieu
Crown Roast of Lamb, Richelieu

Tomate Farcie Genevoise
Stuffed Tomato Genevoise

Têtes de Champignon Duxelles
Mushroom Caps Duxelles

Coeur de Laitue Braisé
Braised Heart of Romaine Lettuce

Pommes de Terre Fondantes
Fondant Potatoes

• • •

Salade d'Endives Vinaigrette
Endive Salad Vinaigrette

• • •

Pêches Napoleon
Peaches Napoleon

• • •

Demitasse

Venison Gourmet Dinners

Venison #1

Première Assiette
La Mousse de Pèlerines, Sauce Cressonette
Scallop Mousse with Watercress Sauce

• • •

Mise en Bouche
Le Consommé de Canard au Gingembre
Clear Duck Broth with Ginger and Julienne of
Vegetables

• • •

Deuxième Assiette
Le Pigeonneaux Braisé à l'Essence de Celeri
Braised Boneless Squab with Celery Puree

• • •

Troisième Assiette
La Pomme de Ris de Beau Gourmand
Braised Sweetbread with Goose Liver
and Asparagus

• • •

Pour se Rafraîchir
Le Sorbet de Goyave au Champagne Rosé
Sorbet of Guava Fruit with Champagne

• • •

Assiette Principale
La Selle de Chevreuil, Grand Veneur
Larded Saddle of Venison served with a
Delicate Game Sauce with Braised Chestnuts
and Gooseberries
La Pomme de Terre Farcie aux Chanterelles
Roast Potato filled with Chanterelle Mushrooms
Les Têtes de Violin
Fiddlehead Ferns
La Courgette Farcie avec la Purée de Carottes
Zucchini Boats filled with Puree of Carrots

• • •

Issue de Table
La Laitue du Kentucky au Coeur de Palmier
à l'Huile Douce et Citron
Kentucky Limestone Lettuce with Hearts of Palm

• • •

Boutehors
La Charlotte Russe
Russian Vanilla Ice Cream
Le Café Kona
Les Truffes au Chocolat
Les Liqueurs et Fines Champagnes Assorties

Venison #2

Consommé de Queue de Boeuf à la Français,
Pailletes au Parmesan
Clear Oxtail Soup, Cheese Straws
• • •

Cassolette de Crevettes
Potted Shrimps
• • •

Selle de Venaison Roti
Gelée de Groseilles Rouges
Roast Rack of Venison
Red Currant Jelly

Pommes de Terre Croquettes
Croquette Potatoes

Chanterelles au Beurre
Chanterelles in Herbed Butter
• • •

Salade Waldorf
Waldorf Salad
• • •

Ananas Frais au Kirsch
Fresh Pineapple with Kirsch

Petits Fours
• • •

Demitasse

Fish/Seafood Gourmet Dinners

Seafood #1

Potage Queue de Boeuf
Clear Oxtail Soup with Sherry
• • •

Coeurs de Palmier et Artichauts Vinaigrett
Hearts of Palm and Marinated Artichoke
Hearts served on a bed of Bibb Lettuce
• • •

Sorbet de Calvados
• • •

Suprême de Saumon Duc de Wellington
Fillet of Salmon wrapped in Fresh Spinach
and baked in Puff Pastry, Served with Sauce
Mousseline

Carottes Vichy
Broccoli
Chou-Fleur au Beurre
• • •

Mousse d'Amaretto avec Amandes
A Light Amaretto Mousse garnished
with Sliced Almonds
• • •

Le Café

Seafood #2

Petite Terrine d'Aubergines avec une Salade
de Lapereau Confit
A Terrine of Eggplant and Slice of Rabbit,
cooked in a Vinegar Sauce
• • •

Ragout de Langoustes aux Champignons des
Bois
Florida Lobster Stew with Sautéed
Wild Mushrooms
• • •

Pâté Pantin de Caille,
son Jus et une Salade Mélangée aux Chapons
Homemade Quail Pâté in its own Juice
and a Salad
• • •

Les Fromages Français
French Cheeses
• • •

Mangue Rotie à la Vanille Fraîche et sa
Glacé
Roasted Mango with Fresh Vanilla and
Homemade Ice Cream
• • •

Tuiles et Mignardises
Coffee

Multiple-Entrées Gourmet Dinners

Multiple #1

Consommé Bonaparte
Chicken Consommé garnished with
Chicken Quenelles

• • •

Saumon Fumé
Sliced Smoked Salmon served with
Cocktail Rye, Capers, and Lemon

• • •

Salade d'Epinards Flambées
Fresh Spinach Tossed with Hot Bacon
Dressing, Fresh Mushrooms, Sour Cream,
and Flamed with Cognac

• • •

Sorbet de Framboise avec Champagne

• • •

Les Medallions de Veau et de Boeuf
Beef Tenderloin with Sauce Périgourdine,
accompanied by
Tender Veal, with Sauce Calvados

• • •

Pommes Persillées
Carottes Julienne
Broccoli au Beurre

• • •

Les Fraises Jubilees
Strawberries Jubilee served over
Vanilla Ice Cream

• • •

Le Café

Multiple #2

Salade de Homard Vanderbilt
Lobster Salad with Julienne of Truffles

• • •

Consommé de Queue de Boeuf Claire,
Rondelles de Pain aux Herbes
Beef Consommé with Herbal Flavored Toast

• • •

Coeurs de Laitue et d'Artichaut, Sauce
Ravigote
Hearts of Bibb Lettuce and Artichokes

• • •

Sorbet au Citron Vert
Lime Sherbet

• • •

Noisette d'Agneau de Printemps et
Medallion de Veau, Sauce Morilles
Fillet of Lamb and Veal
Accompanied by Morel Mushroom Sauce

• • •

Pommes Olivettes, Bouquetiere de Légumes

• • •

Ballon Master Kidd
Currant Sherbet with Freshly
Whipped Cream

• • •

Petits Fours

• • •

Café Roma

Multiple #3

Avocado with Lump Crabmeat
in a Spicy Sauce Presented on Crisp Lettuce

• • •

Consommé Clear with Fine Vegetables, Cheese Straws

• • •

Bibb Lettuce with Palm Hearts, Cherry Tomatoes,
Sliced Mushrooms, Creamy Garlic Dressing

• • •

6-ounce Broiled Rock Lobster Tail, with Drawn Butter
6-ounce Broiled Filet Mignon, with Bordelaise Sauce

Buttered Broccoli
Roasted Potatoes

• • •

Assorted Dinner Rolls

• • •

Vanilla Ice Cream with Fresh Strawberries and
Pineapple, Grand Marnier
Coconut Macaroons

• • •

Beverage

Multiple #4

Le Consommé au Xérès
Consommé with Sherry served with Home Baked Cheese Straws

• • •

Salade Treasure Coast
Bibb Lettuce, Fresh String Beans, Sliced Mushrooms,
Bay Shrimp, and Cherry Tomato

• • •

Caille et Filet de Boeuf
Quail Ladled with a Bing Cherry Sauce, Accompanied by a
Filet Mignon, served with a Béarnaise Sauce

Carottes au Beurre
Fonds d'Artichauts Florentine
Riz Maison

• • •

Mousse d'Amaretto
Served with an Almond Macaroon

• • •

Le Café de Maison Spécial

Multiple #5

Prosciutto avec Melon
Melon, in Season, with Prosciutto Ham

• • •

Escargots aux Champignons
Snails Stuffed into Fresh Mushroom Caps with Herb Garlic
Butter and Shallots

• • •

Salade de Californie
Green Salad Tossed with Bay Shrimp and Diced Avocado, then
Dressed with Peppercream

• • •

Sorbet au Citron

• • •

Le Filet Mignon Cardinal
Broiled Filet Mignon with Medallions of Lobster

Pommes Duchesse
Broccoli au Beurre

• • •

Bananes Flambées

• • •

Le Café

Multiple #6

Pheasant Terrine
or
Consommé of Capon with Rainbow
Trout Julienne

• • •

Escalope of Salmon, Crème aux Herbes

• • •

Trout Normand

• • •

Saddle of Lamb with Veal Mousse,
Sauce au Porto
Bouquetiere of Fresh Vegetables
Saddle of Deer, Sauce Grand Veneur

• • •

Kentucky Limestone Lettuce with Olive Oil,
Lemon, and Fine Herbs

• • •

Brie Cheese with Truffles and
Walnut French Bread

• • •

Pear Helene on Almond Wafer

• • •

Pralines
Coffee

Multiple #7

Roulade of Smoked Salmon with Trout
Mousse

• • •

Cream of Asparagus Soup with
Sausage Quenelles

• • •

Shrimp wrapped in Savoy Cabbage with
Caviar Butter

• • •

Johannesburg Sherbet

• • •

Roasted Partridge on Toast au Jus Naturel
Gratin Dauphinois
Pheasant Breast, Madeira Sauce
Artichoke Bottom with Chestnut Puree

• • •

Cheeses of France

• • •

Individual Chocolate Praline Soufflés Glacés,
Sauce Noisettes

• • •

Mignardises
Coffee

Chapter 22

Reception Menus

The City Square Reception

A spectacular setting decorated in a style indicative of an international town square.

Branching from the park-like setting on all sides will be small shop facades where costumed vendors will "sell" their goods and merchandise.

Guests will be encouraged to visit the shops, relax in the park under umbrellas, and listen to the band play in the gazebo or watch the changing beauty of the water fountain.

The Storefronts Will Include:

The Seafood Market
Where shuckers will show their catch of the day
including:
Fresh Oysters and Clams
Cocktail Sauce, Horseradish, Tabasco, Lemon Stars, and
Oysterettes
Jumbo Prawns, sauté au Pernod, Flambé Mussels,
on the Half Shell, Provençale
• • •

The Butcher
Preparing Tenderloin of Beef Steak Tartare,
Ground to Order and Served on Rye,
Pumpernickel, and Wheat Crackers
Whole Tenderloin of Beef, Marinated in a
Cognac Mustard Sauce with Cracked Peppercorn,
Sliced at the Shop
Shop to be Decorated with Meat Rack and a Side of Beef

The Produce Stand
Where the Greengrocer will display:
Crates and Baskets of Market Fresh Fruits and
Vegetables and serve . . .
Massive Displays of Crudités on Ice Including:
Green Beans, Carrots, Radishes, Celery, Zucchini,
Cauliflower, Dill Dip, Clam Dip, and Onion Dip
And a Variety of Vegetable Salads
In Light Marinades . . .
Red Cabbage Slaw, Brussels Sprouts and Tomato,

Zucchini and Summer Squash with Onion,
Corn with Bell Pepper,
Bite-Size Pieces of Fruit:
Varieties of Apples, Pears, Grapes, Oranges, Melons,
Grapefruit, Kiwi, Pineapple, Strawberries, Pomegranate,
etc., with Brown Sugar, Whipped Cream,
Crème Fraîche, and Chocolate Fondue
• • •

The Cheese Shop
From a Display Case . . .
Larger Wheels and Blocks of
Domestic and Imported Cheeses Including:
Cheddar, Swiss, Havarti, Camembert, Brie, Port du Salut,
Bel Paese, Cheshire, Gouda, Edam, Stilton,
Pont l'Evêque, Boursin, Monterey Jack, Gorgonzola,
Cherry- and Walnut-Flavored Gourmandese
All Cheese cut by the Cheese Merchant and served with a
variety of Breads, Crackers, Lahvosh, and Mustards
Whipped Butter and Fruit Garnish will also be available,
along with a Wine display

The Tea and Spice Shop
With the aroma of:
Fresh Cinnamon Wafting Overhead
A Variety of Hot Teas will be offered, With Cream,
Sugar Cubes, and Lemon Wedges
The Attendant will also prepare Coffees using a variety of:
Liqueurs, Whipped Cream, and the like.
• • •

The Bakery and Pâtisserie
Shelves filled With:
Cakes, Pies, Breads, Pastry, Rolls, and Cookies,
all yours for the asking
Breads Kept Warm in Concealed Units,
Whipped Butters, in Flavors, Jams, Preserves, and
Confitures,
Suitably Placed to encourage a double helping
atop Golden Brown Croissants

French Pastries and Tortes
Pies
Custards
Mousse
Trifle

Onion Rolls, Kaiser Rolls,
Salt Sticks and Bagels,
Whole Loaves of Rye,
Pumpernickel, Swirls,
Boules, Baguettes, Epes,
Batards, etc.

• • •

The Crêpe and Omelette Shoppe
Omelettes Sizzling to Perfection,
as the Guest Requests His Favorite Filling:
Brie, Shrimp and Artichoke, Ratatouille.
Endless Combinations with the same Fillings
Available for Crêpes, Flambé of Course!

• • •

What Town Square would be complete without a Candy Store? Jars and jars of delightful Penny Candy are on view, but they're no match for our homemade Confections, Pralines, and Petits Fours, as well as our Fudge. Presented to guests in small white bags.

Interspersed throughout the Square Shopfronts are an Art Gallery, a Haberdashery, a Drugstore, a Silversmith, and perhaps a Shop with a Florist making small Bouquets and Boutonnieres for guests, or a Calligrapher showing the unique writing craft, or a Silhouette artist doing cuts and mounting them on white backgrounds.

Beverages: Complete Bars would be located around the Square with various shingles hung to denote Spirits, a Wine Shoppe, and a Pub serving only beers. These shops would complement the festive nature of the event.

The European Farmers' Market
Reception

Atop Cubic Constructions, the following will be served:

Hot Dishes
Brochette of Escargot wrapped in Chicken Breast
Veal Stuffed with Crabmeat and Spinach
Duckling Brochette with Kumquat
Shrimp Tempura
Fried Swiss Cheese
Shashlick of Veal, Pork, and Lamb
Mushrooms Stuffed with the Following:
Curried Chicken topped with Coconut, Crab,
Parmesan Cheese, and Sherry
Sweet Breads en Bouchée
Baby Lamb Chops
Kidneys in White Wine

• • •

Cold Dishes
Servuga Caviar Served in Silver Spoons
From Well-Lit Crystalline Ice Blocks,
with Blinis and with Stolichnaya Vodka,
Chilled in Crushed Ice
Marinated Crayfish
Seafood Mélange of Lobster, Crab, and Shrimp
Lachsschinen
Medallions of Beef Tenderloin, Lobster, Eel
Whole Sturgeons and Smoked Salmons
Cold Pheasant Breast
Venison Quenelles
Choice Selection of Pâtés
Elaborate Tropical Fruit and Imported Cheese Display
with Assorted Breads and Crackers

To Include Grapes Garnished with Rock Candy
and Poached Pears Stuffed with Gorgonzola Cheese

• • •

Topiaries of Fresh Vegetables
Served with Fresh Dill, Avocado, Crab, and Clam Dips

• • •

Chocolate Fondue Served with Assorted Fresh Fruits
Glass Bowls of
Whipped Cream, Sour Cream, and Brown Sugar
Assortment of Delicate Sweets

• • •

From a larger than life re-creation
of a European Farmers' Market,
we will display, atop, around, and on triangular and
rectangular cubes, the following:
Masses of Fresh Whole Vegetables "in crate" to include:
Cauliflower, Artichokes, Eggplant, Rhubarb,
Green Spinach, Celery, Watercress, Dill, Tomatoes,
Potatoes, Belgian Endive, Red Cabbage, Mushrooms,
Summer Squash, Zucchini, Beets, Wheat, Corn on the
Stalk and Tiny Whole Corn, Sweet Potatoes, Avocados,
Cucumbers, Broccoli, Asparagus, Chicory Lettuce,
Romaine Lettuce, Boston Bibb Lettuce,
Carrots and Turnips

• • •

Fresh Fruits to include:
Bushels of a variety of Apples, Persimmons, Grapefruits,
Oranges, Pineapple, Cantaloupes, Assorted Melons,
Blueberries, Strawberries, Pears, Assorted Grapes,
Bananas, Plums, Peaches, Coconuts, Tangerines, Kiwis,
Papayas, Red Bananas, and Plantains

• • •

Also Displayed in Overflowing Bushels:
Smoked Oysters, Variety of Fresh and Smoked Clams,
Mussels, Shrimps, Lobsters, Variety of Herring,
Crab Claws, Sardines, Smoked Eel, Smelts, and Crayfish
In Addition, on Giant Blocks of Ice:
Whole Salmon, White Fish, Red Snapper, and Halibut

• • •

Giant Wheels of Cheeses from Around the Globe
Giant Breads of Every Description
International Assortment of Crackers
International Selection of Colossal Sausages,
Both hung and placed accordingly

• • •

Bushels of Shelled Peanuts and Nuts of all Varieties,
Dried Fruits to include Apricots, Dates, etc.

• • •

Carved by Chef,
Whole Steamship Beef with Condiments
and Assorted Rolls

In addition, Displayed and Carved,
Roast Suckling Pigs and Whole Hams
Displays of Varieties of Pâté

• • •

Vegetables Cut and Served with Variety of Dips:
Fresh Dill, Avocado, Crab, and Clam

• • •

Fruits, Cut and Whole,
Served with Whipped Cream and Brown Sugar

• • •

All Seafoods, Sausage, Beef, and Pork,
Served Appropriately on Massive Platters

• • •

Chefs on Stations
To Carve Ham, Beef, and Pig
To Shuck Oysters

The International Cubed Presentation Reception

From a multisided geometric shaped buffet table, a presentation of the following food (Approximately 15 to 16 pieces of hors d'oeuvres per person):

Presented from the Central Buffet Tables, in the Center of the Room

Selection of Cold Hors d'Oeuvres to Include
Mirrored Presentations Garnished with Show Pieces:
Medallions of Beef Tenderloin, Pork, Veal, Pâté,
and Cold Breast of Pheasant

• • •

Individual Crystal Ice Carvings Containing:
Colorful Array of Fresh Fruits to include
Pineapple Cubes, Melon Cubes, Strawberries,
and a Selection of Other Fresh Fruits
accompanied by Brown Sugar, Chocolate Fudge
Fondue, and Whipped Cream

Selection of Hot Hors d'Oeuvres to Include
Presented in Gleaming Silver Rectangular Chafing
Dishes, the following:
Crabmeat Wonton with Selection of Sauces
Barbecued Baby Shrimp en Coquille
Clams Casino
Oysters Rockefeller
Oysters Bienville
Fried Shrimp
Crab Claws Tempura with Plum Sauce, Hot Mustard,
and Teriyaki Sauce

Presented, in Crates, at Another Location Masses of
Fresh Whole Vegetables to include:
Cauliflower, Artichoke, Eggplant, Rhubarb,
Green Spinach, Celery, Watercress, Dill, Tomatoes,
Potatoes, Belgian Endive, Red Cabbage, Mushrooms,
Zucchini, Beets, Wheat, Corn on Stalk
and Tiny Whole Corn, Sweet Potatoes, Avocado,
Cucumbers, Broccoli, Asparagus, Chicory Lettuce,
Romaine Lettuce, Boston Bibb Lettuce,
Carrots and Turnips
Selected Vegetables will be cut up and served with a
variety of Dips to include:
Fresh Dill, Avocado, Crab, Clam,
and Hot Chili Con Queso

Presented from a Special Side Table at Another Separate Location
Bananas Foster, Prepared by two Waiter Attendants

Presented at Two More Separate Locations
We will Provide two Waiters to Prepare at Table Side,
Sautéed Medallions of Venison
with Juniper Berries and Gin

• • •

Chicken Drumettes, Louisiana style,
will be Flambéed with Sour Mash at table side
by Two Additional Attendants

In Addition, at Still Two Additional Locations, We Will Carve
Whole Hot Baked Hams,
served with Buttermilk Biscuits and condiments

Special Decorations: Special decorations will include special neon sculptures (to include a banana, a strawberry, and a carrot), white geometric cubes, clear plexiglass cubes, and mirrored cubes. Further decorations will feature the color scheme of red, white, and black. The focal points of this decor will be two six-foot sculptures of cranes (birds), black columns topped with large glass bowls filled with red calla lillies, and two contemporary illuminated trees. The tops of the buffets will be covered with red wet-look plastic.

Professional Models: The Hotel will provide Professional Models, specially attired to blend with the decor, to greet guests upon arrival.

The Contemporary Cubic Reception

(Approximately 15 to 16 pieces of Hors d'Oeuvres per Person)

We will present, atop, around, and on a rectangular black cubic construction, a culinary display. Approximately fifteen tallow sculptures, at varying levels, will cascade down from the ballroom's mirrored ceiling. In addition, four stations will be presented, extending from the cubic central construction. Those four stations will include:

Station #1
Plexiglass Goldfish Aquarium, on which a Sushi Seafood Display will be presented, with Sweet and Sour Dip, and
Hot Soy Dip
Salmon in Seaweed
Hot Mustard Shrimp
Tuna and Bass
Saki and Plum Wine served at this station
• • •

Station #2
Sliced Tenderloin with Fresh Horseradish Cream (hot)
Skewered Beef Sate (hot)
Steak Tartare
• • •

Station #3
Cold Fruit Fantasy to include:
Dried Pears, Pineapples, Dates, Plums, Apricots, and Peaches
Fresh Kiwi, Pineapple, Strawberries, Cantaloupe, Honeydew, and Papaya with Hot Fudge Fondue, Whipped Cream, and Brown Sugar
Glass Bowls of Shining Red Apples
Fresh Kiwi Display and Petite Tarts
Fresh Strawberry Display and Petite Tarts
Fresh Papaya Display and Petite Tarts
• • •

Station #4
Massive Display of Cheeses from Around the Globe with a Giant Wheel of Selected Cheeses,
Lahvosh, Assorted Crackers, Tabbouleh, Hummus, and Quartered Pita Bread
• • •

From four additional stations elsewhere in the ballroom, we will serve:

Station #5
Assorted Dim Sum (five kinds),
with Plum Sauce and Hot Mustard
Shrimp and Vegetable Tempura
Cantonese Egg Rolls, English Mustard,
Sweet and Sour Sauce
Shumai
Gonzi
Sweet and Sour Pork
Shrimp Toast
• • •

Station #6
Hot and Cold Hors d'Oeuvres:
Cold
Shrimp in Aspic
Cold Jumbo Shrimp with Cocktail Sauce and Lemon Stars
Lobster Medallions
Lump Crabmeat
Canadian Smoked Salmon
Marinated Mussels in Lemon Applejack
Hot
Crab Puffs
Oysters Mexicana
Clams Sicilian
Barbecued Salmon Americus
• • •

Station #7
Smoked Lamb Chops with Hot Peanut Sauce
Pâté en Croûte, decorated with Stuffed Pheasants

Duck Minnesota with Pear Williams Sauce
Smoked Turkey Display

• • •

Section #8
For the Sweet Side of the Evening, a Positive and
Negative Pastry Display
Elevated from the center of this station will be
Black and White Tallow Sculptures of a Seal, a Penguin,
a Zebra, a Black Horse, a White Horse Head,
and Two Panda Bears
The display will include:
Black and White Marzipan Dominos
Black and White Petits Fours
Chocolate Truffles
White Divinity
Dark and White Chocolate-Dipped Strawberries
Dark Black Chocolate Pralines
Large Bowl of Black String Licorice

Black and White Checkerboard Cakes
Silver Service of Coffee, Sanka, and International Teas

Special Decorations: The Hotel will handle all special decorations. We have made arrangements for special decor to include giant dominos for the Positive and Negative Pastry Display, the tallow sculptures described above, a mirrored and clear plexiglass goldfish tank to contain approximately 100 black goldfish, the black cubic construction, neon sculptures of a fish and a beef branding iron, an oriental display consisting of a bamboo gazebo, oriental fans, and brass. In addition, we will provide two floral arrangements of white calla lillies in large glass bowls, to be placed near the tallow sculptures, and two additional large black and white floral arrangements to be placed at the Positive and Negative Pastry Display.

Professional Models: The Hotel will arrange for Professional Models, who will be attired in feminine Tuxedos, to greet the guests upon their arrival.

The Denims and Diamonds Reception

No matter what your attire—blue jeans or black tie—you'll feel right at home as our Chefs bring you the best of both. . . .

From an Elaborately Decorated Southern-Style Smokehouse, We Will Serve
Country Ham, Carved at Buffet
Roasted Beef, on spit
Barbecued Chicken, Baby Pork Riblettes
Assortment of Breads and Baby Rolls, with
appropriate Garnishes

• • •

Baby Ears of Corn on the Cob,
served from large boiling pots

• • •

From a Classical Buffet Table Arrangement, We Will Serve
An Elaborate Selection of Hors d'Oeuvres
to include:
Cheese Fondue, Chocolate Fondue
Sliced Fresh Fruit
Beef, Shrimp, Vegetables Tempura

• • •

Steak Tartare, Freshly made at the Buffet with
Onions, Capers, Eggs, Croutons, Melba Toast

• • •

Guacamole Dip with Assorted Chips

• • •

Plus an International Selection of Cold Canapés

The Don't Be Square Cube Reception

Atop cubic constructions, the following will be served:

Hot Dishes
Brochette of Escargot wrapped in Chicken Breast
Veal Stuffed with Crabmeat and Spinach
Duckling Brochette with Kumquat
Shrimp Tempura
Fried Swiss Cheese
Shashlick of Veal, Pork, and Lamb
Mushrooms Stuffed with the Following:
Curried Chicken Topped with Coconut and Crab,
Parmesan Cheese and Sherry
Sweet Breads en Bouchée
Baby Lamb Chops
Venison Quenelles

• • •

Cold Dishes
Marinated Crayfish
Seafood Mélange of Lobster, Crab, and Shrimp
Lachsschinen
Medallions of Beef Tenderloin, Lobster, and Eel
Whole Sturgeons and Smoked Salmons
Choice Selection of Pâtés

• • •

Elaborate Tropical Fruit and Imported Cheese
Display with Assorted Breads and Crackers

• • •

Topiaries of Fresh Vegetables
Served with Fresh Dill, Avocado, Crab, and Clam Dips

The Welcome to Washington Reception

A culinary welcome to Washington, the World's Capital, America's Home City, and the seat of the world's oldest and most powerful democracy. And now the new spirit of the District of Columbia presents: "The Taste of Washington."

For our Federal City buffet presentation, our Chefs pay a monumental tribute to the nation's tourist city with huge sugar replicas of the Jefferson and Lincoln Memorials, the Washington Monument, the US Capitol, and the White House. Tallow sculptures of our political party symbols, a donkey and an elephant, will also be on display.

Whole Steamship Rounds of Beef,
Carved in the room by Chefs in White Uniforms,
With an assortment of Rye and Pumpernickel Breads,
Miniature Rolls,
Horseradish, Curry Sauce, and other Condiments
• • •
Captured in Large Ice Sculptures, a collection of Raw Seafoods to include:
Cold Jumbo Shrimp, Cold Crab Claws, Mussels, Oysters on the Half Shell, Clams on the Half Shell,
Garnished with Lemon Stars and Parsley,
Accompanied with Rémoulade and Cocktail Sauces
• • •
Multiple presentations, on Mirrors, of International and Domestic Cheeses
Large Wheels of Selected Cheeses,
Garnished with Fresh Fruit and Fresh Flowers,
Accompanied by Baskets of Breads, Lahvosh, and Assorted Crackers
• • •
Pâté de Maison, Chef's selections of Cocktail Pâté,
Surrounded in Aspic,

Garnished with Mallard Ducks, Pheasants,
or other Wildlife
Display of Fresh Vegetables served on crushed ice including:
Zucchini, Mushrooms, Broccoli, Green Beans, Celery,
Cauliflower, and Carrots
Accompanied by a selection of Clam, Cheese,
and Dill Dips
• • •
Presented in Gleaming Silver Chafing Dishes, the following selection of Hot Hors d'Ouevres:
Crabmeat Wontons, with selection of Sauces,
Petite Quiche Lorraine Squares,
Beef Teriyaki Kabobs, Rumaki,
Cantonese Egg Rolls with English Mustard,
Medallions of Crisp Duck, Pepper Sauce
• • •
International Cold Canapés, presented on Large Mirrors,
to include:
Smoked Salmon on Rye, Steak Tartare Canapés,
Variety of Deviled Eggs, Melon and Prosciutto,
Cucumber Rondelles with Seafood Salad,
Anchovies on Toast Points
• • •
For the Sweet Side of the Evening,
presented in Individual Ice Boats, a colorful array of
Fresh Fruits to include:
Assorted Melons, Strawberries, Pineapples, Blueberries,
Garnished with Assorted Nuts,
Accompanied by Giant Champagne Glasses of Whipped
Cream, Brown Sugar, and Petite Chafing Dishes of
Chocolate Fondue

The America the Bountiful Reception

America's abundance is exemplified as we conduct a Food Fantasy Flight from its heartland to its four far-flung geographical corners. As a people, we have been shaped as much by the foods we have eaten as by democratic ideals; we are taller, stronger, healthier than our ancestors. We are, in a sense, a nation that food has made possible.

Join us now, gastronomic traveler, as we enjoy an exciting tour of regional foods.

Elevated in the center of the room will be a huge replica of the symbol of our American Freedom and Independence—The Liberty Bell—surrounded with the flags of all 50 states.

• • •

From the Nation's Heartland

A Mid-America Cheese and Bread Display, to consist of an eleborate selection of Domestic Cheeses in Large Wheels and Chunks,
Garnished with Fresh Fruit and
Accompanied by Baskets of Whole Bread of all Varieties,
Lahvosh, and Assorted Crackers,
Complemented by a Toast to California, serving
Cabernet Sauvignon, Chablis, and Grenache Rosé, Wines of California vintage, charged as consumed
• • •

From the New England States
Fresh Clams and Oysters, shucked to order, served with Cocktail Sauce, Horseradish, Tabasco, Lemon Wedges, and Oysterettes
Crab Claws, Cold Jumbo Shrimp, garnished with Lemon Stars and Parsley, Accompanied with Rémoulade and Cocktail Sauces
Large Round Chafing Dishes of:
Clams Casino on Rock Salt,
Oysters Rockefeller on Rock Salt,
Scallops wrapped in Bacon,
Deep Fried Maine Potato Skins, served with Sour Cream,
Steamship Round of Corned Beef,
Carved in room and served on New York–style Rye Bread with Horseradish, Mustard, and Mayonnaise

• • •

From the South
Ham and Buttermilk Biscuits, Country-Style Sausage and Biscuits, Southern-Style Fried Chicken Drumettes,
Half Ears of Corn, placed on popsicle sticks, heated in the Room in Large Boiling Pot, served with Drawn Butter,
Fried Catfish Pieces with Tartar Sauce,
The Crêpe au Crabe station, Individual Crabmeat Crêpes, Prepared to order, flambéed in the style of New Orleans, with a Taste of the Gulf Shore
Farmer's Market of Fresh Whole Vegetables, Displayed in old crates and baskets, and accompanied with Sliced Fresh Vegetables, served on crushed ice, to include:
Zucchini, Cauliflower, Carrots, Cherry Tomatoes, Celery, Mushrooms, Green Beans, and Broccoli
With Dill, Sour Cream, and Cheese Dips

• • •

From the Great Southwest
A Station for the Preparation of Tacos, made to order by attendant in costume,
Mini Barbecued Texas-style Spare Ribs,
Bowls of Guacamole Dip with Tostadas

• • •

From the West Coast
The Flavor of San Francisco's Oriental population:
Peking-style Duck,
prepared in the room, by attendant in costume
Duck is wrapped in Mandarin Pancakes with Plum Sauce and a sprinkle of Scallions and Chinese Parsley
Whole Poached Kennebec Salmon, presented on Mirrors, with Tronçons de Saumon en Bellevue
Crabmeat and Vegetables in a Flaky Pastry Shell
Crabmeat Wonton with Selection of Sauces
Oriental Spinach Quiche à la San Francisco, a delightful contemporary treatment of a popular French creation,
Oriental Egg Rolls with English Mustard and Sweet and Sour Sauce

• • •

For the Sweet Side of the Evening
Presented in creatively Sculptured Ice Socles,
an Elaborate Display of Fresh Fruits to include:
Pineapple, Assorted Melon, Blueberries, Strawberries, Kiwi, and Mangoes, accompanied by Brown Sugar and Whipped Cream,
Petite Chafing Dishes of Chocolate Fondue

The Chesapeake Bay Reception

A Nautical Buffet Presentation to include: a spectacular whale ice sculpture. Also, tallow sculptures of two fishermen and two large fish.

Raw Bar Presentation,
Featuring Fresh Clams and Oysters, shucked to order, served with Cocktail Sauce, Horseradish, Tabasco, Lemon Wedges, and Oysterettes

• • •

Elegant King Crabmeat Display, on crushed ice, to include:
Crab Claws
Cold Jumbo Shrimp, Garnished with Lemon Stars and Parsley,

Accompanied with Rémoulade and Cocktail Sauces

• • •

Large Round Silver Chafing Dishes to include:
Oysters Rockefeller on Rock Salt
Clams Casino on Rock Salt
Paella
Scallops wrapped in Bacon

• • •

Crêpe au Crabe Station, Individual Crabmeat Crêpes, Prepared to order and Flambéed

The Nightcap Reception

In the center of the room, we will provide six geometric shaped mirrored cubes, with specially designed food table presentations on each end of the buffet arrangements. From this elegant buffet, we will serve the following:

On the East End of the Buffet Arrangement
Variety of Whole Quiches cut in small wedges,
with two waiter attendants
The varieties will include: Spinach Quiche, Broccoli Quiche, Seafood and Bacon Quiche with Onion and Chives

From the West End of the Buffet Arrangement
Crêpes Suzettes
Strawberry Crêpes with Grand Marnier Sauce
Cinnamon, Apple, and Almond Crêpes, Blueberry Crêpes
Prepared to order and accompanied with Whipped Cream,
Chocolate Fudge Fondue, Brown Sugar, Slivers of Rock
Candy, a Variety of Nuts, and Toasted Coconut
Two waiter attendants will assist in preparation

From a Specially Designed Buffet Table on the West End
A variety of Fancy Miniature After Dinner Pastries
(The selection will be of the lighter variety,
due to the late night hour)
Variety of After Dinner Mints
• • •

From a Specially Designed Buffet Arrangement on the East Wall
Specialty After Dinner Coffees will be prepared
appropriately, in the room, by two waiter attendants,
Selections to include: Irish Coffee, Spanish Coffee,
Café Royale, Café à l'Orange, and Chocolate Amaretto
The After Dinner Coffees will be charged as consumed
Additional Regular Coffee will be available in a Silver
Service, and charged on a per gallon basis

The Mardi Gras Extravaganza Reception

Beverages
Hurricane, Mint Julep, and Brandy Milk Punch
Served in personalized Hurricane glasses,
from a colorful center Gazebo
Eight Bars, with Bartenders in Bayou Pirate Costumes,
serve popular Highballs and Cocktails

Oyster Bars
Two stations with original Pirogue Boats,
serving Freshly Shucked Oysters on the Half Shell,
Crawfish and Lake Pontchartrain Crabs

Deli Shoppe
Against a backdrop of an Old World Deli Shoppe, a
Serpentine Buffet Table serves New Orleans' Giant
Muffaletta Sandwiches and Six-Foot Po' Boy Sandwiches
Jambalaya and Seafood Gumbo served from Black Kettles
The staff of Creole Country Kitchen proudly serves
Original Creole and Cajun Sausages:
Chauriz, Boudin, Andouille, Pickled Smoked Sausage,
and Head Cheese

La Fromagerie
An Impressive Display of International and Domestic
Cheeses includes: Stilton with Port Wine, Brie,
Camembert, Cheddar, Swiss, and Port Salut
On both sides of the presentation,

Cornucopias carved from Ice display
an array of Whole Fresh Fruits, in addition to Fresh Cut
Fruit, with Poppy Seed Dip
In the background, Three Wine Racks with
Barrels display an Assortment of Wines,
while Magnums of Mondavi are poured to your guests

Le Grand Buffet
A Three-Tiered Buffet Table is festively lit in Mardi
Gras colors
Silver Chafing Dishes Serve
Coujan of Catfish, Creole Meatballs, Quiche Lorraine,
Beef Kabobs, Chicken Cordon Bleu,
Cajun Stuffed Peppers, Creole Bouchées,
and Sautéed Frog Legs
From Domed Copper Chafers
Hot Spicy Barbecued Shrimp, in the Shell
Two Carving Stations Slice to Order
Steamship Rounds of Beef and Bourbon Glazed Hams
• • •
The table is topped with Two Fleurs-de-Lis Ice Carvings
and a colorful Fountain

Bourbon Street
A 60-foot backdrop depicts Bourbon Street with a New
Orleans Marching Band

Lucky Dog Carts from the French Quarter serve Hot Dogs with Condiments
Fresh Popcorn is prepared in a Popcorn Cart
Chocolate-Covered Bananas and Ice Cream Sandwiches are served from a Roving Ice Cream Cart

Café du Monde
This French Café serves: King Cake, Doberge Cake, Pralines, and Beignets
New Orleans Praline Liqueur is used to make Praline Frappé, dispensed from a Soft Ice Cream Machine, and Topped with Chopped Nuts

The Society Reception

In the Center of the Ballroom, we will present geometric shaped mirrored plexiglass cubic construction culinary displays.

As the guests enter, they will encounter a mirrored plexiglass aquarium, filled with African cichlid fish, on which a mélange of seafood is displayed to include: Giant Shrimp, Langostinos, and Golden Gulf Crabmeat, garnished with Lemon, Mustard, Rémoulade, and Cocktail Sauces.

The focal point of this display will be selected pieces of coral and a 20-pound lobster with Lobster Medallions cascading down the body to the claws.

Whole Nova Scotia Smoked Salmon will be displayed on a marble slab, sliced by two chefs in white uniform, and served with Sourdough and Pumpernickel Breads and the appropriate garniture.

A mosaic display of international cheeses will be artistically arranged on gleaming mirrors, to include: Boursin with Nuts, Montrachet, English Stilton, Dutch Edam, Feta, Port Salut, and French Brie. The cheeses will be accompanied with Baguettes of Sourdough, Pumpernickel, French, Marble, and Italian Breads, along with Assorted Gourmet Crackers and Lahvosh.

A decorated Whole Saddle of Veal will be served with the appropriate condiments.

The special Steak Tartare Display will be prepared in the Ballroom by a chef in white uniform, and served with the appropriate garniture and a variety of Breads.

The deluxe selection of Cold Canapés will be presented on mirrored serving platters.

Four five and a half foot round mirrored buffet tables will be strategically placed around the ballroom. Each will present a crystal ice sculpture in the center of the table, surrounded by gleaming silver chafing dishes serving the following selection of hot hors d'oeuvres: Medallions of Wisconsin Duck, laced with Peppercorn Sauce; Oysters Rockefeller; Clams in Pernod; Escargots Wrapped in Tender Fillet of Chicken; Baby Lamb Cutlets; and Pâté de Fois Gras.

The Welcome to Florida Reception

(Approximately 15 to 16 Total Pieces of Hors d'Oeuvres per Person)

The culinary display will be presented atop, around, and on rectangular mirrored and other Kydex cubic constructions, in the center of the Grand Ballroom, as well as on skirted buffet tables. The "Welcome to Florida" neon sculpture will be the focal point of the buffet. We will serve the following selection of hot and cold hors d'oeuvres:

Presented in Gleaming Silver Chafing Dishes, the Following Selection of Hot Hors d'Oeuvres:
Crabmeat Wontons, with Selection of Sauces
Petite Quiche Lorraine Squares
Beef Teriyaki Kabobs
Rumaki
Cantonese Egg Rolls, with French Mustard
Medallions of Crisp Duck, with Pepper Sauce
• • •

Presented on Round Mirrors, International Cold Canapés, to Include:
Smoked Salmon on Rye
Steak Tartare Canapés
Variety of Deviled Eggs
Melon on Prosciutto
Cucumber Rondelles with Seafood Salad
Anchovies on Toast Points

Captured in a Mirrored and Clear Plexiglass Florida Seafood Bar, a Collection of Raw Seafoods, to Include:
(Eight pieces of Seafood per Person included in the total)
Cold Jumbo Shrimp
Cold Crab Claws
Mussels
Oysters on the Half Shell

Clams on the Half Shell, garnished with Lemon Stars and
Parsley
Accompanied with Rémoulade and Cocktail Sauces
• • •

On Mirrored Platters We Will Present:
International and Domestic Cheese Displays
Large Wheels of Selected Cheese
Garnished with Fresh Fruits
Accompanied by Baskets of Breads, Lahvosh, and
Assorted Crackers
• • •

Pâté de Maison, Chef's Selections of Cocktail Pâtés,
Surrounded in Aspic, Garnished with Mallard Ducks,
Pheasants, or other Wildlife
• • •

Display of Fresh Vegetables, served on Crushed Ice, and
including:
Zucchini, Mushrooms, Broccoli, Green Beans, Celery,
Cauliflower, and Carrots,

Accompanied by a Selection of Clam, Cheese,
and Dill Dips
• • •

From Four Separate Stations:
Four Whole Steamship Rounds of Beef,
Carved in the Room by Four Chefs in White Uniforms,
with an Assortment of Rye
and Pumpernickel Breads and Miniature Rolls,
with Horseradish, Curry Sauce, and other Condiments
• • •

For the Sweet Side of the Evening:
Presented in Individual Ice Boats, a colorful array of
Fresh Fruits to include:
Assorted Melons, Strawberries, Pineapples, Blueberries,
Garnished with Assorted Nuts, and Accompanied by
Mountains of Whipped Cream, Sour Cream, Brown
Sugar, and Petite Chafing Dishes of White
and Dark Chocolate Fondue

The Around the World in 80 Minutes Reception

Minimum Guarantee: 250 Guests
(Can be tailored to fewer guests)
(Approximately 16 to 18 pieces of Hors d'Oeuvres per Person)

Grab your passport as you are about to embark on a taste-tempting trip around the world. Everyone's dream is to tour the world, and this party is the next best thing.

We will be happy to arrange for the appropriate decorations to enhance the international theme. Miniature hot-air balloons can be created to fly over each "country," identifying your destinations. All decorations are at an additional charge.

Welcome Home, Yankee
Whole Roast Steamship Rounds of Beef, accompanied by
Mayonnaise, Horseradish, Chutney, Mustard,
and including
Miniature Rolls, Cocktail Rye, and Pumpernickel,
Chef carver required at an additional expense
• • •

Southern Crispy Fried Chicken Drumettes
• • •

Deep-Fried Maine-style Potato Skins with Bacon Bits and
Cheddar Cheese
• • •

Florida Fish Fingers with Tartar Sauce
• • •

Bonjour, Paris
Pâté de Campagne,
Country Pâté
• • •

Galantine de Canard,
Galantine of Duck
• • •

Escargots Parisiens,
Snails in Aioli Sauce
• • •

Quiche de Fruits de Mer,
Seafood Quiche
• • •

Orient Express

Orient
Rumaki Chicken Liver à l'Orientale
• • •

China
Prawn Egg Rolls, with Sweet and Sour Sauce
• • •

Japan
Mini Steak Teriyaki Kabobs

• • •

Indonesia
Petite Medallions of Sautéed Pork Loin
Bali-Bali, with Spicy Peanut Ginger Sauce

Fiesta Mexicana
Jamón Cancún,
Smoked Ham

• • •

Tostadas

• • •

Chorizo,
Spiced Sausage

• • •

Habichuelas Refritas,
Refried Beans

• • •

Viva Italia
Antipasto Milanese,
A Variety of Fresh Marinated Vegetables

• • •

Mitilos Salsa Marinara,
Marinated Mussels

• • •

Gamberetti con Cipolla e Vino,
Shrimp Scampi

• • •

Salsiccia al Forno,
Baked Mild Italian Sausage Tidbits

• • •

Alpine Festival
Geraucherter Westfalischer Schinken mit Schwarzbrot,
Smoked Westphalian Ham with Pumpernickel

• • •

Weisswurst und Knackwurst in Bier,
White Sausage and Knockwurst, cooked in Beer

• • •

Heisser Kartoffel Salate,
Hot Potato Salad

• • •

Suss Saueres Rot Kraut,
Sweet and Sour Red Cabbage

International Dessert Display
Fromages Assortis,
Assorted Cheeses with French Bread
Pâtisseries Françaises Assorties,
Large Selection of Miniature French Pastries
Galletas,
Mocha, Cherry, and Nut Cookies

Torte de Ricotta y Frutta,
Light Pastry of Raisins, Candied Fruit, and
Ricotta Cheese

Frische Erdbeeren mit Kirschwasser,
Fresh Strawberries in Kirsch

• • •

Allgauer Apfel Strudel mit Vanille Sosse,
Apple Strudel with Brandied Vanilla Sauce

• • •

Selection of International Teas and Coffees

Special Beverages: In addition to open bars, we suggest providing an outstanding selection of International Beers, Wines, and Waters, at an additional cost.

Music: Mariachi guitars . . . Italian violins . . . a German "oom-pah" band . . . some Dixieland jazz will help to create the special mood of the international tour. Prices on request.

Decor: A decor package can be designed in accordance with your budget to include the mystery and intrigue of the Orient, a quaint Bavarian Village, the romance and adventure of Venice, the domination of the Eiffel Tower and a sidewalk café, the colorfulness of old Mexico, and back home at last in the good old USA . . . the Stars and Stripes welcome you to an All-American 4th of July Celebration! Prices on request.

The At Your Service Reception
(Approximately Six Pieces per Person)

White-gloved waitpersons will serve your guests butler-style from silver trays. Food selections will include:

Silver Demitasse Spoons, filled with Salmon Mousse and Caviar

• • •

Snow Peas with Swiss Cheese, rolled with Proscuitto

• • •

Petite Pâté Maison Medallions

• • •

Petite Mushroom Caps Stuffed with Steak Tartare

• • •

Shrimp Mandarin

• • •

Cheese Sushi

The International Reception

Tour several far-off lands without leaving the Resort! Beautiful native floral arrangements represent the countries of your choice. Scenes from distant cities and picturesque places will give the appearance of Europe, the Orient, and old Mexico. Everyone's dream is to tour the world, and this party makes it come true!

Merry Olde England

Roast Round of Aged Hereford Beef, Carved to Order

• • •

Yorkshire Pudding

• • •

Breaded Dover Sole, with Chips

• • •

Chicken Pot Pie, Cheshire Style

• • •

Fresh Pineapple Slices with Triple Sec

• • •

Welsh Trifle

• • •

Fried Cheddar Pieces with Sourdough Bread

• • •

Make Those Stiff British Upper Lips Turn into Smiles!
Pimm's Cup and Bass Ale

Alpine Festival

Bayrische Linsen Suppe
Bavarian Lentil Soup

• • •

***Geraucherter Westfalischer
Schinken mit Schwarzbrot***
Smoked Westphalian Ham with Pumpernickel

• • •

Frische Salate
Crisp Garden Salad, Choice of Dressings

• • •

Diverse Frische Gemuse
Relish Tray and Fresh Vegetables

• • •

Kasseler Rippchen
Smoked Pork Loin

• • •

Weisswurst und Knackwurst in Bier
White Sausage and Knockwurst, cooked in Beer

• • •

Frische Bratwurst
Pan Fried Veal and Pork Sausage

• • •

Heisser Kartoffel Salate
Hot Potato Salad

• • •

Suss Saueres Rot Kraut
Sweet and Sour Red Cabbage

• • •

Frische Erdbeeren mit Kirschwasser
Fresh Strawberries in Kirsch

• • •

Allgauer Apfel Strudel mit Vanille Sosse
Apple Strudel with Brandied Vanilla Sauce

• • •

Turn Your Alpine Fest into an Octoberfest with . . .
Lowenbrau by the keg
Riesling Wines available from Wine List

Orient Express

Rumaki Chicken Liver à l'Orientale

• • •

China
Beef with Oyster Sauce, Cantonese
Mandarin Fried Rice
Prawn Egg Rolls

• • •

Japan
Steak Teriyaki

• • •

Indonesia
Sautéed Pork Loin Bali-Bali
Spicy Peanut Ginger Sauce

• • •

India
Curried Seafood Madras, Condiments

Fortune and Almond Cookies

• • •

Mandarin Oranges with Shredded Coconut

• • •

Make Your Party Inscrutably Delightful!
Imported Chinese Beer
Japanese Sake

Bonjour, Paris

Pâté de Campagne
Country Pâté

Galantine de Canard
Galantine of Duck

Escargots Parisiens
Snails in Aioli Sauce

Quiche de Fruits de Mer
Seafood Quiche

Salade Niçoise

Cuisses de Grenouilles Provençales
Sautéed Frog Legs

Lapin à la Bourguignonne
Fresh Rabbit Stew

• • •

Cotelettes d'Agneau
Lamb Cutlets, Cooked to Order

• • •

Fromages Assortis
Assorted Cheeses with French Bread

Poires Pochées au Porto
Pears in Port Wine

• • •

Pâtisseries Françaises Assorties
Large Selection of Miniature French Pastries

• • •

Absolutely de Rigueur,
Aperitifs:
Dubonnet, Lillet, St. Raphael, Piat d'Or Blanc ou Rouge,
By the Glass

Viva Italia

Antipasto Milanese
A Variety of Fresh Marinated Vegetables

Funghi sotto Aceto
Marinated Mushrooms

Lasagne alla Napolitana

Gamberetti con Cipolla e Vino
Shrimp Scampi

Salsiccia al Forno
Baked Mild Italian Sausage

Maccheroni al Pomodoro
Macaroni with Tomatoes

Peperoni al Forno alla Parmigiano
Baked Italian Peppers

Zucchini alla Romana
Stuffed Zucchini

Pane all' Aglio
Garlic Bread

• • •

Dolci Misti
Desserts
Biscotto Tortoni
Cannoli alla Siciliano

• • •

Esprèsso

• • •

When in Italy, Do Things Italiano!
Chianti Classico by the Glass
Leonardo di Saronno

Fiesta Mexicana

Jamón Cancún
Smoked Ham

Tostadas, Tamales, Enchiladas, Tacos

Chorizo
Spiced Sausage

Camarones al Aji
Shrimp with Tomatoes and Hot Peppers

Habichuelas Refritas
Refried Beans

Paella Valenciana
Baked Chicken with Rice, Shrimp, Clams, and Mussels

• • •

Flan de Coco
Coconut Custard

• • •

Galletas
Mocha, Cherry, and Nut Cookies

• • •

What Mexican Celebration Would be Complete
Without . . .
Mucho Margaritas and Kahlua Coladas

Music: Two bands will play for your enjoyment. You may choose any two of the countries represented and we'll obtain, at your direction, bands that play music particular to those countries. At an additional cost.

Decor: Multicolored flags set the international theme of your party. The staff is costumed in the native dress of each country. The many floral arrangements are comprised of flowers native to the countries represented. To complete the theme, three-dimensional props depicting scenes from far-off lands surround your guests. All decorations are at an additional cost.

Favors: Beer steins, hats, T-shirts, and bandannas will be offered to each guest, at an additional price.

The International Night Reception

From the USA
Steamship Roast of Beef
Baked Whole Virginia Ham
Whole Roast Vermont Turkey
Carved by Chefs, served with Cocktail Bread
and split Hard Rolls
Southern Fried Chicken Drumsticks

From France
Crabmeat Bouchées Diable
Quiche Lorraine
Clams Casino
Salmon Bellevue, Carved by Chef
Bouchées de Fois Gras with Truffles
Cheese and Fruit Tray,
Served with Cocktail Rye and Pumpernickel Bread

From the Orient
Beef Teriyaki
Shrimp Tempura
Chinese Egg Rolls
Barbecued Spare Ribs

From Mexico
Cheese Nachos/Guacamole Dip
Beef Tampico on Skewers
Tacos

From Italy
Miniature Pizzas
Meatballs, Italian Sauce
Prosciutto Romano
Fried Zucchini
Cornets of Genoa Salami

From Germany
Smoked Pork Loin, Carved by Chef
Münchener Sauerbraten
Tiny Cabbage Rolls with Sour Cream
Baby Wiener Schnitzel, German Sausages
German Style Bread and Rolls

Dessert
A Variety of French, German, and Italian Cakes and Pastries
Choice of Beverage

The following ideas are offered to add to the theme of your party. Prices will depend on size of your group and extent of theme involvement.

Music: Mariachi guitars . . . Italian violins . . . a German "oom-pah" band . . . some Dixieland jazz . . . will help create the special mood of each country featured on this international tour.

Decor: Begin your taste-tempting trip around the world at a Fiesta in a colorful Mexican plaza. On to the mystery and intrigue of the Orient, with ancient pagodas and ceremonial dragons. Next, travel to a quaint Bavarian village . . . stroll through the town square to experience a typical German Beer Garden. Your next stop is Italy. The romance and adventure of Venice is recreated with a giant gondola. Your journey continues on to France. The Eiffel Tower dominates the view from your table at a sidewalk café. Back home at last in the good old USA . . . the Stars and Stripes welcome you to an All-American 4th of July celebration!

Favors: A souvenir "Passport" for each of your guests can be used to enhance the "Around-the-World" theme of this party.

The International Marketplace Reception

Italian Station
Spinach Tortellini, with Suprema Sauce
and Marinara Sauce, prepared in room

• • •

Puff Pastry Shells, with Hot Sausage Ragout,
and topped with Chilled Ricotta Cheese, at the station

• • •

Fried Mozarella Marinara,
served from Silver Chafing Dish

• • •

Assorted Deli Meats and Cheeses,
displayed on Wooden Boards,
with appropriate Condiments

German Station
Aufschnitt,
A plate of Various Cold Sausages, sliced and served
with appropriate Condiments and Bread

• • •

Frankfurter Wurstchen,
Bratwurst

• • •

Weisswurst, served from Silver Chafing Dish,
with Mustard and Bread

• • •

Sauerkraut

• • •

/////

German Potato Salad, with Bacon and Onions

• • •

Steak Tartare, made to order,
served with Appropriate Condiments,
Pumpernickel and Rye Bread

• • •

Hot Pretzels

Seafood Station

From a boat filled with ice, we will serve:
Beluga-style American Caviar, with Vodka

• • •

Oysters on the Half Shell

• • •

Clams on the Half Shell

• • •

Jumbo Shrimp

• • •

Snow Crab Claws

• • •

Horseradish, Lemon, Cocktail Sauce, and Tabasco

• • •

Seafood Crêpes, with Baby Shrimp and Scallops,
made to order

Western Station

Spicy Barbecued Chicken and Ribs

• • •

Steamship Round of Beef, carved by Chef
Silver Dollar Rolls,
Horseradish, Mustard

• • •

Hot Mexican Chili

Dessert Station

Assorted French Pastries

• • •

Baumkuchen

• • •

Bananas Cerromar, prepared in room

The Deluxe Reception

(Approximately 18 to 20 pieces of Hors d'Oeuvres per Person)

A culinary display is presented atop, around, and on a special construction of rectangular mirrors and other geometric shapes. Sitting in the center of the Grand Ballroom, the presentation cascades down from a massive ice pyramid, and showcases four of the eight serving stations, as follows:

Station #1   Neon Jumping Sailfish Sculpture

On a Plexiglass Aquarium filled with
African Cichlid Fish,
A Sushi Raw Seafood Display
With Sweet and Sour and Hot Soy Dips,
The Sushi Selection to Include:

Nigiri Sushi
Rice with Raw Fish

Norimaki Sushi
Rice Rolled in Seaweed

Fukusa Sushi
Rice wrapped in Omelette

Inari Sushi
Rice in Fried Bean Curd

Chirashi Sushi
Rice with Seafood and Vegetables

Sashimi
Paper-thin sliced Raw Fish,
garnished with shredded Carrot,
Lettuce, or Cabbage, served with
grated Ginger and Horseradish

• • •

From another location at the same station, from a Large
Ice Carving, we will serve:
Jumbo Shrimp
Golden Gulf Crab Claws
With Rémoulade and Cocktail Sauces, Lemon Crowns

Station #2   Here's the Beef Bull Neon Sculpture

Sliced Tenderloin with Fresh Horseradish Cream (Hot),
carved by Chef in White Uniform,
Sliced Sourdough and Silver Dollar Rolls,
Mayonnaise and French Mustard

• • •

Carpaccio, Prepared by the Waiter,
Sliced Tenderloin with garniture to include:
Balsamic Vinegar, Old Monk Virgin Olive Oil, Sliced
Red Onions, Minced Garlic, Freshly Grated Parmesan
Cheese, Salt and Pepper Grinders, and Mustard,
with Sliced French Bread

• • •

Gleaming Silver Chafing Dishes of
Hot Skewered Beef Sauté

• • •

Station #3   Twin Giant Strawberries Neon Sculpture

Elaborate Tropical Fruit Fantasy, to be presented in
Large Crystal Ice Carvings, and to include:
Kiwi, Pineapple, Strawberries, Cantaloupe, Honeydew,
and Papaya with Hot Dark and White Chocolate
Fondues, Whipped Cream, Sour Cream, Shredded
Coconut, and Choice of Three Sugars

• • •

Display of Dried Fruits to include:
Pears, Pineapples, Dates, Plums, Apricots, Peaches,
Assorted Nuts, and Figs

• • •

French Tartlets of Strawberries, Papaya, Mango, and Kiwi

Station #4   Giant Carrot Neon Sculpture

Eggplant Vases with Carved Vegetable Flowers
Japanese Carved Vegetable Displays
Topiaries of Fresh Vegetables,
Served with Fresh Dill, Madras, Avocado, Crab, and
Clam Dips, served from Vegetable Casings

• • •

The four additional Stations, located strategically around
the room, serve the following:

Station #5   On the South Wall, Large Wheel of Swiss Cheese Neon Sculpture

Mosaic Display of International Cheeses to include:
Boursin with Nuts, Montrachet, English Stilton, Dutch
Edam, Feta, Port Salut, Gorgonzola, and French Brie,
served with Lahvosh and Baguettes of Sourdough,
Pumpernickel, Marble, French, and Italian Bread

• • •

Raclette, prepared in the room, by waiter

Station #6   On the North Wall, Oriental Neon Sculpture

Tempura Station
Fresh Vegetable Assortment and Whole Shrimp,

dipped in Light Oriental Batter, then Cooked in Oil,
served with Spiced Mandarin Sauce,
Prepared Tableside by a Waiter with Two Woks

• • •

Beef Chow Yoke and Oriental Vegetables,
Cooked Tableside on Two Benihana-Style Cooking
Surfaces, to Order, by a waiter

• • •

Silver Chafing Dishes of:
Cantonese Egg Rolls, served with French Mustard,
Sweet and Sour Sauce, and Plum Sauce

Station #7   On the West Wall, "Welcome to Florida" Neon Sculpture

Cold Canapés Displayed on Mirrors:
Crab in Aspic
Lobster Medallions, cascading from a Giant Lobster
Canadian Smoked Salmon
Mussels, in Applejack Brandy
Langostinos

Hot Hors d'Oeuvres Served from Silver Chafing Dishes:
Crab Balls, rolled in Sesame Seeds
Calamari alla Romana
Clams in Sourdough, accompanied with Fennel Sauce
Gravlax, Veal Paupiettes
Duck Medallions in Kiwi Sauce,
Escargot in Bliss

Station #8   On the East Wall, Hershey Chocolate Bar Neon Sculpture
Death by Chocolate Chocaholic Bar

The Orient Express Reception

(Approximately Eight Pieces per Person)

Served from a Buffet:
Oriental Barbecued Spare Ribs

• • •

Chinese Egg Rolls, with Sweet and Sour and Duck Sauces

• • •

Beef with Oyster Sauce, Cantonese

• • •

Sautéed Pork Loin Bali-Bali, with Spicy Peanut Ginger
Sauce

• • •

Dim Sum

• • •

Crab Rangoon

• • •

Rumaki Chicken Liver à l'Orientale

• • •

Passed Butler-Style:
An assortment of Shogun Sushi, Prepared in the room by
a Sushi Chef who is dressed in authentic garments

The Washington Embassy Row
Reception

Japan: Japanese food stands apart from all other Asian cuisines because of its simplicity and purity. It is memorable, not for its richness or spices or complexity of flavors, but rather because it emphasizes basic ingredients, and trains the palate to accept and appreciate food in its most natural state.

Sushi is the Japanese equivalent of the open sandwich. Rice, flavored with a vinegar and sugar dressing, takes the place of bread, and is topped with various kinds of raw fish; rolled around fillings of fish, pickles, mushrooms, or other vegetables; and in some cases enclosed in omelettes or bean curd.

Nigiri Sushi
Rice with Raw Fish

Fukusa Sushi
Rice wrapped in Omelette

Inari Sushi
Rice in Fried Bean Curd

Chirashi Sushi
Rice with Seafood and Vegetables

Norimaki Sushi
Rice rolled in Seaweed

Greece: The beautiful country of Greece had a difficult culinary task throughout the ages, in that its cooks were often asked to satisfy the Gods, as well as mortal men. Their efforts toward heavenly cuisine were not in vain.

The Famed Gyro
Well-seasoned lamb and beef, pressed to form a cone, which is then carved and lightly sautéed
Pita bread with pockets are filled with meat and condiments of:
Feta Cheese, Chopped Tomato, Shredded Lettuce, Vinaigrette Dressing

Lamb Kabobs
Tender pieces of Lamb, skewered with Mushrooms,

Cherry Tomatoes, and Bell Peppers, Served with a Yogurt-Mint Sauce

Spanokopita
Spiced Spinach and Feta Cheese, interspersed between layers of Flaky Filo Pastry

Portugal: Portugal is the homeland of some of the World's greatest explorers. Hence Portuguese cooking is the Iberian Peninsula's interpretation of world cooking.

Whole Roast Suckling Pigs
Presented in Peddler's Carts, Lavishly Garnished and Carved to Order

Chili con Queso Rosales
Served from a Chafing Dish with Baskets of Raw Vegetables to include:
Carrots, Celery, Radishes, Cucumbers, Olives, Peppers, Squash, and Mushrooms

Beef Empanadas
Elaborate Spinach Turnovers, filled with Chopped Beef

Italy: The romance of Southern Italy is exemplified even in its food. Indulge yourself in a love affair with these exquisite offerings.

Pasta Bar
Ribbons of green and white fettucini, Cooked "al dente" and tossed at the buffet with a choice of:
Pesto Sauce, Provençale Sauce, White Clam Sauce, or Fresh Cream
Served with Grated Parmesan and Garlic Bread

Mozzarella Balls
Deep Fried at the buffet, and offered with a Raspberry Dipping Sauce

Triangles of Pizza Bianco
Light Crusty Pizza, topped with Cheese and Spices

Spicy Italian Sausages

Trinidad and Tobago: Come to the islands—a culinary voyage to the Caribbean.

The Caribbean Islands stretch some 2,600 miles, from Florida to Venezuela. When Columbus first viewed this chain of islands, he thought he had found the Garden of Eden. "Always the land was of the same beauty," he wrote, "and the fields very green and full of an infinity of fruits, as red as scarlet, and everywhere there was the perfume of flowers and the singing of birds."

Still today, beauty, fruitfulness and culture abound in this paradise on earth, and are especially exemplified through the cuisine. Herewith is a sampling of these foods, so rich in exotic spices, fruits and fish.

Bakes and Accra

Bakes are indigenous to the Lesser Antilles and are simply baking powder biscuits. They can be served with butter or jellies, but also can take on a spectacular flavor sensation when served with Accras. Accras are salt cod, or bacaloas, dipped in seasoned batter and quickly deep-fried in peanut oil, and then stuffed into the Bakes. In Jamaica this combination is called "Stamp and Go"—a real crowd pleaser, especially during Carnivale.

Roti

The Caribbean Indians fashioned flat round unleavened bread on a hot stone and rolled this bread with a variety of condiments, including Curried Beef, Chicken, Mango Chutney, and Split Pea Puree—native Trinidadians will re-create these popular dishes at the buffet.

Fresh Fruit Oasis

No trip to the islands would be complete without a sampling of the exotic fruits so abundant in the Caribbean. A favorite way to enjoy these is done beautifully in Trinidad and Tobago where cuts of mango, banana, kiwi, pineapple, and papaya are served together in a large wooden bowl, sprinkled with shredded coconut, dark rum and assorted nuts, all laced with honey.

Germany: The basic Meat 'n' Potatoes Cuisine of Germany is generally robust and hearty, and always satisfying in its earthy goodness.

Made to Order Reubens
Rashers of Corned Beef, Melted Muenster, Sauerkraut, Thousand Island Dressing and Sliced Rye and Pumpernickel Breads

Sliced Cucumbers
In Tart Sour Cream

Warmer Kartoffel Salate
German Potato Salad made with Oil and Vinegar and Bacon

Spätzle Salate
Fresh Spätzle cooked "al dente," tossed with Crisp Vegetables, Spicy Vinaigrette, and Cheese

Sauerbraten
Carved to Order, at the buffet

Ivory Coast: In days of long ago, there were societies of men without countries. They often sought refuge in the small Ivory Coast of Africa, but they were men who called the sea their home. This station is dedicated to the adventurous pirates, buccaneers, and swashbucklers.

The riches of the deep blue sea are offered here in a variety of ways to include:

Shrimp, Oysters, and Scallops
Dipped in Beer Batter and Fried at the buffet

Grilled Swordfish Fingers
With Tartar Sauce

North Atlantic Salmon
Poached Whole in White Wine

France: Our tour of Embassy Row is complete with a visit to a Sidewalk Café in Paris for coffee and dessert.

Thin Crêpes
Offered with a Choice of Fillings to include:
Apple-Raisin, Chocolate Kahlua, Bananas Foster

Cherries Jubilee
With Fresh Whipped Cream

Beignets
Deep Fried at the buffet, and Dusted with Powdered Sugar

Espresso
Served with a Choice of Flambéed Liqueurs to include:
Grand Marnier, Amaretto, Kahlua, Vandermint,
Irish Whiskey, in Sugar Rimmed Glasses

The Cocktail Buffet Reception

Iced Shrimp on Horseback

• • •

Clams Casino

• • •

Oysters Rockefeller

• • •

Quiche Lorraine

• • •

Long Grain and Wild Rice

• • •

Lamb Shish Kabobs

• • •

Teriyaki Beef Skewers

• • •

Mandarin Duck

• • •

Fresh Petite Rolls and Butter

• • •

Domestic and Imported Cheeses

• • •

Fresh Fruit

The Ports of the World Reception

This culinary trip around the world offers authentic, native specialties.

Acapulco, Mexico
Baskets of Corn Chips with Guacamole Dip

• • •

Ceviche Acapulco

• • •

Create Your Own Taco with:
Spicy Beef, Shredded Lettuce, Cheddar Cheese, Diced Green Onions, Diced Tomatoes, and Our Own Special Hot Salsa

• • •

Chicken Burritos

Naples, Italy

Antipasto
Antipasto Trays served on Beds of Crisp Lettuce, with Marinated Beef, Salami, Marinated Cauliflower, Celery, Peppers, Black Olives, Artichoke Hearts, Sweet Red Peppers, Mortadella, Hard-Cooked Eggs, Provolone Cheese, Anchovies, Roasted Red Peppers in Oil

• • •

Pasta
Fettucine Alfredo, prepared tableside
Tortellini and Farfalle
Red Clam Sauce, Sauce Bolognese
Spicy Italian Sausage
Pesto and Fresh Grated Parmesan

New Orleans, USA
Raw Vegetable Crudités, with Dips

• • •

French Quarter Creole Bouillabaisse

• • •

Cajun Barbecued Shrimps

• • •

Cajun Blackened Beef

Hong Kong, Far East
Stir-Fried Shark, prepared in Wok

• • •

Cantonese Spring Rolls with Sweet and Sour Sauce and Hot Spicy Mustard

• • •

Shrimp Tempura

Desserts from Around the Globe
Display of Fresh Tropical Fruits,
Melons, Pineapple, Kiwi, Papaya, and Star Fruit

• • •

Fresh Strawberry Trees,
with Bitter Chocolate Fondue

• • •

Mango Mousse

• • •

Pecan Pies

• • •

Variety of Tortes

• • •

Key Lime Pie

• • •

Selection of International Teas and Coffees

Beverages: In addition to full bar service, we suggest a selection of international wines, beers, and waters, charged as consumed.

Decorations: Elaborate props and authentic costumes, featuring the countries represented, are available at additional cost.

The Rhapsody in Seafood Reception

This five-station reception features the best in seafood from around the nation.

From Sea to Shining Sea
A beautiful handcrafted wooden Periwinkle Boat is the backdrop for this delightful Raw Bar
Cold Boiled Shrimp

• • •

Fresh Shucked Oysters

• • •

Fresh Shucked Clams

• • •

Stone Crabs, in Season

• • •

Cocktail Sauce and Mustard Sauce
(Eight pieces per person)

New England
Boston Clam Chowder

• • •

Lobster Newburg, in Pastry Shell

• • •

Fried Scallops, Sauce Rémoulade

• • •

Steamed Clams

• • •

Mushrooms Nantua

America's South
Cajun Barbecued Shrimps

• • •

Monkfish with Crêpes

• • •

Smoked Fish Display

• • •

Fried Grouper Creole

Pacific Splendor
Stir-Fried Shark, prepared in Wok

• • •

Barbecued Swordfish Kabobs

• • •

Mahi Mahi

• • •

Cold Poached Salmon with Watercress Sauce

• • •

Not So Fishy
Sliced Pork Tenderloin, with Peppercorn Sauce

• • •

Cajun Blackened Beef, Carved to Order

• • •

Miniature Rolls

The Luxuriant and Sumptuous Reception

Wild Game Station
This Wild Game Station will be decorated with Stuffed Animals, and a Woods Motif will be created.
The following will be served:
Quail Breast Sautéed in Cognac

• • •

Venison Medallions, Juniper Berry Sauce

• • •

Roasted Duck, Carved to order, served with Gin Sauce

• • •

Roasted Turkey, Carved to order

• • •

Roasted Pheasant in Puff Pastry

• • •

Seafood Station
This Station will be decorated with
Authentic Fishing Nets, strung with Lobsters and Starfish
A Boat Display will enhance the Raw Bar

Snow Crab Claws
Cold Jumbo Shrimp
Clams and Oysters on the Half Shell,
Served with Cocktail Sauce,
Horseradish Sauce, and Lemon Wedge

• • •

Shrimp Sautéed in Garlic Butter

• • •

Caviar with Vodka

• • •

Seafood Crêpes with Scallops

• • •

Smoked Side of Salmon,
served with Capers, Chopped Onions, Black Bread

• • •

Montage of Fillet of Trout, Displayed on Mirrors

• • •

Lobster Montage

International Cheese Board
Assorted Domestic and Imported Cheeses including:
Edam, Brie, Swiss, Cheddar, Port Salut, Camembert,
Boursin au Poivre, Decorated with Fresh Fruits and
Crackers

• • •

Cheese Fondue, Served with French Bread

• • •

Fresh Fruit, Displayed in Baskets to include:
Apples, Oranges, Tangerines, Pears, Figs, and Persimmons

• • •

Pastry Station
Crêpes Suzette, with Almond Paste, Made to Order

• • •

Strawberries, Fresh Pineapple, Melons,
and other Fruits in Season,
served with Honey-Yogurt Dip

• • •

Chocolate Fettucini

• • •

Assorted Cakes and Petits Fours

The Across the Nation Reception

From New England
Jumbo Shrimp
Snow Crab Claws
Clams and Oysters on the Half Shell
The above will be displayed on ice and served with:
Horseradish, Cocktail Sauce, and Lemon Wedges

• • •

Smoked Side of Salmon, Carved in the Room,
Served with Capers, Onions, Chopped Eggs,
Parsley, and Rye Bread

• • •

From the Mid-West
International Cheese Board,
Assorted Domestic and Imported Cheeses including:
Edam, Brie, Swiss, Cheddar, Port Salut, Camembert,
Boursin au Poivre,
Decorated with Fresh Fruits and Crackers

• • •

Whole Steamship Round of Beef
Roast Turkeys
Carved in the Room by Uniformed Chefs,
Served with Miniature Rolls
and Appropriate Condiments

• • •

From the South/Southwest
Sugar-Glazed Virginia Hams,
Carved in the Room by our Uniformed Chefs,
Served with Mustard, Mayonnaise, and Biscuits

• • •

Gruyère Cheese Puffs

• • •

Spinach and Feta Cheese Pies

• • •

Spicy Fried Chicken Drumettes

• • •

Chili and Black Beans, Served with Chopped Onions,
Sour Cream, and Corn Bread

• • •

Taco Bar
To include:
Taco Shells, Ground Beef, Chopped Tomato, Onions,
and Lettuce, Shredded Sharp Cheese

• • •

Chili con Queso

• • •

Nachos

• • •

Wok Station
Beef, Chicken, and Shrimp Sate, Served with Peanut Sauce

• • •

Pastry Station
Bananas Cerromar,
Made to Order from the following:
Vanilla Ice Cream, Sliced Bananas,
Amaretto Liqueur, Banana Liqueur,
Coconut, Raisins, Almonds, Brown Sugar, and Butter

• • •

Loukoumades (Fried Dough),
with Honey Syrup or Powdered Sugar

• • •

Assorted French Pastries

• • •

Crêpes, Made to Order, with Assorted Fruit Fillings

• • •

Assorted Cookies and Truffles

The Executive Reception

Waiters in white gloves will pass the following selections of hors d'oeuvres and canapés.

Cold
Florida Lobster Medallions, on Buttered Toast Rounds
Snow Peas filled with Herb Cheese
Pâté de Foie Gras, on Toasted French
Bread Rounds
Lump Crabmeat, on Cucumber Rondelles
White Asparagus, wrapped in Westphalian Ham

• • •

Hot
Mushroom Caps filled with Escargots
Crispy Sweet and Sour Duck Tidbits
Fried Artichoke Hearts, with Parmesan
Traditional Clams Casino
Miniature Brochettes of Beef Teriyaki

• • •

The Buffet
Complimentary Ice Carving adorned with Flowers and
Greens
Stone Crab Claws, Jumbo Shrimp, Littleneck Clams, and
Plump Oysters, Displayed on Crushed Ice,
Brandied Seafood Sauce, Dijon Mustard Sauce, Tabasco,
Gauzed Lemon, Horseradish,
Crisp Crackers, and Oysterettes

• • •

The Ice Socles
A Display of Three Domestic Caviars:

Red, Black, and Golden With Sour Cream and Warm
Buckwheat Blinis, Accompanied by a Selection of
California Champagnes, on ice:
Piper Sonoma, Blanc de Noirs, Domaine Chandon,
Chandon Brut, Schramsberg, Blanc de Blancs

• • •

Our Chef Will Prepare to Order
Medallions of Steak au Poivre,
Cognac Flambé

• • •

Baby Lamb Chops Sauté,
Mint Sauce

• • •

Carved at the Buffet
Whole Sides of Puget Sound Honey-Cured Salmon,
Traditional Garniture to include:
Baby Sour Capers, Shredded Eggs, Minced Onions,
Buttered Toast Triangles,
Stolichnaya, Absolut, and Finlandia Vodkas,
Displayed from an Ice Block with Frosted Pony Glasses

• • •

A Captain Will Prepare to Order
Canapés of Steak Tartare,
Traditional Garniture, Rye and Pumpernickel Tartines

• • •

Deluxe Selection of Mixed Nuts, on Cocktail Tables

• • •

A Full Bar Featuring Premium Brands,
and Complimentary Bartender

Other Possible Reception Stations

Eastern Shore Waterman's Station

Maryland's Famous Hard Shell Blue Crabs
Steamed with Beer and Vinegar
Covered with Old Bay Seasoning and Coarse Sea Salt

Plump Salty Chincoteague Oysters
Shucked to Order by some of the fastest men you've ever
seen this side of the Mississippi Delta

Tender Soft Clams
Known to locals as "Steamers"
Raked from the shallow beds of the Chesapeake
tributaries

Now opening their shells without resistance as they are
steamed in a well-balanced Court Bouillon
To complement this Array of Exquisite Seafoods,
we offer:
Cocktail Sauce, Rémoulade Sauce, Lemon Wedges,
Drawn Butter, Parslied Garlic Butter, Old Bay Seasoning,
White Vinegar, Oyster Crackers, Saltines
And all the condiments to create your own sauce:
Tabasco, Worcestershire, Ketchup, Horseradish,
Lemons

Uniforms: Staff to wear T-Shirts that read: "Maryland is
for Crabs"

Three-Ring Circus Station

Old-Fashioned Popcorn
Machines are featured here as they turn with the sounds
of Fresh Corn Kernels crackling away with a new twist,
An offering of flavors to include:
Taco
Sour Cream and Chives
New York Deli Rye
Barbecue
and, of course, the old-time favorite,
Butter and Salt,
served in authentic cones or boxes

• • •

America's Own Hot Dog!
The Coney Island Foot Long variety with:
Fresh Buns that almost fit
Condiments of:
Brown, Yellow, and Dijon Mustards, Pickle Relish,
Chopped Onion, Grated Cheese, Texas Chili,
and Sauerkraut

Down Home Country Buffet Station

Beef Rib Bones
Marinated in a zesty Teriyaki Sauce overnight,
Brushed with a Brown Molasses-Based Barbecue Sauce,
Cooked over an Open Pit Charcoal Grill

Delmarua Chickens
Cut into quarters, then turned, and turned over red hot
coals,
Constantly basted with a Southern-Style Tomato-Based
Barbecue Sauce

Virginia Smithfield Hams
Carved to order at the buffet,
Offered with Beaten Biscuits and Peach Chutney

Baltimore-Style Cole Slaw
Hand-Cut Cabbage and Carrots
Bound with Mayonnaise and well-balanced seasoning

Old-Fashioned Potato Salad
This will bring back memories of Grandmother's Hearty
Potato Salad,
Garnished with wedges of Hard-Boiled Eggs,
Diced Bacon, Ripe Olives, and Parsley

Three Bean Salad
Red Kidney Beans, Fresh Green Beans, and Chick Peas
Marinated in a zesty Vinaigrette

• • •

Curried Apple-Raisin Salad
Cucumbers Bound in a Creamy Yogurt–Sour Cream
Dressing
Marinated Mushrooms and Artichoke Hearts
Tomatoes and Bermuda Onions with Basil Vinaigrette
Corn on the Cob with Whipped Sweet Butter
Baked Beans with Brown Sugar and Bacon
Crispy Hush Puppies
Zucchini and Yellow Squash American
Sally Lunn Bread
Beaten Buttermilk Biscuits
Corn Muffins
Tubs of Sweet Whipped Butter

The All-American Dessert Extravaganza Station

Stars and Stripes Forever
One Hundred Pound Replica of Old Glory made into a
Strawberry Shortcake
Sponge Cake is cut to effect the waving of our flag,
With Stripes of Strawberries and Whipped Cream, and a
Corner Field of Blueberries, with Whipped Cream Stars

Mom's Apple Pie, and The Girl Next Door's Cherry Pie
Offered à la Mode

The Good Humor Man Cometh
With Cherry, Lemon, Orange Popsicles, Nutty Buddies,
Toasted Almonds, Chocolate Eclairs, Banana Splits on
Stick

Sno-Cones
Flaked Ice Topped with syrups you couldn't get as a
youngster:
Strawberry Liqueur
Melonball Liqueur
Peppermint Schnapps
Chambord
Blackberry Brandy
Cointreau

Champagne Royale Bar
Champagne mixed with a variety of Beverages
To Create exciting new Tastes:
Cubair with Campari
Pimm's Royale with Pimm's #1 Cup
Black Velvet with Guiness Stout
Kir Royel with Crème de Cassis
Champagne with Whidbey's Liqueur
Mimosa with Orange Piece and Cointreau

• • •

Coffee, Tea, Decaffeinated Coffee, Cream, Sugar, Lemon

Other Reception Suggestions

Selection of International Hot and Cold Appetizers

When planning your reception, it is suggested that at least eight pieces per person be included for the first hour of service, and seven pieces per person during the second hour of service.

Cold Canapés

Cucumber Rondelles, with Seafood Salad
Variety of Deviled Eggs
Cornets of Genoa Salami
Artichoke Bottoms with Ham Mousse
Roast Beef and Cornichon Roulades
Lump Seafood Canapés
Steak Tartare Canapés
Ham and Asparagus Roulades
Smoked Salmon on Rye
Shrimp Imperial, Stuffed Cherry Tomatoes
Smoked Salmon and Boursin Cheese in Cucumber Cups
Tiny Shrimp Canapés
Prosciutto Ham and Melon
Ham Mousse en Bouchée
Walnut and Port Cheese Balls
Sliced Pâté Maison
Celery with Roquefort
Herring Tidbits on Rye Rounds
Profiteroles with Chicken Liver Mousse au Cognac
Smoked Oysters on Melba Rounds
Caviar Canapés
Sardine and Egg on Rye Rounds
Spiced Salami and Cheese Canapés
Spiced Cheese on Pea Pods
Roast Beef Rolls with Horseradish
Lobster Medallions with Truffles
Artichoke Bottoms filled with Caviar
Smithfield Ham wrapped around Fresh Melon
Chicken Breast Tarragon
Fresh Sushi
Country Pâté Triangles
Crabmeat and Avocado Canapés
Smoked Salmon Cornets
Chicken Pâté in Aspic
Seafood Mousse on Melba Toast
Pâté Cubelets en Gelée
Anchovies on Toast Points
Cracked Crabs
Rondelles of Mousse of Foie Gras
Smoked Salmon on Mini Bagels
Crab Puffs Admiral
Skewers of Fresh Fruit and Cheese
Petite Tomato Timbales

Salmon Pâté
Chou Puffs filled with Avocado Salmon Salad
Eggs à la Russe
Turkey with Orange
Beef Salami Butterfly
Julienne Vegetable Pile
Penguin-Shaped Turkey Pâté
Smoked Salmon with Cream Cheeses
Reubennettes
Bird of Paradise Cheese Canapés
Roast Beef and Cheese Rollups
Stuffed Cherry Tomatoes with Turkey Breast
Chicken Liver Mousse on Melba Toast
Sausage and Cheese en Brochette
Tuna Fish Mousse on Pumpernickel
Lox and Cream Cheese Lily
Heart of Palm Roulades
Shrimp and Egg Canapés
Decorated Cream Cheese and Lox
Scallop Suprême Canapés
Fancy Egg Baskets
Artichoke Petals with Crabmeat
Smoked Oyster and Egg on Rye Rounds
Artichoke Petals with Dilled Shrimp Mousse
Fancy Baby Shrimp Canapés
Medallions of Lobster on Toast
Belgian Endive Leaves filled with Crabmeat
Snow Peas filled with Roquefort Mousse
Papaya wrapped in Prosciutto
White Asparagus wrapped in Westphalian Ham
Pâté de Foie Gras on Toasted Petite French Rounds
Silver Demitasse Spoons filled with Salmon Mousse and
 Black Caviar
Ricotta Pesto on Belgian Endive
Shrimp Mandarin
Cucumber Rounds stuffed with Gorgonzola
Shrimp wrapped in Snow Peas with Honey-Mustard Sauce
Assorted Figs, Melons, and Pears wrapped in Prosciutto
 and Smoked Turkey
Smoked Salmon Rosettes with Dill on Pumpernickel
California Crostini
Mediterranean Swordfish in Endive
Pasta Shells stuffed with Sour Cream and Caviar
Skewered Ham and Papaya
Trout Pâté on French Toast
Veal or Beef Carpaccio
Prosciutto-wrapped Hearts of Palm
Three-Cheese Filo
Sugar Snaps with Herb Cheese
Spicy Crabmeat in a Corn Shell
Truffle Mousse Pâté on Toast

Brie Cheese with Smoked Salmon and Dill
Gravlax with Dill Mustard Sauce
Cucumber Sticks with a Curry Yogurt Shrimp Dip
Lobster Medallions with Aioli
Smoked Trout Mousse on English Cucumber Slices with Golden Caviar
Rolled Smoked Ham with Cashews and Cream Cheese
Salmon Mousse in Cherry Tomatoes, Belgian Endive Leaves, Cucumber Rounds, and Pea Pods
Fresh Fruit Skewers with Poppy Seed Dip
Skewered Tortellini and Mussels Marinara
Smoked Salmon Pâté
Grilled Chicken Fingers with Honey-Mustard Sauce
Smoked Salmon with Capers, Onions, and Cream Cheese
Grilled Swordfish, Tuna, or Halibut Skewers with Ginger Garlic
Pâté on Apple Slices with Cornichons
Chilled Poached Scallops with Blueberry Mayonnaise
Cherry Tomatoes with Smoked Oysters and Clams
Smoked Salmon and Avocado Sushi Rolls
Cherry Tomatoes with Sour Cream and Red Caviar
Snow Peas with St. Andre Cheese

Hot Hors d'Oeuvres

Cantonese Egg Rolls with English Mustard and Sweet and Sour Sauce
Fried Shrimp
Petite Vegetable Quiche Squares
Crabmeat Wonton with Selection of Sauces
Stuffed Mushroom Caps
Chicken Fingers
Fried Fish Puffs
Zucchini Pizza Squares
Rumaki
Shumai
Gulf Shrimp Italienne
Escargot Chablis
Bacon-wrapped Chicken Livers
Petite Kabobs of Chicken Livers
Petite Kabobs of Chicken Oriental
Deviled Crab in Small Shells
Medallions of Crisp Duck, with Pepper Sauce, Sprinkle of Scallions, and Chinese Parsley
Petite Beef Kabobs, Grecian Style
Bouchées of Chicken Bengale
Crab Remick en Croustade
Cocktail Franks en Croûte
Barbecued Baby Pork Ribs
Snails in Profiteroles Bourguignonne
Petite Fried Fish Fingers, Tartar Sauce
Petite Hawaiian Brochettes with Pineapple and Chicken
Dinghy Baked Clams
Oysters Wrapped in Bacon, Broiled, served on Herbed Toast Points

Barquettes of Lobster Thermidor
Coconut Chicken
Clams Oreganato
Tempura Fried Vegetables
Bouchées of Brie
Teriyaki Chicken
Brochettes of Sausage, Peppers, and Onions
Shrimp Pakora
Stuffed Mushroom Caps Provençale
Sweet and Sour Meatballs
Crisp Chicken Drumettes
Mahi-Mahi Brochettes
Pizza Napoletana
Baby Sausages in Puff Pastry
Fried Swiss Cheese Amandine
Coconut Fried Shrimp
Croustades St. Jacques
Chicken and Pineapple Tidbits
Chicken Tidbits Maryland
Petite Beef Balls
Mushroom Bouchées
Barbecued Baby Franks
Mushroom Caps filled with Sausage
Onion and Mushroom Barquettes
Croque Monsieur
Goyzo
Baby Lamb Chops Diablo
Baked Oysters Marinara
Brochettes of Tenderloin Shoyo
Stuffed Large Shrimps Imperial
Frog Legs Provençale
Scampi Bombay
Swedish Meatballs, Sweet and Sour Sauce
Shrimp Tempura, Honey-Mustard Sauce
Mushrooms filled with Seafood Mornay
Teriyaki Brochettes
Scampi in Garlic Butter
Crabmeat Lorenzo in Patty Shells
Cheese Croquettes
Chicken Croquettes
Bitki, Small Meatballs served in a Sour Cream Sauce
Oyster Puffs
Mushroom Caps stuffed with Cheese and Nuts
Mandarin Teriyaki
Spring Rolls
Belgian Seafood Croquettes
Fritto Misto, Chicken Chunks, Zucchini, Artichoke Hearts, dipped in Beer Batter and Deep Fat Fried
Pineapple Medallions with Roquefort and Pinenuts
Scallop-Zucchini Brochettes
Clam Linguini Puffs
Bacon and Water Chestnuts
Tidbits of Duckling Curaçao
Escargots served with Assorted Mushrooms, in a Patty Shell

Hot Hors d'Oeuvres (continued)

Brochettes of Vegetable Beef Chinoiserie
Crabmeat Balls Neptune
Polynesian Breaded Chicken Wing Drumettes
Petite Burritos with Cheese
Pepperoni Pizza Mini Bagels
Fried Potato Skins with Bacon Pieces and Cheddar Cheese
Spinach and Feta Cheese Grecian Triangles
Petite Chiles Rellenos
Fried Pasta Angaloti with Salsa–Sour Cream Sauce
Bacon-wrapped Water Chestnuts
Bite-Size Quiches with Vegetables
Chicken Fingers with Sweet and Sour Sauce
Fish Goujonettes, Sauce Tartar
Petite Kabobs of Chicken Oriental
Spicy Buffalo Chicken Wings
Almond Chicken Chunks with Sweet and Sour Sauce
Crabmeat Rangoon with Honey and Mustard Sauce
Fried Wontons with Beef or Shrimp and a Selection of Sauces
Seafood Turnovers Bombay
Tenderloin of Beef Wellington
Stuffed Mushrooms with Seafood
Bite-Size Quiches with Shrimp
Deep-Fried Scallops with Tartar, Cocktail, or Shallot Sauces
Seafood en Brochette
Escargots in Mushroom Caps with Scampi Butter
Cajun Barbecued Shrimp
Miniature Brochettes of Beef Teriyaki
Roast Oysters topped with Foie Gras and Vegetable Julienne
Almond Fried Shrimp with Plum Sauce
Petite Crab Cakes with Tartar Sauce
Fried Calamari with Marinara Sauce and Lemon
Chorizo Sausage in Puff Pastry
Conch Fritters with Sauce Rémoulade
Small Red Bliss Potatoes with Escargot, topped with Melted Camembert
Honey Coconut Shrimp
Grouper Fingers in Beer Batter or Tempura-Style
Beef Sirloin and Onion Kabobs
Chicken Fingers with Raspberry Sauce
Poached Scallops in White Wine with Dill Sauce
Maryland Crab Cakes with Orange-Tarragon Mayonnaise
Veal and Prune Kabobs
Pecan-Stuffed Mushrooms

Cajun Seafood in Pastry
Grilled Shrimp Kabobs, with Orange, Plum, Lemon, or Chili-Apricot Sauce
Crabmeat Imperial Barquettes
Skewered Peanut Chicken
Date and Almond Rumaki
Crabmeat and Conch Fritters with Pineapple Piquant Sauce
Mushrooms Stuffed with Walnuts and Cheese
Shrimp in Almond Batter with Orange-Mustard Sauce
Mushrooms Florentine
Veal Picadillo in Baby Pattypan Squash
Skewered Shrimp Wrapped in Bacon
Fresh Grouper Fingers with Cocktail Sauce
Cheese Mushroom Fingers
Curried Chicken Spring Rolls with Apricot Dip
Hearts of Artichoke Tempura with Sauce Béarnaise
Mushrooms Filled with Crabmeat
Curried Chicken, Papaya, and Pineapple Kabobs
Philippine Lumpia with Sweet and Sour Dressing
Wild Mushroom Pâté in Mushroom Caps
Skewered Veal Nuggets with Salsa Verde
Beef Sirloin on Pita with Basil Sauce
Pineapple Cubes and Water Chestnuts Wrapped in Bacon
Mushrooms Filled with Sweet Italian Sausage
Seafood-Stuffed Mushrooms
Mushrooms Filled with Brie and Pistachios
Miniature Quiches—Lorraine, Spinach, and Broccoli
Mushrooms Stuffed with Minced Clam
Bacon-Wrapped Chutney Bananas
Mexican Chicken Fingers with Guacamole Sauce
Mushrooms and Zucchini with Herbed Dipping Sauce
Grilled Quail Quarters with Currant Sauce
Seafood Croustades
Mesquite Veal Skewers
Coquilles St. Jacques
Brie Shells with Chutney
Tortellini Skewers with Locatelli Romano
Bacon-Wrapped Scallops
Wild Mushroom Tartlets
Swedish Mini Pancakes with Caviar and Sour Cream
Conch Fritters with Cocktail Sauce
Chicken Sate with Spicy Peanut Sauce
Quesadillas with Salsa Dip
Caviar, Potato Crisp, and Sour Cream
Sesame Oysters
Barbecued Shrimp

Reception Embellishments to Enhance Your Cocktail Reception

Chef Carver Required
Whole Roast Steamship Round of Beef
Including Miniature Rolls, Cocktail Rye, and
Pumpernickel,
Accompanied by Mayonnaise, Horseradish, and Chutney
• • •

*Whole Sliced Marinated Roasted Beef Tenderloin en
Croûte*
With Sauces Béarnaise and Choron
• • •

Suckling Pig
Decorated, Garnished, and Wrapped in Banana Leaves
• • •

Whole Smoked Nova Scotia Salmon on Display
Carved to Order at the Buffet Table with Capers,
Sliced Tomatoes, Onions, and Cream Cheese,
served on Black Bread and Bagels
• • •

*Whole Roast Turkey or Whole Sugar-Cured Baked
Ham*
Including Miniature Rolls, Cocktail Rye, and
Pumpernickel,
Accompanied by Mayonnaise and Mustard
• • •

Whole Roast Baron of Veal
With Marjoram
• • •

Whole Glazed Corned Brisket of Beef
Including Miniature Rolls, Cocktail Rye, and
Pumpernickel,
Accompanied by Mustard and Mayonnaise

The Marketplace
Fresh Crudité Display
Presented on Crushed Ice, including Zucchini,
Mushrooms, Broccoli, Radishes, Celery, Cauliflower,
Green Beans, and Carrots, Accompanied by a Selection of
Cheese, Clam, and Dill Dips
• • •

Fresh Fruit Fondue Display
Presented on Crushed Ice, including Pineapple Cubes,
Melon Cubes, Strawberries, and a Selection of other
Fruits, Accompanied by Brown Sugar, Sour Cream,
Dark Chocolate and White Chocolate Fondues
and Whipped Cream
• • •

Pâté Maison Display
To include an Assortment of Pâtés and Terrines,
Appropriately Garnished
• • •

Swiss Vegetable Fondue
Presented with Crisp Vegetables, French Bread, and a
Traditional Cheese Fondue
• • •

International Cheese Display
With a Variety of Crackers, Lahvosh, and Sliced French
Bread and Garnished with Fruit
• • •

Tray of International Cheeses
With a Variety of Crackers, Lahvosh, and Sliced French
Bread and Garnished with Fruit
• • •

The Florida Seafood Bar
Freshly Shucked Clams and Oysters on the Half Shell,
with Cocktail Sauce, Horseradish, and Lemon Stars,
Shucker optional, at an additional cost
• • •

Shrimp Sauté Provençale
• • •

Florida Stone Crabs, in Season
On Ice, Mustard Sauce
• • •

Clams Casino or Oysters Rockefeller
• • •

Cold Jumbo Gulf Shrimp on Ice
With Rémoulade and Cocktail Sauces, Lemon Stars
• • •

Sushi Bar
Featuring Raw Oriental Seafood Specialties with Spicy
Sauces and Rice Cakes
• • •

Golden Gulf Crab Claws on Ice
With Rémoulade and Cocktail Sauces, Lemon Stars

Reception Specialties

Sautéed Pepper Steak
Tender Cubes of Fillet in Peppercorns, Flamed in Brandy
• • •

Baby Lamb Chops
With Dijon Sauce

• • •

Make Your Own Taco Bar
With all the Fixin's

• • •

Carpaccio
Finely Shaved Raw Sirloin topped with Finely Grated
Parmesan Cheese and Ground Peppercorns,
served with Mustard-Mayonnaise Sauce

• • •

Tempura Station
Fresh Vegetable Assortment, Chicken Fingers,
Whole Shrimp, Dipped in Light Oriental Batter,
then Cooked in Oil, served with Spiced Mandarin Sauce

• • •

Assorted Fancy Finger Sandwiches
Ham, Turkey, Cheese, Tuna, and Watercress,
Egg and Tomato, Chicken Salad, Checkerboard,
Salmon and Cream Cheese, Open-Face Cucumber,
and Fillet of Beef with Sauce Béarnaise

• • •

Petite Filets Mignons
Cooked to Order and served on Miniature Rolls with
Sauces Béarnaise and Choron

• • •

Steak Tartare
Freshly Prepared at the Buffet, Appropriate Garniture

• • •

Four-Foot Italian Hero Combination
With Fifteen Items

• • •

American Black or Gold Caviar
10 ounces, with appropriate Garniture, served from an Ice
Carving

• • •

Finger Foods
Fingers of Zucchini, Squash, and other Seasonal
Vegetables Deep-Fried, and served Hot with
Bacon-Horseradish Sauce and Mustard-Mayonnaise Dips

• • •

Wok Mania
Vegetables Stir Fried to order, Beef Chow Yoke,
Ginger Pork with Pinenuts, Sweet and Sour Chicken with
Almonds, Steamed Mussels in White Wine with Garlic

• • •

Assorted Fancy Petite French Pastries

• • •

Flaming Coffees

• • •

Wine and Cheese Party
Domestic and Imported Cheeses with a Fine Selection of
Wines, Selected by the Resort for the Occasion

• • •

Snack and Dip
Pretzels, Roasted Nuts, Potato Chips, and Corn Chips
with Salsa, Clam, and Onion Dips

• • •

Dry Snacks by the Pound
Mixed Nuts
Dry Roasted Nuts
Potato Chips or Corn Chips
Salsa, Clam, Onion, Curry, or Guacamole Dips

The Final Touches

Ice Carvings: Appropriate Designs may be carved to highlight your buffet.

Floral Centerpieces: These will add the final finished touch to the overall table presentation.

Service Charges: All receptions with a minimum of food service will incur a waiter service charge per waiter for three (3) hours and an additonal charge for each hour thereafter. One (1) waiter required for each one hundred (100) guests.

Nightcap Parties

(Price is based on a one hour duration)

Bienvenue à Paris

Your Choice of Crêpes Flambées Made to Order:
Suzette, Jubilee
Banana
Confiture
Peach
Strawberry
Pineapple
Prepared with the Appropriate Liqueurs and Condiments

Coney Island Express

Your Ice Cream Parlor consists of:
Four Flavors of your Favorite Ice Cream or Sherbet,
Heaped High on Cones,
Old-Fashioned Favorite Sundaes,
Served with all the Trimmings
Ice Cream Sodas and Cherry Colas

Vienna by Night

Apple Strudel, with Brandied Vanilla Sauce
Assortment of Mini Pastries and Fruit Tartlets
Sacher Torte
Linzer Torte
Black Forest Cake
Ladyfinger Cake
Cheesecake with Fruit Toppings
Chocolate Cake
Assorted Continental Cookies
Strawberry Friandises
Petits Fours
Chocolettes
Viennese Coffee
Darjeeling, Orange Pekoe, and Jasmine Tea

International Coffees Flambées

Optional at additional price
(Check with your Catering Executive)
Café Napoleon
Café Irlandais
Café Mexicaine
Café Hollandaise
Café Jamaique

Café la Crêpe

Crêpes Suzettes, with Orange-Butter Sauce
• • •
Crêpes Nancy, with Cinnamon, Apples, and Almonds
• • •
Crêpes Myrtille, with Blueberries
• • •
Crêpes Victoria, with Strawberries
• • •
Miniature French Pastries
• • •
Petits Fours
• • •
A Large Decorated Mirror of
Assorted Fresh Fruit and Berries of the Season
• • •
Dark Chocolate Fondue
White Chocolate Fondue
• • •
Brandied Peaches and Bananas Foster
To be served with Vanilla Ice Cream,
Attractively Displayed in a Specially Made Ice Socle

An International Water Station Featuring

Imported splits of Perrier, Poland Spring,
and Vichy Waters,
All served with Fresh Lime and Lemon Wedges

Coffees of the World

Optional at additional price
(Check with your Catering Executive)
Irish Coffee, with Irish Whiskey
Viennese Coffee, with Nutmeg and Kirsch
Dutch Coffee, with Cinnamon Sticks and Vandermint
Fresh Whipped Cream for the above
• • •
Regular Hot Coffee

Chapter 23

Low-Cholesterol, Low-Fat, Low-Sodium Menus

Continental Breakfasts

Continental Breakfast #1

Governor's Smile
Orange Juice, Marshmallow, Lime Juice,
and Honey
• • •
Crunchy Granola or Whole Grain Cereals,
With Seasonal Berries,
Skim Milk or Yogurt
• • •
Freshly Brewed Coffee, Decaffeinated Coffee,
Herbal Teas

Continental Breakfast #2

Half Papaya Filled with Fresh Fruits
or
A Selection of Fruit-Flavored Yogurts
• • •
Assorted Muffins Made with
Corn Oil Margarine,
Preserves and Marmalade
or Smucker's Low-Sugar Jelly
• • •
Freshly Brewed Coffee, Decaffeinated Coffee,
Herbal Teas

Note: Corn oil margarine to be served

Breakfasts

Breakfast #1

Papaya Nectar and White Grape Juice
• • •
Sunshine Cereal,
Oatmeal Blended with Skim Milk, Honey, Apple, Pecans,
Raisins, and Yogurt,
Served Chilled and Decorated with Strawberries
• • •
Cholesterol-Free Scrambled Eggs with Mushrooms*
Tomato Provençale
• • •

Assorted Muffins, Prepared with Corn Oil Margarine,
Preserves and Marmalade
or
Smucker's Low-Sugar Jelly
• • •
Freshly Brewed Coffee, Decaffeinated Coffee, Herbal
Teas

*Optional: Egg Beaters or similar product
Note: Corn oil margarine to be served

Breakfast #2

Freshly Squeezed Orange Juice or
Grapefruit Juice

• • •

Herbed Scrambled Cholesterol-Free Eggs,
on Crispy Cheese Bread*
with Fresh Fruit Garnish

• • •

Freshly Brewed Coffee, Decaffeinated Coffee,
Herbal Teas

*Suggest Boboli Crust

Breakfast #3

Raspberry Banana Drink

• • •

Western Omelette with Cholesterol-Free
Eggs*
Breakfast Potatoes,
Prepared with Corn Oil Margarine

• • •

Breakfast Breads,
Including Date Nut, Zucchini, and
Banana Breads,
Preserves, Marmalade, and Honey
or
Smucker's Low-Sugar Jelly

• • •

Freshly Brewed Coffee, Decaffeinated Coffee,
Herbal Teas

*Egg Beaters or similar product
Note: Corn oil margarine to be served

Breakfast #4

Seasonal Fresh Fruit with Lime Juice

• • •

Poached Egg Florentine
Low-Sodium Bacon
Toasted English Muffin

• • •

Breakfast Breads to include:
Whole Grain Rolls,
Preserves and Marmalade
or
Smucker's Low-Sugar Jelly

• • •

Freshly Brewed Coffee, Decaffeinated Coffee,
Herbal Teas

Breakfast #5

Half Grapefruit Glazed with Brown Sugar

• • •

Whole Wheat French Toast,* with Maple
Syrup
Beef Bacon
Fruit Garnish

• • •

Freshly Brewed Coffee, Decaffeinated Coffee,
Herbal Teas

*Made with Egg Beaters and Skim Milk
Note: Corn oil margarine to be served

Breakfast #6

Freshly Squeezed Orange Juice

• • •

Delicate Buckwheat Pancakes,
Filled with Maple-Margarine,
Served with Crisp Low-Sodium Bacon
Fresh Fruit Garnish

• • •

Breakfast Breads,
Zucchini and Date Nut Bread

• • •

Freshly Brewed Coffee, Decaffeinated Coffee,
Herbal Teas

Breakfast #7

Melon Crown
Fresh Melon Filled with Melon Balls,
Marinated in Grenadine Syrup

• • •

Belgian Waffle,
Topped with Your Choice of
Maple Syrup, Low-Fat Yogurt, or
Strawberries

• • •

Seven Grain Rolls,*
Preserves and Marmalade
or
Smucker's Low-Sugar Jelly

• • •

Freshly Brewed Coffee, Decaffeinated Coffee,
Herbal Teas

*Optional

Breakfast #8

Tomato Cocktail or V-8 Juice

• • •

German Apple Pancake,
Dusted with Powdered Sugar,
and served with Lean Canadian-Style Bacon

• • •

Breakfast Breads,
Zucchini and Date Nut Breads

• • •

Freshly Brewed Coffee, Decaffeinated Coffee,
Herbal Teas

Note: Corn oil margarine to be served

Breakfast #9

Yogurt Melon Wedge
Melon Wedge Filled with Raspberry-Flavored Yogurt

• • •

Poached Egg in a Pastry Shell, with Mushrooms Sautéed in
Corn Oil Margarine, Lean Canadian-Style Bacon

• • •

Breakfast Breads including Quick Breads Made with
Corn Oil Margarine, Preserves and Marmalade
or
Smucker's Low-Sugar Jelly

• • •

Freshly Brewed Coffee, Decaffeinated Coffee, Herbal Teas

Note: Corn oil margarine to be served

Lazy Susan Breakfast

Lazy Susan Breakfast

The following items will be displayed on a
Lazy Susan in the center of each table:

• • •

Carafes of Freshly Squeezed Orange Juice,
Grapefruit Juice, and Skim Milk, on Shaved Ice

• • •

Assorted Cereals to include:
Shredded Wheat, Raisin Bran, Wheaties, and Special K

• • •

Individual Natural Fruit Shells Filled with Cubed
Honeydew Melon, Cantaloupe Melon, Sliced Peaches,

Fresh Strawberries or other Seasonal Berries, Dry Raisins,
Apricots, Walnuts, Brown Sugar, Honey
Preserves and Marmalade
or
Smucker's Low-Sugar Jelly

• • •

Baskets of Assorted Breakfast Breads:
Pumpernickel, Petit Pain, Whole Grain Roll,
Corn Oil Margarine

• • •

Freshly Brewed Coffee, Decaffeinated Coffee, Herbal Teas

Buffet Breakfast

Buffet Breakfast #1

An Attractive Display of Chilled Orange and Grapefruit
Juices

• • •

A Variety of Fresh Sliced Fruits to include:
Honeydew Melon, Cantaloupe Melon, Watermelon,
Assorted Exotic Fruits, Fresh Seasonal Berries

• • •

Assorted Cereals to include:
All-Bran, Raisin Bran, Shredded Wheat,
Accompanied with Skim Milk, Fruit-Flavored and Plain
Low-Fat Yogurt

• • •

Freshly Scrambled Cholesterol-Free Eggs,*
Seasoned with Fresh Herbs,
Accompanied with your Choice of Toppings,
Onions and Mushrooms Sautéed in Corn Oil Margarine,
Fresh Diced Tomatoes, and Spicy Salsa

• • •

Basket of Whole Wheat and Bran Muffins, Preserves,
Corn Oil Margarine

• • •

Freshly Brewed Coffee, Decaffeinated Coffee,
Herbal Teas, and Skim Milk

*Egg Beaters or other similar product

Luncheons

Lunch #1

Ceviche
Scallops Marinated with Lime Juice and Fresh Cilantro
• • •

Grilled Chicken Brochette
Brochette of Chicken,
Grilled and Served Over Fresh Spinach Leaves,
with a Yogurt-Cucumber Sauce
• • •
Chilled Papaya Slices, with Lime Sherbet
• • •
Freshly Brewed Coffee, Decaffeinated Coffee, Herbal Teas

Lunch #2

Consommé d'Angeli
Beef Consommé with Angel Hair Pasta
• • •

Cold Breast of Chicken
Glazed with Tarragon Aspic,
Waldorf Salad with Creamy Low-Fat Ricotta Cheese
• • •
Sliced Fresh Fruits, Topped with Lemon Sherbet
• • •
Freshly Brewed Coffee, Decaffeinated Coffee, Herbal Teas

Lunch #3

Pineapple and Melon Supreme
Fresh Pineapple and Melon,
Marinated in Grenadine Syrup, Served in a Pineapple Shell,
Decorated with Fresh Mint
• • •

Chicken Kung Pao
Stir-Fried Chicken with Pea Pods, Chili Peppers,
Fresh Ginger, and Peanuts, Steamed Rice
• • •
Orange Sherbet with Litchi
• • •
Freshly Brewed Coffee, Decaffeinated Coffee, Herbal Teas

Lunch #4

Shrimp Cocktail
Chilled Shrimp Marinated in V-8,
Seasoned with Jalapeño Pepper,
and Served in a Tomato Crown
• • •

Poached Breast of Chicken
Served in Champagne Sauce,
with Fresh Vegetable Julienne,
Spinach Noodles
• • •

Almond Pastry Basket
Filled with Fresh Berries in Season,
on a Raspberry Coulis
• • •
Freshly Brewed Coffee, Decaffeinated Coffee,
Herbal Teas

Lunch #5

Avocado and Crabmeat Salad
Crabmeat Blended with Low-Fat Yogurt,
and Seasoned with Fresh Tarragon,
Served on a Star of Avocado Wedges
• • •

Grilled Breast of Chicken Oreganato*
Marinated with Lemon Juice and Oregano
Ratatouille Niçoise
• • •

Orange Amaretto
Orange Slices with Amaretto,
Decorated with White Seedless Grapes and
Low-Fat Ricotta
• • •
Freshly Brewed Coffee, Decaffeinated Coffee,
Herbal Teas

* Breast of chicken must be skinless.

Lunch #6

Minestrone Soup

• • •

Veal Piccata with Lemon
Delicate Veal Medallion,
Sautéed in Margarine and Laced with Lemon
Juice and Capers,
Broccoli Flowerettes,
Saffron Rice

• • •

Spumoni
Italian Water Ice

• • •

Freshly Brewed Coffee, Decaffeinated Coffee,
Herbal Teas

Lunch #7

Spinach-Mushroom Salad
Crisp Spinach Leaves and Fresh Sliced
Mushrooms, with Red Bell Pepper and Water
Chestnuts,
Yogurt-Lime Dressing

• • •

Chilled Poached Salmon Medallion
Horseradish Ricotta Sauce,
Dill Cucumber Salad

• • •

Raspberry Strudel, Made from Filo Dough

• • •

Freshly Brewed Coffee, Decaffeinated Coffee,
Herbal Teas

Lunch #8

Chilled Apricot Nectar

• • •

Baked Fillet of Boston Scrod, Lemon Sauce
Braised Celery
Imported Belgian Carrots

• • •

Baked Apple in Cider

• • •

Coffee

Lunch #9

Mushroom Trio
Shiitake, Chanterelle and Button Mushrooms,
Sautéed in Lemon Margarine,
Served on Toast Points, with Fresh Chopped Chives

• • •

Poached Salmon à la Nage, with Fresh Herbs
Asparagus Tips
Parslied Potatoes

• • •

Raisin Pineapple Rice Pudding, Prepared with Skim Milk

• • •

Freshly Brewed Coffee, Decaffeinated Coffee, Herbal Teas

Lunch #10

Tomato and Mozarella Slices
Sliced Tomato and Skim Milk Mozarella,
With Basil Vinaigrette

• • •

Veal Saltimbocca
Veal Medallion with Sage, Sautéed in Corn Oil Margarine
Fresh Zucchini
Spaghetti with a Creamy Low-Fat Ricotta Sauce

• • •

Rainbow Sherbet

• • •

Freshly Brewed Coffee, Decaffeinated Coffee, Herbal Teas

Lunch #11

Melon Bora Bora
Honeydew, Cantaloupe, Watermelon, and Papaya,
with Honey Yogurt, Served in a Melon Basket

• • •

Roasted Cold Breast of Chicken with Cranberry Sauce,
Fillet of Smoked Trout with Horseradish Ricotta,
Cold Sliced Tenderloin of Beef with Mustard,
Green Bean Salad, Angel Hair Pasta,
Presented on a Wooden Board

• • •

Timbale Montmorency, with Bing Cherries, Orange Sauce

• • •

Freshly Brewed Coffee, Decaffeinated Coffee, Herbal Teas

Lunch #12

Salad Rosemarie
Orange, Grapefruit, and Avocado with Vinaigrette Dressing

• • •

Grilled Fresh Swordfish Steak
With Fennel Margarine

Grilled Marinated Vegetables
Zucchini, Tomato, Onion, Whole Mushrooms,
and Yellow Squash

• • •

Fresh Strawberries Nicholi
Strawberries with Low-Fat Ricotta Honey and Vanilla

• • •

Freshly Brewed Coffee, Decaffeinated Coffee, Herbal Teas

Lunch #14

Fresh Asparagus Tips, Marinated in
Corn Oil Vinaigrette

• • •

Steamed Halibut Fillet
Served with Yellow and Red Bell
Pepper Sauce
Parslied Potatoes

• • •

Fresh Melon Slices in Season
Cantaloupe, Honeydew, Casaba, Santa Claus,
Served with Honey-Yogurt Dressing

• • •

Freshly Brewed Coffee, Decaffeinated Coffee,
Herbal Teas

Lunch #13

Fresh Fruit Salad

• • •

Dutch Cold Platter
Roasted Cold Breast of Turkey, Cranberry Sauce

• • •

Vegetable Salad
Carrots, Beans, Wax Beans,
and Raw Celery in Low-Cal Dressing

• • •

Rye Crisps and Margarine

• • •

Cheese Chiffon Cake

• • •

Coffee

Lunch #15

Chilled Grape Juice

• • •

Broiled Breast of Capon
With Creole Sauce
Brown Rice
Cling Peach

• • •

Fruit Goblet
Cubes of Orange and Lemon
Jello over Fruit Segments

• • •

Coffee

Luncheon Buffet

Luncheon Buffet

Tossed Garden Salad
Iceberg Lettuce, Romaine, Celery, Cucumber,
and Plum Tomatoes

• • •

Chicken Salad
Sliced Breast of Chicken
With a Yogurt-Tarragon Vinaigrette Dressing

• • •

Salmon Salad
Flaked Salmon with Snow Peas,
Yellow and Red Bell Peppers, and Sliced Mushrooms,
with a Fresh Herb Dressing

• • •

Variety of Breads to include
Whole Grain, Pumpernickel, Rye, and Seven Grain

• • •

Display of Whole and Sliced Fruits, served with Brown Sugar, Honey, Low Fat Yogurt, or Sherbet

• • •

Freshly Brewed Coffee, Decaffeinated Coffee, Herbal Teas

Special Note: Corn oil margarine to be served

Additional Buffet Suggestions

Cold Beef Salad
Julienne of Roast Sirloin,
Marinated in Olive Oil Vinaigrette, with Capers

• • •

Tabbouleh
Bulgur Wheat Mixed with Diced Tomato, Mint,
Parsley, and Onion,
Seasoned with Lemon Juice and Olive Oil

• • •

Greek Salad
Romaine, Tomato, Cucumber, Onions, and Olives, with
Oregano Dressing,
Topped with Low-Fat Goat Cheese

• • •

Tomato and Mozzarella Slices
Laced with a Basil Vinaigrette

• • •

Pasta Salad
Linguine or Spaghetti Tossed with,
Fresh Garden Vegetables,
Olive Oil and Cilantro Vinaigrette

• • •

Spinach Salad
Tender Spinach Leaves with Strips of Red Bell Pepper,
Fresh Sliced Mushrooms, and Water Chestnuts,
Yogurt Dressing

A variety of the following soups can be added:

Cold

Gazpacho
Yogurt-cucumber soup
Kaltschale (German cold fruit soup)
Spicy Mandarin shrimp soup

Hot

Fat-free consommé
Minestrone—specialty
Clear vegetable soup
Kansas City steak soup (made with lean beef)

If cream soups are used, be sure to make the roux with corn oil margarine or Ole; do not add heavy cream, but use skim milk.

Dinner

Dinner

Chilled Cocktail of Fruits de Mer
Flakes of Saltwater Fish in a Wine Lemon Dill Marinade,
topped with Bay Shrimp

• • •

Roast Prime Ribs of Blue Ribbon Beef
Au Jus to be in Sauceboat on Side

Broccoli Polonaise
Baked Tomato

• • •

Caesar Salad, Caesar Dressing in sauceboat

• • •

Whole Bartlett Pear in Claret Wine Sauce

• • •

Coffee, Tea, Milk

Chapter 24

The Fantasy Factory® Theme Menus

Creative Strategies for More Profitable Theme Parties

There are few things in the life of a meeting less appreciated than an uninspired food function, but that axiom's mirror image is also true. Few things are more appreciated than a food function with a life of its own.

Sure, memorable meals take lots of time, effort and, saddest of all, money. But food functions with thematic tie-ins can prove rewarding both to attendees, who get a break from monotony, and to you, the function's planner, if you like to implement your sense of creativity.

The "Fantasy Factory" is designed to provide you with some basic information and ideas that will enable you to decide upon themes and to make them work. We will also look at food theme decor and show you how to enhance the "flavor" of the foods through appropriate decorations, costumes, novelties, and entertainment. These are at least as important as the food itself for the thematic success.

In planning a theme party, put together all manner of necessary materials to make your function as simple or complex as you can afford. And speaking of affordability, for the budget-conscious planner (and who really isn't?) there are alternatives.

The best advice is to create your theme first, then look for ways to bring it to life without skimping on anything, and finally begin to cut back. When you have pared your plans down to the point where your budget can accommodate them—and have made sure at the same time that they are not too threadbare—then you have a theme function that your people will love and that you can live with.

We should take a look at the marketing techniques for aggressive retailing as practiced by stores like Bloomingdale's. These stores create an immedi-ate competitive marketing impact by shipping a complete festival package to all their locations. The package includes posters, store decorations, special merchandising pieces, media advertising formats, and detailed directions for putting the event on. The result is a professional, first-class production carried out throughout the store and in all departments.

Developing Theme Packages

To create an aggressive theme program in your hotel, you need to approach it in the same way, involving the entire food and beverage department. Some things you will want to consider in developing your theme packages are as follows:

A. If your hotel does not already have a food festival program, you should develop one. It can serve two important functions: First, it helps you sell the hotel's food and beverage services to the local market; this can be accomplished rather dramatically by a blitz advertising method. Second, the festivals can become a permanent part of the catering sales kit, offering special appeal to incentive groups. In developing a food festival kit, you should include the following:
  1. Newspaper advertising:
     a. Full page
     b. Entertainment section insert
     c. Press release
  2. TV spots
  3. Radio spots
  4. Souvenir menus
  5. Table tents
  6. Posters
  7. Lobby displays
  8. Catering albums
  9. Festival decor panels
  10. Murals
  11. Buffet centerpieces

12. Food photos
13. Decor/setup photos
14. Recipe manuals
15. Blueprints
16. Costume plans
17. Entertainment
18. Skirting/tablecloths
19. Centerpieces
20. Napkins/coasters

B. Think of theme meals the hotel can prepare especially well and how they would lend themselves to your theme ideas.

C. Think of theme meals that have had great success, and of the meals that have bombed.

D. Consider which local or regional specialty foods can be included in your theme ideas. Perhaps you can even cook up a theme meal based solely on these dishes if they are plentiful and unusual.

E. Are any local wines highly recommended? How can they contribute to your theme ideas? In many cases, a regional theme requires the addition of wines that have traditionally accompanied certain foods.

F. How well do various foods you may have in mind hold up on a buffet table or during the trek from the kitchen to the function room? Let's face it, some dishes lose their appeal from too long a wait, so you need to determine those and avoid them.

G. Price everything before committing yourself to a client. Theme meals and their various support items can become unexpectedly expensive for the hotel, instead of profitable, if you fail to keep abreast of the details and the changes.

H. When planning theme decorations, you should determine what your hotel has in the way of props and costumes left over from prior events; does the hotel have any silk flower arrangements or other centerpieces; what about culinary pieces the hotel may have such as sugar, tallow, or shortening pieces? Which colors are available in linens, and which colors must be rented? Also, look into outside suppliers. What specific props do they have on hand and which props would have to be built to your specifications and then rented? The most important consideration with regard to decor is what works best in your facility. You need to develop practical means for getting your theme ideas to work within the context of your facility.

I. When developing a new theme, you need to prepare a sample test meal consisting of everything you have selected for that theme meal. Then check it for size of portions, compatibility of food colors, tastes and textures, nutrition value, and style of service, including the time needed for preparation and warming. All such tests are recommended so there will be no surprises when your groups are served the same meal.

Surely the most common food function theme these days is the ethnic or nationality theme. In fact, the idea has been around for quite a few years, often used as a last resort by meeting planners who decide at the eleventh hour to "throw in" a theme party and can't think of anything except along ethnic lines.

Meeting goers do like ethnic-themed parties, however, because they are the basis for a good time. And they give you, the catering executive, an opportunity to put local atmosphere into your show.

So yes, the ethnic theme survives, but it comes to us now with a plea, personified: Use me well or not at all. It begs for your respect.

Whether your ethnic theme is from South of the border, the Continent, or some small Island Paradise in a corner of the Globe nearly forgotten, it will work only if you treat it well.

An ethnic theme deserves your careful attention, not only to its menu, but to appropriate and tasteful decoration. If well thought out and augmented by the proper decor and atmosphere, any ethnic theme meal can still be exotic, as well as delicious.

Creative catering has become something of a hackneyed expression in the meeting business. Its goal, to inject excitement into a group meal experience, is certainly valid, but efforts to reach that goal often take the form of empty razzmatazz, jazzing up what amounts to plain old mashed potatoes.

As with the meeting business itself, creative "Show Biz" catering is really effective only when it is grounded in tangible practices, each with an explainable raison d'être.

Group meals can have many purposes—fun, a stage for announcements, relaxation, a gearing up for the evening ahead, or plain nourishment. The meeting planner should determine the appropriate goal and then let the catering executive help him or her plan carefully to achieve that objective.

To see it from the caterer's perspective is like comparing the preparation of a menu to the way in which an artist creates a painting. First, you have to select your materials, colors, and tools. Then you decide whether you want it to be primitive, traditional, or modern. If your picture elicits approval, you are an artist. So, too, with menus. In putting together a work of art, one must think of foods that are compatible, and that must involve all of your senses. The appeal to the senses covers everything that goes into a meal, from condiments to glassware, and all aspects must be carefully matched to produce harmony.

With this in mind, this section was developed into a "Fantasy Factory" of ideas with panache and flair and all at an affordable price! Remember: "If we can dream it—we can achieve it!" So gather your most creative staff together, form your own band of Dream Merchants for theme parties, and manufacture your dreams!

The "Fantasy Factory" contains brief descriptions of some of the most popular themed parties that you might arrange for selected groups. Each description includes a detailed menu, along with beverage options. These parties have proven to be successful. And depending on your group's tastes and preferences, any one of them is guaranteed to be talked about for a long time to come.

Dream Merchants, your fantasy awaits.

A Very Sheik Affair

Each of your guests will feel like an oil-rich sheik as he or she enters the sultan's multicolored tent for an evening to long be remembered. The family-style dinner is served on low tables with your guests seated on tufted pillows. They will eat only with their hands, as there will be no utensils, for complete authenticity. Persian rugs will adorn the floor and special decor pieces will complement the decor offered. We can also arrange for an authentic Arabian band to provide the intoxicating musical interludes while your guests are charmed and entranced by bejeweled belly dancers.

Mezzah—Appetizers

Warak Enab
Stuffed Vine Leaves

Koubaba
Ground Lamb stuffed with Pinenuts

Sambousak
Pastries stuffed with Cheese

Kebbe Krass
Lamb Tartare with Bulgur

Fatayers
Pastries stuffed with Meat and Spinach

Fattoush
Mixed Salad with Toasted Bread

Salitit Khyaar Bi Laban
Cucumber with Laban

Hummus
Chickpea Salad

Baba Ghanouj
Eggplant Salad

Assorted Black and Green Olives

Fresh Lemon and Lime Slices

Tabbouleh
Mint and Parsley Salad

Arabic Bread

Entrées

Shish Kabob
Lamb Skewers

Shish Taaowk
Chicken Skewers

Jemberi Mashwi
Shrimp Skewers

Kofta Kabob
Ground Lamb and Beef

Kharoof Mashi
Roasted Stuffed Baby Lamb

Kabsa
A Traditional Saudi dish of Spiced Lamb Chunks over Arabic Rice

Couscous
Lamb Braised with Vegetables, served with Couscous

Tajin of Chicken
Braised Chicken with Onion, Garlic, and Olives

Stuffed Pigeon
with Freek

Halfoot Mashi
Stuffed Cabbage

Kousa Mashi
Stuffed Zucchini

Arabic Mixed Vegetables
Fresh Vegetables with Potatoes in Tomato Sauce

Grilled Lamb Chops

Desserts

Fresh Fruits with Pâtés

Mhalabya
Almond Flavored Pudding

Crème Caramel

Arabic Pastries

Ashayariha
Milk Curd Marinated in Rose Water Syrup and Chopped Pistachios

Arabic Tea with Fresh Mint

Arabic Coffee with Cardamon

Special Beverages: We suggest free-flowing service of specially selected Arabic wines, at an additional charge.

Menus with a Floridian Theme

Palm trees sway in the tropical Floridian breezes while white sandy beaches and blue-green waters perfect the backdrop for a vacationer's paradise.

Special Beverages: May we suggest fresh squeezed Florida orange and grapefruit juice with vodka to get the party started right? In addition to Screwdrivers and Greyhounds, we recommend an open bar. Or how about serving a Hot Florida O.J. Sipper to each guest? Prices on request.

Music: Music for all interests . . . for listening and dancing as you enjoy the tropical atmosphere about you.

Floridian Seated Breakfast

Tropical Fresh Fruit Cup
Topped with Shredded Coconut and a Whole Fresh Strawberry

• • •

Venice of America Eggs
Potato Pancake, Sliced Apple,
Two Poached Eggs, Hollandaise Sauce
Smoked Whitefish
Papaya with Kiwi Garnish

• • •

Brioche, Croissants, Petite Danish Pastry,
Butter and Assorted Fruit Preserves

• • •

Coffee, Tea, Decaffeinated Coffee, or Milk

South Florida-by-the-Sea Seated Luncheon

Chilled Fresh Grapefruit Slices,
with Cointreau

• • •

Supreme Florida Pompano, Amandine
Parsley Potatoes
Broccoli Polonaise
Yellow Squash

• • •

Key West Lime Pie

• • •

Coffee, Tea, Decaffeinated Coffee, or Milk

Welcome to Florida Reception

A culinary welcome to South Florida, extending a sophisticated, contemporary elegance with its spectacular, innovative buffet presentation. Your guests will come away ready to bask in our sun-drenched days and tropical moonlit evenings, enjoy the delicacies from our native waters, and revel on our beach landscape.

Atop, around, and on a square and rectangular mirrored and stark white cubic construction, our culinary display will be presented in the center of your assigned ballroom. This presentation will include approximately 18 pieces of total hors d'oeuvres per person, and will feature the following stations:

Station #1   Neon Jumping Sailfish Sculpture

Mélange of Seafood
Presented on a Plexiglass Six-Foot by Thirty-Inch
Aquarium filled with Jumbo Goldfish,
Seafood Selections to include:
Jumbo Shrimp, Langostinos, and Golden Gulf Crabmeat,

Garnished with Lemon, Mustard, Rémoulade, and
Cocktail Sauces
The Focal Point of this Display will be
Selected Pieces of Coral and a Giant Lobster
with Lobster Medallions cascading down the body, to the
claws and beyond

Station #2   Here's the Beef Bull Neon Sculpture

Carpaccio, Prepared by a Waiter
Finely Shaved Beef Tenderloin
With Garniture to include: Balsamic Vinegar,
Old Monk Virgin Olive Oil, Sliced Red Onions,
Minced Garlic, Freshly Grated Parmesan Cheese,
Salt and Pepper Grinders, and Mustard,
With Sliced French Bread

Station #3   Twin Giant Strawberries Neon Sculpture

Elaborate Tropical Fruit Fantasy
Presented in a Large Crystal Ice Carving and including:

/////

Kiwi, Pineapple, Strawberries, Cantaloupe,
and Honeydew
With Hot Dark and White Chocolate Fondues,
Whipped Cream, Sour Cream, Shredded Coconut, and
Brown Sugar

Station #4   Giant Carrot Neon Sculpture

Topiaries of Fresh Vegetables
Served with Fresh Dill, Madras, Avocado,
and Clam Dips Served from Vegetable Casings

From four additional stations, strategically located around
the room, we will serve the following:

Station #5   Large Wheel of Swiss Cheese Neon Sculpture

Mosaic Display of International Cheeses
To include: Boursin with Nuts, Montrachet,
English Stilton, Dutch Edam, Feta, Port Salut,
Gorgonzola, and French Brie,
Served with Lahvosh, Baguettes of Sourdough,
Pumpernickel, and Sliced French Bread

Station #6   Oriental Neon Sculpture

Tempura Station
Fresh Vegetable Assortment and Whole Shrimp,
Dipped in Light Oriental Batter, then Cooked in Oil,
Served with Spiced Mandarin Sauce,
Prepared Tableside by a Waiter with Two Woks

• • •

Beef Chow Yoke and Oriental Vegetables
Cooked Tableside on Two Benihana-Style Cooking
Surfaces, To Order, by a Waiter

Station #7   "Welcome to Florida" Neon Sculpture

Cold Canapés Displayed on Mirrors
Cucumber Rondelles with Seafood Salad
Smoked Salmon on Rye
Spiced Cheese on Pea Pods
Celery with Roquefort
Prosciutto Ham with Melon
Tiny Shrimp Canapés
Roast Beef and Cornichon Roulades
Steak Tartare Canapés

Hot Hors d'Oeuvres Served from Silver Chafing Dishes
Cantonese Egg Rolls, Served with French Mustard,
Sweet and Sour Sauce and Plum Sauce
Pepperoni Pizza on Mini Bagels
Medallions of Crisp Duck, with Pepper Sauce,
Sprinkle of Scallions, and Chinese Parsley
Fried Potato Skins with Bacon Bits and Cheddar Cheese
Petite Beef Kabobs, Grecian Style
Mushroom Caps Stuffed with Italian Sausage
Crabmeat Wontons with Selection of Sauces
Chicken Fingers with Sweet and Sour Sauce

Station #8   Neon Hershey's Chocolate Bar Sculpture

Death by Chocolate Chocoholic Bars

Florida Sunset Clambake Buffet

From an Elaborately Decorated Buffet Table, we'll be
pleased to serve the following:

Seafood Market Chowder with Oyster Crackers

• • •

Mixed Garden Salad of Selected Romaine and Spinach
Leaves, Bouquet of Watercress, and Sliced Tomatoes,
Choice of Three Dressings

• • •

Fresh Oysters on the Half Shell

• • •

Beer-Steamed Clams with Special Sauces

• • •

Wine-Simmered Jumbo Shrimp in the Shell

• • •

Fresh Florida Lobster, cut in Half, with Drawn Butter

• • •

Broiled Barbecued Chicken
Corn on the Cob with Drawn Butter

• • •

Boiled Redskin Potatoes

• • •

Sliced French Bread and Creamery Butter

• • •

Florida Key Lime Pie

• • •

Watermelon, in Season

• • •

Assorted Pies and Cakes

• • •

Coffee, Tea, Decaffeinated Coffee, or Milk

• • •

We suggest Pitchers of Ice Cold Draft Beer on each table,
price on request

Key West Festival of the Sunset Dinner

(See Photo on Page 69)

Key West is a circus of color and characters with the sunset splashing a golden path across the blue-green waters of the Gulf of Mexico. You'll actually feel the 60's-style antiestablishment atmosphere, created by Key West's aging flower children, while you sample the delicacies harvested from the crystal blue-green of the Keys.

Freshly Shucked Raw Bar of Oysters, Clams, and Conch

• • •

Garden Fresh Crudités on Ice

• • •

Sliced Tomato and Cucumber Salad

• • •

Creamy Cole Slaw

• • •

Seafood Quiche

• • •

Red Snapper in Lemon Butter

• • •

6-Ounce Rib Eye Steaks

• • •

Seafood Stew with Savory Rice

• • •

Sautéed Squash

• • •

Parslied New Potatoes

• • •

Fresh Rolls and Creamery Butter

• • •

Key West Lime Pie

• • •

Fresh Tropical Fruit

• • •

Coffee, Tea, Decaffeinated Coffee

Special Beverages: In addition to an open bar, we suggest specialty drink bars serving: Hurricanes, Key West Coolers, Birds of Paradise, Key West Sundowners, and our own Special Rum Punch served in a hollowed-out pineapple. Prices on request.

Music/Entertainment: In order to help set the proper atmosphere, we suggest a variety of street vendors, musicians, and performers, available at an additional expense.

Favors: Street vendors can give away woven hats, conch shells, and Key West T-Shirts, at an additional cost.

Decor: The decor prices will depend upon the size of your group and the extent of the theme involvement. To help create a suitable atmosphere, we suggest elaborate decorations, which we will arrange for you at an additional charge. The special decor package costs can be increased or decreased, depending upon the amount of display materials used. Consult with your Catering Executive.

Costume Rentals: Costume prices available on request.

Florida Reception

Reception: As guests enter the Reception area, we will provide a Florida Tropical decor.

In the center of the Reception area, a Multisided Mirrored Plexiglass Construction of geometric shapes will present, at varying levels, the culinary selections listed below.

The Buffet will be accented with silk coconut palm trees, silk banana trees, pink flamingos, and a "Welcome to Florida" neon sculpture.

Approximately 15 to 16 pieces of total hors d'oeuvres per person will be served.

Station #1

Presented on a Mirrored and Clear Plexiglass Seafood Bar:
Large Fish and Coral Crystal Ice Carving, displaying, on a bed of Crushed Ice, the following Seafood Delicacies:
Freshly Shucked Clams on the Half Shell
Freshly Shucked Oysters on the Half Shell

Large Shrimp
Golden Gulf Crab Claws
Decorated with Seaweed and
Garnished with Cocktail, Rémoulade, and Aurora Sauces,
Lemon Crowns

Station #2

Steak Tartare, prepared in front of the Guests by a Waiter, with Condiments to include:
Chopped Eggs, Anchovies, Garlic, Capers, Parsley, Paprika, Salt and Pepper Grinders

Station #3

Terrines and Pâtés, Elegantly Displayed on Mirrors and Decorated with Plumage and Wildlife

Station #4

From Two Separate Round Mirrored Buffet Tables with
Gleaming Silver Chafing Dishes:
Florida Frog Legs Provençale
Clams Casino on Rock Salt
Oysters Rockefeller on Rock Salt

Reception Decor to Include: Mirrored seafood bar, ice carving, silk banana and coconut palm trees, neon, wildlife, and pink flamingos.

Tuxedo rental for waiters and white-glove service at an additional expense. Also, service charge and tax not included in reception per-person prices.

Menus with an All-American Theme

The sounds of Americana fill the air with a carnival atmosphere as the colorful Country Fair swings into action. Fast-paced excitement, combined with the best of Down-Home America, makes for a casual and fun-filled party.

Special Beverages: In addition to full open bar service, we suggest draft beer stations, charged per keg. Price on request.

Music: A vibrant Country Fair atmosphere will be enhanced by a Dixieland Band in red and white striped jackets and straw skimmers. Maybe even a Barbershop Quartet singing "The Ol' Songs."

Americana Country Fair Reception

Using a Country Fair theme
and from multiple buffet tables, we would serve
the Tastes of the Midway to include:
Miniature Cocktail Hamburgers, Mini Hot Dogs,
with Hot Dog Rolls and Hamburger Buns, Mustard,
Mayonnaise, Ketchup, Chopped Onions, Chili,
and Shredded American Cheese

• • •

Soft, Salt Pretzels with Mustard and Cheese Spread

• • •

Cotton Candy, Made in the Room

• • •

Boxes of Cracker Jacks

• • •

Popcorn, Freshly Popped in the Room

• • •

Assorted Bags of Potato and Banana Chips

• • •

Four-Foot Italian Hero Super Submarine Sandwiches,
with Fifteen Ingredients, Sliced and Served by the Slice

• • •

Jumbo Chocolate Chip Cookies

• • •

Chocolate-Covered Bananas on Sticks

• • •

Ice Cream Station serving Popsicles, Drumsticks,
Fudgesicles, Ice Cream Sandwiches, Eskimo Pies,
and Dreamsicles

• • •

Assorted French Pastries

• • •

Fried Elephant Ears, Dusted with Powdered Sugar

• • •

Authentic Sicilian Pizza
Prepared Whole and Cut at the Buffet

• • •

Iced Glow Trays with Topiaries of Fresh Vegetables
to include:
Zucchini, Mushrooms, Broccoli, Radishes, Celery,
Cauliflower, Green Beans, and Carrots

• • •

International Cheese Displays, with a variety of Crackers,
Lahvosh, and Sliced French Bread
and Garnished with Fruit

• • •

Displays of Fresh Sliced Fruits,
Presented on Crushed Ice,
including Pineapple Cubes, Melon Cubes, Strawberries,
and a Selection of Other Fruits, Accompanied by
Sour Cream, Brown Sugar, Dark Chocolate
and White Chocolate Fondues, and Whipped Cream

• • •

Assorted Soft Drinks, on Tap, from Several Locations

• • •

International and Regular Coffees

All-American Buffet Dinner

Michigan Celery

· · ·

Colorado Carrots

· · ·

California Olives
New Jersey Pickles

· · ·

Texas Sliced Tomatoes and Onions
All-American Mixed Green Salad,
Choice of Dressings

· · ·

Lone Star Potato Salad

· · ·

Whole Cold Oregon Poached Salmon, Sauce Mousseline

· · ·

Midwest Roast Baron of Beef, Carved on Buffet

· · ·

Maryland Southern Fried Chicken

· · ·

Creole Jambalaya

· · ·

Wisconsin and Minnesota Cheeses

· · ·

Confederate Green String Beans with Bacon Pieces

· · ·

Maine Potatoes Lyonnaise

· · ·

Freshly Baked Rolls and Buttermilk Biscuits

· · ·

Pennsylvania Dutch Apple Pie

· · ·

George Washington Cherry Tarts
Indiana Black Walnut Layer Cake

· · ·

New York Cheesecake with Sauce

· · ·

All-American Old-Fashioned Strawberry Shortcake

· · ·

Hawaiian Kona Coffee

America the Bountiful Reception

America's abundance overwhelms us as we conduct a Food-Fantasy Flight from America's Heartland to its Four Far-Flung Geographical Corners. We Americans have been shaped by the bountiful menu our land provides; we are taller, stronger, healthier than our ancestors. So join us now, gastronomic traveler, as we enjoy an exciting tour of regional foods (approximately 16 to 18 total pieces of hors d'oeuvres per person).

Special Beverages: In addition to some selected California wines, we recommend Open Bars throughout the ballroom.

Music: Mariachi guitars . . . Dixieland jazz . . . strolling violins . . . a harpist . . . will help to create the special moods of each section of these United States.

From the Nation's Heartland

A Mid-America Cheese and Bread Display to consist of
An elaborate selection of Domestic Cheese in large
Wheels and Chunks,
Garnished with Fresh Fruit and Accompanied by Baskets
of Whole Bread Varieties, Lahvosh and Assorted Crackers,
Complemented by a Toast to California,
serving Cabernet Sauvignon,
Chablis and Rosé Wines of California vintage
(Wine prices on request, charged as served)

· · ·

From the New England States

Fresh Clams and Oysters shucked to order,
served with Cocktail Sauce, Horseradish,
Lemon Wedges, and Oysterettes
(Six pieces of Seafood per Person Included in the Total)

· · ·

Large Round Chafing Dishes of:
Clams Casino on Rock Salt, Oysters Rockefeller
on Rock Salt, Scallops Wrapped in Bacon

· · ·

Deep-Fried Maine Potato Skins Served with Sour Cream

· · ·

Steamship Round of Corned Beef,
Carved in Room and Served on New York–style Rye Bread
with Horseradish, Mustard, and Mayonnaise

· · ·

From the South

Ham and Buttermilk Biscuits

· · ·

Country-Style Sausage and Biscuits

· · ·

Southern-Style Fried Chicken Fingers

· · ·

Half Ears of Corn, placed on popsicle sticks,
Heated in the Room in Large Boiling Pot,
Served with Drawn Butter

· · ·

Fried Catfish Pieces with Tartar Sauce

· · ·

The Crêpe au Crabe Station,
Individual Crabmeat Crêpes, Prepared to Order,
Flambéed in the style of New Orleans,
with a Taste of the Gulf Shores

· · ·

Farmer's Market of Fresh Whole Vegetables,
Displayed in Old Crates and Baskets
and Accompanied with Sliced Fresh Vegetables,
Served on Crushed Ice and to include:
Zucchini, Celery, Mushrooms, Green Beans, Broccoli
with Dill, Sour Cream, and Cheese Dips

· · ·

From the Great Southwest

A station for the Preparation of Tacos Made
to Order by Attendant in Costume, price on request

· · ·

Mini Barbecued Texas-Style Beef Spare Ribs

· · ·

Bowls of Guacamole Dip with Tostadas

· · ·

From the West Coast

We present the Flavor of San Francisco's Oriental
population

Peking-style Duck, Prepared in the Room by Attendant
in Costume (price on request)
Duck is Wrapped in Mandarin Pancakes, with Plum
Sauce and a Sprinkle of Scallions and Parsley

· · ·

Whole Poached Kennebec Salmon Presented on Mirrors,
with Tronçons of Salmon en Bellevue

· · ·

Crabmeat Wontons with Selection of Sauces,
Oriental Mixture of Crabmeat and Vegetables,
Captured in a Flaky Pastry Shell

· · ·

Spinach Quiche à la San Francisco,
a delightful contemporary treatment
of a popular French creation

· · ·

Oriental Egg Rolls, French Mustard and Sweet and Sour
Sauce

For the Sweet Side of the Evening

Presented in Creatively Sculptured Ice Socles,
an elaborate Display of Fresh Fruit to include:
Pineapple, Assorted Melon, Blueberries, Strawberries,
Kiwi, and Mangoes,
Accompanied by Brown Sugar, Sour Cream,
Whipped Cream, and Petite Chafing Dishes
of White and Dark Chocolate Fondue

· · ·

Carvers and Shuckers, price on request

Menus with an International Theme

Culinary Cruise Around the World Reception

Board a Culinary Cruise that stops at Ports from the Far East to the Greek Isles. Indulge in American Favorites before sailing on to Italian Delights, French Cuisine, Delicacies from Deutschland, and Spicy Mexican Morsels. For the true Epicure who enjoys a varied and bounteous banquet. Bon Voyage!

Special Beverages: We suggest an Open Bar, including a selection of International and Domestic Wines, Beers, and Waters.

Music: Mariachi guitars . . . Italian violins . . . a German "oom-pah" band . . . some Dixieland jazz . . . will help to create the special mood of each country featured on this International Cruise.

North America

New York
Manhattan Clam Chowder, served from Crocks,
Oysterettes, Pilot Wafers, and Saltines

· · ·

Texas
Mini Barbecued Texas-Style Spare Ribs

· · ·

Louisiana
Jambalaya

· · ·

Culinary Cruise Around the World
Reception (continued)

Canada
Roasted Goose with Cranberry and Nut Sauce

• • •

New England
Fresh Clams and Oysters, Shucked to order, served with
Cocktail Sauce, Horseradish, Tabasco, Lemon Wedges,
and Oysterettes

• • •

Idaho
Deep Fried Potato Skins served with Sour Cream

• • •

Tennessee
Country-Style Sausage and Biscuits

• • •

Virginia
Smithfield Ham and Buttermilk Biscuits

• • •

Vermont
Whole Roast Turkey, Served with Cocktail Bread and
Split Hard Rolls and Condiments
(Carver required, price on request)

• • •

Georgia
Southern Chicken Drumsticks, Fried in Peanut Oil

• • •

Kansas
Whole Steamship Round of Beef, Carved in the Room by
Chefs in White Uniforms, with an Assortment of Rye
and Pumpernickel Breads, Miniature Rolls, with
Horseradish, Curry Sauce, and other Condiments
(Carver required, price on request)

• • •

Near and Middle East

Jordan
Bulgur Pilaf,
Rice with Minced Lamb

• • •

Iran
Cucumber-Yogurt Salad with Pita Bread, quartered

• • •

Saudi Arabia
Chicken à la Rijad, Cooked with Dates and Figs

• • •

Turkey
Shish Kabob,
Lamb Brochette

• • •

Greece
Mihski Malhuf,
Stuffed Grape Leaves

• • •

Egypt
Kousa Mahski,
Stuffed Squash, Tomato Sauce

• • •

Israel
Falafel,
Small Finger Croquette made of ground Chickpeas,
Fried in Olive Oil

• • •

Europe

Germany
Weisswurst und Knackwurst in Bier,
White Sausage and Knockwurst cooked in Beer

• • •

England
Fish n' Chips,
Breaded Sole Fingers with French Fries

• • •

Belgium
Waterzooie,
A simply Delicious Chicken Stew

• • •

Norway
Kalvefilet Med Sur Flote,
Sautéed Veal Scallops in Sour Cream Sauce

• • •

France
Quiche de Fruits de Mer,
Seafood Quiche

• • •

Hungary
Puszta Gulyas,
Beef Goulash

• • •

Italy
Fettucini Ticata,
Spinach Noodles, Sautéed in Butter with Prosciutto,
Blended with Cream,
Seasoned with Parmesan and Freshly Ground Pepper

• • •

Latin America

Brazil
Impada Amorda Bras,
Petite Patty Shells Stuffed with Spiced Chopped Shrimp

• • •

Colombia
Ceviche de Mazattan,
Marinated Spiced Scallops

• • •

Argentina
Empanadas,
Meat-Filled Pastries

• • •

Mexico
Tacos Rellenos,
Prepared to Order with Tortilla Shells, Spicy Beef,
Tomato, Lettuce, Onions, Green Peppers,
Shredded Cheese, and Salsa

• • •

Guatemala
Burritos de Bollo,
Flour Tortilla folded with a Savory Chopped Meat

• • •

Venezuela
Arroz con Pollo,
Rice and Chicken Casserole

Far East

China
Medallions of Crisp Duck, Pepper Sauce, Sprinkle of
Scallions and Chinese Parsley
Cantonese Shrimp,
Lobster and Pork Egg Rolls, Hot French Mustard, Soya
Sauce, Sweet and Sour Sauce, and Duck Sauce

• • •

Hong Kong
Sweet and Sour Shrimp,
Balanced flavor of Sweet and Pungent Sauce
with Whole Shrimp

• • •

India
Murghi Palao,
Curried Chicken with Rice, Shredded Coconut,
and Mango Chutney

• • •

Indonesia
Roasted Pork Loin Surabaja,
Served with a Spicy Peanut-Ginger Sauce

• • •

Japan
Beef Teriyaki, Prepared to order

• • •

International Dessert Display

Wisconsin
Old-Fashioned Ice Cream Parlor, with all the Trimmings

• • •

China
Almond and Fortune Cookies

• • •

Austria
Viennese Table Display,
Enjoy Austria's Finest Cakes, Tortes,
and Assorted Pastries

• • •

Germany
Black Forest Cake

• • •

Belgium
Quartered Waffles
with Lingonberry and Gooseberry Sauces

• • •

Greece
Baklava, Filo pastry, Spices, and Chopped Nuts with a
Spiced Honey-Lemon Syrup

• • •

Washington
Chocolate-Covered Cherries, stem on

• • •

Pennsylvania
Dutch Crumb Apple Pie

• • •

Hawaii
Fresh Pineapple, Coconut, Papaya Spears, and Guava

• • •

New York
Original Recipe Cheesecake

• • •

Selection of International Teas and Coffees

• • •

Selection of International Cheeses, Garnished with Fruit,
with a Variety of Crackers, Lahvosh,
and Sliced French Sourdough Bread

• • •

International Beers and Wines: At an additional cost,
we would be happy to provide an outstanding selection of
International Beers and Wines, including Wines from Argentina, Chile, Germany, France, Italy, New York State,
Virginia, and California. Prices on request.

Taste of the Globe Reception

Grab your Passport: You are about to embark on a Taste-Tempting Trip Around the World. Everyone's dream is to Tour the World, and this party is the next best thing.

Welcome Home, Yankee

Whole Roast Steamship Round of Beef

• • •

Whole Roast Vermont Turkey

• • •

Whole Sugar-Cured Baked Virginia Ham
Accompanied by Mayonnaise, Horseradish, Chutney,
and Mustard
Including Miniature Rolls, Cocktail Rye,
and Pumpernickel
(Chef Carvers Required)

• • •

Southern Crispy Fried Chicken Drumsticks

• • •

Deep-Fried Maine-Style Potato Skins
Served with Sour Cream and Chives

• • •

Catfish Tidbits with Tartar Sauce

Bonjour, Paris

Pâté de Campagne
Country Pâté

• • •

Galantine de Canard
Galantine of Duck

• • •

Escargots Parisiens
Snails in Aioli Sauce

• • •

Quiche de Fruits de Mer
Seafood Quiche

• • •

Salade Niçoise

• • •

Cuisses de Grenouilles Provençales
Sautéed Frog Legs

• • •

Lapin à la Bourguignonne
Fresh Rabbit Stew

• • •

Cotelettes d'Agneau
Lamb Cutlets, Cooked to Order

Orient Express

Orient
Rumaki Chicken Liver à l'Orientale

• • •

China
Beef with Oyster Sauce Cantonese
Mandarin Fried Rice
Prawn Egg Rolls

• • •

Japan
Steak Teriyaki

• • •

Indonesia
Sautéed Pork Loin Bali-Bali,
With Spicy Peanut-Ginger Sauce

• • •

India
Curried Seafood Madras, With Condiments

Fiesta Mexicana

Jamón Cancún
Smoked Ham

• • •

Tostados

• • •

Tamales, Enchiladas, Tacos

• • •

Chorizo
Spiced Sausage

• • •

Camarones al Aji
Shrimp with Tomatoes and Hot Peppers

• • •

Habichuelas Refritas
Refried Beans

• • •

Paella Valenciana
Baked Chicken with Rice, Shrimp, Clams, and Mussels

• • •

Viva Italia

Antipasto Milanese
A Variety of Fresh Marinated Vegetables

• • •

Funghi sotto Aceto
Marinated Mushrooms

Calameretti con Cipolle
Marinated Squid

• • •

Mitilo Salsa Marinara
Marinated Mussels

• • •

Lasagne alla Napolitana

• • •

Gamberetti con Cipolla e Vino
Shrimp Scampi

• • •

Salsiccia al Forno
Baked Mild Italian Sausage

• • •

Maccheroni al Pomidoro
Macaroni with Tomatoes

• • •

Peperoni al Forno alla Parmigiano
Sautéed Italian Peppers

• • •

Zucchini alla Romana
Stuffed Zucchini

• • •

Pane all' Aglio
Garlic Bread

• • •

Alpine Festival

Bayrische Linsen Suppe
Bavarian Lentil Soup

• • •

Geraucherter Westfalischer Schinken mit Schwarzbrot
Smoked Westphalian Ham with Pumpernickel

• • •

Frische Salate
Crisp Garden Salad, Choice of Dressings

• • •

Diverse Frische Gemuse
Relish Tray and Fresh Vegetables

• • •

Kasseler Rippchen
Smoked Pork Loin

• • •

Weisswurst und Knackwurst in Bier
White Sausage and Knockwurst cooked in Beer

• • •

Frische Bratwurst
Pan-Fried Veal and Pork Sausage

• • •

Heisser Kartoffel
Hot Potato Salad

• • •

Suss Saueres Rot Kraut
Sweet and Sour Red Cabbage

International Dessert Display

Fresh Pineapple Slices with Triple Sec

• • •

Fried Cheddar Pieces with Sourdough Bread

• • •

Welsh Trifle

• • •

Fromages Assortis
Assorted Cheeses with French Bread

• • •

Poires Pochées au Porto
Pears in Port Wine

• • •

Pâtisseries Françaises Assorties
Large Selection of Miniature French Pastries

• • •

Fortune and Almond Cookies

• • •

Mandarin Oranges with Shredded Coconut

• • •

Flan de Coco
Coconut Custard

• • •

Taste of the Globe Reception (continued)

Galletas
Mocha, Cherry, and Nut Cookies

• • •

Torte de Ricotta y Frutta
Light Pastry of Raisins, Candied Fruit, and Ricotta Cheese

• • •

Profiteroles au Chocolat
Cream Puff Balls filled with Coffee Kahlua Custard, then covered with a Rich Creamy Chocolate Mousse Covering

• • •

Frische Erdbeeren mit Kirschwasser
Fresh Strawberries in Kirsch

• • •

Allgauer Apfel Strudel mit Vanille Sosse
Apple Strudel with Brandied Vanilla Sauce

• • •

Special Beverages—Waters of the World: In addition to Open Bars, we suggest an International Water Station. We will be pleased to offer a complete selection of bottled Mineral and Sparkling Waters from around the world, to include: Evian, Saratoga, Poland Spring, Vichy, Apollanaris, Perrier, and Calistoga, at an additional charge.

Music: Mariachi guitars . . . Italian violins . . . a German "oom-pah" band . . . some Dixieland jazz . . . will help to create the special mood of the International Tour. Prices on request.

Decor: A decor package can be designed in accordance with your budget to include the Mystery and Intrigue of the Orient, a Quaint Bavarian Village, the Romance and Adventure of Venice, the Domination of the Eiffel Tower and a Sidewalk Café, the Colorfulness of Old Mexico, and Back Home at last in the Good Old USA . . . the Stars and Stripes welcome you to an All-American 4th of July Celebration!

Mexican Fiesta

(See Color Insert and Photo on Pages 68)

Fiesta in any language means Feast and this is no exception. The Hot-Blooded and Colorful Image of Mexico surrounds us as we feast in the Spanish tradition of an age-old ceremony. From south of the Rio Grande, we offer:

Mexican Bean Salad

• • •

Guacamole Salad

• • •

Cilantro-Herbed Tomatoes

• • •

Frijoles Salad

• • •

Raw Vegetables with Guacamole Dip

• • •

Salsa Dip, Tortillas, Tostadas, and Nacho Chips

• • •

Make-Your-Own Taco Bar, with all the Fixin's

• • •

Paella

• • •

Chicken Mole Poblano

• • •

Enchiladas with Meat Sauce

• • •

Tenderloin Tips in Chipotles

• • •

Mexican-Style Refried Beans

• • •

Spanish Rice, Zucchini Mexicana

• • •

Hot Sauce

• • •

Spanish Breads and Butter

• • •

Mousse de Mango

• • •

Assorted Mexican Cookies

• • •

Spanish Flans

Special Beverages: With all this spicy food, you'll enjoy an Open Bar as well as Pitchers of our Homemade Sangria and Tequila Punch. Prices on request.

Music: A strolling Mariachi band in authentic costumes can be contracted for an additional cost.

Favors: Mexican sombreros could be provided for an additional charge.

Menus with a Deli Theme

Mel's Best of the Wurst Delicatessen
Luncheon

(See Color Insert)

The freshly baked bagels, salads, and whitefish, liver-wurst, and pastrami, cream cheese and dill pickles. It's hectic, it's frenzied, it's sensational. It's a New York Deli—and the atmosphere may be less-than-luxurious, but where else would pastrami on rye taste as good?

From Deli-style Cases and Counters
We Will Serve and Prepare Sandwiches using:
Corned Beef, Pastrami, Kosher Salami, Roast Beef,
Turkey Breast, Swiss Cheese, Chopped Chicken Livers,
Tuna Fish Salad

• • •

Varieties of Breads and Rolls,
Mayonnaise, Mustard, Ketchup
served in Jars or Pump Bottles

• • •

Kosher Hand-Packed Pickles

• • •

Chicken Noodle Soup

• • •

Herring in Sour Cream

• • •

Potato Salad and Cole Slaw

• • •

Fruit Salad

• • •

Pickled Eggs with Beet Juice

• • •

Red Horseradish

• • •

Bags of Potato Chips

• • •

Baked Beans with Molasses

• • •

New York Style Cheesecake

• • •

Chocolate-Covered Joya

• • •

Slim Jims

• • •

Life Savers

• • •

Cartons of Milk

• • •

Coffee and Iced Tea

Special Beverages: We suggest a large selection of International and Domestic Beers, Dr. Brown's Celray Cream Soda, Diet Raspberry, Pepsi Cola, and Perrier. Prices on request.

Music: Only a radio is needed, tuned to an ethnic radio station.

Irving's Delicatessen

East side, west side, all around the town known as the Big Apple. It's like no other city in the world. You'll feel the excitement, swear you see the sights and hear the sounds, as you walk down the streets of New York and sample the following:

Chopped Chicken Livers

• • •

Tuna Fish Salad

• • •

Lox and Cream Cheese

• • •

Herring in Sour Cream

• • •

Potato Salad and Cole Slaw

• • •

Fruit Salad

• • •

Pickled Eggs in Beet Juice

• • •

Red Horseradish

• • •

Cold Kosher Pickles

• • •

Hot Pastrami

• • •

Turkey Breast

• • •

Hot Corned Beef

• • •

Kosher Salami

• • •

Hot Roast Beef

• • •

Swiss Cheese

• • •

Chicken Noodle Soup

Bags of Potato Chips

• • •

Baked Beans with Molasses

• • •

Varieties of Breads and Rolls
Mayonnaise, Mustard, Ketchup,
Served in Jars or Pump Bottles

• • •

New York Style Cheesecake

• • •

Chocolate-Covered Joya

• • •

Slim Jims

• • •

Cartons of Milk

• • •

Coffee and Iced Tea

Special Beverages: We suggest serving a large selection of International and Domestic Beers, Dr. Brown's Celray Cream Soda, Cola, Diet Cola, and Perrier. Prices on request.

Music: We suggest an array of street musicians to bring the streets alive, contracted for an additional cost.

Favors: We can arrange for souvenir "I Love New York" T-shirts, at an additional charge.

Seventh Avenue Deli

A scrumptious display of Europe's most tantalizing cheeses, breads and rolls, relishes, pickles, sausages, wursts, fresh fruits, and fresh vegetables, such as:

Corned Beef

• • •

Braunschweiger

• • •

Kosher Salami

• • •

Sausage from Lyon

• • •

Zungenwurst

• • •

Fleischwurst

• • •

Landjager

• • •

Beerkase,
Boursin aux Fines Herbes,

Brie, Camembert, Swiss, Gruyère, and Roquefort Cheeses

• • •

Giant Kosher Dills

• • •

Poppy Seed, Curry, Clam, Onion, and Caraway Seed Dips

• • •

Fresh Cauliflower Buds

• • •

Red Pepper Relishes

• • •

Scallions and Carrots

• • •

Cherry Tomatoes

• • •

Thousand Island Dressing

• • •

Whole Fresh Mushrooms, Cherry Peppers

• • •

Pumpernickel, Rye, and Sourdough Breads, Sesame Buns

Menus with a Schutzenfest Theme

The joyous carnival air of a Deutsch Oktoberfest will intoxicate your senses. The charm of the Old Country, coupled with the delights of the Bavarian kitchen, create a festive and sumptuous atmosphere.

German Theme Seated Luncheon

Lentil Soup with Ham

• • •

Braised Sauerbraten
Potato Pancakes
Red Cabbage with Apples

• • •

Black Forest Cake

• • •

Coffee, Tea, Decaffeinated Coffee, or Milk

Schutzenfest Theme Buffet Dinner

Cold

String Bean Salad

• • •

Crisp Garden Salads with Choice of Dressings

• • •

Relish Tray and Fresh Vegetables
Dill Pickles

• • •

Assorted Wursts: Salami, Thuringer, Blood Sausage,
Veal Liverwurst, Tongue Sausage, Headcheese, Beerwurst
Assorted Bavarian Cheeses
Smoked Westphalian Ham

• • •

Tidbits of Marinated Herring

• • •

Old-Fashioned Cucumber Salad

Hot

Sauerbraten, Bavarian Style

• • •

Bratwurst

• • •

Knockwurst

• • •

Whole Roasted Leg of Milk-Fed Veal

• • •

Smoked Pork Loin

• • •

Sauerkraut Swaben Style

• • •

Sweet and Sour Red Cabbage

• • •

Hot German Potato Salad

• • •

Potato Pancakes with Hot Applesauce

Desserts

German Chocolate Cake and Fruit Tarts

• • •

Fresh Strawberries in Kirsch

• • •

Schwarzwalder Kirsch Torte (Black Forest Cake)

• • •

Apple Strudel with Brandied Vanilla Sauce

• • •

Coffee, Tea, Decaffeinated Coffee, or Milk

Special Beverages: With the dinner, we recommend a vintage Riesling wine. In addition to an Open Bar, we also suggest Lowenbrau by the keg. Prices on request.

Music: Enjoy an authentic oom-pah-pah played by a Bavarian-costumed band and dancers . . . and why not include a bell ringer and yodeler for added fun (at an additional charge)?

Favors: Give each guest a Bavarian-style felt hat as they enter (at an additional charge).

A French Menu

Ah! Paris in the Springtime! Paris and amour! Paris and food and drink! Whether in the best French restaurant or a quaint sidewalk café on the Seine, dining is an art form in France—be part of this masterpiece.

You'll be singing "I Love Paris in the Springtime" as you feel the romantic atmosphere while you sample an array of specialty dishes. From your sidewalk café you can view the Eiffel Tower in the background and the many things that make Paris unique in all the world.

Bonjour, Paris Buffet Dinner

Pâté de Campagne
Country Pâté

• • •

Galantine de Canard
Galantine of Duck

• • •

Escargots Parisiens
Snails in Aioli Sauce

• • •

Quiche de Fruits de Mer
Seafood Quiche

• • •

Salade Niçoise
Salad Niçoise
• • •

Cuisses de Grenouilles Provençales
Sautéed Frog Legs

Lapin à la Bourguignonne
Fresh Rabbit Stew
• • •

Cotelettes d'Agneau
Lamb Cutlets Cooked to Order
• • •

Fromages Assortis
Assorted Cheeses with French Bread
• • •

Poires Pochées au Porto
Pears in Port Wine
• • •

Pâtisseries Françaises Assorties
Large Selection of Miniature French Pastries
• • •
Demitasse

Special Beverages: In addition to an Open Bar, we suggest a vintage French wine to be served with dinner, as well as offering Vichy waters and an array of international coffees. Prices on request.

Music: Let us arrange a string ensemble or the most romantic of all musical instruments—a harp—for an additional charge.

Favors: We can arrange for berets for each guest, as well as a sidewalk artist to caricature your guests.

A Nostalgic Menu

Glamour, excitement, and the sounds of the 20's provide the ambience of the Great Gatsby Era. Lose yourself in the luxury and opulence of days gone by and taste the forbidden fruits of Prohibition. "The Way We Were" is the way you'll want to be again!

The Way We Were Supper

Continuous Buffet Attended by White-Gloved Waiters From a Variety of Buffet Tables and Service Stations,

We Will Be Pleased to Serve From Four Separate Stations:

Preparation of Steak Tartare using a Hand Meat Grinder, Beef Presentation and mixing in a Wooden Bowl with the following ingredients:
Chopped Onion, Raw Egg, Capers, Anchovies, Mustard, Lea & Perrins, Tabasco, Salt, Freshly Milled Pepper, served atop Tartines of Rye and Pumpernickel and Toast Triangles
• • •

Preparation of Jumbo Prawns, Sautéed with Pernod, Flambé, accompanied by Rice Florentine
(six prawns per person)
• • •

Preparation and Service of Caesar Salad, Romaine Lettuce, Anchovy, Mustard, Garlic, Fresh Lemon, Fresh Ground Pepper, Tabasco,

Parmesan Cheese, Olive Oil and Toasted "Homemade" Croutons, Tossed in a Wooden Bowl
• • •

Station for Carving and Service of:
Whole Roast Tenderloin of Beef rolled in Cracked Peppercorns and Marinated in Cognac-Mustard Sauce, Accompanied by Cognac-Mustard Sauce
• • •

From a Large Oval Buffet Table, We Will Serve:

Canadian Smoked Salmon,
with Tartines of Rye and Fresh Toast Points, Capers, Chopped Parsley, Chopped Red Onion, Chopped Egg Yolk, and Chopped Egg White, garni
• • •

Pâté Maison Display, Decorated with Plumage
• • •

Display of Galantine Duck, Garni
• • •

Display of Saddle of Cold Venison

• • •

The Marquis Selection of Cold Canapés

• • •

Petite Displays of Vegetable Crudités,
Garnish of Carved Fresh Vegetables

• • •

Marinated Mussels on the Half Shell
(four mussels per person)

• • • •

From Gleaming Silver Chafing Dishes:

Boneless Breast of Chicken, en Croûte

• • •

Scallopini of Veal, Française

• • •

Sweetbreads in Petite Puff Pastry Shells

• • •

Petite Frenched Lamb Chops

• • •

And Accompanied By:

Fresh Artichoke Salad, Vinaigrette

• • •

Fresh Fennel Salad

• • •

Waldorf Salad

• • •

Whole Fresh Green Beans Wrapped in Westphalian
Ham

• • •

Zucchini Boats Filled with Puree of Gingered Carrot

• • •

Tomato Crowns Filled with Mushroom Duxelles

• • •

Parkerhouse Rolls, Petite Pumpernickel and Rye Rolls,
Molded Butter, Currant Jelly, and Orange Marmalade

• • •

From an Additional Buffet Table, We Will Serve:

Select Fresh Strawberries, with stem on

• • •

Fresh Blueberries, Raspberries, Cherries,
Dates, Whole Poached Figs, Ripe Pears,
Accompanied by White and Dark Chocolate Fondue,

Sour Cream, Whipped Chantilly Cream,
and Brown Sugar

• • •

Stilton Cheese with Port Wine

• • •

Wheels of Brie with Toasted Almonds

• • •

Homemade Melba Toast, Biscuits, Crackers,
and French Bread

• • •

**In a Corner of the Room, We Will Recreate a
1920's Drug Store Soda Fountain Featuring:**

Vanilla, Butter Pecan, Strawberry,
and Chocolate Ice Creams,
Whipped Cream, Cherries, Chopped Nuts,
Chocolate Jimmies, Strawberry Sauce,
Marshmallow Topping, Hot Fudge, Butterscotch Sauce,
and Crushed Pineapple, Bananas, and Sugar Cones

• • •

In addition, a soda-dispensing unit for Coca Cola, Sprite,
Root Beer, and Club Soda
Chocolate Syrup and Crushed Ice will also be provided

• • •

From Still an Additional Station:

Coffee Service with Demitasse
Sugar Cubes

• • •

Fancy Cookies and Petits Fours

• • •

Unfiltered Cigarettes

• • •

Carvers, price on request

Special Beverages: We suggest having Flapper Girls pass Pink Champagne to all arriving guests. Throughout the evening, Full Bar Service will provide Premium Brands of Liquor from Silver Urns into coffee cups. Bars will also be stocked with Red and White Wines, as well as Pink Champagne.

Toward the end of the Supper service, we will pass Fine Cognac to guests attending this affair. Prices on request.

Music: We suggest a full orchestra, a female torch singer, and strolling strings.

Menus with a Polynesian Theme

From the lush Tropical Island Paradise where palm trees are swaying in the cool ocean breeze, lovely native girls in grass skirts and brightly colored muumuus greet you with an "Aloha" and a necklace of orchids.

Hawaiian Paradise Buffet Reception

(Approximately 16 to 18 Pieces of Hors d'Oeuvres per Person)

Barbecued Beef on Bamboo Sticks

• • •

Beer-Battered Banana Fritters

• • •

Fried Pineapple Slices

• • •

Sautéed Bananas, Prepared at buffet

• • •

Hawaiian Egg Rolls, Sweet and Sour Sauce

• • •

Petite Chicken and Pineapple Kabobs

• • •

Sweet and Pungent Shrimp

• • •

Polynesian Barbecued Spareribs with Polynesian
Barbecue Sauce

• • •

Shrimp Imperial Stuffed Cherry Tomatoes

• • •

Herring Tidbits on Rye Rounds

• • •

Smoked Oysters on Melba Rounds

• • •

Sardine and Egg on Rye Rounds

• • •

Spiced Cheese on Pea Pods

• • •

Green Onions and Celery Curls

• • •

Banana Chips with Avocado Dip

• • •

Date Teasers

• • •

Skewered Fruits

Polynesian Luau Buffet Dinner

Snow Mountain and Cheese Trees

• • •

Cold Hors d'Oeuvres

• • •

Assorted Hawaiian Salads

• • •

Zucchini Mousse

• • •

Polynesian Poi Poi

• • •

Polynesian Barbecued Ribs

• • •

Egg Rolls

• • •

Bola Bola Balls

• • •

Fried Shrimp

• • •

Jamaki

• • •

Pork Pineapple

• • •

Beef Kon Tiki

• • •

Sautéed Chicken with Mushrooms and Chinese Greens

• • •

Broiled Mahi Mahi, Hawaiian

• • •

Luau Fried Rice

• • •

Mixed Chinese Vegetables

• • •

Mai Tai Soufflé

• • •

Coconut Pudding

• • •

Rum Cakes

A whole roast suckling pig, decorated, can be added for an additional charge.

The Polynesian Luau is decorated with mementos of the South Seas and is served by Waiters in Hawaiian costumes. Also, a Hawaiian Band and Native Dancers can be contracted for an additional charge.

Special Beverages: In addition to an Open Bar, we suggest an Aloha Welcome Cocktail, a Mai Tai, served in a whole chilled pineapple. Price on request.

Music: Ukuleles ring out and island drums boom while the island girls sway sensuously as they invite you to join in the Hula and other native dances. Remember, the story is in the hands, not the hips.

A Gambler's Menu

The pace is quick, the stakes are high, and the air is charged with the titillating excitement Lady Luck brings with her. The only sure thing here is the quality of food and drink.

Casino Night Reception

From a Specially Designed Buffet Table, we will serve:

Approximately 18 to 20 pieces per person

• • •

Mirror Presentation of Canapés to Include:
Cherry Tomatoes Stuffed with Tuna Mousse

• • •

Cucumber Rondelles Topped with Baby Shrimp

• • •

Ham Mousse en Bouchées

• • •

Cornets of Salami Stuffed with Cream Cheese

• • •

A Display of Crisp Vegetables to Include:
Zucchini, Carrots, Celery, Scallions, Green Pepper, Radishes, Cauliflower, Broccoli, and Green Beans Accompanied by Clam, Cheese, and Dill Dips

• • •

From Gleaming Chafing Dishes we will serve:

Chinese-Style Steamed Dumplings (Dim Sum), with Scallion and Soy Dipping Sauce

• • •

Chinese-Style Spare Ribs

• • •

Petite Squares of Quiche Lorraine

• • •

Deep-Fried Potato Skins with Sour Cream

From Separate Stations, we will prepare and serve:

Peking Duck,
With Oriental Service person to Carve and Serve
(Attendant, Price on Request)

• • •

Shrimp Scampi, Sauté Provençale,
Laced with Pernod and Flambéed

• • •

Steamship Round of Beef,
Carved by White-Coated Chef Carver
(Price on Request)

• • •

Whole Side of Salmon Sliced in the Room,
Garni of Capers, Chopped Onions, Chopped Parsley,
Chopped Hard-Cooked Egg White and Egg Yolk

• • •

Raw Bar to serve:

Clams, Oysters, Mussels, Shrimp, Crab Claws
Garni of Cocktail and Rémoulade Sauces, Oysterettes,
Lea & Perrins and Tabasco Sauces
(Shucker required, Price on Request)

Dessert Table to Include:

Baklava, Black Forest Torte,
Assorted French Pastries, English Trifle,
Assorted Pastry Fruit Tarts,
Fresh Strawberries with Whipped Cream
and Brown Sugar

• • •

Demitasse

Special Beverages: The high rollers must have a Free-Pouring Open Bar serving only Premium Brands. Price on request.

Music: Lounge-type music with a backup band and dancing girls available at an additional cost.

Menus with a Western Theme

The zest of the Old West will assault your senses in the most pleasing and exhilarating attack ever. Smells, sights, and sounds of this unique influence are sure to give you an incurable case of Texas Fever (see Color Insert).

Grand Prairie Seated Breakfast

Freshly Squeezed Orange Juice,
Garnished with a Whole Strawberry

• • •

Texas Golden Buck Eggs with Canadian
Bacon

• • •

Poached Eggs on Pastry Shell with Cheese
Topping

• • •

Hash Brown Potatoes

• • •

Hot Biscuits, Corn Bread, Breakfast Pastries,
Creamery Butter, Honey, Jams, and
Marmalade

• • •

Coffee, Tea, Decaffeinated Coffee, or Milk

Big "D" Seated Lunch

Orange Sections with Watermelon Cubes,
on Leaf Lettuce,
Avocado-Yogurt Dressing

• • •

Chicken Fried Steak
Mashed Potatoes and Homemade Pan Gravy
Fried Okra
Corn on the Cob

• • •

Corn Bread, Biscuits, Butter
and Honey

• • •

Strawberry Biscuit Shortcake with Whipped
Cream

• • •

Coffee, Tea, Decaffeinated Coffee, or Milk

Western Buckboard Cookout

10-Ounce Charcoal-Broiled Smoked Brisket Steak* to be
Cooked over Fire and Sliced at Buffet,
Barbecue Sauce

• • •

Barbecued Sausage

• • •

Barbecued Chicken Cooked over Open Fire

• • •

Barbecued Texas Ribs Served from Chafing Dishes

• • •

Bourbon Baked Beans with Salt Pork

• • •

Corn on the Cob with Drawn Butter

• • •

Freshly Made Western-Style Cole Slaw

• • •

Jalapeño Chilies

• • •

Chili Con Carne

• • •

Okra and Tomatoes

• • •

Hot Peppers

• • •

Red Bean Salad

• • •

Watermelon Boats of Fresh Fruits of
the Season

• • •

Mixed Green Salad with
Raw Onions and Green Pepper Slices,
Oil and Vinegar Dressing

• • •

Western Loaves of Bread,
Cowboy Soda Biscuits,
Sheepherders' Rye Bread

• • •

Open Apple and Cherry Turnovers

• • •

Strawberry Shortcake

• • •

Pecan Tassies Tarts

• • •

Pecan-Stuffed Date Cookies

• • •

Coffee, Tea, Decaffeinated Coffee, or Milk

Special Beverages: With Breakfast, how about Bullshots and Bloody Marys? At the Mid-Day Grub Time, what could go better than a bucket of iced Lone Star Beer on each table or even pitchers from the keg? After a day on the trail, we suggest Texas Bloody Marys, served in half-pint fruit jars. Prices on request.

Music: How about a real bluegrass band for lazy-listenin' or foot-stompin'?

*Charcoal-Broiled Prime Aged Sirloin Steak (12 ounces) can be served instead of Smoked Brisket Steak, Sliced (Price on request).

Texas Shoot-Out Western Buffet Dinner

Big "D" Salad Bar
Crates of Seasoned Salad Greens,
with Farmers' Raw Vegetables,
Fresh Herb Dressing and Vinaigrette Dressing
• • •
Assortment of Southern Pickled Peppers,
Cucumber Salad, Sliced Beefsteak Tomatoes,
Garbanzo Beans, Carrot Salad, Cole Slaw, Zucchini,
and Squash Salad, Alfalfa Sprouts, Garlic Croutons,
Sliced Olives, and Shredded Cheddar Cheese
• • •
Bowls of Hot Chili Cooked by
International Chili Champion,* Lone Star Chili Willi,
Served with Diced Onions, Jalapeño Peppers,
Shredded Cheddar Cheese, and Crackers
• • •
Texas Spiced BBQ Brisket of Beef, carved at Buffet
• • •
Grilled Chicken; Fried Gulf Shrimp
• • •
Smoked Beef and Pork Ribs
• • •
Corn on the Cob with Drawn Butter
• • •
Okra and Tomatoes
• • •
Bourbon Baked Beans with Salt Pork
• • •

Enchiladas, Burritos, Tamales
• • •
Corn Bread Muffins, Onion Rolls,
Sourdough Biscuits, and Creamery Butter
• • •
Sliced Watermelon
• • •
Pecan Pie, Apple-Raisin Pie
• • •
Caramel Custard
• • •
Strawberry Biscuit Shortcake
• • •
Cherry Turnovers
• • •
Six Shooter Coffee, Tea, Decaffeinated Coffee, or Milk
(Carvers, price on request)

The "Texas Shoot-Out" Western Buffet Dinner includes decorations of authentic wagon wheels, wooden barrels, post and rails, checkered red and white tablecloths and napkins, hurricane lamps, and western costumes. A Western Band can be contracted for an additional charge.

*Special Appearance: A special appearance by the International Chili Champion, Lone Star Chili Willi, a crotchety old Chuck Wagon Cook from Lizard Tail, Texas, can be arranged at an additional cost. He boasts his chili is better because he does it with spice. Appearance price on request.

Texas Western Buffet Dinner

Lone Star Potato Salad
• • •
Texas Cole Slaw
• • •
Pickles, Sliced Tomatoes, and Sweet Onions
• • •
Pinto Bean Salad
• • •
Pickled Beets, Assorted Relish Trays
• • •
Texas Spiced Baron of Beef, Carved on Buffet
• • •
Barbecued Chicken and Spare Ribs
• • •
Smoked Shredded Beef Brisket
• • •
Country Corn on the Cob
• • •

Smoked Barbecued Beans
• • •
Ranch-Style Potatoes
• • •
Hush Puppies
• • •
Corn Muffins, Sourdough Biscuits
• • •
Selection of Southern Fried Pies
• • •
Prairie Cake
• • •
Pecan Tarts
• • •
Strawberry Mousse
• • •
Six Shooter Coffee

Texas Hill Country Cookout

Crates of Seasoned Salad Greens,
with Farmer's Raw Vegetables,
Fresh Herb Dressing and Vinaigrette Dressing

• • •

Red Bean Salad

• • •

Garbanzo Beans

• • •

Freshly Made Western-Style Cole Slaw

• • •

Jalapeño Chilies

• • •

Hot Peppers

• • •

Texas Spiced BBQ Smoked Brisket of Beef,
Carved at Buffet, Barbecue Sauce

• • •

Disjointed Barbecued Chicken

• • •

Barbecued Texas Ribs

• • •

Corn on the Cob with Drawn Butter

• • •

Bourbon Baked Beans with Salt Pork

• • •

Okra and Tomatoes

• • •

Bowls of Lone Star Chili Willi's
International Award Winning Hot Chili,

served with Diced Onions, Red Beans,
Sliced Jalapeño Peppers, Shredded Cheddar Cheese,
and Crackers, on the side

• • •

Western Loaves of Bread, Cowboy Soda Biscuits,
Sheepherder's Rye Bread, Corn Bread Muffins,
and Creamery Butter

• • •

Sliced Watermelon

• • •

Strawberry Biscuit Shortcake

• • •

Pecan Pie

• • •

Apple-Raisin Pie

• • •

Six Shooter Coffee

Special Beverages: After a day on the trail, we suggest Texas Bloody Marys, served in half-pint fruit jars, or a bucket of iced Lone Star Beer on each table. Prices on request.

Music: How about a real bluegrass band for lazy-listenin' or foot-stompin', at an additional charge?

Favors: Cowboys are issued western straw hats and bandannas and the cowgirls get bonnets, arranged at an additional cost.

Menus with a Southern Theme

You can almost smell the magnolia blossoms as the lure of the charming South captures your heart. Dixieland Fever will pervade your senses with toe-tappin', hand-clappin' excitement.

Southern Hospitality Buffet Breakfast

Carafes of Fresh Squeezings of Sun-Ripe
Florida Oranges and Grapefruits,
Displayed on Crushed Ice

• • •

Fresh Orange and Grapefruit Slices

• • •

Melon Pieces and Berries, in Season

• • •

Grilled Ham Steak topped with Fluffy Scrambled Eggs
mixed with Diced Peppers and Onions

• • •

Southern-Style Grits and Red Eye Gravy

• • •

Broiled Hot Sausage Patties

• • •

Crisp Thick Bacon Strips

• • •

Home Fried Potatoes

• • •

On the Table, Baskets of Hot Biscuits, Croissants,
Corn Bread, Bran Muffins, Assorted Breakfast Bakeries,
Creamery Butter, Marmalade, Jams, Honey

• • •

Coffee, Tea, Decaffeinated Coffee, or Milk

Southern Comfort Plantation Buffet
Dinner

Southern Hospitality—and plenty of it—comes alive with Home Cookin' Specials set out Buffet Style.

Georgia Peanut Soup
Crayfish Chowder

• • •

Freshly Tossed Garden Greens with Fresh Spinach Leaves, Assorted Dressings

• • •

Creamy Cole Slaw

• • •

Sliced Tomatoes

• • •

Green Onions and Radishes

• • •

Cottage Cheese

• • •

Roast Pork Tenderloin

• • •

Brunswick Stew
or
Creole Fried Chicken

• • •

Barbecued Backstrap Ribs

• • •

Baked Country Ham, Carved to Order

• • •

Spoonbread

• • •

Candied Yams

• • •

Hush Puppies

• • •

Confederate Pole Beans with Onions and Bacon Bits

• • •

In Baskets, on each Table: Freshly Baked Corn Bread, Buttermilk Biscuits, Country-Style Butter and Honey

• • •

Old-Fashioned Biscuit Strawberry Shortcake

• • •

Southern-Style Pecan Pie made with Chocolate

• • •

Fresh Jam Cake, Cherry Cobbler, Chantilly

• • •

Watermelon

• • •

Coffee with Chicory, Tea, Sanka,
Lemonade, Iced Tea, or Milk

• • •

(Carvers, price on request)

Special Beverages: We recommend a good old-fashioned Open Bar, serving plenty of Jack Daniels and Southern Comfort, to accompany your luncheon or dinner. For breakfast you may wish to serve Bloody Marys and Screwdrivers, passed on Silver Trays by waiters. Also, our Specialty Drink service will insure the South will rise again, and will include:

Mint Juleps, Orange Blossoms
Scarlett O'Haras and Rhett Butlers
(Prices on request)

Music: We recommend starting the party with the strolling violinists and then being joined by a full orchestra, to make your gal feel like the Belle of the Ball.

Country Hoedown Jamboree Reception

Join in the fun down on the farm with toe-tappin' merriment. It's a real Hoedown, and you'll be caught up in the spirit of an excitement-filled barnyard.

Large Display of Whole Fresh Vegetables in Old Crates and Baskets

• • •

Fresh Sliced Vegetables to include:
Zucchini, Cauliflower, Carrots, Cherry Tomatoes, Celery, Mushrooms, Green Beans, Broccoli, Avocados, and Cucumbers,
with Dill, Sour Cream, and Cheese Dips

• • •

Large Display of Whole Fresh Fruit in Bushel Baskets and Crates

• • •

Fresh Cut and Whole Fruit to include:
Apples, Oranges, Grapefruit, Pineapple, Cantaloupe, Berries in Season, Strawberries, Pears, Assorted Grapes, Bananas, Coconuts, and Kiwi, Served with Whipped Cream, Chocolate Fondue, and Brown Sugar

• • •

Barbecued Chicken Drumettes

• • •

Baby Pork Riblettes

• • •

Slices of Baked Ham on Buttermilk Biscuits

• • •

Sausage Patties on Buttermilk Biscuits

• • •

Sliced Charcoal-Broiled Flank Steak

• • •

Whole Steamship Rounds of Beef, Served with
Miniature Rolls, Cocktail Rye, and Pumpernickel,
Accompanied by Mayonnaise and Mustard

• • •

Country Hams Carved at Buffet by Chef, Served with
Miniature Rolls, Cocktail Rye, and Pumpernickel,
Accompanied by Mayonnaise and Mustard

• • •

Half Ears of Corn placed on Popsicle Sticks,
Heated in the Room in a Large Boiling Pot,
Served with Drawn Butter

• • •

Whole and Sliced Fresh Baked Bread,
as part of a Large Bread Display,
Butter, Honey, Marmalade, Preserves

• • •

International and Domestic Cheese Display,
with a Variety of Crackers, Lahvosh, Sliced French Bread

• • •

International Selection of Colossal Sausages

• • •

From a Separate Dessert Table:
Individual Strawberry Shortcakes

• • •

Assorted Cookies

• • •

Fudge Brownies

• • •

Coffee, Tea, Decaffeinated Coffee

• • •

(Carver, price on request)

Georgia Country Bash

Southern Hospitality—and plenty of it—comes alive with
Home Cookin' Specials set out Buffet Style.

Georgia Peanut Soup

• • •

Roast Barbecued Pork

• • •

Baked Southern Beans

• • •

Hoppin' John Country Chicken

• • •

Kernel Corn

• • •

Barbecued Country Ribs

• • •

Brunswick Stew

• • •

Hush Puppies

• • •

Spinach Salad, Creamy Cole Slaw

• • •

Honey and Biscuits, Corn Bread and Butter

• • •

Pecan Pie, Peach Pie

Special Beverages: In addition to an Open Bar, we
would be most pleased to serve Beer on Draft or
Moonshine served in wide-mouth fruit jars. Prices on
request.

Music: We suggest a country and western or bluegrass
band. The fiddles, guitars, and banjos will play foot-
stompin' tunes for a real eye-opener. And you may
consider a clogging dance group to keep everyone movin'.

Christmas in the Old South Reception

(Based on 700 Guests)

Combine Southern Hospitality with the Holiday Spirit and
you are assured the "South Will Rise Again!" Because the
Old South especially exemplifies itself through its unique
cuisine, we are featuring three of the most distinctive and
exhilarating variations of "Home-Cooked Southern-Style"

vittles that will ring out with the words, "You All Come
Back Now, Hear!?"

Approximately 16 bite-size pieces of hot and cold hors
d'oeuvres per person, as described, will be provided. In
addition, 2,800 total pieces of freshly shucked clams and

oysters on the half shell, a total of 2,550 pieces of cold jumbo Gulf shrimp and golden Gulf crab claws, 4 steamship rounds of beef, and 6 bourbon-glazed hams will be served, included in the total per person price. From the Plantation Mansion station, with its red brick and columns we will feature the cuisine of:

Georgia on My Mind

You can almost smell the magnolia blossoms as the lure of the charming South captures your heart. Dixieland Fever will pervade your senses with toe-tappin', hand-clappin' excitement.

Come relive the good life at an Antebellum Southern Plantation. The Old South enjoyed a charming elegance, "Gone With The Wind" and now recaptured for your and your guests' enjoyment. You stroll the formal gardens in the company of Graceful Hoopskirted Belles and Chivalrous Gentlemen. Your every need is catered to in the true sense of Southern Hospitality.

Southern Soup station to include:

Georgia Peanut Soup

• • •

Okra Gumbo

• • •

Crayfish Bisque

• • •

Miniature Chicken Fried Steak and Biscuit Sandwiches

• • •

Country Sausage Patties and Biscuit Sandwiches

• • •

Crisp "Catfish-Fried" Chicken Drumsticks,
with a Crunchy Cornmeal Coating,
and then Fried in Peanut Oil

• • •

Barbecued Country Baby Back Ribs

• • •

Hush Puppies

• • •

Confederate Pole Beans with Onions and Bacon Bits

• • •

Candied Yams with Raisins and Marshmallows

• • •

Pickled Watermelon Rind

• • •

Hoppin' John

• • •

Freshly Baked Corn Bread, Farmhouse Potato Bread,
Buttermilk Biscuits, Country-Style Butter, Honey,
Apple Butter, and Sorghum

• • •

Bayou I Wanna Be

From a soft, moody re-creation of a Louisiana Bayou, with fireflies twinkling, mist rising from the marshy grasses,

and tall trees dripping with Spanish moss, we will feature Back Country Cookin'. Come way back in the swamp, where the city folks never go, and kick up your heels in the Bayou with an old-fashioned buffet with its Home Cookin' Specials.

A total of 2,800 pieces of freshly shucked clams and oysters on the half shell, served with cocktail sauce, horseradish, Tabasco, lemon wedges, and oysterettes.

Some of the clams and oysters will be preshucked. In addition, we will have two shuckers, at an additional charge, shucking fresh clams and oysters to order, from iced glow trays.

A total of 2,550 pieces of cold jumbo Gulf shrimp, on ice, and golden Gulf crab claws, on ice, will be served with Rémoulade and cocktail sauces and Lemon Stars.

• • •

Dipped Catfish
Dipped in Cornmeal and Pan Fried

• • •

Barbecued Backstrap Boneless Pork Loin

• • •

Red Beans and Rice

• • •

Boiled New Potatoes with Jackets

• • •

Stewed Apples

• • •

Old Man River

From the deck of our Paddlewheel Riverboat, the Mississippi Queen, we will feature River Country Cuisine. You'll enjoy Cajun Cookin' and other Down Home Specialties as your inhibitions lower and your appetites increase. As sure as you can beat your feet on the Mississippi mud, you'll be wagerin' Cajun is your favorite cuisine.

Blackened Redfish with Creole Mustard Sauce

• • •

Seafood Jambalaya

• • •

Barbecued Shrimp

• • •

Blackened Tuna, with Light Lemon Dressing

• • •

Creole Sausage Tidbits

• • •

Seafood Etoufée

• • •

Beef Kabobs, Louisiana Style

• • •

Giant Muffaletta Sandwiches, by the Slice

• • •

Six Foot Po' Boy Sandwiches, by the Slice

• • •

Christmas in the Old South Reception (continued)

From Separate Carving Stations:

Four (4) Whole Steamship Rounds of Beef,
With Miniature Silver Dollar Rolls, Cocktail Rye, and
Pumpernickel,
Accompanied by Mayonnaise, Horseradish, Mustard, and
Chutney
Carving to Order by Two Chefs in Crisp White
Uniforms, from Two Carving Stations

• • •

Six Bourbon-Glazed Hams with Pickled Peach Glaze,
With Miniature Silver Dollar Rolls, Cocktail Rye, and
Pumpernickel,
Accompanied by Mayonnaise, Horseradish, and Mustard
Carving to Order by Two Chefs in Crisp White
Uniforms, from Two Additional Carving Stations

Scarlett's You'll Never Be Hungry Again Dessert Display

In the foyer, within a Grand Garden Gazebo, strung with lights and trimmed with green garlands, wreaths, and ribbons, we will feature the Southern sweet display consisting of:

King and Doberge Cakes

• • •

Fresh Jam Cake

• • •

Southern-Style Pecan Pie with Chocolate

• • •

Beignets

• • •

Hot Cherry Cobbler

• • •

Lattice-Topped Raspberry Pie

• • •

Angel Food Cake with Strawberries and Brown Sugar Sauce

• • •

Pralines

• • •

Old-Fashioned Biscuit Strawberry Shortcake

Georgia Peach Pie

• • •

Watermelon Cubes

• • •

Hot Apple Brown Betty

• • •

Cheese and Fruit Display

Display of Imported and Domestic Cheeses
to include: Camembert, Swiss, Cheddar, American,
Port Salut, and Stilton with Port Wine, Fruits,
Grapes, Homemade Melba Toast, Biscuits,
Crackers, and Sliced French Bread

• • •

Coffee, Tea, Decaffeinated Coffee

For the carving stations, there will be a total of four chefs, in whites, carving, and at the clam and oyster station, there will be a total of two shuckers. Additional charges for the chefs and the shuckers.

Suggested Special Beverages: Good old-fashioned Open Bar serving plenty of Jack Daniels and Southern Comfort. Also, to insure the South will rise again, we will serve, from two specialty drink bars, Mint Juleps, Orange Blossoms, Scarlett O'Haras, and Rhett Butlers.

And listen, when you're in the swamp, you don't insult someone's hound dog and you don't refuse his "Mountain Dew." So stranger, you don't have no choice but to order plenty of that . . . Swamp Water or White Lightning, served in Half-Pint Mason Canning Jars, of course, at an additional expense. The dummy still in the background dispenses "legal booze," in case you're too much of a "City Feller!"

Southern Gentlemen's Seated Luncheon

Louisiana Shrimp Gumbo

• • •

Crispy Southern Pan-Fried Chicken
Barbecued Country Baby Back Ribs
Corn on the Cob
Tomato Filled with Black-Eyed Peas
Hush Puppies
Buttermilk Biscuits, Corn Bread, Whipped Butter, and Honey

• • •

Georgia Peach Cobbler

• • •

Lemonade, Iced Tea, and Coffee with Chicory

Menus with a Fiesta Theme

Fiesta in any language means Feast and this is no exception. The hot-blooded and colorful image of Mexico surrounds us as we Feast in the Spanish Tradition of an Age-Old Ceremony (see color insert and photo on page 68).

When You're Hot . . . You're Hot
Seated Mexican Luncheon

Iceberg Lettuce Salad,
with Sliced Red Onion and Jalapeño Peppers
Avocado Dressing

• • •

Enchiladas with Meat Sauce

• • •

Twin Beef Tacos with Hot Sauce passed
Mexican-Style Refried Beans
Zucchini Mexicana
Baskets of Tortillas, Tostadas, and Nacho Chips,
on each Table with Salsa Dip

• • •

Mousse de Mango

• • •

Coffee, Tea, Decaffeinated Coffee, or Milk

Special Beverages: With all this spicy food, you'll enjoy an Open Bar as well as pitchers of our Homemade Sangria and Tequila Punch. Prices on request.

Music: A strolling Mariachi Band in authentic costumes can be contracted for an additional cost.

Lone Star Chili Willi's South of the Border Reception
(Menu proposal based on 600 guests)

Tex-Mex at its best, with our own Chili Champion cookin' up a storm, makes this reception an event to be remembered!

Approximately 14 bite-size pieces of hot and cold hors d'oeuvres per person, as described, will be provided. In addition, cold Gulf of Mexico shrimp and hot steamship rounds of beef, as indicated under the menu description, will be served and included in the total per-person price. From the Mexican Banditos Cantina, we will serve:

Make-Your-Own Fajita Fever Bar, with Two Costumed Attendants
Slices of Spicy, Marinated and Grilled Beef Skirt Steak, Wrapped in a Warm Floured Tortilla with Pico de Gallo, Picante Sauce, Guacamole, Shredded Cheese, Beans, Shredded Lettuce, and Chopped Onions

• • •

Make-Your-Own Chicken and Beef Taco Bar, with Two Costumed Attendants
Shredded Mexican Chicken and Spicy Beef, Tortilla Shells, Shredded Lettuce and Cheese, Diced Tomatoes, Onions, and Mild and Hot Sauces

• • •

3,600 Pieces of Cold Gulf of Mexico Medium-Size Shrimp
with Rémoulade and Cocktail Sauces,
Lemon Stars
(Stagger service throughout the reception)

• • •

Tostadas and Nacho Chips,
with Guacamole and Salsa Dips,
Chili con Queso

• • •

Miniature Enchiladas, with Meat Sauce

• • •

Mexican-Style Refried Beans

• • •

Miniature Burritos
Raw Vegetable Display,
with Guacamole, Cheese, Clam, and Ranch Dips

• • •

Jalapeño Peppers

• • •

Mexican Bean Salad

• • •

Corn Relish

• • •

International Cheese Display with a Variety of Crackers, Lahvosh, and Sliced French Bread and Garnished with Fresh Fruit

• • •

From two additional stations, complete with stucco-finished Mexican facades with tile roofs, we will present and serve:

Petite Pieces of Chicken Mole Poblano

• • •

Mexican Rice

• • •

Mushrooms Stuffed with Mexican-Style Sausage

• • •

Homemade Tamales, wrapped in Corn Husk

• • •

Mexican Pizza
Layered between Tortillas
Chicken, Beans, Cheese, Tomatoes, and Peppers

• • •

Corn and Pepper Salad

• • •

Just north of the Rio Grande, on the Main Street of a 100-year old western town, we will present and serve the following:

Bowls of Texas 3-Alarm Chili,
Cooked by International Chili Champion,
Lone Star Chili Willi,
Served with Diced Onions, Jalapeño Peppers,
Shredded Cheddar Cheese, and Crackers

• • •

Miniature Barbecued Chicken Drumsticks

• • •

Bourbon Baked Beans,
with Salt Pork

• • •

Barbecued Sausage Tidbits

• • •

Fried Rio Grande Catfish Pieces, with Tartar Sauce

• • •

Barbecued Baby Texas Pork Ribs

• • •

Petite Corn Fritters

• • •

From three separate and elaborately decorated carving stations, we will present and serve:

Three Whole Steamship Rounds of Beef,
Served with Miniature Silver Dollar Rolls,
Cocktail Rye, and Pumpernickel,
Accompanied by Mayonnaise, Horseradish, Mustard, and
Chutney
Carving to order will be done by Three Chefs
in Crisp White Uniforms

• • •

In the Foyer, we will present and serve the following elaborately decorated display:

Texas Pecan Pie

• • •

Sliced Fresh Fruit with Warm Cajeta Sauce

• • •

Apple Brown Betty

• • •

Pralines

• • •

Kahlua Pie

• • •

Sopaipillas

• • •

Margarita Pie

• • •

Spanish Flans

• • •

Assorted Mexican Cookies

• • •

Mousse de Mango

• • •

Cherry Turnovers

• • •

Strawberry Shortcake

• • •

Pecan-Stuffed Date Cookies

• • •

Caramel Custard

• • •

Rio Grande Mexican Cake

• • •

Freshly Brewed Coffee, Tea, Freshly Brewed
Decaffeinated Coffee

Special Appearance: A special appearance of the International Chili Champion, Lone Star Chili Willi, a crotchety 87-year-old Chuck Wagon Cook from Lizard Tail, Texas, has been arranged. He will appear in front of Lone Star Chili Willi's Chili Parlor and sing while the band is on breaks, to provide continuous music. His many songs will include "To All the Girls I've Loved Before."

Beverages: We will provide good old-fashioned Hosted Bars and Bartenders serving unlimited name brands, to include plenty of Jack Daniels and Southern Comfort, along with a complete selection of highballs and cocktails, domestic beer and wine, imported beer, mineral water, and soft drinks.

In addition, to insure that "The South Will Rise Again," we will serve, from additional Specialty Drink Bars, free-flowing Margaritas.

The number charges are based on the Food Function Guarantee, or the Number in Attendance, whichever is greater.

Special Note to Client: Flat Rate Bar opens and closes promptly at the given times.

Bartenders and specialty drinktenders are included in the flat rate.

If alcoholic beverages are to be served on the Hotel premises (or elsewhere under the Hotel's alcoholic beverage license), the Hotel will require that beverages be dispensed only by Hotel servers and bartenders. The Hotel's alcoholic beverage license requires the Hotel to (1) request proper indentification (photo ID) of any person of questionable age and refuse alcoholic beverage service if the person is underage or if proper indentification cannot be produced, and (2) refuse alcoholic beverage service to any person who, in the Hotel's judgement, appears intoxicated.

Mexican Fiesta Buffet Dinner

Corn Relish

• • •

Mexican Bean Salad

• • •

Guacamole Salad

• • •

Fiesta Cole Slaw

• • •

Cilantro Herbed Tomatoes

• • •

Raw Vegetables with Guacamole Dip

• • •

Jalapeño Peppers

• • •

Picadillo

• • •

Tortillas, Tostadas, and Nacho Chips, Salsa Dip

Make-Your-Own Taco Bar, with all the Fixin's

• • •

Mexican Rice with Shellfish

• • •

Chicken Mole Poblano

• • •

Enchiladas with Meat Sauce

• • •

Stuffed Pork Chops

• • •

Mexican-Style Refried Beans

• • •

Zucchini Mexicana

• • •

Hot Sauce

• • •

Mousse de Mango

• • •

Assorted Mexican Cookies

• • •

Spanish Flans

• • •

Coffee, Tea, Decaffeinated Coffee, or Milk

The Mexican Fiesta is complemented with authentic piñatas, red and white checkered tablecloths and napkins, wooden barrels, fences, and cactus plants. A strolling Mariachi Band in authentic costumes can be contracted for an additional charge.

Mexican Cantina Buffet Dinner

Enchiladas with Meat Sauce

• • •

Chicken Mole

• • •

Beef Tacos

• • •

Stuffed Pork Chops

• • •

Chiles Rellenos

• • •

Arroz con Pollo

• • •

Chopped Steaks Ranchero

• • •

Snapper Fingers

• • •

Refried Beans

• • •

Zucchini Mexicana

• • •

Spanish Rice

• • •

Hot Sauce

• • •

Guacamole Salad

• • •

Mexican Cole Slaw

• • •

Stuffed Jalapeños

• • •

Relishes

• • •

Hot Peppers

• • •

Picadillo

• • •

Corn Relish

• • •

Mexican Bean Salad

• • •

Tomatoes

• • •

Tostadas and Tortillas

• • •

Mousse de Mango

• • •

Mexican Flans

• • •

Fried Bananas

• • •

Assorted Mexican Cookies

• • •

Capiliotadas

• • •

Coffee

With all this spicy food, you will enjoy pitchers of our home-made Sangria and Tequila Punch, at an additional charge.

Menus with a Tropical Islands Theme

(See Photo on Page 69)

The heady perfume of lush exotic flowers scents the air while palm leaves sway to the rhythm of tropical breezes. The beat of the Caribbean is felt in the intoxicating pleasure of a lazy, languid lifestyle, which finds its only peer in the lovely islands of the South Pacific.

Caribbean Islands Blazing Pineapples
Seated Luncheon

As guests enter this luncheon, there will be a major focal display of island palms and greens, with a whole pineapple surrounded by dry ice and flames.

An Island Seafood Salad
With Crab and Shrimp, served in Half Pineapples,
Presented on Special Matting,
with Banana, Poppy Seed, and Honey Dressing

• • •

Fresh Assorted Rolls and Butter

• • •

Whole Smoked Pork Roast
Rubbed in Garlic and Wrapped in Banana Leaves,
Lean Slices Served on Banana Leaves,
Accented with Island Salt, Garnished with Crabapple

• • •

Layers of Banana, Pineapples, Litchi Nuts,
Baked in Bubbling Brown Sugar

• • •

Island Fried Celery with Water Chestnuts, Pea Pods,
and Bamboo Shoots

• • •

Coconut Coma
Blend of Rich Ice Creams,
Toasted French Coconut

• • •

Chopped Macadamia Nuts and Passion Fruit served in
Coconut Shell,
Garnished with sticks of Sugar Cane and a Fresh Vanda
Orchid

• • •

Coffee, Tea, Decaffeinated Coffee, or Milk

Fantasy Island Reception

From a specially designed buffet, a total of 16 pieces per person of the following:

Caribbean Egg Rolls, Sweet and Sour Sauce

• • •

Sweet and Sour Shrimp

• • •

Barbecued Spareribs Martinique,
with Caribbean Barbecue Sauce

• • •

Petite Chicken and Pineapple Kabobs

• • •

Beer-Batter Banana Fritters

• • •

Fried Pineapple Slices

• • •

Mirrors of Caribbean Cold Canapés

• • •

Display of Sliced Fresh Tropical Fruit to include:
Melon Cubes, Pineapple Wedges,
Strawberries, and other Island Fruit

• • •

Cold Jumbo Gulf Shrimp, on Ice (six shrimp per person),
with Rémoulade and Cocktail Sauces,
Lemon Stars

• • •

Prepared to Order at Buffet:
Sautéed Bananas

• • •

Cooked on Hibachis:
Barbecued Beef Antigua on Bamboo Sticks,
Served with Fried Rice

• • •

Special Presentation, at an Additional Price:
A Suckling Pig, Decorated, Garnished,
and Wrapped in Banana Leaves, served Hot and Sliced
(Carver required, Price on request)

Night in the Tropics Reception

Approximately 16 total pieces of hors d'oeuvres per person:

Barbecued Beef Antigua on Bamboo Sticks

• • •

Beer-Batter Banana Fritters

• • •

Fried Pineapple Wedges

• • •

Sautéed Bananas, Prepared at Buffet

• • •

Caribbean Egg Rolls, Sweet and Sour Sauce

• • •

Petite Chicken and Pineapple Kabobs

• • •

Sweet and Sour Shrimp

• • •

Petite Bahamian Conch Fritters

• • •

Barbecued Spareribs Martinque, with Caribbean
Barbecue Sauce

• • •

Deep-Fried Fish and Shrimp Tidbits,
with Ginger-Flavored Peanut Sauce

• • •

Tropical Raw Vegetables with Island Dips

• • •

Shrimp Imperial Stuffed Cherry Tomatoes

• • •

Banana Chips, Avocado Dip

• • •

Date Teasers

• • •

Skewered Fruit

• • •

Displays of Tropical Fruit and Coconut Meat au
Liqueur,
Served from Sculptured Ice Canoes,
with Whipped Cream, Brown Sugar, and Sour Cream–
Honey Dressing

• • •

Puerto Rican Flan

• • •

Tropical Nut Bread

• • •

At an Additional Price, from Separate Carving Stations,
we will serve:
Whole Roasted Suckling Pig
Decorated, Garnished, and Wrapped in Banana Leaves;
Served Hot and Sliced at the Buffet by Chef

• • •

Caribbean Steamship Rounds of Beef,
including Miniature Rolls, Bahamian Rye, and
Pumpernickel,
Accompanied by Mayonnaise, Horseradish, and Chutney

• • •

(Carvers, price on request)

Goombay Paradise Buffet Dinner

An Elaborate Buffet Presentation of Island Greens surrounded by mounds of Whole Fresh Tropical Fruit to include:
Bananas, Persimmons, Pineapples, Guava, Kiwi, Mangoes, and Papaya

• • •

Sweet and Pungent Pork Pineapple

• • •

Tahitian Barbecued Spareribs

• • •

Shrimp in Lobster Sauce, Fried Rice

• • •

Polynesian Barbecued Young Chicken

• • •

Baby Snow Peas

• • •

Cantonese Beef and Mushrooms
Tender Sliced Beef Cooked with Mushrooms, Water Chestnuts, and Bamboo Shoots

• • •

Egg Foo Yung
A delectable Chinese Omelet of Eggs, Mushrooms, Bean Sprouts, with Pork and Shrimp

• • •

Tossed Salad with Iceberg Lettuce, Spinach Leaves, Toasted Croutons, and Toasted Coconut, Sweet and Sour Pineapple Dressing

• • •

Island Chicken Salad

• • •

Fresh Tahitian Halibut Salad

• • •

Multicolored Lobster Chips

• • •

From Sculptured Ice Canoes, we will serve an Assortment of
Bite-Sized Fresh Island Fruit including:
Papayas, Casaba Melon, Oranges, Pineapples, Mangoes, Bananas, Strawberries, Grapes, Persimmons, Guava, and Kiwi, with Brown Sugar, Whipped Cream, Rock Candy and Sour Cream–Honey Dressing

• • •

Magnificent Ice Tiki Pyramid Sculpture

• • •

Assorted Dinner Rolls and Butter

• • •

Island Banana and Pineapple Pie

• • •

Coconut Layer Cake

• • •

South Seas Coconut Pudding

• • •

Banana Pound Cake

• • •

Coconut Ambrosia with Chocolate Sauce

• • •

Coffee, Tea, Decaffeinated Coffee, or Milk

Special Beverages: In addition to an Open Bar, we suggest Specialty Drink Bars serving: Bahama Mamas, Hurricanes, Birds of Paradise, Tahitian Sunsets, Navy Grogs, Vanda Daiquiris, Mai Tais, and our Special Island Rum Punch served in a hollowed-out pineapple. Prices on request.

Music: Calypso rhythms will set the mood, with steel drums beating out the island sounds. Adding a Limbo Dancer can create audience participation for more fun. Include a Fire Dancer to complete the evening. Prices on request.

A Mardi Gras Extravaganza Menu

Revel in the colorful excitement only a New Orleans Mardi Gras can create. You'll enjoy Cajun cooking and other bayou specialties as your inhibitions lower and your appetites increase.

New Orleans Mardi Gras Buffet Dinner

From a Grand Center Buffet,
Topped with Giant Floral Ice Carvings:
Goujon of Catfish

• • •

Creole Meatballs

• • •

Sautéed Frog Legs

• • •

Quiche Lorraine

• • •

Beef Kabobs, Louisiana-Style

• • •

Creole Bouchées

• • •

Cajun Stuffed Peppers

• • •

Chicken Cordon Bleu

• • •

Barbecued Shrimp

• • •

From Four Separate Carving Stations:

Steamship Rounds of Beef and Bourbon-Glazed Hams,
Including Miniature Rolls, Cocktail Rye, and
Pumpernickel
Accompanied by Mayonnaise, Horseradish, Mustard,
and Chutney

From a Deli Shop:

Giant Muffaletta Sandwiches, by the Slice

• • •

Six Foot Po' Boy Sandwiches, by the Slice

• • •

Jambalaya

• • •

Boudin

• • •

Chauriz

• • •

Andouille

• • •

Pickled Smoked Sausage

• • •

Hoghead Cheese

• • •

From Two Separate Oyster Stations:

Freshly Shucked Oysters on the Half Shell,
with Cocktail Sauce, Horseradish, and Lemon Stars
(Shuckers, price on request)

• • •

Cheese and Fruit Display:

Display of Imported and Domestic Cheeses to include:
Camembert, Brie, Swiss, Cheddar, American, Port Salut,
and Stilton with
Port Wine, Fruits, Grapes, Homemade Melba
Toast, Biscuits, Crackers, and French Bread

• • •

Café du Monde Buffet:

King and Doberge Cakes

• • •

Pralines

• • •

Praline Frappé with Chopped Pecans

• • •

Chocolate-Covered Bananas

• • •

Ice Cream Sandwiches

Special Beverages: An Open Bar is a must, with a variety of bottled wines served at the Buffet. We would suggest a Specialty Drink Bar. Prices on request.

Music: New Orleans Jazz Band to keep the tempo up and steppin' lively. Price on request.

A Shogun Party

(See Color Insert)

A resonant, ceremonial gong announces each guest in the world of 17th century Japan. Japanese food stands apart from all other Asian cuisines because of its simplicity and purity. It is memorable, not for its richness or spices or complexity of flavors, but rather because the emphasis is on the basic ingredients, training the palate to accept and appreciate food in its most natural state.

Sushi Bar: Sushi is the Japanese equivalent of the open sandwich. Rice flavored with a vinegar and sugar dressing takes the place of bread, and is topped with various kinds of raw fish, is rolled around fillings of fish, pickles, mushrooms, or other vegetables, and in some cases, is enclosed in omelettes or bean curd. In Japan exquisitely arranged boxes of sushi can be bought to take home, as Westerners buy boxes of chocolates. Sushi always forms part of any picnic lunch.

The Shogun Selection Buffet

The Sushi Selections

Nigiri Sushi
Rice with Raw Fish

• • •

Norimaki Sushi
Rice rolled in Seaweed

• • •

Fukusa Sushi
Rice wrapped in Omelette

• • •

Inari Sushi
Rice in Fried Bean Curd

• • •

Chirashi Sushi
Rice with Seafood and Vegetables

• • •

Cold Buffet

Sashimi
Paper-Thin Sliced Raw Fish
Garnished with Shredded Carrot, Lettuce, or Cabbage,
served with Grated Ginger and Horseradish

• • •

Kyurimomi
Cucumber Salad

• • •

Tsukemono
Pickled Mustard Cabbage and Daikon

• • •

Kobachi
Cucumber and Crab Salad

• • •

Taramabushi
Tuna-Cod Variety

• • •

Hot Buffet

Yakitori
Grilled Chicken on Skewers

• • •

Wakadori Tehayaki
Fried Chicken with Sesame Seeds

• • •

Onigariyaki
Large Prawns, Cut in Half, Marinated in Soya Sauce,
Grilled on Skewers

• • •

Tempura
A variety of Seafood and Vegetables Dipped
in Batter and Deep-Fried

Special Beverages: In addition to an Open Bar, we suggest serving Green Tea, Plum Wine, Kirin and Asahi Beers, Hot Sake and our Rising Sun Exotic drink. Prices available on request.

Music: Authentic entertainment is available to enhance the Oriental atmosphere. Delicate as the scent of jasmine, musical notes drift from oriental strings. Prices on request.

A Menu with an Old English Theme

Rob from the Rich and give to the Poor? There's no need of that when you join this Merry Band. The bountiful assortment of dishes will prove more than enough for everyone in Sherwood Forest, even if Friar Tuck is invited!

Evening in Sherwood Forest Reception and Seated Theme Dinner

Reception

From Market Stall and Wagon, we will Serve the Following:
Crêpes Portofino

• • •

Assorted Crudités to include:
Cauliflower, Broccoli Buds, Whole Mushrooms,
Celery Sticks, Carrots Julienne, with
a Variety of Dipping Sauces

• • •

Assorted Cheeses including:
Stilton au Porto

• • •

Sausages

• • •

Variety of Breads, Sliced

• • •

Fresh Fruit in Season

• • •

Assorted Deluxe Canapés, to be passed Butler Style,
by Waiters in Costume
(Costume prices, on request)

Seated Dinner

Salmon Nottingham in Dill
With Creamed Horseradish and Melba Toast

• • •

King Richard's Gin Tomato Soup
Served in Tureens en Croûte

• • •

Maid Marion Salad
Chicory on Bibb Lettuce and Artichoke Hearts,

Served with Mustard Dressing

• • •

Sherwood Forest Saddle of Venison
With Mushroom Sauce
English Bread Dumplings
Honey-Glazed Carrots
Braised Fennel

• • •

Friar Tuck's Temptation
Zuppa Inglaise Pudding

• • •

Devil's Coffee

Special Beverages: Plenty of beverages flowing from an Open Bar, as well as a varied selection of wines. Price on request.

Music and Entertainment: A roaming magician, a juggler, acrobats, wench fights, a wandering minstrel, and sword fights are all available. A flutist might play in between courses. Prices on request.

A Greek Menu

The beautiful country of Greece presented its cooks with a difficult task throughout the ages: They were often asked to satisfy the Gods as well as mortal men. Their efforts to provide a heavenly cuisine were not in vain.

Zorba the Greek Seated Theme Dinner

Fish Broth with Red Snapper and Sorrel

• • •

Vegetable Greek Salad
Romaine and Cucumber with Dill, Greek Olives,
Quality Feta Cheese, Tomato Wedges, Dolmas,
Broccoli Flowerettes, Cauliflower Buds

• • •

Grilled Steak, Greek Style
Marinated and Grilled Fillet of Tenderloin,
with a light Lemon Demi Butter Sauce

Greek Orzo (pasta)
With Tomato, Onion, and Lamb with Cheese

Peas Polita
Peas and Diced Onions with Dill Olive Oil and a

Cream Sauce, Stuffed in Artichoke Hearts
and Topped with Braised Shredded Carrots
Braised Celery with Egg Lemon Sauce
Baby Eggplant,
Stuffed with Onion and Cheese with Breadcrumbs

• • •

Mixed Bread Basket, with Quartered Pita Bread,
Citrus and Raisin Bread, Hard Rolls and Butter

• • •

Baklava with Orange Sections au Kirsch

• • •

Coffee

Special Beverages: Selected Wines, as well as an Open Bar, are recommended.

Music: A full orchestra will ensure you can dance the night away.

Menus with an Italian Theme

Enjoy the Old-World charm of Italy and its passionate delights. Gondolas, quaint sidewalk cafés, and gastronomical pleasures beyond your dreams will transport you to a land where every season speaks of romance (see color insert).

Italian Seated Luncheon

Minestrone with Parmesan Cheese

• • •

Veal Cacciatore
Fettucini Milanaise
Baked Zucchini

• • •

Neapolitan Ice Cream Cake

• • •

Coffee, Tea, Decaffeinated Coffee, or Milk

That's Italian Buffet Luncheon

Deluxe Salad Bar
Roman Antipasto with Provolone,
Salami, Mozzarella, Anchovies, Sardines,
Raw Vegetables, Olives, and Artichoke Hearts

• • •

Eggplant Salad

• • •

Cucumber Salad

• • •

Garden Green Salad with a delightful Garlic, Egg,
Mustard, and Anchovy Dressing

• • •

Fettuccine Salad

• • •

Sliced Tomatoes

• • •

Marinated Squash and Zucchini

• • •

Assorted Salami and Cheeses

• • •

From Gleaming Chafing Dishes, we will serve:

Italian Sausage with Green Peppers and Onions

• • •

Crabmeat Cannelloni Florentine

• • •

Manicotti Stuffed with Cheese

• • •

Ravioli

• • •

Osso Bucco

• • •

Spaghetti Bolognese

• • •

Our Special Pizza with Pepperoni, Mushrooms, Peppers,
Onions, and Extra Cheese

• • •

Garlic Broiled Bread, Italian Bread, Bread Sticks, Butter

• • •

Cannoli

• • •

Cake Galliano

• • •

Biscuit Tortoni

• • •

Italian Pastries

• • •

A variety of Italian Cheeses with Fresh Fruit

• • •

Espresso, Tea, Decaffeinated Coffee, or Milk

Operatic Rigoletto Buffet Dinner

Let us orchestrate this Italian street scene of small quaint shops serving their hearty Italian food, to include:

Antipasti Regionali—Assorted Antipasto from Italy

Gamberetti Marinara
Tiny Shrimp Marinated in Sauce Louis

• • •

Peperonchini Arrosto
Roasted Green and Red Peppers with Garlic

• • •

Carciofi alla Romana
Artichokes with Garlic Stuffing

• • •

Funghi Triffolata
Baked Mushrooms and Garlic

• • •

Cozze Italiano
Mussels in White Wine Marinade

• • •

Prosciutto San Daniele
Thin Sliced Smoked Ham with Lemon and Oil

• • •

Salami e Cappricoala Italiano
A Selection of Sausages from Italy

• • •

Minestra—Soups

Zuppa de Verdura
Assorted Vegetable Soup

• • •

Capelli d'Angelo in Brodo
Very Fine Hair-like Pasta in Chicken Broth

• • •

Insalate—Salads

Insalate Misto
A Combination of Romaine, Red Cabbage,
Julienne of Carrot, Sliced Mushrooms, Black Olives,
Onions, Parsley, and Tomatoes in a Delightful
Garlic, Egg, Mustard, and Anchovy Dressing

• • •

Insalate Legumi Cotti
Cold Cooked Vegetables in Italian Dressing

Specialita Trattoria—Specialties of the House

Calzone Ripieno
An Inverted Pizza Filled with Shaved Ham,
Mozzarella, and a Touch of Tomato Oregano Sauce

• • •

Saltimbocca alla Romano
Two Slices of Veal Piccata with Thin Prosciutto Ham
together, Sautéed in a Light Sage and Butter Sauce

• • •

Suprema de Pollo alla Valdostana
A Chicken Breast with Sage Sautéed and Covered with
Melted Bel Paese Cheese,
Served on a Bed of Rice Milanaise

Manicotti Torino
Pasta Shells Filled with Ricotta and Mozarella,
Served in a Tomato Sauce with Mushrooms

Pesce—Fish

Trotelle con Cozze e Vino Bianco
Trout Sautéed with Mussels, Parsley, and White Wine

• • •

Pastas—Pasta

Bricciolini Milanese
Green Ravioli Stuffed with Ham, Cream,
and Parmesan Cheese

• • •

Spaghetti alla Vongole
Spaghetti with Fresh Clams

• • •

Legumi—Vegetables

Fagiolini e Zucchini Fritate
Beans and Thin Sliced Zucchini, French Fried

• • •

Frutta e Dolci—Fruits and Sweets

Chocolate Profiteroles
Tiny Cream Puff Balls Filled with Custard,
Choice of: Chocolate, Coffee Kahlua,
Mocha, Butterscotch, or Pineapple, then covered with
a Rich Creamy Chocolate Mousse Covering

• • •

Zuppa Inglese
A Bread Custard and Chocolate Combination with
Rum

• • •

Macedonia di Frutta
Assorted Fresh Fruits with a Dash of your Favorite
Liqueur: Kirsch, Rum, or Grenadine

• • •

Torte di Ricotta e Frutta
A Light Pastry of Raisins, Candied Fruit, and
Ricotta Cheese

• • •

Espresso
Coffee

Menus with a Carnival Theme

A Carnival in Munich and Rome

The unusual combination of culinary specialties from two great cities, set out buffet style with enough for seconds.

Lasagna Romana

• • •

Bavarian-Style Sauerbraten

• • •

Scallopini alla Romana

• • •

Ravioli Fra Diavolo

• • •

Linguini with Clam Sauce

• • •

Grilled Bratwurst

• • •

Antipasto Salad Buffet

• • •

Caraway Bread Dumplings

• • •

Pickled Noodle Salad

• • •

German Potato Salad

• • •

Red Cabbage

• • •

Marinated Cauliflower Salad

• • •

Fresh Rolls and Butter

• • •

Cold Sabayon

• • •

Assorted Mousses

• • •

Honey-Almond Cake

• • •

Assorted Pastries

Special Beverages: To add zest to a most authentic culinary theme, please don't overlook carafes of Chianti and pitchers of chilled beer from your own tap.

We suggest, in addition to an Open Bar, at Lunch, you serve Pitchers of Beer at each Table. For Dinner, we recommend you serve a Chianti Classico and Leonardo di Saronno Amaretto with the Coffee. Prices on request.

Music: Lovely strains of Italian melodies throughout the evening played by Neapolitan Strollers, in costume, to help set the festive mood. You may want to add an Italian singer or a complete show.

Carnival from Rio

From the lush tropics of South America, we offer foods with the influence of early inhabitants and conquerors, the Indian, European, and African Cultures. When explorers and settlers came to this part of the New World, their food heritage mixed with the native diet. The result: An array of spicy stews, grilled and roasted meats, abundant fruits and vegetables.

Fish and Shrimp in Ginger-Flavored Peanut Sauce

• • •

Ceviche

• • •

Escabeche

• • •

Watercress Salad

• • •

Avocado Salad

• • •

Goat Cheese

• • •

Arroz con Pollo

Rice and Chicken with Tomatoes,
Red and Green Sweet Peppers,
Garnished with Peas, Young Artichokes

• • •

Empanadas

Meat-Filled Turnovers

• • •

Sliced Loin of Pork, Garni

• • •

Rio Beef Roll Stuffed with Eggs, Carrot, Spinach,
Onion, and Parsley, and Roasted

• • •

Curried Duck with a Blend of Long Grain and Wild Rice

• • •

Humitas
Pureed Corn with Scallion, Green Pepper, and Cheese

• • •

Displays of Tropical Fruits to include:
Melons, Bananas, Mango, Papaya, Pineapple, Oranges,
and Coconut with Chocolate Fudge Sauce

• • •

Strongly Brewed Coffee with Heavy Cream and Sugar

Special Beverages: We suggest serving Capiroshak's to each guest to insure a celebration, at an additional cost.

Music: We can arrange the appropriate music to samba by, contracted for an additional cost.

Favors: Issue masks and noisemakers as your guests enter, to get everyone into the celebratory mood, for an additional charge.

Chapter 25

Kosher Menus

All kosher menus are prepared in strict accordance with Hebrew Dietary Laws and under the orthodox supervision of the Rabbinical Council.

Kosher Breakfast Menu Suggestions

Seated Breakfasts

Appetizers (Choice of One)

Assorted Chilled Fruit Juices

• • •

Citrus Fruit Cup

• • •

Orange Sections

• • •

Grapefruit Sections

• • •

Entrées (Choice of One)

Eggs, Any Style

• • •

Beef Fry and Eggs

• • •

Lox, Eggs, and Onions

• • •

Kosher Cheese Omelettes

• • •

Accompaniments (Choice of One)

Home Fries

• • •

French Fries

• • •

Grits

• • •

Hash Brown Potatoes

• • •

Garnishes (Choice of One)

Half Baked Apple

• • •

Sun-Dried Fruit

All seated breakfasts include assorted breakfast rolls, assorted bagels, croissants, assorted miniature Danish, vegetable spread, kosher butter, service of coffee, tea, and sanka.

Buffet Continental Breakfast

Assorted Chilled Juices:
Orange, Tomato, Grapefruit

• • •

Assorted Bagels, Assorted Danish Pastries, Cream Cheese, Kosher Butter, Preserves

• • •

Coffee, Tea, or Sanka

To accompany any Kosher breakfast or brunch, we suggest passing platters of

Smoked Whitefish and Lox,
Sliced Tomatoes and Onions,
Bagels, Chived Cream Cheese Molds
(at an additional charge)

Full Buffet Breakfasts

(Minimum 100 Guests)

Buffet Breakfast #1

Assorted Fruit Juices:
Orange Juice, Apple Juice, Prune Juice,
Tomato Juice, Pineapple Juice, and
Grapefruit Juice

• • •

Fresh Vegetable Platters:
Lettuce, Tomato, Cucumber, Green Peppers,
Onions

• • •

Breads:
Assorted Breakfast Rolls, Assorted Bagels,
Croissants

• • •

Scrambled Eggs with Spanish, Mushroom,
and Onion Toppings
Home Fries, Margarine and Vegetable Spread

• • •

Assorted Miniature Danish, Cookies, Fruit
Tarts, and Rugalach

• • •

Service of Coffee, Tea, and Sanka

Buffet Breakfast #2

Assorted Fruit Juices:
Orange Juice, Apple Juice, Prune Juice,
Tomato Juice, Pineapple Juice, and
Grapefruit Juice
or
Fruit Salad

• • •

Cheese Blintzes served with
Sour Cream and Blueberry Toppings

• • •

Fruit Blintzes with Assorted Toppings

• • •

Assorted Breakfast Rolls, Assorted Bagels

• • •

Cream Cheese and Margarine Spreads

• • •

Assorted Miniature Danish, Miniature
Cookies, Fruit Tarts, Rugalach

• • •

Fruits:
Watermelon, Cantaloupe, Honeydew,
Green and Red Grapes, Strawberries

• • •

Service of Coffee, Tea, and Sanka

Kosher Bruncheon Menu Suggestions

Seated Bruncheons

Appetizers (Choice of One)

Individual Fresh Fruit Cup

• • •

Garden Fresh Vegetable Salad, with Choice of
Dressings

• • •

Entrées (Choice of One)

Eggs Florentine, with Spinach and
Hollandaise Sauce

• • •

Western Omelette

• • •

Corned Beef Hash

• • •

Chicken à la King, served on a Bed of Rice

• • •

Accompaniments

Tomato Gratiné

• • •

Assorted Breakfast Rolls and
Bagels, Margarine and Vegetable Spreads

• • •

Dessert

Choice of Sherbet

• • •

Service of Coffee, Tea, and Sanka

Buffet Bruncheon Menus

Buffet Brunch #1

Melon Wedge, in season, with
Strawberry Garnish

• • •

Spinach Quiche
Fresh Asparagus
Grilled Tomato

• • •

Bagels and Cream Cheese, Onion Rolls,
Kosher Butter

• • •

Assorted Cookies

• • •

Double Chocolate Brownies

• • •

Coffee, Tea, or Sanka

Buffet Brunch #2

Display of Fresh Fruit of the Season

• • •

Assorted Relishes and Fresh Vegetables

• • •

Eggs Florentine

• • •

Cheese Blintzes with Fruit Compotes

• • •

Potato Pancakes with Apple Sauce

• • •

Display of Lox with Sliced Red Onions and Tomato

• • •

Display of Gefilte Fish

• • •

Herring in Sour Cream

• • •

Smoked Whitefish

• • •

Pickled Herring

• • •

Bagels and Cream Cheese,
Assorted Bread and Onion Rolls,
Kosher Butter

• • •

Coffee Cake

• • •

Coffee, Tea or Sanka

Buffet bruncheons under the minimum requirement will incur an additional $ _____ charge for each 20 guests under the minimum, added to the per-person buffet price.

Kosher Luncheon Menu Suggestions

Seated Luncheon Menus

Appetizers (choice of one)

Fresh Florida Fruit Salad

• • •

Mushroom Barley Soup

• • •

Melon in Season

• • •

Consomme of Chicken Noodle

• • •

Chilled Florida Grapefruit Half

• • •

Chilled Tomato Juice

• • •

Chopped Liver (chicken and beef)

• • •

Garden Fresh Vegetable Soup

• • •

Fresh Florida Citrus Cup

• • •

Chilled Grapefruit Juice

• • •

Supreme Orange Sections

• • •

Fresh Sliced Fruit in a Grapefruit Basket

• • •

Fresh Sliced Pineapple, laced with Kirsch

• • •

Orange Sections, Laced with Kirsch

• • •

Marinated Herring in Wine Sauce

• • •

Entrée Selections (choice of one)
Dairy Entrées:

Broiled Fillet of Sole, served with Lemon, Parsley, and Butter, with choice of Vegetable and Potato

• • •

Salmon Salad Served on a Bed of Lettuce, Sliced Tomato, and Onion, with Lemon and Olive, Garni

• • •

Triple Salad Plate: Chopped Liver Salad, Egg Salad, Chicken Salad, Appropriately Garnished

• • •

Primavera Salad, made with
Kosher Pasta, to include: Spinach Rotelli,
Pasta Shells, Zucchini, Broccoli Buds, Cherry
Tomatoes, Black Olives, Red Pepper Ring,
Garni, Served on Chilled Glass Salad Plate

• • •

Egg Salad, Served on a Bed of Lettuce,
Sliced Tomato, Potato Salad, Cole Slaw, and
Sliced Pickle

• • •

Tuna Fish Salad, Served on a Bed of Lettuce,
Sliced Tomato, Marinated Health Salad,
Potato Salad

• • •

Combination Platter: Tuna Fish Salad,
Egg Salad, Salmon Served on a Bed of Lettuce,
Sliced Tomato, Cole Slaw, and Potato Salad

• • •

Smoked Fish Platter: Sliced Nova Scotia, and
Whitefish Salad Served on a Bed of Lettuce,
Sliced Tomato, Onion, and Cream Cheese

Meat Entrées:

Boneless Breast of Chicken,
Stuffed with Kishke (Derma), Kosher Wine Sauce

• • •

Chopped Beef Steak, Mushroom Gravy

• • •

Boneless Breast of Chicken Continental,
Stuffed with Wild Rice, Kosher White Wine
Sauce

• • •

Broiled Rib Eye Steak, Pan Roasted Potatoes

• • •

Kosher Chicken Breast à la Kiev,
Kosher White Wine Sauce

• • •

Broiled "Catch of the Day,"
Variety of Fresh Kosher Fish

• • •

Boneless Breast of Chicken,
Kosher Wine Sauce

• • •

Brisket of Beef à la Jardiniere

• • •

Assorted Deli Platter: Choice of Corned Beef,
Roast Beef, Pastrami, Turkey Breast, and Tongue

• • •

Broiled Fish Fillet of Sole, Lemon, Parsley,
Tartar Sauce

• • •

Beef Stroganoff with Noodles

• • •

Chicken Fricassee, on a Bed of Rice

• • •

Half Roast Chicken, Peach Garni

• • •

Chicken Chow Mein, Rice Pilaf

• • •

Pepper Steak, Rice Pilaf

• • •

Accompaniments (choice of three)

Baby Carrots, Green Beans Amandine,
Creamed Spinach, Buttered Mixed Vegetables,
Sweet Peas and Pearl Onions, Fresh Sliced
Carrots, Peas with Mushrooms and Slivered
Almonds, Broiled Tomato, Tiny Belgian
Carrots, Broccoli with Herbed Breadcrumbs,
Half Tomato Du Barry, Honey-Glazed Carrots,
Hand-Turned Carrots Sauté

• • •

Rice Pilaf, Oven Roasted Potatoes, Pan
Roasted Potatoes, Noodles Kugel, Valencia Rice,
Potatoes Kugel, Parslied Potatoes,
Rissolées Potatoes, Au Gratin Potatoes,
Baked Idaho Potato, Mashed Potatoes

Desserts (choice of one)

Sherbet, Choice of Kosher Ice Cream, Apple Pie,
Fruit Tarts, Apple Strudel with Warm Vanilla
Sauce, Lemon Meringue Tart, Marble Pound
Cake, Brownies, Apple Crumb Cake, Fruit
Compote, Lemon Fruit Ice with Crushed
Strawberries, Pineapple Lemon Sherbet (Parve),
Chilled Cream of Mint Sauce, Black Forest Cake
(Parve), Fresh Apple Strip, Mocha Mousse
(Parve), Vanilla Ice Cream (Parve) with
Strawberry Sauce, Double Chocolate Mousse
Cake Roll, with Chocolate Fudge Sauce (Parve)
and Whipped Cream passed

• • •

Coffee, Tea, or Sanka

Buffet Luncheon Menus

Buffet Luncheon—Meat
(Choice of Two)
BBQ Ribs, Southern Fried Chicken, Beef
Stroganoff, BBQ Chicken, Chicken à la King,
Steak Teriyaki, Chicken Chow Mein,
Sautéed Cabbage, Chinese Pepper Steak,
Swedish Meatballs, Hawaiian Chicken,
Tongue Polonaise, Italian Meatballs,
Liver Sauté

(Choice of Two)
Potato Kugel, Stir-Fried Vegetables,
Buttered Noodles, Broccoli Soufflé, Fried Rice,
Egg Barley, Kasha Varnishkas,
Oven Brown Potatoes, Sweet Noodle Kugel,
Spinach Kugel, Spaghetti

Breads
Assorted Dinner Rolls, Challah, and Margarine
Rosettes

Vegetables (Choice of Three)
Garden Fresh Vegetables with Choice of
Dressing
Health Salad, Beet Salad, Cucumber Salad,
Pasta Primavera, Hearts of Palm

Fruit Display
Watermelon, Cantaloupe, Honeydew, Green and
Red Grapes, Strawberries, Bananas

Baked Desserts (Choice of Three)
Eclairs, Napoleons, Black Forest Cake,
Pound Cake, Marble Cake, Blueberry Crunch
Cake
Service of Coffee, Tea, and Sanka

Buffet Luncheon—Dairy
Fishes (Choice of Two)
Lox and Nova, Whitefish Salad, Sable,
Tuna Salad, Salmon Mousse

Hot Dishes (Choice of Two)
Eggplant Parmigiana, Lasagna, Broccoli-
Mushroom Quiche, Baked Ziti,
Assorted Fruit Blintzes with Toppings,
Cheese Blintzes with Sour Cream

Breads
Assorted Luncheon Rolls, Bagels,
and Dinner Rolls
Butter, Margarine, and Cream Cheese Spreads

Cakes
Miniature Danish, Cookies, Rugalach,
Assorted Fruit and Guava Tarts

Fruit Display
Watermelon, Cantaloupe, Honeydew, Green and
Red Grapes, Strawberries, Bananas
Service of Coffee, Tea, or Sanka

Kosher Hors d'Oeuvres and Smorgasbord Suggestions

We suggest, for your reception, an excellent selection of Kosher hot and cold appetizers. You may make your selection from the following. We suggest at least eight pieces per person for one hour of butler-style service, and at least nine pieces per person for one hour of buffet table service. For a smorgasbord, we suggest at least twelve pieces per person for one hour of Buffet Table Service.

Hors d'Oeuvres Suggestions

Cold Canapés

Cornets of Salami and Olives
Rondelles of Smoked Whitefish
Finger Toast of Smoked Salmon
Bite-sized Gefilte Fish on Frill Picks, Beet Horseradish
Matjis Herring in Wine Sauce with Sliced Onion Rings
Celery with Chopped Chicken Liver
Barbecued Turkey Canapés
Finger Toasts of Anchovies
Stuffed Deviled Eggs
Chopped Herring on Toast
Breast of Wisconsin Duckling en Gelée
Rondelles of Chopped Chicken Liver
Finger Toasts of Smoked Whitefish
Tuna Pâté

Hot Hors d'Oeuvres

Stuffed Mushroom Caps Florentine
Chicken Livers Wrapped in Pastrami
Miniature Patty Shells Stuffed with Poultry
Cantonese-Style Chicken Bits in Sweet and Sour Sauce
Cubed Beef Tongue, Benedictine Sauce
Cocktail Franks en Croûte
Meatballs in Wine Sauce, on Frill Picks
Water Chestnuts Wrapped in Pastrami
Fillet of Sole l'Orly

Miniature Chicken Kabobs
Stuffed Puffed Pastries
Chicken Wings in Barbecue Sauce
Sweet Breads and Sliced Mushrooms in Wine Sauce
Chow Mein with Sliced Water Chestnuts
Croquettes of Halibut
Chinese Egg Rolls
Cubed Corned Beef Brisket with Pineapple, on Frill Picks
Liver Knishes
Barbecued Beef Ribs
Rumaki Wrapped in Pastrami
Potato Knishes
Whole Sweet and Sour Stuffed Cabbage Rolls
Extra Crisp Boneless Duckling
Tidbits Curaçao
Combination of Chicken and Beef Teriyaki
Fresh Mushroom Caps Stuffed with Mushroom Duxelles
and Spinach
Imitation Shrimp
Vegetable Knishes
Steak Tidbits
Beef Shish Kabobs
Fresh Vegetable Tempura
Oriental Franks
Potato Latkes
Italian Meatballs
Liver Puffs, Chicken Tidbits

Smorgasbord Suggestions

Hot Selections	Side Selections	Cold Suggestions
Barbecued Ribs	Potato Pudding	Chopped Liver Mold
Beef Lo Mein	Stir-Fried Vegetables	Gefilte Fish Platter
Beef Stroganoff	Buttered Noodles	Chopped Herring Platter
Chicken à la King	Rice Pilaf	Chopped Eggplant Platter
Chicken Cacciatore	Fried Rice	Curried Rice Salad
Chicken Chow Mein	Kasha Varnishkas	Fresh Vegetable Platter,
Chinese Pepper Steak	Oven Browned Potatoes	served with Avocado, Techina,
Hawaiian Chicken	Sweet Noodle Kugel	and Curry Dips
Italian Meatballs	Spaghetti	
Liver Sauté	Egg Barley	
Southern Fried Chicken		
Steak Teriyaki		
Stuffed Cabbage		
Swedish Meatballs		
Tongue Polonaise		

Kosher Reception
Embellishments to Enhance
Your Cocktail Reception

The Carvery (Chef Carver Required)

Smoked Scotch Salmon on Display, Carved to
Order at the Buffet Table, with Black Bread
Tartines and Bagels, with Appropriate Garniture

• • •

Glazed Corned Brisket of Beef,
including Miniature Rolls, Cocktail Rye, and
Black Bread,
Accompanied with Appropriate Condiments

• • •

Petite Filets Mignons, Cooked to Order,
Served on Miniature Rolls

• • •

Miniature Baby Lamb Chops en Manchette

The Marketplace

Fresh Vegetable Display, presented on crushed
ice,
Including Zucchini, Mushrooms, Broccoli,
Radishes, Celery, Cauliflower, Green Beans, and
Carrots, Accompanied by Onion Dip (no cream
or butter) and Vinaigrette Dip

• • •

Display of Fresh Sliced Fruit, presented on
crushed ice,
Including Pineapple Cubes, Melon Cubes,
Strawberries, and a Selection of Other Fruits,
Accompanied by Brown Sugar, Dark Chocolate
Fondue (Parve)

Kosher Dinner Menu Suggestions

Seated Dinners

Appetizers (Choice of One)

Fresh Sliced Melon, in Season, with Strawberry
Garnish

• • •

Minestrone Soup,
Chicken Soup with Knaidels

• • •

Chilled Citrus Sections

• • •

Light Vegetable Barley Soup,
Chilled Fresh Fruit

• • •

Melon Wedge with Strawberry Garnish

• • •

Marinated Herring in Wine Sauce,
Mushroom Soup with Barley

• • •

Half Cantaloupe with Scalloped Edges,
Filled with Litchi Nuts, Fresh Strawberries,
Assorted Melon Balls, Kiwi Fruits, Fresh

Pineapple, Sprinkled with Grand Marnier and
Topped with Grated Coconut

• • •

Chilled Fresh Fruit Laced with Cointreau

• • •

Light Vegetable Julienne, Barley Consommé

• • •

Velouté Alexandra
Cream of Chicken Soup with
Julienne of Lettuce and Quenelles of Chicken

• • •

Pineapple Ambrosia

• • •

Homemade Gefilte Fish, served with Red Beet
Horseradish

• • •

Indian River Florida Grapefruit,
Honeydew au Citron

• • •

Seated Dinners (continued)

Beef and Chicken Chopped Liver

• • •

Baked Jellied Carp, Tongue Polonaise

• • •

Baked Whitefish in Creole Sauce

• • •

Stuffed Cabbage, Chicken Fricassee

• • •

Moussaka

• • •

Matzoh Ball Soup, Vegetable Pea Soup

• • •

Kreplach Soup

• • •

Salads (Choice of One)

Tossed Garden Salad with Sliced Mushrooms
and Cucumber, Chef's Dressing

• • •

Romaine and Spinach Salad, with Sliced Tomato,
Mushrooms, and Artichoke Hearts,
Vinaigrette Dressing

• • •

Tossed Selection of Green Leaves, Sliced
Mushrooms, Sliced Cucumber, and Cherry
Tomatoes, Vinaigrette Dressing

• • •

Salade Normande
Salad Endive, Watercress, Lettuce,
Hearts of Palm, Sliced Fresh Mushrooms, and
Toasted Croutons,
Oil and Vinegar Dressing

• • •

Tossed Garden Salad, with Sliced Mushrooms
and Tomato,
Vinaigrette Dressing

• • •

Spinach Salad, Sprinkled with Chopped Egg,
Olive Oil and Lemon Dressing

• • •

Spinach Salad, Sprinkled with Walnuts and
Chopped Egg,
Olive Oil and Lemon Dressing

• • •

Lettuce Wedge, Tomato and Cucumber Salad,
Thousand Island Dressing

• • •

Caesar Salad with Croutons (no cheese),
Caesar Dressing

• • •

Salad Viltoft
Bibb Lettuce, Fresh Sliced Mushrooms,
Alfalfa Sprouts, Tomato, and Cucumber Wedge,
Chef's Herb Cream Dressing

• • •

Leaf Iceberg Lettuce Salad, with Hearts of Palm,
Quartered Artichoke Heart, Freshly Sliced
Mushrooms, and Cherry Tomatoes,
Chef's Herb Cream Dressing

• • •

Mixed Green Salad,
Appropriately Garnished,
Oil and Lemon Dressing

Entrées (Choice of One)

Braised Tournedo of Veal aux Chanterelles,
on a Sautéed White Bread Crouton,
and a Breast of Duckling aux Abricot

• • •

Rack of Veal Prince Orloff

• • •

Double Breast of Capon Wellington, Sauce
Périgourdine

• • •

Kosher Boneless Rock Cornish Game Hen,
Stuffed with Wild Rice

• • •

Broiled "Catch of the Day"
Variety of Fresh Kosher Fish

• • •

Brisket of Beef à la Jardiniere

• • •

Kosher Chicken Breast à la Kiev, Kosher White
Wine Sauce

• • •

Sliced Barbecued Turkey

• • •

Roast Prime Rib of Beef au Jus

• • •

Boneless Breast of Chicken, Kosher
Wine Sauce

• • •

Broiled Rib Eye Steak

• • •

Roast Half Spring Chicken

• • •

Boneless Chicken Breast Continental, Stuffed
with Wild Rice,
Kosher White Wine Sauce

• • •

Filet Mignon au Champignon, Sauce
Périgourdine

• • •

Broiled Baby Lamb Chops, Frenched

• • •

Fresh Fillet of Sole, Lemon, Parsley, and Tartar
Sauce

• • •

Boneless Breast of Chicken, stuffed with Kishke
(Derma),
Kosher Wine Sauce

• • •

Fresh Fillet of Red Snapper

• • •

Sautéed Pompano Parisienne

• • •

Accompaniments (Choice of Three)

Whole Baby Green Beans, Honey-Glazed
Carrots, Broccoli Flowerettes, Fresh Sliced
Carrots, Stuffed Derma, String Beans Amandine,
Julienne of Fresh Vegetables, Carrots Tzimmes,
String Beans Sauté, Half Tomato Du Barry,
Stuffed with Cauliflower, Hand-Turned Carrots
Sauté, Asparagus Spears, Artichoke with Puree
of Carrots, Hand-Turned Potatoes Sauté,
Tomato Rose in Lemon Basket, Salsify Sauté,
Freshest Vegetables of the Season, Berny
Potatoes, Long Grain and Wild Rice, Roasted
Potatoes, Plaza Rice, Potato Kugel, Noodles
Kugel, Rice Pilaf, Pan-Roasted Potatoes,
Valencia Rice, Barley Kugel

• • •

Relish Trays

Celery Sticks, Carrot Curls, Green and Black
Olives, Radish Rosettes, and Baby Corn

• • •

Desserts (Choice of one)

Platters on each table of:
Petits Fours, Halvah, Special Chocolates,
Sugared Almonds, and Strawberries Dipped in
Chocolate

• • •

Flaming Strawberry Crêpes

• • •

Lemon Ice, with Fresh Strawberries and Kiwi

• • •

Profiteroles Filled with Kosher Ice,
Chocolate Rum Sauce, Passed

• • •

Fruit Ices, Served with a Cookie

• • •

Chocolate Mousse (Parve)

• • •

Vanilla Ice Cream (Parve), with Strawberry
Sauce

• • •

Fresh Apple Strips

• • •

Raspberry Sherbet (Parve)

• • •

Double Chocolate Mousse Cake Roll, with
Chocolate Fudge Sauce (Parve) and Whipped
Cream passed

Kosher Parve Viennese Table

An elaborate Viennese Sweet Table is suggested
toward the end of the evening, to include such
items as:

Marbelized Halvah, Black Forest Cake,
Double Chocolate Mousse, Almond Mocha
Torte, Eclairs, Napoleons, Orange Cream Tortes,
Open-Face Tortes, French Apple Strip,
Mini Cream Puffs, Petits Fours,
Miniature Assorted Fruit Tarts,

Banana Cream Pie, Parve Cheesecake,
Fresh Summer Fruits, Chocolate-Covered Mints,
Hot Apple Crêpes, Cinnamon Crêpes

• • •

Watermelon Baskets, Filled with Honeydew,
Cantaloupe, Green and Red Grapes,
Strawberries, and Pineapple

• • •

Hot Coffee

Kosher Wine List

White Wines

Kedem—Dry White Bordeaux
Crisp, dry white wine from the world-renowned Bordeaux region of France.

Kedem—Semi Dry White Bordeaux
Mild, medium dry, with fresh fruity bouquet, from Bordeaux, France.

Bartenura Soave
A Kedem Italian import. A dry, mild, most popular wine.

Abarbanel Rioja White
A Kedem Spanish import, rich and mellow.

Kedem—Chenin Blanc
A California varietal wine, crisp with breed and bouquet.

Kedem—Seyval Blanc
A dry white wine made from French-American New York State hybrid grapes.

Kedem—Blanc de Blancs
Demi-sec, light, pleasant bouquet, similar to a Riesling. From New York State.

Kedem—Chablis
A superb, very dry New York State wine.

Rosé Wines

Kedem—Vin Rosé
Combines the dry asperity of red wines and the light freshness of white wines. From New York State.

Red Wines

Kedem—Dry Red Bordeaux
The kind of wine, a dry, smooth red with a full bouquet, from Bordeaux, France.

Bartenura Valpolicella
Light red wine imported from Italy, from the world-renowned Verona region, a Kedem Selection.

Abarbanel Rioja Red
A Kedem import, full-bodied dry red wine, bottled in Spain's famed Rioja Alavesa region.

Kedem—de Chaunac
Full-bodied, mellow, dry red wine, made from the finest French-American hybrid grapes of New York State.

Kedem—Zinfandel
A dry red California varietal wine with a rich bouquet.

Kedem—Burgundy Royale
A dry, clear, ruby-red New York State burgundy wine.

Sparkling Wines

Bartenura Asti Spumante
A light, semi-sweet sparkling wine imported from Italy by Kedem.

Kedem—White Champagne
A semi-dry wine with a mild bouquet, from New York State.

Kedem—Pink Champagne
Demi-sec, from New York State.

About the Author

G. Eugene Wigger, CPCE, the author of *Catering to Every Whim, A Complete Guide to Catering Sales, Administration and Operations,* literally wrote the book in this profession. His textbook is used to educate hospitality professionals worldwide. Wigger has designed and produced thousands of special events and social affairs for nine of our last ten U.S. presidents, many foreign heads of state, royalty, dignitaries, celebrities, business and industry leaders, and countless elected and appointed officials. Wigger served as chairman of several special event committees for the Summit of the Americas, the first-ever hemispheric meeting of 34 democratically elected heads of state and government, hosted by President Bill Clinton in December, 1994.

Wigger was awarded the designation of Certified Professional Catering Executive, CPCE, the highest level of competence as a catering professional, and he has over 30 years of experience in food and beverage management. His professional credits include serving the White House Military Protocol Office for four years as a member of the elite U.S. Air Force Presidential Honor Guard. He was also one of the finalists seriously considered by President Ronald W. Reagan for U.S. chief of protocol.

Currently, Wigger is the director of catering and convention services at the Adam's Mark Hotel Dallas, the ninth largest hotel in America—with 1,730 guest rooms and a total of 210,000 square feet of meeting and banquet space, including a ballroom of 41,000 square feet, the largest in Texas. (Hotel expansion to be completed Fall, 1998.) While at the Adam's Mark Hotel Dallas, Wigger has created and designed Theme Dreams®, a new level of thematic excellence with a touch of magical excitement. Theme Dreams is the most comprehensive program for thematic guest event experiences ever created, one where dreams become reality. Incorporated into this ingenious concept, Theme Dreams presents a magical marketing program that includes selected thematic events supported by innovative theme menus, staff costumes, suggested attire for attendees, all forms of entertainment suggestions, and elaborate, sophisticated three-dimensional props—all at an affordable total price per person. In some cases, the decor is animated, or even interactive, but it is always unique and on the cutting edge.

Theme Dreams is presently being offered by the Adam's Mark Hotel Dallas in the Dallas/Fort Worth Metroplex, and this innovative program has elevated the thematic experience to an art form.

During his distinguished career, Wigger has participated in the opening of 15 hotels and resorts across the United States and Europe, representing four major hotel corporations: Hilton, Hyatt, Sheraton, and Marriott. Wigger is widely recognized as one of the most innovative and creative catering executives and special event authorities in the nation. He also has experience as a meeting planner of corporate incentive travel, sales meetings, and conventions.

Wigger also provided catering and creative expertise as executive director of catering sales and service of Euro Disney Resort, now known as Disneyland Paris. As the Euro Disney corporate catering dream merchant, Wigger designed and developed the catering menus for all six American-themed resort hotels, as well as a million-dollar theme and meeting break program complete with resort-owned decor, costumes, and entertainment.

The Disney assignment occurred during the six years that Wigger had his own catering consulting firm, Creative Catering Concepts, Ltd., in South Florida. CCC, Ltd. provided consultation, catering sales development, menu and theme concepts, marketing strategies, lectures, planned special events and corporate meetings, as well as conducted catering and marketing seminars for the hospitality industry nationwide.

Wigger's experience includes serving as senior producer of the nationally televised series, *The Best of Modern Cuisine with Robin Leach.* Wigger holds a master's degree in mass communications and he has served as a television newscaster, radio station program director, and radio personality. He also has been a frequent guest lecturer at Cornell University and Florida International University and adjunct professor of catering for Nova Southeastern University.

For Wigger, who is known as the "Wigger of Ah-h-h's," a special event is not a different kind of banquet, but every banquet is a different kind of special event!